THE GREAT HADASSAH WIZO COOKBOOK

THE GREAT HADASSAH WIZO COOKBOOK

Compiled by Members of Edmonton Hadassah-WIZO
Introductions by Sara Waxman

Hurtig Publishers Ltd.
Edmonton

Hurtig Publishers Ltd.
10560 – 105 Street
Edmonton, Alberta

Canadian Cataloguing in Publication Data

Main entry under title:

The Great Hadassah-WIZO cookbook

   Includes index.
   ISBN 0-88830-219-3

   1. Cookery, Jewish.   I. Hadassah-WIZO
Organization of Edmonton. Ami Chai Chapter.
TX724.G73   641.5'676   C82-091198-4

Food Photography
Arrangements by Elexis Schloss
Photography by McDermid Studios
Food prepared by Denis Dion of The Mayfield Inn
Food supplied by Woodward's Stores Limited
Tableware supplied by Bowring Brothers Ltd.
Photographed at The Mayfield Inn

Printed and bound in Canada
by T.H. Best Printing Co. Ltd.

Hadassah-WIZO Organization of Edmonton

To our past leaders,
whose commitment and perseverance
built a strong and viable organization
for today and the future.

Contents

Introduction

Delve into this book with the enthusiasm and joy that Ami Chai Chapter (Edmonton) and Edmonton Hadassah-WIZO have had in preparing it for you. For over two years, we have been collecting recipes from our members, testing and refining them, and selecting only the very best to make up a comprehensive, exciting, and innovative cookbook.

What is Hadassah-WIZO?

Hadassah-WIZO is a volunteer charitable organization in Canada whose primary aim is to assist the people of Israel to improve their quality of life. The material and moral support extended by the Hadassah-WIZO movement includes the funding of medical care and social services, and the provision of academic and vocational education facilities. Founded in 1917 as Hadassah, the movement affiliated in 1921 with the Women's International Zionist Organization, and is now known as the Hadassah-WIZO Organization of Canada. It has grown from a mere handful of concerned women to a membership of over seventeen thousand volunteers across Canada. Their enthusiasm, ingenuity, and commitment create a stream of services for countless thousands of young and old.

Edmonton Hadassah-WIZO, established in 1921, is a vital force in the national organization, with over four hundred women in eight chapters. Ami Chai is one of the newest of these chapters, and boasts as its members an energetic group of young women, who elected to make this cookbook a major fund-raising project.

Why produce a cookbook?

Hadassah-WIZO and its members have a reputation for fine cooking and baking. Everywhere in North America, the public is well acquainted with their major fund-raising events—the annual bazaars, held coast to coast, which showcase the staple foods and mouth-watering delicacies of Jewish tradition.

Edmonton's Annual Hadassah-WIZO Bazaar is now in its twenty-second year, and the display and sale of Jewish foods is always the focus of the event. Year after year, requests for recipes are made at these bazaars. "Why don't you publish a cookbook?" Year after year, the question is asked; so when publisher Mel Hurtig approached us to do such a cookbook, we agreed it would be a welcome addition to many cookbook collections.

A committee composed of members of Ami Chai Chapter was formed, and the mammoth task of collecting the recipes was begun.

Why *The Great Hadassah-WIZO Cookbook?*

The recipes in this book are the very best from among the hundreds and hundreds received from our members. The fine array of foods offered at the bazaars is only a sampling of the treasures available from their kitchens. Members submitted many more of their favourite recipes, some of which had been handed down from their mothers and grandmothers, and others of which are modern creations geared to the busy career woman.

We are proud of the enormous range of recipes included in this book. Traditional Jewish dishes have been incorporated alongside the contemporary. Quick and easy dishes ideal for a brunch or light family supper appear together with complicated and expensive creations for spectacular entertaining. The recipes cover everything from hearty staples to delicious delicacies.

We have tried to make this a cookbook for all occasions and for all types of foods. If we have succeeded, then this is, truly, a great cookbook.

The book has been organized to be your extra hand for your daily cooking activities. Its major divisions are the categories of food that you might wish to prepare—Appetizers, Soups, Vegetables and Side Dishes, and so on. We have tried to make the index detailed, to help you find recipes as quickly and easily as possible.

All the recipes in this book were tested and closely scrutinized before being approved for inclusion. Many of the traditional recipes, handed down through the generations, had to be transcribed from their colourful but approximate proportions—"a teacup of honey," "a handful of flour," "a few pinches of spice"—to more accurate measurements. All recipes were tested in imperial measures, but metric equivalents have been added for convenience. To maintain Jewish heritage, all recipes conform to the traditions of Jewish dietary law.

There is no one section called "Traditional Foods," since we consider traditional dishes to be part of daily fare, and not symbolic foods to be served on special occasions alone. Most of these dishes evolved to satisfy an economic need; almost all of our favourite Jewish dishes are, in some form, recipes to stretch a limited amount of expensive ingredients to feed a hungry family. At the same time, the recipes reflect their countries of origin, as the same basic idea was adapted to fit the local style of cooking and the ingredients found easily at hand.

Some of the traditional foods were, indeed, created to meet a religious requirement or to symbolize a holiday celebration. The last section of this book contains sample menus of dishes traditionally associated with special Jewish holidays or rituals, although the recipes themselves will appear in the relevant section elsewhere in the book. Passover, with its special dietary restrictions, is in a class of its own; dishes "kosher for Passover" do appear separately, also in the last section of the book. We are particularly proud of the unusual, imaginative, and delicious dishes we have been able to include for Passover.

Several people have spent untold hours completing this book, from the first planning group (Shelley Alexander, Tryna Rudolph, Molly Shugarman, Helen Paull, Elaine Lyons, Jackie White) to those members of the cookbook committee, and the many others, who helped get the manuscript to finished form, especially Allie Greenberg and Mae Pasternack, who typed the recipes; Freda Schachter, who did much of the conversion from imperial to metric measurements; Vicki Mishna, who kept track of the recipes out for testing; Sharon Cairns and Selma Linzer, who liaised with the Chapter and Hadassah-WIZO executive and who assisted with a number of administrative decisions; Rabbi Saul Hyman, who provided the information for the last section of the book. Thanks to Elexis Schloss, for her magic in helping with the photography, and to Cecille Shaw, for her assistance with proofreading. A special thanks is extended to José Druker of Hurtig Publishers, without whose help the book would not have been possible. To all, Hadassah-WIZO says thank you.

And I have a very special personal thank-you to Ricky, Alisa, and Adam, for all their love and encouragement.

Susie Lyons

Appetizers & Hors d'Oeuvres

Appetizers are the overture to the meal. Often served as "finger food" prior to sitting down at table, these delicious morsels serve a two-fold purpose: to whet the appetite of the indifferent, and to appease the palate of the ravenous.

Pleasing to the eye and to the taste, appetizers and hors d'oeuvres set the tone of what is to come. A light hors d'oeuvre such as a savoury dip with fresh vegetables may signify that a substantial main course is to follow, whereas a hot, flaky cream-filled vol-au-vent served as an appetizer at the table may be the introduction to a lighter main course.

Time was when the repertoire of appetizers in the traditional Jewish home consisted of not much more than chopped liver or chopped herring. In the last few decades, accessibility to the foods and cultures of other countries has broadened our horizons. As a result, new and exciting dishes have found a niche and created greater variety in the Jewish *forshpize* glossary.

The charm of the appetizer is its versatility. An independent group, appetizers can stand on their own: a selection may be prepared for a sophisticated light lunch, an after-theatre snack, or a tasty Sunday brunch. An attractive platter of canapés will delight family members and keep their hunger at bay and their spirits up till the dinner hour. Terrines and patés made several days in advance and left to season in the refrigerator till serving time can free a clever hostess on party day. Crisp puff pastries may be made dozens at a time, frozen, and reheated to their flaky delicious best to be served with cocktails on the spur of the moment.

Has there ever existed a Jewish home where "a little something to eat" has not been offered to a guest? Irresistible antipastos, spreads, and savouries are easy to whip up and may be served with flair and confidence. The varieties of their flavours and textures will please even the most discriminating gourmet.

CUCUMBER CHEESE DIP

½ lb.	cream cheese	250 g
4 tbsp.	sour cream	60 mL
2 tbsp.	cucumber, grated	30 mL
½ cup	slivered almonds	125 mL

Thin cheese with cream, then blend in cucumber and nuts. Serve with crackers, potato chips, or raw vegetables for dipping.

BLUE CHEESE DIP

8 oz.	cream cheese	250 g
3 oz.	blue cheese	100 g
3 tbsp.	cream	45 mL
1 tsp.	chives, chopped	5 mL
½ tsp.	Worcestershire sauce	2 mL

Mix all ingredients together until well blended. Excellent as a chip dip.

MEXICAN DIP

2	tomatoes	2
2	green onions	2
1 lb	Jack cheese, grated	500 g
12 oz.	black olives, sliced	340 mL
7½ oz.	green chili peppers	210 mL
	parsley	
2½ oz.	Italian dressing mix	70 g

Chop tomatoes and green onions. Combine all ingredients and mix well.

PINK CHEESE DIP

½ lb.	cream cheese	250 g
2 tbsp.	cream	30 mL
2 tbsp.	French dressing	30 mL
⅓ cup	ketchup	75 mL
1 tbsp.	onion, grated	15 mL
¼ tsp.	salt	1 mL

Mix all ingredients together well.

SPINACH DIP

8 oz.	creamed spinach	250 g
1 tsp.	salt	5 mL
¼ tsp.	onion flakes	1 mL
1 cup	mayonnaise	250 mL
½ cup	sour cream	125 mL
2 drops	Tabasco sauce	2 drops
	pinch of garlic powder	

Combine all ingredients, and mix well. Let stand overnight before serving. (If frozen spinach is used, it must be fully thawed before mixing.) Serve as a vegetable dip.

TAHINI HOUMOUS

19 oz.	chick peas, drained	540 mL
4 oz.	tahini (sesame paste)	113 g
1	green onion, chopped	1
	salt	
	pepper	
⅓ cup	lemon juice	75 mL
2 cloves	garlic, crushed	2 cloves
¼ tsp.	cayenne pepper	1 mL
½ tsp.	cumin	2 mL

Mash chick peas until smooth. Add tahini and mix until smooth. Add remaining ingredients. Season to taste. Serve with pita bread or fresh vegetables for dipping. (Note: ¼ cup (50 mL) oil may be substituted for the tahini.)

CELERY BOUQUET

1 bunch	celery	1 bunch
4 tbsp.	butter	60 mL
	salt	
	pepper	
4 tbsp.	blue cheese	60 mL
4 tbsp.	cream cheese	60 mL

Separate celery stalks, trim ends, wash, and dry thoroughly. Cream half the butter with cream cheese and half with blue cheese. Season with salt and pepper. Stuff smallest stalk with cream cheese mixture, then next smallest stalk with blue cheese mixture and press firmly into first stalk. Continue filling and pressing stalks together, alternating cheese mixtures, until all the celery is formed back into a bunch. Tie with string, wrap in wax paper, and chill. Slice thinly and serve on rye bread. Garnish with chopped olives.

Variation
Other suggested fillings: peanut butter; chopped liver; salmon or tuna spread; other cheese mixtures.

AVOCADO SPREAD

2	avocado pears	2
	lemon juice	
1	egg, hard-boiled	1
1 tbsp.	mayonnaise	15 mL
1	green onion, chopped	1
	salt	
	Tabasco sauce	

Choose ripe avocados, not too soft. Peel, and mash the pulp. Squeeze lemon juice over pulp to prevent darkening. Mash egg and add together with salad dressing. Add onion and season to taste. Mix well. Serve chilled. Store in a tightly covered jar.

GUACAMOLE

2	avocado pears	2
2 tbsp.	lemon juice	30 mL
4	green onions	4
2 medium	tomatoes	2 medium
1/2 tsp.	Tabasco sauce	2 mL
	salt	

Peel and pit avocados and save one pit. Mash avocado pulp until lumpy, not smooth. Immediately add lemon juice to prevent darkening. Finely slice the green onions; peel, seed, and chop tomatoes. Combine all ingredients. Place in a bowl with pit in centre, to retard further discoloration. Serve with chips or crackers.

AVOCADO CANAPÉS

white bread, thinly sliced
rye bread, thinly sliced
margarine
mayonnaise
salt
pepper
cold roast beef, thinly sliced
cold turkey or chicken, thinly sliced
avocado, thinly sliced

Remove crusts from bread. Spread with margarine and seasoned mayonnaise. Place wafer-thin slices of cold meat on white bread and then add a layer of avocado. Top with dark bread. Wrap in a damp towel and refrigerate a few hours. Cut into small wedges. Set upright in tiny pyramids on a tray ringed with parsley. Hold the wedges together with toothpicks.

STUFFED DILLS

dill pickles
pimento cream cheese

Select large dill pickles. Carefully remove centres with an apple corer, and stuff the cavities with pimento cream cheese. Chill. Cut diagonally into slices.

EGGPLANT CAVIAR

1 medium	eggplant	1 medium
1	tomato	1
1	onion	1
1/2	green pepper	1/2
1/2 tsp.	salt	2 mL
	pepper	
	pinch of sugar	
1 tsp.	oil	5 mL

Wash, dry, and prick eggplant in several places (to prevent it exploding in the oven). Bake at 350°F (180°C) for 45 minutes or until soft. Scoop out pulp and chop with the tomato, onion, and green pepper. Season to taste with salt, pepper, sugar, and oil. Store in a tightly covered jar in the refrigerator.

EGGPLANT SPREAD

1 medium	eggplant	1 medium
1	onion	1
1 clove	garlic	1 clove
1/4 cup	oil	50 mL
1/4 cup	white vinegar	50 mL
1 1/2 tsp.	salt	7 mL
1 tsp.	pepper	5 mL

Prick eggplant with a fork. Bake at 375°F (190°C) for 20 minutes; cool, then peel. Grind eggplant and onion. Crush garlic and add. Whip in the oil and vinegar with salt and pepper. Store in a jar in refrigerator but do not freeze. Serve as a dip or spread.

GRATED BLACK RADISH

2	black radishes, peeled	2
1	onion	1
1/4 cup	schmaltz or oil	50 mL
1 1/2 tsp.	salt	7 mL
1/4 tsp.	pepper	1 mL

Grate radish and onion fairly coarse. Add the schmaltz, salt, and pepper. Toss lightly. Chill. Serve with crackers.

CHOPPED SARDINES

1 slice	white bread	1 slice
2 tbsp.	vinegar	30 mL
8 1/2 oz.	Brunswick sardines	240 g
1	egg, hard-boiled	1
1 small	onion, grated	1 small
1/4 tsp.	salt	1 mL
1 small	apple, grated	1 small
1/2 tsp.	sugar	2 mL

Soak bread in vinegar. Combine all ingredients and chop until fine. Serve with crackers or rye bread.

CHOPPED LIVER

1 lb.	liver	500 g
1 large	white onion	1 large
2 tbsp.	oil	30 mL
3 tbsp.	schmaltz or oil	45 mL
1 1/2 tsp.	pepper	7 mL
2 tsp.	salt	10 mL

Use beef, calf, or chicken livers, according to preference. Broil liver until well cooked. Slice onion, and fry in oil until tender and golden brown. Grind liver and onions together and mix with other ingredients. Serve cold on lettuce as a spread or appetizer. (Note: Instead of schmaltz, 2 chicken bouillon cubes and 2 tbsp. (30 mL) margarine may be used.) Serves 6.

CHOPPED CHICKEN LIVERS

1/4 cup	shortening	60 mL
2	onions, sliced	2
1 lb.	chicken livers	500 g
2	eggs, hard-boiled	2
1 1/2 tsp.	salt	7 mL
1/4 tsp.	pepper	1 mL

Melt the shortening in a skillet. Add onions and sauté for 10 minutes, stirring often. Remove the onions and set aside. Wash and drain livers. Broil chicken livers until well done. Remove gristle, and grind the livers with the onions and egg yolks. Add salt and pepper and mix well. Chill.

MOCK CHOPPED LIVER

1 small	onion, sliced	1 small
2 tbsp.	schmaltz or oil	30 mL
1 lb.	green beans, cooked	500 g
8	walnuts	8
1	egg, hard-boiled	1
	salt	
	pepper	
	cinnamon	

Fry onion in schmaltz. Mince with the beans, egg, and nuts. Season, and mix in some fat in which the onions have been fried. Spread onto a platter and decorate with slices of tomato, egg, and cucumber.

LIVER IN RYE ROLL

| 1 loaf | salty rye bread | 1 loaf |
| | chopped liver | |

Scoop out centre of a long, salty rye bread. Fill with chopped liver. Chill overnight. Cut into slices ½'' (1 cm) thick.

CHOPPED BRAINS

2	calf's brains	2
1 tbsp.	vinegar	15 mL
2 tsp.	salt	10 mL
2	onions, chopped	2
4 tbsp.	olive oil	60 mL
3 tbsp.	lemon juice	45 mL
¼ tsp.	pepper	1 mL

Wash brains. Place in a saucepan with water to cover. Add vinegar and salt. Bring to a boil, cover, and cook over low heat for 30 minutes. Drain well. Remove the membrane and chop the brains. Add remaining ingredients, mixing well. Chill.

CHOPPED PICKLED HERRING

8 oz.	pickled herring	250 g
1 large	apple	1 large
1	egg, hard-boiled	1
1 slice	white bread, toasted	1 slice
2 tbsp.	sweet wine	30 mL

Drain herring and onions. Peel and core apple. Grind all ingredients together and blend with wine.

CHOPPED HERRING

3	herring	3
1 large	onion	1 large
1	green pepper	1
4	eggs, hard-boiled	4
2 slices	white bread	2 slices
	pepper	
	oil	
	vinegar	

Soak herring overnight in water to cover, changing water twice. Drain. Remove skin, and fillet. Grind herring, onion, green pepper, eggs, and bread. Add pepper, oil, and vinegar to taste and mix well. Refrigerate in a sealed jar.

ANCHOVY BALLS

4 oz.	anchovy paste	112 g
2	eggs, hard-boiled	2
5 drops	Worcestershire sauce	5 drops
	cayenne pepper	
½ cup	parsley, minced	125 mL

Mash anchovy paste with eggs. Season with Worcestershire sauce and cayenne pepper, and add ¼ cup (50 mL) of the parsley. Form into balls. Roll in remaining parsley.

HOT TUNA FISH CANAPÉS

12 slices	bread	12 slices
1 cup	flaked tuna	250 mL
4 tbsp.	mayonnaise	60 mL
1 tbsp.	ketchup	15 mL
1 tbsp.	vinegar	15 mL
	pepper	
1	cucumber	1
	paprika	

With a cookie cutter or large glass, cut rounds from bread to make approximately 3 dozen. Toast on one side. Mix tuna, mayonnaise, ketchup, vinegar, and pepper to taste. Peel cucumber, flute sides with a fork, and slice. Dip edges in paprika. Place a slice of cucumber on untoasted side of bread. Pile a little tuna fish mixture in centre of each. Garnish with green pepper strips and pimento. Heat under broiler. Serve hot.

MUSHROOM ALMOND PATÉ

1 cup	slivered almonds	250 mL
4 tbsp.	butter	60 mL
3/4 lb.	fresh mushrooms	375 g
1 small	onion, sliced	1 small
1 clove	garlic, minced	1 clove
3/4 tsp.	salt	3 mL
1/4 tsp.	thyme, ground	1 mL
1/8 tsp.	pepper	0.5 mL
2 tbsp.	oil	30 mL

Toast slivered almonds over a medium-low heat in a wide frying pan about 5 to 7 minutes, stirring frequently until lightly browned. Turn nuts out of pan to cool. Melt butter in pan, add sliced mushrooms, onions, garlic, salt, thyme, and pepper. Cook over medium-high heat, stirring occasionally, until most of the liquid evaporates. Chop 2 tbsp. (30 mL) of the almonds and set them aside. Whirl remaining nuts in a blender until finely ground. Continue blending, gradually adding oil, until creamy and smooth. Add mushroom mixture and blend until smooth. Stir in chopped nuts. Serve at room temperature with crackers or raw vegetables.

CREAM CHEESE CAVIAR APPETIZER

6	eggs, hard-boiled	6
1 1/2 tbsp.	mayonnaise	22 mL
	salt	
	pepper	
1 1/2 tbsp.	Spanish onion, grated	22 mL
1/2 lb.	cream cheese	250 g
1 1/2 tbsp.	milk	22 mL
1 3/4 oz.	black lumpfish caviar	50 g

This is beautiful presented on a glass pedestal plate with a small edge; otherwise, serve on a large round plate.

Grate the eggs, not too fine, and combine with mayonnaise and seasonings. Spread over bottom of plate. Sprinkle grated onion over the egg layer. Blend cream cheese and milk and spread over the onion. If making this ahead of time, stop here, cover with plastic wrap and refrigerate. Just before serving, drain the caviar and spread on top of cheese mixture. Serve with crackers. (Note: 1 1/4 cups (300 mL) sour cream may be substituted for the cream cheese and milk.)

ANTIPASTO

14 oz.	white tuna chunks	400 g
24 oz.	sweet pickles	682 mL
6 oz.	sweet onions	188 mL
24 oz.	stuffed green olives	682 mL
10 oz.	button mushrooms	284 mL
10 oz.	chili sauce	285 mL
11 oz.	ketchup	360 mL
1 tbsp.	lemon juice	15 mL
1/2 tsp.	dry mustard	2 mL
	dash of Worcestershire sauce	

Blanch tuna. Chop pickles and onions into large chunks, and slice olives. Combine all ingredients. Chill.

ANTIPASTO

1	cauliflower	1
1	green pepper, diced	1
1/2 cup	pimento, diced	125 mL
12 oz.	pickled sweet onions	375 mL
24 oz.	sweet mixed pickles	500 mL
12 oz.	gherkins, sliced	375 mL
14 oz.	cut green beans	398 mL
2 oz.	anchovies, chopped	50 g
10 oz.	mushrooms, sliced	284 mL
19 1/2 oz.	flaked tuna	552 g
20 oz.	ketchup	568 mL
1/2 cup	oil	125 mL

overleaf:
Chopped Liver (page 14); Seviche (page 19)

Drain liquids from canned ingredients and discard. Break cauliflower into flowerettes. Combine all ingredients in a large pot and simmer for 1 hour. May be frozen, or kept in refrigerator for up to 6 weeks.

ANTIPASTO

16 oz.	cauliflower	455 mL
12 oz.	green olives	341 mL
7 oz.	black olives	200 mL
14 oz.	tuna, drained	396 g
8 oz.	button mushrooms	227 mL
24 oz.	sweet mixed pickles	682 mL
13 oz.	pearl onions	375 mL
15 oz.	ketchup	450 mL
15 oz.	hot ketchup	450 mL
10 oz.	chili sauce	285 mL
	horseradish	

Chop fine or process with grater blade of food processor. Mix all together.

SEVICHE

1 lb.	fillet of sole or flounder	500 g
8 oz.	bottled lemon juice	250 mL
1	English cucumber	1
4	tomatoes	4
1 large	onion	1 large
1 cup	celery	250 mL
14 oz.	canned tomatoes	375 mL
4 tbsp.	lemon juice	60 mL
	salt	
	pepper	
	Tabasco sauce	

Cut fish into 1'' (2 cm) cubes. Pour bottled lemon juice over. Cover and refrigerate at least 24 hours. Strain, and discard juice. Peel cucumber and cut in cubes. Chop fresh tomatoes, onion, and celery. Drain canned tomatoes, reserving juice, and chop. Mix vegetables and fish together. Combine reserved tomato juice with lemon juice, seasoning to taste. Pour over fish. Chill well. Serve as an appetizer or side dish. Serves 4.

SALMON SPREAD APPETIZER

7¾ oz.	sockeye salmon	220 g
½ lb.	cream cheese	250 g
1 tsp.	white horseradish	5 mL
¾ tsp.	liquid smoke	3 mL
1 tsp.	lemon juice	5 mL
2 tbsp.	onion flakes	30 mL

Drain salmon and combine well with other ingredients. Chill. Serve with crackers.

LAYERED TACO SPREAD

14 oz.	refried beans	398 mL
	garlic	
	chili powder	
2 small	avocado pears	2 small
½ tsp.	lemon juice	2 mL
¾ cup	sour cream	175 mL
1	tomato, chopped	1
7 oz.	black olives, chopped	200 mL
3	green onions, chopped	3
	Cheddar cheese, grated	

This dish is assembled in layers on the serving plate.

Mash beans and fry with garlic and chili powder until dry. Spread onto the plate as the first layer. Mash avocados with lemon juice; spread on. Add a layer of sour cream. Mix chopped tomato, olives, and green onion, and spread over. Top with cheese. Serve with crackers.

HOT ARTICHOKE SPREAD

14 oz.	canned artichoke hearts	398 mL
½ cup	mayonnaise	125 mL
½ cup	Parmesan cheese, grated	125 mL
7½ oz.	green chilis	213 mL

Drain and chop the artichokes. Mix all ingredients together. Bake in a casserole at 350°F (180°C) for 30 to 45 minutes. Serve with crackers.

CHOPPED EGGS AND ONION

2 small	onions	2 small
8	eggs, hard-boiled	8
1 1/2 tsp.	salt	7 mL
1/4 tsp.	pepper	1 mL
4 tbsp.	schmaltz or oil	60 mL

Chop onions very fine. Add eggs and continue chopping. Add salt, pepper, and schmaltz. Mix lightly. Serve with crackers.

SARDINE DEVILLED EGGS

3	eggs, hard-boiled	3
1 tbsp.	mayonnaise	15 mL
1 tsp.	prepared mustard	5 mL
1 tsp.	onion, minced	5 mL
4 1/4 oz.	sardines, mashed	120 g
1 tsp.	capers	5 mL
	salt	
	pepper	

Halve eggs lengthwise. Remove yolks and mash. Combine with rest of ingredients. Mix well and re-fill whites. Garnish with parsley and capers and serve on lettuce leaves.

PRETZEL TWIGS

1/4 lb.	cream cheese	112 g
	salt	
	pepper	
	Tabasco sauce	
24	pretzel twigs	24
	pistachio nuts, chopped	

Cream the cheese with salt, pepper, and Tabasco sauce to taste. Take a spoonful of the cheese. Twirl the end of a pretzel in the cheese in the spoon. Roll the dipped portion in finely chopped nuts. The twigs should be prepared just before serving. Do not chill, as they will soften. (Note: Instead of pistachio nuts, toasted blanched almonds, chopped finely, may be used.)

APPETIZER OR CANAPÉ PASTRY

1 cup	butter	250 mL
1 2/3 cups	flour	400 mL
1/2 lb.	cream cheese	250 g

Rub butter into flour and bind with cheese. Knead into a smooth pastry and store in refrigerator until required. Roll pastry thinly, cut into squares, and fill. Roll up or fold into triangles (depending on filling), and bake in a hot oven for 10 minutes. (This pastry may also be cut into cookie shapes, brushed with beaten egg, sprinkled with sugar, and baked as cookies.)

Suggested Fillings

- Asparagus seasoned with salt and cayenne pepper.

- Grated cheese flavoured with cayenne pepper on a drop of mayonnaise.

- Sardines mashed with seasonings and mayonnaise.

- Hard-boiled eggs mashed with seasonings and mayonnaise.

- Anchovies and egg.

MUSHROOM VOL-AU-VENTS

2 medium	onions, diced	2 medium
1/2 cup	green pepper, diced	125 mL
1 cup	celery, diced	250 mL
1 lb.	fresh mushrooms	500 g
2 tbsp.	flour	30 mL
1 cup	milk	250 mL
	patty shells	

Sauté onions, green pepper, and celery until golden brown. Add mushrooms, and cook 5 minutes. Sprinkle with flour. Stir, then add milk. Keep hot in the top of a double boiler until ready to fill shells and serve. Serves 6 – 8.

CHEESE CRISPS

2 cups	Cheddar cheese, grated	500 mL
1/2 cup	soft margarine	125 mL
1 cup	flour	250 mL
	salt	
	pepper	
1/2 tsp.	dry mustard	2 mL
1/4 tsp.	paprika	1 mL
1/3 cup	sesame seeds, toasted	75 mL

Cream the margarine and cheese together. Add flour and seasonings, blending well. Roll into 3/4'' (2 cm) balls, roll in sesame seeds, and bake on an ungreased cookie sheet at 425°F (220°C) for 15 minutes. May be served as an appetizer or as a side dish with a light dairy dinner.

CHEESE PUFFS

1 cup	sharp cheese, grated	250 mL
1 tbsp.	butter	15 mL
	salt	
	pepper	
1 cup	flour	250 mL
2 tsp.	baking powder	10 mL
1	egg	1
3/4 cup	milk	175 mL

Cream cheese and butter. Add salt and pepper to season well. Add flour and baking powder and rub through the fingers. Beat egg, and add enough milk to make up 1 cup (250 mL). Add gradually to cheese mixture. Dough must be very soft. Drop by the spoonful onto a greased cookie sheet and bake at 425°F (220°C) for 7 to 10 minutes. Yields 24.

CHEESE OLIVE SNACKS

10 oz.	vol-au-vent pastry	283 g
1 cup	Cheddar cheese, grated	250 mL
1/2 cup	stuffed olives, sliced	125 mL
3 tbsp.	butter	45 mL
1 1/2 tbsp.	onion, chopped	20 mL
1	egg	1

Roll each pastry round into a square 1/8'' (0.25 cm) thick. Cut each into 4 triangles. Place flat on a greased cookie sheet. In mixing bowl, combine remaining ingredients. Equally divide cheese mixture between the triangles, spreading to within 1/4'' (0.5 cm) of edges. Fold points in. Bake at 375°F (190°C) for 13 to 20 minutes. Remove from pan. Serve hot. Yields 24 triangles.

CHEDDAR CHEESE BALLS

2 cups	Cheddar cheese, grated	500 mL
2 tbsp.	sherry	30 mL
1/3 cup	mayonnaise	75 mL
	walnuts, crushed	

Mix cheese, sherry, and mayonnaise. Chill. Shape into balls and roll in chopped nuts.

CHEESE SNACKS

1/2 lb.	cream cheese	250 g
1 cup	butter	250 mL
	cayenne pepper	
2 cups	flour	500 mL
	paprika	

Cream together cheese, butter, and a dash of cayenne. Work in the flour with fingertips. Refrigerate until cold. Make small balls and place on foil-lined cookie sheets. Pinch up. Sprinkle each with paprika and bake at 375°F (190°C) for 15 minutes.

CHEESE RYE BREAD

2 cups	Cheddar cheese, grated	500 mL
3 1/2 oz.	olives, chopped	105 g
1/2 cup	green onion, chopped	125 mL
1 tsp.	curry powder	5 mL
2 tbsp.	mayonnaise	30 mL

Combine ingredients, using just enough mayonnaise to moisten. Spread on party rye bread. Bake at 350°F (180°C) for 10 minutes or until bubbly.

VEGETARIAN EGG ROLLS

Prepare 15 paper-thin blintzes, using the batter on p. 52.

Filling

1¼ oz.	dried mushrooms	35 g
16 oz.	canned bean sprouts	500 mL
10 oz.	canned water chestnuts	284 mL
1 cup	canned bamboo shoots	250 mL
2 tsp.	peanut oil	10 mL
2 tsp.	sesame seeds	10 mL
½ tsp.	monosodium glutamate	2 mL
	salt	
	pepper	

Soak mushrooms 2 to 3 hours. Drain and chop coarsely. Drain canned ingredients, and chop or slice finely. Combine with all ingredients for filling. Place 1 tbsp. (15 mL) of mixture in the centre of each pancake. Fold over 3 sides and roll. Make a paste of flour and warm water, and seal flap. Deep fry in hot oil.

Variation
For chicken egg roll, add 2 cups (500 mL) cooked shredded chicken.

COCKTAIL BLINTZES

Use blintz batter (page 52). Make 12 to 15 blintzes, about the size of a bread plate. Cut them in half, for very small blintzes.

Meat Filling

1 lb.	cooked meat	500 g
1	onion	1
	salt	
	pepper	
	schmaltz or oil	

Fry onion. Mince with meat. Add seasoning and schmaltz to moisten. Place 1 tbsp. (15 mL) in the middle of each blintz, fold over 3 sides and roll. Fry until lightly browned.

BARBECUE SAUCE FOR COCKTAIL WIENERS

1 cup	onion, chopped	250 mL
1 clove	garlic	1 clove
4 tbsp.	oil	60 mL
1 cup	green pepper, chopped	250 mL
¾ cup	celery, chopped	175 mL
½ cup	chili sauce	125 mL
1 tbsp.	prepared mustard	15 mL
1½ tsp.	sugar	7 mL
1 tbsp.	Worcestershire sauce	15 mL
½ tsp.	salt	2 mL

Fry onion and garlic in oil until golden brown. Add remaining ingredients and cook 5 to 10 minutes.

FINGER DRUMSTICKS

3 lb.	chicken wings	1.5 kg
½ cup	sugar	125 mL
3 tbsp.	cornstarch	45 mL
1 tsp.	salt	5 mL
½ tsp.	ginger	2 mL
¼ tsp.	pepper	1 mL
¾ cup	water	175 mL
⅓ cup	lemon juice	75 mL
¼ cup	soy sauce	50 mL

Cut wings in half. Bake in a 400°F (200°C) oven for 30 minutes. Turn once. Mix sugar, cornstarch, salt, ginger, and pepper in a pan. Stir in remaining ingredients. Cook until thick, and boil 3 minutes. Brush over chicken. Continue baking, turning and brushing, for another 40 minutes until richly glazed.

Soups

Beautiful soup so rich and green,
Waiting in a hot tureen.
Who for such dainties would not stoop,
Soup of the evening, beautiful soup!

Venerated by the Mock Turtle in *Alice in Wonderland*, soups are for all seasons and senses.

Hot, cold, clear, creamy or chunky. Be it exuberant Gazpacho as a first course or a hearty Beet Borscht as the main event, soup satisfies! The school lunch standby of hot soup and sandwich graduates to luncheons of iced soup and salad, or is transformed into late-night suppers of crusty cheese-baked onion soup.

The faith of Jewish mothers in the nutritious value of soups, particularly chicken soup, has been the butt of many a Catskill comedian's humour. Yet "Jewish penicillin" has indeed been proven by scientists to relieve the symptoms of the common cold.

Not to be taken lightly is the economical factor. A real *balabosta* knows how to make a few ounces of meat, a few root vegetables, and some herbs into an extraordinarily delicious broth. In many countries, a large soup-kettle stands permanently on the back burner of the stove, simmering languidly. The meat and vegetable trimmings from each day's meal preparations are invested in the pot, along with an appropriate amount of water and seasonings. *Voilà*! The family "soup du jour."

At any family gathering or formal dinner, one of the highlights is surely the moment when the hostess lifts the lid from the soup tureen and ladles the aromatic contents into bowls to serve her eager guests.

CHICKEN SOUP

4 lb.	chicken	1.8 kg
8 cups	cold water	2 L
1 large	white onion	1 large
5 tsp.	salt	25 mL
1 1/2 tsp.	pepper	7 mL
1 tbsp.	sugar	15 mL
4 stalks	celery, with tops	4 stalks
4 large	carrots	4 large
3 sprigs	fresh parsley	3 sprigs
1	parsnip, peeled	1

Place chicken and onion in cold water in a large soup pot. Add seasonings. At high temperature, bring just to the boil, reduce heat to a low simmer and add remaining ingredients. Simmer for 2 to 3 hours, removing the parsnip after 1 hour. Skim the top before serving. (For very clear broth, strain through cheesecloth and discard vegetables that have been cooked with soup.)

GAZPACHO

2/3 cup	tomatoes, finely diced	150 mL
1/3 cup	green pepper, finely diced	75 mL
1/3 cup	celery, finely diced	75 mL
1/3 cup	cucumber, finely diced	75 mL
3 tbsp.	green onion, finely diced	45 mL
4 cups	tomato paste	1 L
1/4 tsp.	Tabasco sauce	1 mL
1/2 tsp.	Worcestershire sauce	2 mL
1 tsp.	basil	5 mL
1 clove	garlic, finely chopped	1 clove
1 tsp.	salt	5 mL
1/4 tsp.	pepper	1 mL
3 tbsp.	oil	45 mL
3 tbsp.	wine vinegar	45 mL
1 tbsp.	lemon juice	15 mL
2 cups	tomato juice	500 mL
3 tbsp.	parsley, chopped	45 mL

Combine all ingredients and chill several hours before serving. Garnish the soup with chopped parsley and garlic croutons. Traditionally, the soup is served with additional finely diced vegetables passed in small bowls so that guests may add more to the soup to suit their tastes. Serves 8.

MOCK TWO-MINUTE GAZPACHO

1 large	cucumber	1 large
4 cups	buttermilk	1 L
14 oz.	condensed tomato soup	398 mL
	salt	
	pepper	
1 tsp.	sugar	5 mL
1 tsp.	curry powder	5 mL
	Tabasco sauce	

Chop cucumber finely and mix with buttermilk and undiluted tomato soup. Add seasonings. Chill and serve. Serves 10.

BLENDER GAZPACHO

28 oz.	stewed tomatoes	796 mL
1 1/2	cucumbers, peeled	1 1/2
1	green pepper	1
2 cloves	garlic	2 cloves
3 stalks	celery	3 stalks
1 small	Spanish onion	1 small
2 tsp.	Worcestershire sauce	10 mL
1 tbsp.	vinegar	15 mL
	tomato juice	

Chop vegetables in blender. Add Worcestershire sauce and vinegar, and thin with tomato juice. Garnish with pieces of cucumber and green pepper.

BEET BORSCHT

2 lb.	short ribs or brisket	1 kg
2 pieces	sour salt	2 pieces
6	beets	6
2 medium	onions	2 medium
2 tbsp.	sugar	30 mL
1 clove	garlic	1 clove
	salt	
	pepper	

Simmer beef in water to cover. Skim to clear. When no more scum rises to the top, add sour salt, peeled and sliced onions and beets, sugar, and seasoning. Mince garlic; add to broth. Cook about 3 hours until meat is tender. Correct seasonings. Serve hot. (Note: Juice of 1 large lemon may be substituted for the sour salt.)

COLD BEET BORSCHT

6	beets with greens	6
8 cups	water	2 L
1 tsp.	salt	5 mL
2 tbsp.	lemon juice	30 mL
2 tsp.	sugar	10 mL
2	eggs	2

Wash beets and greens thoroughly. Boil in water for 15 minutes. Remove beets and grate. Return grated beets to liquid. Add salt to taste, lemon juice, and sugar to taste. Simmer slowly another 15 minutes. Allow to cool for 30 minutes. Beat eggs well in a large bowl. Slowly pour a small amount of warm borscht into the beaten eggs, stirring constantly. Add remaining borscht to egg mixture, stirring constantly to prevent the egg from curdling. Serve cold with sour cream, boiled potato, chopped scallions, or hard-boiled eggs as desired.

BEET AND RHUBARB BORSCHT

6 large	beets, peeled	6 large
1½ lb.	rhubarb	750 g
1 large	onion, diced	1 large
1 lb.	short ribs with bone	500 g
	water	
¾ cup	sugar	175 mL
2 tbsp.	lemon juice	30 mL
	salt	
	pepper	

Place whole beets, rhubarb, onion, and short ribs in a 4 quart (4 L) soup pot. Add cold water to fill three-quarters of the pot. Boil gently for 3 to 4 hours. Remove beets, dice, and return to soup. Season to taste with sugar, lemon juice, and salt and pepper.

QUICK TCHAV

12 oz.	frozen chopped spinach	340 g
4 cups	water	1 L
	salt	
3 tbsp.	lemon juice	45 mL
1	egg	1

Place spinach in a deep pot of boiling salted water. Bring to a boil again and add lemon juice. Skim foam from surface, partly cover, and cook for about 1 hour. Cool slightly. Beat egg and gradually add to spinach soup. Mix well, and cool. When cool enough, place in refrigerator to chill.

Serve garnished with sour cream, hard-boiled eggs, scallions, diced cucumber, or with a hot boiled potato, according to preference.

VICHYSSOISE

4	leeks, thinly sliced	4
2	white onions, sliced	2
½ cup	butter	125 mL
6	potatoes, halved	6
1 tsp.	salt	5 mL
	pepper	
1 cup	cream or sour cream	250 mL
1 cup	milk	250 mL
1 tbsp.	chives, chopped	15 mL

Sauté leeks and onion in butter for 5 minutes in a deep saucepan. Add potatoes, salt, pepper, and enough cold water to cover. Bring to a boil. Reduce heat. Cover and simmer for 45 minutes. Press through sieve or purée. Stir in cream and milk. Chill.

Variations

Avocado Vichyssoise
Blend one avocado and add to vichyssoise. Liquidize one large bunch of parsley. Add to soup with

lemon juice and a small amount of white wine to taste.

Cucumber Vichyssoise

Peel one medium cucumber, slice thinly and remove seeds. Salt the slices and put them under a weight for half a day, then drain and add to vichyssoise. Add one small bunch of parsley, chopped, and leaves of one medium bunch of dill. Chill well before serving.

SWEET AND SOUR CABBAGE SOUP

2 lb.	cabbage, shredded	1 kg
1 lb.	soup bones	500 g
28 oz.	tomatoes	796 mL
1	onion, minced	1
1 clove	garlic, minced	1 clove
16 cups	water	4 L
1 piece	sour salt	1 piece
2 tbsp.	raisins	30 mL
	salt	
	pepper	
	sugar	

Combine all ingredients in a pot and cook about 2 hours. Season to taste.

FAVOURITE BARLEY SOUP

1/2 cup	medium barley	125 mL
1/2 cup	lima beans	125 mL
1/4 cup	split peas	50 mL
8 cups	water	2 L
1 lb.	short ribs	500 g
1	onion, cut up	1
1	carrot, grated	1
4 – 5	dried mushrooms	4 – 5
	salt	
	pepper	

Thoroughly rinse the barley, lima beans, and split peas. Cook with meat about 1 hour in boiling water. Add onion, carrot, and mushrooms. Simmer another 1 1/2 hours, stirring occasionally. Add salt and pepper. Soup will be quite thick when done.

BEAN AND BARLEY SOUP

1 cup	white beans	250 mL
1 cup	orange lentils	250 mL
1/3 cup	pearl barley	75 mL
1/2 cup	split green peas	125 mL
1 medium	onion, chopped	1 medium
1 stalk	celery, sliced	1 stalk
2	carrots, diced	2
1 tbsp.	onion soup mix	15 mL
1 tbsp.	chicken soup mix	15 mL
1 tbsp.	vegetable soup mix	15 mL
10 cups	water	2.5 L
1 tbsp.	margarine	15 mL
	salt	
	pepper	
1 tsp.	sugar	5 mL

Soak beans overnight. Combine all ingredients and cook for 1 to 1 1/2 hours.

CUCUMBER SOUP

3 tbsp.	butter	45 mL
3 cups	pareve chicken bouillon	750 mL
1	onion, grated	1
	salt	
	pepper	
3 large	cucumbers	3 large
1/2 cup	cream	125 mL

Heat butter until softened. Pour in bouillon. Add onion, salt, and pepper. Cool. Chop cucumber and stir into soup together with cream. Chill.

STEAK SOUP

4 stalks	celery	4 stalks
2	parsnips	2
3	carrots	3
2 small	potatoes	2 small
1 lb.	chuck steak, sliced	500 g
4 cups	beef broth	1 L
1 tbsp.	flour	15 mL
1 tbsp.	margarine	15 mL

Cut all vegetables into uniform cubes, about ½'' (1 cm). Brown steak, and add to broth with all vegetables. Cook 1½ hours. Brown flour with margarine and add this roux to thicken the soup.

HEARTY VEGETABLE SOUP

2 lb.	chuck	1 kg
12 cups	water	3 L
2 ears	fresh corn	2 ears
8 oz.	string beans	250 g
8 oz.	peas	250 g
1	parsnip	1
2	tomatoes	2
3	carrots	3
3 stalks	celery	3 stalks
1	onion	1
3 stems	parsley	3 stems
	salt	
½ cup	fine noodles	125 mL

Bring meat and water to a boil; skim top. Cut corn off cobs, dice vegetables, and add to soup. Cook slowly for 2 hours. Adjust seasoning. Add noodles and boil for 20 minutes more.

VEGETABLE MILK SOUP

4	carrots, grated	4
1 cup	peas	250 mL
4 stalks	celery	4 stalks
2 small	onions	2 small
2	potatoes, diced	2
3 oz.	vegetable soup mix	85 g
4 tbsp.	butter	60 mL
4 cups	water	1 L
4 cups	milk	1 L
	salt	
	pepper	

Combine vegetables with soup mix, 2 tbsp. (30 mL) of the butter, and water. Cook over medium heat for 1 hour. Add milk and remaining butter, and season to taste. Cook another 1 to 1½ hours until vegetables are tender.

TUNA CORN CHOWDER

14 oz.	flaked tuna	398 mL
2 medium	onions, diced	2 medium
2 tbsp.	butter	30 mL
3 medium	potatoes, diced	3 medium
	salt	
	pepper	
1½ cups	water	375 mL
2 cups	milk	500 mL
14 oz.	cream-style corn	396 mL

Drain tuna well. Sauté onions in butter in the soup pot. Add potatoes, salt and pepper, and water. Cook, covered, for 15 to 20 minutes until potatoes are done. Add milk, corn, and tuna. Heat until simmering and serve.

FISH CHOWDER

2 fillets	haddock or halibut	2 fillets
5	potatoes, cubed	5
2	onions, chopped	2
2 cups	whipping cream	500 mL
2 tbsp.	butter	30 mL
	salt	
	pepper	

Steam fish until it flakes when tested with a fork, approximately 10 minutes. Place potatoes and onions in a soup pot with water to cover, and boil just until tender. Add fish and more water, just enough to cover. Add remaining ingredients and heat 20 minutes. Do not boil. Serves 6.

TOMATO SOUP

57 oz.	canned tomatoes	1.6 L
1 tsp.	salt	5 mL
⅛ tsp.	pepper	0.5 mL
1 tsp.	sugar	5 mL
1 tsp.	baking soda	5 mL
2½ cups	milk	625 mL
2 tbsp.	butter	30 mL
2 tbsp.	flour	30 mL

Break up tomatoes and combine with seasonings, sugar, and baking soda in the top of a double boiler. Heat, stirring, until smooth. Keep hot but do not boil. Combine butter and flour in a saucepan and heat, gradually adding the milk, until hot. Again, do not boil. Mix in tomato mixture and keep hot. Serve immediately. Serves 8.

CURRIED TOMATO SOUP

20 oz.	condensed tomato soup	560 mL
2 cups	cold water	500 mL
1 1/4 cups	sour cream	300 mL
1 tbsp.	horseradish	15 mL
1 tsp.	curry powder	5 mL
1/2 cup	dry sherry	125 mL

Blend ingredients together thoroughly. Chill at least 4 hours before serving.

TOMATO CONSOMMÉ

10 oz.	beef bouillon	284 mL
20 oz.	condensed tomato soup	568 mL
10 oz.	tomato juice	284 mL
4 cups	water	1 L
1 tbsp.	onion, finely grated	15 mL
1/2 cup	dry sherry	125 mL

In a large saucepan, combine first 5 ingredients. Heat thoroughly. Add sherry, heat again, and serve.

HOT TOMATO BOUILLON

20 oz.	condensed tomato soup	568 mL
20 oz.	beef bouillon	568 mL
20 oz.	water	568 mL
1/4 tsp.	oregano	1 mL
1/8 tsp.	garlic powder	0.5 mL

Combine ingredients in a saucepan. Bring to simmer. Serve.

Variation
Add vodka and serve cold as a cocktail.

TOMATO AND RICE SOUP

4	soup bones	4
4 cups	water	1 L
20 oz.	canned tomatoes	568 mL
1	onion, diced	1
	salt	
	pepper	
1/2 cup	rice, uncooked	125 mL

Place bones in water. Bring to a boil and skim. Add tomatoes, onion, and seasonings. Simmer for 1 1/2 hours. Add rice and cook 20 minutes longer. Remove bones. Serves 6.

TOMATO CHOWDER

2 cups	potatoes, diced	500 mL
3/4 cup	onion, diced	175 mL
1 cup	celery, chopped	250 mL
3 cups	tomatoes, chopped	750 mL
3 1/2 tsp.	salt	17 mL
1/2 tsp.	pepper	2 mL
1 tsp.	oregano	5 mL
2 1/2 cups	boiling water	625 mL
3 tbsp.	butter	45 mL
1/4 cup	flour	50 mL
1/2 tsp.	dry mustard	2 mL
2 cups	milk	500 mL
1 tsp.	Worcestershire sauce	5 mL
1 1/2 cups	Cheddar cheese, grated	375 mL
1 tbsp.	parsley, chopped	15 mL

Combine vegetables with 2 tsp. (10 mL) of the salt, 1/4 tsp. (1 mL) pepper, oregano, and water in a large pot. Bring to boil. Cover and simmer until vegetables are tender, approximately 15 minutes. Melt butter in a saucepan. Sprinkle in flour, remaining salt, pepper, and mustard, and stir to blend. Remove from heat and add milk all at once. Stir in Worcestershire sauce. Cook over moderate heat, stirring constantly, until thick and smooth. Add cheese and continue heating gently, stirring until cheese is melted. Add to vegetable soup. Mix in parsley. Bring to boiling and serve. Serves 6 – 8.

TOMATO BORSCHT

5 lb.	beef chuck or short ribs	2.5 kb
4 medium	onions	4 medium
6	beets	6
1/2 medium	cabbage	1/2 medium
3 large	carrots	3 large
10 oz.	condensed tomato soup	284 mL
14 oz.	canned tomatoes	398 mL
4 tbsp.	lemon juice	60 mL
1/3 cup	sugar	75 mL
	salt	
	ketchup	

Set meat in a pot about half-full of water, bring to a boil, and cook for 1 1/2 hours. Shred the onions, beets, cabbage, and carrots, and add to the meat. Cook for another hour. Together with tomato soup, undrained tomatoes, and lemon juice, add sugar, salt, and ketchup to taste. Cook for a further hour. (Note: Sour salt may be substituted for the lemon juice.)

SPLIT PEA SOUP

3 lb.	short ribs	1.5 kg
10 cups	water	2.5 L
2	onions	2
4	carrots	4
4 stalks	celery, with leaves	4 stalks
1 1/2 lb.	split peas	680 g
2 tbsp.	salt	30 mL
1 tsp.	pepper	5 mL
1 tsp.	peppercorns	5 mL
1 tbsp.	garlic	15 mL

In a large soup pot, cover meat and bones with water and bring to a boil; discard water. Add the 10 cups (2.5 L) cold water, whole fresh vegetables, dried peas, and seasonings. Boil gently for 2 to 2 1/2 hours. Remove meat and carrots, and reserve. Process soup through a blender, then pour into sealers to store. Divide meat and carrots between the jars, chopping or leaving whole as desired. To serve: Thin with boiling water to make soup the preferred consistency, and garnish with sliced salami.

VEGETARIAN SPLIT PEA SOUP

1 lb.	split peas	454 g
8 cups	cold water	2 L
2 stalks	celery, sliced	2 stalks
2	carrots, diced	2
2 small	onions, chopped	2 small
2 tsp.	salt	10 mL
1 tsp.	pepper	5 mL
1 tbsp.	parsley	15 mL

Combine peas and water in a dutch oven or soup pot, and boil gently until peas are soft. Add remaining ingredients and cook until vegetables are tender, approximately 30 minutes.

CREAM OF MUSHROOM SOUP

1 lb.	fresh mushrooms	500 g
	salt	
	pepper	
1 medium	onion, diced	1 medium
2 tbsp.	butter	30 mL
1/2 cup	water	125 mL
4 tbsp.	tomato paste	60 mL
1 large	potato, diced	1 large
1 cup	cream	250 mL

Wash mushrooms well, dry and slice them. Sprinkle with salt and pepper. In a saucepan, brown onion in butter. Add mushrooms and cook about 5 minutes, adding water if mushrooms become dry. Stir in tomato paste and potato. Simmer, covered, over very low heat until potatoes are soft. Add cream. Heat and serve. Serves 6.

MUSHROOM SOUP

1 1/2 lb.	fresh mushrooms	750 g
2 tbsp.	margarine	30 mL
2 tbsp.	onion, minced	30 mL
6 cups	chicken bouillon	1.5 L
1/2 tsp.	salt	2 mL

| 1 tsp. | lemon juice | 5 mL |
| 1 | lemon, thinly sliced | 1 |

Wash mushrooms and chop finely. Melt margarine in a large saucepan. Sauté onion until translucent. Add mushrooms and cook 5 minutes longer, stirring occasionally. Pour in bouillon. Bring to a boil, then reduce heat and simmer uncovered for 30 minutes. Cool. Strain soup through a coarse sieve, pressing mushrooms firmly to extract all the liquid. (The strainer must be coarse enough to let specks of mushrooms through.) Season with salt and lemon juice, and garnish individual bowls with lemon slices.

MAST VA KHIAR (PERSIAN YOGURT SOUP)

½ cup	raisins	125 mL
2½ cups	yogurt	625 mL
½ cup	cream	125 mL
1	hard-boiled egg, chopped	1
6	ice cubes	6
1	cucumber, chopped	1
¼ cup	green onion, chopped	50 mL
2 tsp.	salt	10 mL
½ tsp.	pepper	2 mL
1 cup	cold water	250 mL
1 tsp.	parsley, chopped	5 mL
1 tsp.	fresh dill, chopped	5 mL

Soak raisins in cold water for 5 minutes. Combine yogurt in a big mixing bowl with cream, egg, ice cubes, chopped cucumber, green onions, salt, and pepper. Drain raisins and add. Mix in cold water. Refrigerate 2 to 3 hours before serving. Garnish with parsley and dill. Serves 4 – 5.

FRUIT SOUP

2 lb.	apricots	1 kg
1 lb.	peaches or pears	500 g
5	apples	5
4 cups	water	1 L
16 oz.	orange juice concentrate	500 mL
6	ice cubes	6
	sugar	

Cook fruit 15 to 20 minutes until soft. Add concentrate and purée. Add ice cubes and sugar to taste, garnish with sour cherries or sliced fruit, and serve with a dollop of sour cream or yogurt.

MANDLEN (SOUP NUTS)

3	eggs	3
2 tbsp.	oil	30 mL
2 cups	flour	500 mL
1 tsp.	salt	5 mL

Mix all ingredients, using only enough flour to make a soft dough just firm enough to roll with the hands. Divide dough into 2 or 3 parts and roll into ropes ³/₈'' (1 cm) thick. Cut into ½'' (1 cm) pieces. Bake on a well-greased cookie sheet at 375°F (190°C) until golden brown. Shake pan occasionally or turn nuts so that they brown evenly on all sides.

Salads

Imagination and a head of lettuce. Add tomato and avocado slices for chunky firmness, celery for crunch, elegant English cucumber for body and, for sincerity, grated Cheddar cheese. Enhance with a pungent creamy garlic dressing, toss with gay abandon, and enjoy a perfect marriage of nature's bounty in a bowl.

The days of the victory vegetable patch in the back yard, nurtured and weeded till vine-ripened tomatoes and tender lettuce were presented as the first summer salad, are only nostalgia now. From South and Central America, as well as the U.S. and Australia, the most exotic fruits and vegetables are trucked to our local markets. Produce of every description abounds, in season and out. Endive, artichoke, and avocado have become as commonplace as carrot and celery. The varieties of lettuce alone are enough to create salad excitement.

Fashions in salads have changed as well, and there is a salad for every season. A cool, beautiful summer luncheon buffet, casually served out of doors or more formally laid out in the dining room, may be arranged easily and with elegant results: Beet Borscht Mould with sour cream; the lemon mint pizzaz of Tabbouleh; marinated vegetables; several bowls of vivacious greens; and for dessert, a shimmering Ginger Ale and Fruit Mould. Irresistible and impressive.

January and February appreciate salads with a different point of view: hearty Mexican Salad with cheese and pinto beans, or tasty Artichoke and Chick Pea Salad, is a menu brightener for those wintry days.

A cheerful herb garden in the kitchen window or an adventurous dried herb collection will work magic on salads, and reward them all year round with snippets of freshness.

BIBB LETTUCE SALAD WITH GRAPES

3 heads	bibb lettuce	3 heads
1 lb.	grapes	500 g
1/8 tsp.	salt	0.5 mL
1/4 tsp.	pepper	1 mL
1/8 tsp.	oregano	0.5 mL
1 clove	garlic, minced	1 clove
5 tbsp.	olive oil	75 mL
1 tbsp.	red wine vinegar	15 mL

Wash lettuce and pat leaves dry with paper towels. Break into bite-sized pieces in a salad bowl. Gently toss with grapes. Add salt, pepper, oregano, and garlic. Mix oil and vinegar, and sprinkle over salad. Toss gently.

FRENCH SALAD

6 tbsp.	oil	90 mL
2 tbsp.	lemon juice	30 mL
1/2 tsp.	salt	2 mL
1 tbsp.	prepared mustard	15 mL
	tarragon leaves	
1 clove	garlic	1 clove
1 tbsp.	parsley, chopped	15 mL
2	green onions, chopped	2
1 head	lettuce	1 head
2 bunches	watercress	2 bunches
1 bunch	endive	1 bunch

With a wooden spoon, mix first 5 ingredients together to make the dressing. Rub bowl with garlic. Pour in dressing. Add chopped parsley and green onions, then salad greens. Toss salad just when serving.

SUPER TOSSED SALAD

6 oz.	marinated artichoke hearts	175 mL
3 oz.	marinated mushrooms	75 mL
	assorted kinds of lettuce	
	cherry tomatoes	
1	cucumber, peeled and sliced	1
1	avocado pear	1

Drain artichokes and mushrooms, reserving liquid. Slice avocado and dip in lemon juice to prevent discolouring. Toss greens together. Arrange other vegetables on top. Cover with plastic wrap and refrigerate until needed. Combine dressing ingredients with enough reserved liquid to make 3/4 cup (175 mL). Toss salad with dressing and serve.

Dressing

1/3 cup	oil	75 mL
2 tbsp.	vinegar	30 mL
1/2 tsp.	salt	2 mL
1/4 tsp.	paprika	1 mL
1/2 tsp.	sugar	2 mL
1/8 tsp.	dry mustard	0.5 mL
1/8 tsp.	garlic salt	0.5 mL

MEXICAN SALAD

1 head	lettuce	1 head
3	tomatoes	3
1	onion	1
1 lb.	Cheddar cheese	500 g
14 oz.	canned pinto beans	398 mL
	spicy sweet French dressing	
10 oz.	tortilla chips, crushed	300 g

Shred the lettuce, chop the tomatoes and onion, and grate the cheese coarsely. Wash and drain the pinto beans. Combine all ingredients, adding chips last.

SPINACH SALAD

3	eggs	3
1/2 tbsp.	dry mustard	7 mL
1 clove	garlic, crushed	1 clove
	salt	
	pepper	
1 tbsp.	Parmesan cheese, grated	15 mL
1/2 cup	lemon juice	125 mL
	dash of Worcestershire sauce	
1/2 cup	oil	125 mL
1 lb.	fresh spinach	500 g
3	green onions, chopped	3

Boil 2 of the eggs until hard. Mix remaining raw egg with seasonings and cheese. Add lemon juice and Worcestershire sauce and, lastly, the oil. Mix thoroughly and refrigerate. Wash and trim spinach leaves. Tear into bite-sized pieces. Chop hard-boiled eggs and mix 1 – 2 tbsp. (15 – 30 mL) of the chopped egg with the green onion. Add to spinach, then add dressing. Toss and sprinkle with the rest of the egg. Serves 6 – 8.

CHICK PEA SALAD

38 oz.	canned chick peas	1 L
1 cup	green pepper, chopped	250 mL
1/2 cup	onion, chopped	125 mL
1 clove	garlic, finely chopped	1 clove
2 tbsp.	parsley, finely chopped	30 mL
2 cups	cider vinegar	500 mL
3 tbsp.	lemon juice	45 mL
1/3 cup	oil	75 mL
1/4 cup	sugar	50 mL
1 tsp.	salt	5 mL
1/2 tsp.	pepper	2 mL

Drain the chick peas, discarding liquid. Mix all ingredients together and refrigerate at least 12 hours. Drain. Garnish with onion rings and chopped parsley. Serves 6 – 8.

ARTICHOKE AND CHICK PEA SALAD

28 oz.	canned artichoke hearts	796 mL
14 oz.	canned red kidney beans	398 mL
20 oz.	canned chick peas	568 mL
1	red onion, chopped	1
1 tsp.	fresh basil	5 mL
1 tsp.	fresh parsley	5 mL
1 1/2 tsp.	fresh chives	7 mL
1/2 tsp.	fresh thyme	2 mL
1/2 cup	vinaigrette dressing	125 mL

Drain vegetables and rinse. Toss all ingredients together in a serving bowl. Refrigerate. Serves 8 – 10. (Note: For dried herbs, use one-quarter of the amounts given. For dressing, see page 42.)

PIQUANT CARROT SALAD

1 1/2 lb.	carrots	750 g
1	onion	1
1	green pepper	1
1/4 cup	white or cider vinegar	50 mL
3 tbsp.	sugar	45 mL
3 tbsp.	oil	45 mL
1 tbsp.	ketchup	15 mL
1/2 tsp.	seasoning salt	2 mL
1/2 tsp.	celery seed	2 mL
1/2 tsp.	Worcestershire sauce	2 mL
1/2 tsp.	prepared mustard	2 mL

Cut carrots in 1/4'' x 3'' (0.5 x 7 cm) strips and cook, covered, in boiling water just until tender, about 5 minutes. Drain, and cool quickly under cold water. Slice onion and green pepper in rings. In a large serving bowl, layer carrots, onion, and green pepper. Combine remaining ingredients in a small jar, shake well, and pour over vegetables. Cover, and chill at least 4 hours, stirring often. Flavour improves with longer marination. This salad keeps well in refrigerator for at least 1 week.

CREAMY CUCUMBER SALAD

1	English cucumber, chopped	1
2 tsp.	salt	10 mL
3/4 cup	plain yogurt	175 mL
1/2 cup	sour cream	125 mL
1 clove	garlic, crushed	1 clove
2 tsp.	green onion, chopped	10 mL
3/4 tsp.	lemon juice	3 mL
3/4 tsp.	white wine vinegar	3 mL
1/8 tsp.	pepper	0.5 mL
1 1/4 tsp.	dill weed	6 mL
1/4 tsp.	prepared mustard	1 mL

Sprinkle cucumber with salt. Place on paper towels. Let stand about 10 minutes, and pat dry. Mix remaining ingredients, adding lemon juice, vinegar, and dill to taste. Fold in cucumber. Refrigerate covered, where it will keep 2 to 3 days. (Note: All yogurt may be used instead of sour cream.)

PEA SALAD

2 lb.	frozen peas, thawed	1 kg
6 stalks	celery, sliced	6 stalks
3	green onions, chopped	3
10 oz.	water chestnuts, diced	284 mL
1/2 cup	mayonnaise	125 mL
1/2 cup	sour cream	125 mL
	imitation bacon bits	

In a 2 1/2 quart (2 L) serving bowl, arrange thin layers of peas, celery, green onions, and water chestnuts, repeating layers until all vegetables are used up and ending with peas. Spread mayonnaise mixed with sour cream on top. Cover. Refrigerate overnight. Before serving, toss and sprinkle with bacon bits. Serves 15.

FARMER'S SALAD

1 lb.	creamed cottage cheese	500 g
4 tbsp.	sour cream	60 mL
1	green onion, diced	1
4	radishes, sliced	4
1	cucumber, diced	1
	salt	
	pepper	

Mix cottage cheese and sour cream. Combine with vegetables. Refrigerate until ready to serve.

BANANA CELERY NUT SALAD

3 cups	celery, sliced	750 mL
2	bananas, sliced	2
1/2 cup	pecan nuts, chopped	125 mL
3 tbsp.	mayonnaise	45 mL
3 tbsp.	sour cream	45 mL
1 1/2 tsp.	lemon juice	7 mL
3/4 tsp.	salt	3 mL

Sprinkle a small amount of the lemon juice on the bananas to keep them from discolouring. Combine celery, bananas, and nuts. Blend remaining ingredients and fold in. Serves 6 – 8.

PARTY VEGETABLE SALAD

3 heads	cauliflower	3 heads
2 lb.	mushrooms	1 kg
2	red peppers	2
2	green peppers	2
3	sweet onions	3
	seasoning salt	
	salt	
	pepper	
	sugar	
3/4 cup	oil	175 mL
3/4 cup	vinegar	175 mL
1	avocado pear	1
1	cucumber	1
1/2 lb.	cherry tomatoes	250 g

Break up cauliflower; slice mushrooms, peppers, and onions. Arrange in layers in a tall glass bowl. Sprinkle each layer with seasonings, sugar, and 2 tbsp. (30 mL) each of oil and vinegar until layers are practically covered. Cover and chill. About 1 hour before serving slice avocado, cucumber, and tomatoes, and arrange attractively down the sides and on top. Cover and refrigerate. Drain marinade to serve. Serves 35. (Note: Marinade may be stored in refrigerator and reused.)

MARINATED VEGETABLES

2 cups	water	500 mL
1 cup	sugar	250 mL
2 cups	vinegar	500 mL
1 tsp.	dill weed	5 mL
1 tbsp.	pickling salt	15 mL
1 clove	garlic, crushed	1 clove
2 tbsp.	oil	30 mL
2 heads	cauliflower	2 heads
2	Spanish onions	2
2	green peppers	2
3 – 4	carrots	3 – 4
1/2 lb.	fresh mushrooms	250 g

Combine water, sugar, vinegar, and dill in a saucepan and bring to boil. Remove from heat to add salt and garlic. Blend in oil. Break up cauli-

overleaf:
Avocado Vichyssoise (page 25)

flower, and slice remaining vegetables in strips or rings. Combine vegetables, pour sauce over, and marinate in refrigerator at least 2 days before using. Keeps indefinitely in refrigerator. Serves 15.

MARINATED VEGETABLE SALAD

2 cups	cabbage, shredded	500 mL
2 large	onions, sliced	2 large
1 large	carrot, grated	1 large
1	green pepper, chopped	1
1	cucumber, thinly sliced	1
3 tbsp.	vinegar	45 mL
3 tbsp.	oil	45 mL
3 tbsp.	sugar	45 mL
1 tbsp.	salt	15 mL

Arrange vegetables in dish. Combine remaining ingredients for dressing and mix thoroughly. Pour over vegetables. Mix or toss to ensure all are covered. Cover tightly and refrigerate at least overnight.

MIXED VEGETABLES IN MARINADE

1/2 cup	olive oil	125 mL
1/4 cup	wine vinegar	50 mL
1 clove	garlic, crushed	1 clove
2 tbsp.	parsley, chopped	30 mL
2 tsp.	chives, chopped	10 mL
1/8 tsp.	dried tarragon	0.5 mL
1/2 tsp.	salt	2 mL
1/8 tsp.	pepper	0.5 mL
3	tomatoes	3
1	cucumber	1
14 oz.	canned artichoke hearts	398 mL
1 lb.	asparagus, cooked	500 g
1/2 lb.	fresh mushrooms	250 g

Combine oil, vinegar, garlic, herbs and spices in a shallow 3 quart (3 L) glass baking dish. Stir well to combine. Peel tomatoes and cucumber, and slice thickly. Drain artichokes and asparagus, slicing

asparagus if necessary. Wash and drain the mushrooms. Add vegetables to the dressing in the baking dish, and marinate at least 2 hours, stirring occasionally so that all pieces absorb the marinade. Chill until time to serve. Serves 8 – 10.

MARINATED BEAN SALAD

14 oz.	canned kidney beans	398 mL
14 oz.	canned wax beans	398 mL
14 oz.	canned green beans	398 mL
1/2 cup	green pepper, chopped	125 mL
1 large	Spanish onion, sliced	1 large
3/4 cup	sugar	175 mL
2/3 cup	vinegar	150 mL
1/3 cup	oil	75 mL
1 tsp.	salt	5 mL
1 tsp.	pepper	5 mL
	tarragon	
	basil	
	parsley	
	dry mustard	

Drain vegetables and wash. Mix all ingredients together. Marinate 2 or 3 days before serving.

Variation
Adding canned button mushrooms and chick peas gives the salad a different and interesting taste.

SWEET AND SOUR BEAN SALAD

14 oz.	canned green beans	398 mL
14 oz.	canned yellow beans	398 mL
14 oz.	canned kidney beans	398 mL
19 oz.	canned chick peas	540 mL
1	green pepper, chopped	1
1	onion, chopped	1
3/4 cup	sugar	175 mL
1 tsp.	salt	5 mL
1/2 tsp.	pepper	2 mL
1/3 cup	oil	75 mL
2/3 cup	vinegar	150 mL

Drain beans and chick peas, and combine in a large bowl. Add green pepper and onion. Mix remaining ingredients in a separate bowl, pour onto bean combination, and refrigerate overnight. Garnish with a few Spanish onion rings.

PARTY COLE SLAW

3 lb.	cabbage	1.5 kg
6	carrots	6
2	green peppers	2
12	green onions	12
1 cup	oil	250 mL
1 cup	vinegar	250 mL
1/2 cup	sugar	125 mL
1 1/2 tsp.	salt	7 mL
1 tbsp.	celery salt	15 mL
1 tbsp.	garlic salt	15 mL
1 tbsp.	prepared mustard	15 mL

Shred cabbage and carrots. Cut green peppers in strips, and chop green onions finely. Combine vegetables. Boil oil, vinegar, and sugar together for 5 minutes. Add seasonings. Pour hot over cabbage. Chill.

GINGER ALE SALAD

1 tbsp.	gelatine	15 mL
1/4 cup	cold water	50 mL
1/4 cup	orange juice	50 mL
1/4 cup	sugar	50 mL
	dash of salt	
1 cup	ginger ale	250 mL
1 1/2 tbsp.	lemon juice	22 mL
1 cup	grapes, peeled	250 mL
1	peach, peeled	1
1	apple, peeled and cored	1
1	pear, peeled and cored	1

Soak gelatine in cold water for 5 minutes. Heat orange juice to boiling and add gelatine. Stir until dissolved. Add sugar, salt, ginger ale, and lemon juice. Chill until mixture begins to set. Dice fruit and add. Pour into mould. Chill until set. Unmould on lettuce and serve with fruit salad dressing (see page 44).

VEGETABLE MOULD

6 oz.	lime gelatine	170 g
1 cup	hot water	250 mL
1/4 cup	lemon juice	50 mL
2 tbsp.	vinegar	30 mL
2 tbsp.	onion juice	30 mL
	pinch of salt	
1/2 tsp.	horseradish	2 mL
1/4 cup	cucumber, diced	50 mL
1/2 cup	carrot, grated	125 mL
1/4 cup	cabbage, shredded	50 mL

Dissolve gelatine in hot water. Add lemon juice, vinegar, onion juice, salt, and horseradish. Cool. Add vegetables, pour into a greased 1 quart (1 L) mould, and chill several hours until firm. Unmould. Serves 6 – 8. .

MOULDED GAZPACHO

1/2 oz.	unflavoured gelatine	14 g
20 oz.	tomato juice	568 mL
3	tomatoes	3
1/2	green pepper	1/2
1	cucumber	1
1/8 cup	onion, minced	25 mL
1 clove	garlic	1 clove
1/4 cup	wine vinegar	50 mL
8 drops	Tabasco sauce	8 drops
3/4 tsp.	salt	3 mL

Soften gelatine in tomato juice, then heat until dissolved. Cool. Peel and chop the vegetables. Add to juice with vinegar and seasonings. Mix, and pour into a small ring mould. Chill until set.

BORSCHT MOULD

2 cups	beet borscht	500 mL
6 oz.	cherry gelatine	170 mL
2 cups	sour cream	500 mL
1/2 tsp.	dill weed	2 mL

Drain borscht, reserving beets. Bring juice to a boil and pour over gelatine. Stir until dissolved.

Refrigerate until slightly thickened, then add sour cream and whisk well. Fold in beets and dried dill. Pour into a ring mould and refrigerate. Serves 8 – 10.

FRUIT SALAD MOULD

3 oz.	raspberry gelatine	85 g
2 cups	grape juice	500 mL
3 oz.	lemon gelatine	85 g
14 oz.	fruit cocktail	398 mL
8 oz.	cream cheese	250 g
1 cup	sour cream	250 mL

Dissolve raspberry gelatine in heated grape juice. Cool slightly and pour into the bottom of a mould. Drain fruit cocktail, reserving 1 cup (250 mL) of the juice. Heat juice to dissolve lemon gelatine. Cool. Add cheese and sour cream. Whip, and fold in fruit. Pour over grape layer in mould. Chill.

STRAWBERRY AND RHUBARB MOULD

15 oz.	frozen rhubarb	425 g
1/4 cup	water	50 mL
6 oz.	strawberry gelatine	170 g
14 oz.	crushed pineapple	398 mL
15 oz.	frozen strawberries	425 g

Cook rhubarb in water. Dissolve gelatine in hot rhubarb. Add remaining ingredients. Pour into a greased mould and refrigerate until set.

PINEAPPLE AND SOUR CREAM MOULD

6 oz.	lime gelatine	170 g
2 cups	boiling water	500 mL
2 cups	sour cream	500 mL
14 oz.	crushed pineapple	398 mL

Stir gelatine into boiling water. Let cool slightly.

Beat in sour cream with an egg beater. Drain pineapple; add to mixture. Turn into a well-greased mould and refrigerate several hours to set.

Variation

Blueberry Mould

Use any berry-flavoured gelatine. Before adding sour cream, whip partially cooled gelatine and fold in 14 oz. (398 mL) canned blueberries and 1 tsp. (5 mL) lemon juice. Fold in sour cream and set. Omit pineapple.

Cranberry Mould

Use raspberry-flavoured gelatine, adding rind of 1 orange. Beat partially cooled gelatine then add pineapple, 1 cubed orange, 14 oz. (398 mL) canned cranberries, and 1 – 2 tbsp. (15 – 30 mL) chopped nuts. Omit sour cream. (Substitute 1/2 cup (125 mL) pineapple or orange juice for equivalent amount of water, if desired.)

MOULDED CHEESE LOAF

1 tbsp.	gelatine	15 mL
1/4 cup	cold water	50 mL
1 cup	cottage cheese	250 mL
1 cup	cream	250 mL
1/4 cup	stuffed olives, chopped	50 mL
1/4 cup	pickles, chopped	50 mL

Soak gelatine in water 5 minutes. Dissolve over hot water. Combine cheese with 1/2 cup (125 mL) of the cream and stir in olives and pickles. Add dissolved gelatine and remaining cream, whipped. Pour into a loaf pan or mould and chill until firm, preferably overnight. Unmould on lettuce and surround with fresh vegetables.

TABBOULEH SALAD

1/4 cup	bulgar wheat	50 mL
2 cups	parsley, chopped	500 mL
1 large	tomato, chopped	1 large
1/4 cup	cucumber, sliced	50 mL
1/2 cup	green onion, chopped	125 mL

Cover bulgar wheat with cold water and let stand for 1 hour. Drain. Combine with remaining ingredients. Pour on dressing. Serves 6 – 8.

Dressing

¼ cup	olive oil	50 mL
⅓ cup	lemon juice	75 mL
1 tsp.	salt	5 mL
½ tsp.	pepper	2 mL
	dash of basil	
	dash of oregano	
¼ tsp.	dried mint	1 mL

BULGAR SALAD

2 cups	bulgar wheat	500 mL
1	tomato, diced	1
¼ cup	cucumber, diced	50 mL
2 tbsp.	parsley, chopped	30 mL
¼ cup	onion, diced	50 mL
1 tsp.	salt	5 mL
½ tsp.	pepper	2 mL
1 clove	garlic, crushed	1 clove
¼ cup	oil	50 mL
2 tbsp.	vinegar	30 mL

Cover bulgar wheat with cold water and let stand for 1 hour. Drain well. Combine with tomato, cucumber, parsley, and onion. Mix remaining ingredients together for dressing. Toss well with salad.

DILL SOUR CREAM POTATO SALAD

4 cups	cooked potatoes, diced	1 L
1 cup	celery, sliced	250 mL
3	green onions, sliced	3
3 tbsp.	vinegar	45 mL
3 tbsp.	oil	45 mL
¼ tsp.	seasoning salt	1 mL
¼ tsp.	pepper	1 mL
2 sprigs	dill, chopped	2 sprigs
¾ cup	sour cream	175 mL
½	green pepper, diced	½
½	red pepper, diced	½

Combine potato, celery, and green onions. Mix vinegar, oil, seasonings, and dill. Pour onto potato mixture and toss. Refrigerate several hours. Mix in sour cream and pepper pieces. Garnish with dill sprigs and tomato wedges. Serves 4 – 6. (If using dried dill weed, use only ½ tsp. (2 mL).)

SPECIAL POTATO SALAD

5 large	potatoes	5 large
	salt	
	pepper	
1	onion, chopped	1
1	pickled cucumber, grated	1
1 long	radish, grated	1 long
3	green onions, chopped	3
2	eggs, hard-boiled	2
	mayonnaise	
	parsley, chopped	

Boil potatoes in jackets. Cool, peel, dice, and season. Add onion, pickled cucumber, radish, and green onions. Chop 1 egg, and add with sufficient mayonnaise to cover thoroughly. Garnish with parsley and finely sliced hard-boiled egg.

CRUNCHY POTATO SALAD

1½ lb.	cooked potatoes	750 g
3	eggs, hard-boiled	3
½ cup	celery	125 mL
1 tbsp.	onion	15 mL
1 tbsp.	sweet pickles	15 mL
1 tbsp.	cucumber	15 mL
2	carrots	2
¾ cup	mayonnaise	175 mL
2 tbsp.	prepared mustard	30 mL
	salt	
	pepper	
	caraway seeds	
	celery salt	
2 tbsp.	cider or tarragon vinegar	30 mL

Coarsely chop the potatoes and eggs; dice the celery, onion, pickles, and cucumber; grate the carrots coarsely. Combine all ingredients, seasoning to taste. Decorate with parsley and red and green pepper rings.

COLD RICE SALAD

2 cups	cooked rice, cold	500 mL
1/4 cup	mushrooms, chopped	50 mL
1/4 cup	celery, chopped	50 mL
1/4 cup	Spanish onion, chopped	50 mL
1/4 cup	cooked peas, cold	50 mL
1/4 cup	red pimento, chopped	50 mL

Toss all ingredients together and dress lightly with Italian dressing.

VERMICELLI SALAD

1 lb.	vermicelli noodles	500 g
2 tbsp.	green onion, chopped	30 mL
2 tbsp.	parsley	30 mL
1/4 tsp.	basil	1 mL
1/4 tsp.	oregano	1 mL
1 cup	Italian dressing	250 mL
1 1/4 cups	mayonnaise	300 mL

Cook noodles according to package directions. Drain, and rinse thoroughly with cold water. Combine dressings with green onion and herbs and toss with noodles. Keep refrigerated. Serve cold.

TUNA SALAD FOR 40

105 oz.	canned tuna	3 kg
20	eggs, hard-boiled	20
1 stalk	celery	1 stalk
50 oz.	pineapple chunks	1.4 L
1 cup	sour cream	250 mL
1/2 tsp.	garlic powder	2 mL
	mayonnaise	

Blanch tuna and flake. Chop eggs, dice celery,

and drain pineapple. Add to tuna. Combine remaining ingredients for dressing, using enough mayonnaise to moisten. Mix well and garnish with blanched, toasted almonds.

TUNA SALAD MOULD

3 oz.	lime gelatine	85 g
1/4 tsp.	salt	1 mL
1 cup	boiling water	250 mL
3/4 cup	cold water	175 mL
2 tbsp.	vinegar	30 mL
2 tsp.	onion, grated	10 mL
1/2 cup	cucumber, diced	125 mL
1/2 cup	celery, diced	125 mL
2 tbsp.	pimento, chopped	30 mL
2 tbsp.	stuffed olives, sliced	30 mL
7 oz.	flaked tuna, drained	198 g

Dissolve gelatine and salt in boiling water. Add cold water, vinegar, and onion. Chill until very thick. Stir in remaining ingredients. Pour into individual ring moulds or a 1 quart (1 L) ring mould. Chill until firm. Unmould on crisp salad greens. If desired, serve with additional tuna, and top salads with mayonnaise. (Note: 1/2 cup (125 mL) chopped tomato may be substituted for the pimento and half the celery.) Serves 4.

ANCHOVY EGG SALAD

2 cups	lettuce, shredded	500 mL
1/2 cup	celery, diced	125 mL
4	hard-boiled eggs, chopped	4
10	anchovy fillets	10
	French dressing	
	salt	
	pepper	

Toss together lettuce, celery, and eggs. Cut the anchovy fillets in small pieces and add. Toss with French dressing (see page 42) to moisten well, and season to taste. Serve on crisp lettuce with mayonnaise. Serves 4.

SALAD DRESSINGS

BASIC FRENCH DRESSING

3 parts	oil	3 parts
1 part	tarragon vinegar	1 part
	salt	
	pepper	
	prepared mustard	

Shake together well. Store in a bottle in refrigerator.

MAYONNAISE

2	egg yolks	2
1 tsp.	salt	5 mL
1 tsp.	dry mustard	5 mL
1/4 tsp.	pepper	1 mL
1 tsp.	sugar	5 mL
2 tsp.	boiling water	10 mL
1 cup	oil	250 mL
1 tbsp.	vinegar	15 mL
1 tbsp.	lemon juice	15 mL

Beat egg yolks with seasonings and sugar. Add water. Beating continuously, add oil slowly, a little at a time. Boil vinegar and lemon juice and add slowly to mixture when cool.

ALTERNATIVE MAYONNAISE

1	egg	1
1 tsp.	salt	5 mL
1/4 tsp.	pepper	1 mL
1 tsp.	dry mustard	5 mL
1/8 tsp.	paprika	0.5 mL
	cayenne pepper	
1 tsp.	sugar	5 mL
2 tbsp.	vinegar	30 mL
2 tbsp.	lemon juice	30 mL
1 1/2 cups	oil	375 mL

Break egg into a bowl. Beating thoroughly after each addition, add seasonings, sugar, and 1 tsp. (5 mL) of the vinegar. Add oil slowly in a thin stream, beating continuously, until dressing begins to thicken. Then add remaining oil, vinegar, and lemon juice all at once.

TARTAR DRESSING

1 cup	mayonnaise	250 mL
1	gherkin, chopped	1
2	green onions, chopped	2
1 tsp.	horseradish	5 mL
1 tsp.	parsley, chopped	5 mL

Combine all ingredients together well.

SOUTHERN DRESSING

1 cup	mayonnaise	250 mL
1	hard-boiled egg, chopped	1
3	green onions, chopped	3
1 tbsp.	parsley, chopped	15 mL
1 tbsp.	olives, chopped	15 mL
1 tbsp.	chili sauce	15 mL

Combine all ingredients well.

VINAIGRETTE DRESSING

1 cup	vinegar	250 mL
1/2 cup	oil	125 mL
1 tbsp.	seasoning salt	15 mL
1 tsp.	mixed peppers	5 mL
1 tbsp.	sugar	15 mL
2 tsp.	onion powder	10 mL
1 tsp.	garlic powder	5 mL
1 tsp.	salt	5 mL
	shake of paprika for colour	

Combine ingredients in a jar with a tight seal. Shake well. Keep refrigerated.

NICOISE DRESSING

1 cup	mayonnaise	250 mL
1 tsp.	dry mustard	5 mL
1 tbsp.	anchovies	15 mL
1 tbsp.	capers	15 mL
1 tbsp.	parsley	15 mL
1	egg, hard-boiled	1

Combine mayonnaise and mustard. Chop remaining ingredients and add, mixing well.

TOMATO FRENCH DRESSING

10 oz.	condensed tomato soup	284 mL
1/3 cup	sugar	75 mL
1 tsp.	salt	5 mL
1 tsp.	paprika	5 mL
1 tsp.	dry mustard	5 mL
1/2 cup	vinegar	125 mL
1/2 cup	oil	125 mL
1 tbsp.	Worcestershire sauce	15 mL
1 clove	garlic, crushed	1 clove

Combine ingredients in a 1 quart (1 L) sealer. Cover tightly and shake well. Chill.

THOUSAND ISLAND DRESSING

2	eggs	2
1 tbsp.	sugar	15 mL
1 tsp.	salt	5 mL
1/2 tsp.	dry mustard	2 mL
	pinch of pepper	
	pinch of paprika	
	pinch of cayenne pepper	
2 cups	oil	500 mL
1 cup	sweet mixed pickles	250 mL
2	pimentos	2
1/2 cup	ketchup	125 mL

Beat eggs with sugar and seasonings. Beating continuously, add oil in a thin stream until mixture thickens. Chop pickles and pimento, and stir into dressing with ketchup.

SOUR CREAM DRESSING

1 1/4 cups	milk	300 mL
1 cup	buttermilk	250 mL
2 1/4 cups	mayonnaise	550 mL
1/4 cup	cider vinegar	50 mL
1/2 cup	Parmesan cheese, grated	125 mL
1/4 tsp.	pepper	1 mL
1 tbsp.	garlic salt	15 mL
1 1/2 cups	sour cream	375 mL

Combine all ingredients except sour cream in a mixing bowl. Mix well with a wire whisk. Fold in sour cream, leaving mixture lumpy. Refrigerate in a tightly closed container.

CELERY SEED DRESSING

1/2 cup	sugar	125 mL
1 tsp.	dry mustard	5 mL
1 tsp.	salt	5 mL
1/2 tsp.	onion juice	2 mL
1/3 cup	vinegar	75 mL
1 cup	oil	250 mL
1 tbsp.	celery seed	15 mL

Mix sugar, mustard, and salt. Add onion juice and half the vinegar. Gradually pour in oil, beating constantly. Lastly add remaining vinegar and celery seed.

BLENDER CAESAR DRESSING

1 cup	wine vinegar	250 mL
2 cloves	garlic, chopped	2 cloves
1 oz.	anchovies	25 g
1 tsp.	seasoning salt	5 mL
1 tsp.	salad seasoning	5 mL
1 tsp.	pepper	5 mL
3 tbsp.	Parmesan cheese	45 mL
2	eggs (raw)	2
2 cups	oil	500 mL

Pour just enough vinegar into blender to cover blade. Add garlic, anchovies, and seasonings, and blend. Add cheese and eggs. Blend at high speed for 2 minutes, then slowly add oil. (Note: This makes a thick dressing that may also be served as a dip.)

CAESAR DRESSING

½ cup	olive oil	125 mL
1½ tbsp.	red wine vinegar	20 mL
2 tsp.	lemon juice	10 mL
¼ tsp.	dry mustard	1 mL
2 oz.	anchovies, drained	50 g
2 cloves	garlic, crushed	2 cloves
1 tsp.	pepper	5 mL
5 drops	Tabasco sauce	5 drops
	dash of Worcestershire sauce	
1	egg yolk (raw)	1

Blend all ingredients together well.

MOCK SOUR CREAM

¼ cup	buttermilk	50 mL
1 cup	skim milk cottage cheese	250 mL

Combine buttermilk and cottage cheese in a blender. Blend at high speed, stopping often to scrape down sides, until smooth and creamy.

Can be used in dips, with fruit, or on baked potatoes. Makes approximately 1 cup (250 mL).

(Note: Do not use in any recipe that requires baking, as mock cream will separate.)

FRUIT SALAD DRESSING

2	eggs	2
¼ cup	sugar	50 mL
¼ cup	pineapple juice	50 mL
¼ cup	lemon juice	50 mL
½ cup	whipping cream	125 mL

Beat eggs, adding sugar, pineapple and lemon juice. Cook in top of double boiler, stirring constantly until thick. Cool. Just before serving, fold in whipped cream.

GREEK SALAD DRESSING

1 cup	oil	250 mL
¼ cup	white vinegar	50 mL
3 cloves	garlic	3 cloves
¼ lb.	brick cheese, diced	125 g
5 tbsp.	Parmesan cheese, grated	75 mL
¼ tsp.	oregano	1 mL
	Worcestershire sauce	
1½ tsp.	salt	7 mL
½ tsp.	pepper	2 mL

Combine all ingredients in a blender and mix. Pour on top of a salad of green lettuce, spinach, cucumber, and Feta cheese.

CREAMY GARLIC DRESSING

½ cup	mayonnaise	125 mL
½ cup	sour cream	125 mL
½ cup	milk	125 mL
	salt	
	pepper	
1 tsp.	sugar	5 mL
1 tsp.	Worcestershire sauce	5 mL
½ tsp.	dry mustard	2 mL
1 tbsp.	lemon juice	15 mL
4 cloves	garlic, crushed	4 cloves

Combine all ingredients well in blender or shake in a jar.

Variation

Creamy Blue Cheese Dressing
Decrease garlic to 1 clove, crushed, and add ¼ lb. (125 g) blue cheese.

Eggs & Cheese

Nature's gift to mankind's table, the egg comes to us faultlessly gift-wrapped in a snap-top container. A perfect food, with no waste, it can be boiled, poached, fried, scrambled, or baked.

The egg is an affable traveller, and enjoys going to picnics or school lunches cooked in the shell and eaten naturally whole, sprinkled with salt, or mashed with mayonnaise or sliced in a sandwich.

For the indecisive but ravenous appetite, immediate gratification can be achieved with Hopple Poppel or an omelette of any kind—smoked salmon, mushroom, or any other imaginative filling.

Unite the egg with its best friend, cheese, and there is a marriage made in heaven. Baked in a Quiche, Cheese and Onion Pie, or Cheese Strata, it becomes the basis of a full-course meal. Cheese may be served on its own, to complement a full meal or supplement a sparse one. As a snack, it is without equal; and because of the infinite varieties to choose from, cheese is never boring.

And then there are dishes, the methods learned from watching mothers and grandmothers, that elevate the improvisation of cheese to ambrosial heights. Cheese Blintzes. A melding of cottage cheese, eggs, sugar and cinnamon, enveloped by a delicate crepe and lavished with sour cream. In the Yiddish language, the word *blintzes* exists only in the plural: it was inconceivable that a person would eat just one. And the same holds true for Varenickes, Linivnikes, Minichkes, and Knishes.

Recipes long forgotten are once again emerging at the most elegant luncheons, and it is these old-country *maicholim* for which a hostess will be long remembered.

HOPPLE POPPEL

2½ cups	salami, diced	625 mL
½ cup	onion, chopped	125 mL
2	tomatoes, sliced	2
½ cup	green pepper, diced	125 mL
2 tsp.	salt	10 mL
¼ tsp.	pepper	1 mL
12	eggs, slightly beaten	12

Mix all ingredients thoroughly. Pour into a greased 9" x 13" (3 L) pan. Bake at 400°F (200°C) for 20 to 30 minutes until set. Serves 12.

BAKED TOMATOES AND EGGS

7 tbsp.	butter	105 mL
¼ tsp.	curry powder	1 mL
5 tbsp.	flour	75 mL
¾ tsp.	salt	3 mL
¼ tsp.	pepper	1 mL
2 cups	milk	500 mL
4 large	tomatoes, peeled	4 large
6	eggs, hard-boiled	6
¼ cup	green onion, chopped	50 mL
¾ cup	cheese, grated	175 mL
1 cup	bread cubes	250 mL

Grease an ovenproof utility pan. Melt 3 tbsp. (45 mL) of the butter in a saucepan. Add curry and cook gently 2 minutes. Sprinkle in 3 tbsp. (45 mL) of the flour, and salt and pepper. Stir, then remove from heat. Stir in milk all at once. Stirring continuously, return to heat and cook until boiling, thickened, and smooth. Keep warm. Heat 2 tbsp. (30 mL) of the butter in a large skillet. Cut tomatoes into thick slices. Dip into remaining flour to coat, and fry in skillet 1 minute on each side. Remove from heat. Press eggs through a sieve. Using half the quantities at a time, layer the tomato slices, eggs, onions, sauce, and cheese in the baking dish, in that order. Repeat layers. Brown bread cubes in remaining butter and spread over top. Bake at 350°F (180°C) for 30 minutes until tomatoes are tender and sauce bubbles. Serves 4 as a main dish.

COMPANY SCRAMBLED EGGS

12	eggs	12
½ cup	milk	125 mL
10 oz.	canned mushrooms	284 mL
3 tbsp.	butter	45 mL
2 large	tomatoes, cut in wedges	2 large
1 cup	Cheddar cheese, diced	250 mL
1 tsp.	seasoning salt	5 mL

Beat eggs with milk. Drain mushrooms and add. Melt butter in a frying pan. Add eggs and move gently with a spatula as they start to set. Sprinkle with tomatoes, cheese, and seasoning salt. Keep moving gently until set. Serves 8 – 12.

SPANAKOPITA

1 cup	butter	250 mL
1	onion, chopped	1
7	green onions, chopped	7
1 lb.	Feta cheese	500 g
1 lb.	cottage cheese	500 g
20 oz.	fresh spinach, chopped	570 g
½ cup	dill weed, chopped	125 mL
6	eggs, beaten	6
1 lb.	phyllo dough	500 g
	salt	
	pepper	
¼ cup	flour	50 mL

Melt half the butter in a saucepan. Add onion and sauté until transparent, then add green onion and sauté 1 minute more. Combine Feta cheese, cottage cheese, spinach, and dill weed in a large bowl. Stir in onion mixture. Add eggs gradually, stirring constantly. Season with salt and pepper, sprinkle in flour, and mix well. Melt remaining butter. Lay 1 sheet of dough flat and cut in half lengthwise. Brush with butter. Place ½ cup (125 mL) of cheese-spinach filling in one corner of dough. Fold over to make a triangle and continue to fold from side to side to retain triangular shape to the end. Seal end and brush top with butter. Repeat until all the mixture is used. Bake at 350°F

(180°C) for 30 minutes until golden brown. (If not to be used immediately, freeze before baking.)

EGGS FLORENTINE

10 oz.	frozen spinach	280 g
½ tsp.	salt	2 mL
1 cup	white sauce	250 mL
½ cup	Cheddar cheese, grated	125 mL
½ tsp.	dry mustard	2 mL
4 – 8	eggs, poached lightly	4 – 8

Cook spinach with salt as directed, being careful not to overcook. Drain, and press between two plates to remove all moisture. Chop. Spread in the bottom of a greased 8'' x 8'' (2 L) baking dish. Prepare a white sauce according to standard recipe for medium thickness, stirring in cheese and mustard. Arrange poached eggs on top of spinach and cover with sauce. Bake at 350°F (180°C) for 15 to 20 minutes until bubbly. Serves 4.

Variations
Asparagus, French-style beans, or chopped broccoli may be used instead of spinach.

MOCK SOUFFLÉ

8 slices	bread (slightly dry)	8 slices
3 tbsp.	butter, softened	45 mL
1 lb.	Cheddar cheese, grated	500 g
6	eggs, slightly beaten	6
2½ cups	milk, scalded	625 mL
1 small	onion, grated	1 small
½ tsp.	dry mustard	2 mL
½ tsp.	seasoning salt	2 mL
½ tsp.	salt	2 mL
⅛ tsp.	pepper	0.5 mL
1½ tsp.	brown sugar	7 mL
½ tsp.	Worcestershire sauce	2 mL

Butter bread. Cube 6 of the slices; remove crusts from remaining 2 slices, and cut each into 4 triangles. Alternate layers of bread cubes and cheese in a well-greased 2 quart (2 L) baking dish. Top with the 8 triangles arranged around the edge of the dish with the points toward the centre. Combine remaining ingredients. Pour over bread and cheese. Chill for several hours or overnight. Stand at room temperature for 15 minutes before baking at 325°F (160°C) for 1 hour. Should be puffy and golden. Serve hot. Serves 6.

SEAFOOD PUFF

18 slices	bread	18 slices
14 oz.	canned salmon, drained	396 g
1 cup	green pepper, chopped	250 mL
1 cup	onion, chopped	250 mL
1½ cups	celery, chopped	375 mL
1 cup	mayonnaise	250 mL
12	eggs	12
3 cups	milk	750 mL
10 oz.	cream of mushroom soup	284 mL
½ cup	Cheddar cheese, grated	125 mL

Cube 9 slices of bread, with crusts, and cover the bottom of an ovenproof dish. Mix fish with green pepper, onion, celery, and mayonnaise. Spread on top of bread layer. Cover with 9 slices of crustless bread. Beat eggs with milk. Pour over bread. Cover with wax paper and refrigerate overnight. Allow to come to room temperature, and then top with mushroom soup. Sprinkle with grated cheese. Bake at 350°F (180°C) for 1½ hours. Serves 10.

CHEESE CASSEROLE

9 slices	rye bread	9 slices
½ lb.	Jarlsberg cheese	250 g
2¾ cups	milk	675 mL
4	eggs	4
1 tsp.	salt	5 mL
¼ cup	butter, melted	50 mL

Remove crusts from bread, and cut into 1'' (2 cm) cubes. Grate the cheese. In a 2 quart (2 L) baking dish, layer bread cubes and cheese. Combine milk, eggs, and salt, and pour over bread and cheese. Pour melted butter over top. Cover. Refrigerate overnight. Bake uncovered at 350°F (180°C) for 50 minutes until firm. Serve immediately.

EGG LOAF

1/4 oz.	gelatine	7 g
1/4 cup	cold water	50 mL
2 tbsp.	lemon juice	30 mL
1 cup	mayonnaise	250 mL
8	eggs, hard-boiled	8
1/2 cup	celery, diced	125 mL
2 tbsp.	green pepper, diced	30 mL
2 tbsp.	pimento	30 mL
3 tbsp.	sweet mixed pickles	45 mL

Dissolve gelatine in cold water for 5 minutes, then place over hot water until completely dissolved. Add lemon juice; let stand until it begins to set. Whip mayonnaise, and add gelatine. Cut eggs into big pieces, and fold into mayonnaise with remaining ingredients, finely diced. Pour into loaf tin or mould. Refrigerate until set. Unmould, garnish, and serve.

CHEESE QUICHE

1 (9'')	pie shell, unbaked	1 (1 L)
	prepared mustard	
1 1/3 cups	Jack cheese, grated	325 mL
1/2 cup	onion, chopped	125 mL
2 tbsp.	butter	30 mL
2/3 cup	milk	150 mL
1	egg	1
1	egg yolk	1
	salt	

Line pie shell with foil. Bake at 375°F (190°C) until light golden. Remove from oven and paint bottom of shell with mustard. Sprinkle on half the cheese. Sauté onions in butter until soft. Spread onions over cheese in shell, and sprinkle on remaining cheese. Mix milk, egg, and salt; pour over cheese and bake 40 minutes.

ASPARAGUS QUICHE

1 (9'')	pie shell, unbaked	1 (1 L)
1/2 cup	onion, chopped	125 mL
1/2 lb.	fresh asparagus, cooked	250 g
1 1/2 cups	Havarti cheese, grated	375 mL
3	eggs	3
1 cup	cream	250 mL
1/2 cup	milk	125 mL
1/4 tsp.	pepper	1 mL
1 tsp.	salt	5 mL
1/2 tsp.	dry mustard	2 mL
	dash of cayenne pepper	

Sauté onion in butter and sprinkle on bottom of pie shell. Arrange drained asparagus spears, spoke fashion, in shell. Beat remaining ingredients together well, and pour into pie shell. Bake at 375°F (190°C) for 45 minutes. Serve hot. Serves 6 – 7. (If using canned asparagus, use a 12 oz. (350 mL) can and drain well.)

CHEESE AND ONION PIE

1 (9'')	pie shell, unbaked	1 (1 L)
1/2 lb.	Swiss cheese, grated	250 g
1 large	onion, sliced	1 large
4	eggs, lightly beaten	4
2 tbsp.	flour	30 mL
1 cup	cream	250 mL
1 cup	milk	250 mL
1/2 tsp.	curry powder	2 mL
1/4 tsp.	nutmeg	1 mL
3 drops	Tabasco sauce	3 drops
1 tsp.	salt	5 mL
	pepper	

Sprinkle cheese over shell. Arrange onion rings on top of cheese. Beat eggs slightly with remaining ingredients. Pour over onions. Bake at 350°F (180°C) for 45 minutes.

COTTAGE CHEESE PIE

1/2 cup	butter	125 mL
1/2 cup	sugar	125 mL
3	eggs	3
3/4 cup	milk	175 mL
1 1/4 cups	flour	300 mL
1 tsp.	baking powder	5 mL
1/2 tsp.	salt	2 mL
1 lb.	dry cottage cheese	500 g

Cream butter. Beat in half the sugar, then 2 eggs. Add milk slowly. Stir in dry ingredients. Mixture should be like batter. Combine cottage cheese with remaining egg and sugar, and additional salt to taste. Pour half the batter into a greased 8'' x 8'' (2 L) pan. Spread cheese mixture on top and cover with remaining batter. Bake at 350°F (180°C) for 55 minutes. Cool slightly before cutting. Serve with sour cream and berries or apple sauce.

SALMON MUSHROOM QUICHE

1 (10'')	pie shell, unbaked	1 (1.5 L)
2 cups	fresh mushrooms, sliced	500 mL
2 tbsp.	chives, chopped	30 mL
7³/₄ oz.	canned salmon	220 g
1 tbsp.	butter	15 mL
¹/₂ tsp.	salt	2 mL
¹/₈ tsp.	pepper	0.5 mL
¹/₄ tsp.	tarragon	1 mL
2 tbsp.	dry white vermouth	30 mL
4	eggs	4
³/₄ cup	cream	175 mL
¹/₂ cup	Swiss cheese, grated	125 mL

Prick shell and bake at 400°F (200°C) for 8 minutes. Cool.

Cook mushrooms and chives lightly in butter. Do not brown. Drain and flake salmon, reserving liquid but discarding skin and bones. Add salmon and seasonings to mushroom mixture. Add vermouth and let mixture boil up for just a minute. Add cream to salmon liquid to make up 1 cup (250 mL). Beat eggs in a mixing bowl and add cream. Spread salmon-mushroom mixture evenly in partially baked pie shell. Sprinkle with grated cheese. Pour egg mixture over all. Bake at 400°F (200°C) for 30 to 35 minutes, until golden brown and a knife inserted in the centre comes out clean. Serves 6. (Note: For cocktail canapés or hors d'oeuvres, double this recipe, baking the quiche in a 13'' x 12'' (4 L) jelly roll pan at the same temperature for the same amount of time. Cool, and cut into bite-sized pieces to serve.)

CREAM CHEESE AND LOX QUICHE

1 (9'')	pie shell, baked	1 (1 L)
¹/₄ lb.	lox	125 g
1	egg	1
3	egg yolks	3
¹/₂ lb.	cream cheese	250 g
²/₃ cup	cream	150 mL
	salt	
	pepper	
3 small	tomatoes	3 small

Arrange pieces of lox on the bottom of the shell. Beat egg and yolks. Add softened cream cheese, and continue beating until mixture is smooth. Gradually beat in cream. Season, and pour over lox. Peel and slice tomatoes; arrange on top. Bake in centre of oven at 400°F (200°C) for 20 minutes or until set. Garnish with additional pieces of lox.

SPINACH QUICHE

1 (9'')	pie shell, baked	1 (1 L)
10 oz.	frozen spinach	280 g
¹/₂ cup	Mozzarella cheese, diced	125 mL
¹/₂ cup	whipping cream	125 mL
	salt	
	pepper	
6 slices	Mozzarella cheese	6 slices

Cook and drain spinach. Mix with Mozzarella cubes and cream. Season to taste. Fill pie shell, and top with Mozzarella slices. Bake at 350°F (180°C) for 10 minutes.

SMOKED SALMON QUICHE

1 (9'')	pie shell, baked	1 (1 L)
¹/₄ lb.	smoked salmon	120 g
¹/₄ cup	green onion, chopped	50 mL
¹/₂ cup	Swiss cheese, grated	125 mL
3	eggs	3
1 cup	milk	250 mL
¹/₂ tsp.	salt	2 mL
¹/₈ tsp.	pepper	0.5 mL
1 tbsp.	butter	15 mL

Chop salmon coarsely. Combine with green onion and cheese, and spread in bottom of shell. Blend eggs, milk, and seasoning. Pour into pie shell, dot with butter, and bake at 350°F (180°C) 30 to 35 minutes until a knife inserted in the centre comes out clean.

SPECIAL SMOKED SALMON QUICHE

1 (10'')	pie shell, unbaked	1 (1.5 L)
1	egg white, slightly beaten	1
1/2 lb.	smoked salmon	250 g
1 cup	Swiss cheese, grated	250 mL
4	eggs	4
1 1/4 cups	cream	300 mL
1 tbsp.	fresh dill, snipped	15 mL
1/2 tsp.	salt	2 mL
1/4 tsp.	pepper	1 mL

Brush pastry shell with egg white, and bake at 400°F (200°C) for 5 minutes. Cool slightly. Arrange salmon over bottom of pastry shell and sprinkle with grated cheese. Beat remaining ingredients together and pour over. Bake at 450°F (230°C) for 15 minutes. Reduce oven temperature to 350°F (180°C) and continue baking until golden brown, approximately 15 minutes. Serves 6 – 8. (Note: Use 1 tsp. (5 mL) dried dill weed if fresh dill is unavailable.)

ZUCCHINI MUSHROOM QUICHE

Pastry

1 cup	flour	250 mL
1/2 cup	shortening	125 mL
	pinch of salt	
2 tbsp.	cold water	30 mL

Rub shortening into flour and salt. Add water. Shape into a ball. Place dough in the middle of a greased quiche pan or pie plate and press onto the bottom and up sides with fingers. Chill while making filling.

Filling

3 stalks	celery	3 stalks
1/4 lb.	fresh mushrooms	125 g
3 medium	zucchini	3 medium
	parsley	
	dill weed	
	nutmeg	
	salt	
	pepper	
1/3 cup	cashew nuts, chopped	75 mL
8 slices	Jack cheese	8 slices
3	eggs	3
1/2 cup	milk	125 mL

Slice celery, mushrooms, and peeled zucchini; sauté in butter until soft. Season with parsley, dill weed, nutmeg, salt, and pepper to taste. Sprinkle pie shell with nuts. Spread vegetables over nuts, and cover with cheese slices. Beat eggs and milk and pour over cheese. Sprinkle with parsley. Bake at 350°F (180°C) approximately 50 minutes. Let stand 15 minutes before serving.

ZUCCHINI QUICHE

1 (9'')	pie shell, unbaked	1 (1 L)
1 small	onion, chopped	1 small
1 1/2 cups	Cheddar cheese, grated	375 mL
1 medium	zucchini	1 medium
3	eggs	3
1/2 cup	milk	125 mL
1/2 tsp.	salt	2 mL
1/4 tsp.	pepper	1 mL
1/4 tsp.	nutmeg	1 mL
	basil or oregano	

Sauté onion in oil over medium heat until soft. Place in bottom of pie crust and sprinkle with cheese. Steam zucchini until soft. Slice and arrange in pie shell. Beat eggs with milk and seasonings, and pour on top of zucchini. Bake at 400°F (200°C) for 10 minutes, then reduce oven to 375°F (190°C) and bake until mixture is firm and golden, about 30 minutes. Serves 6 – 8.

Variation
Add 1/4 cup (50 mL) fresh mushrooms, sliced.

SMOKED SALMON OMELETTE

1 oz.	smoked salmon	30 g
1	green onion, sliced	1
1/4 cup	sour cream	50 mL
1/2 tsp.	prepared mustard	2 mL
3	eggs	3
	salt	
	pepper	
1 tbsp.	water	15 mL
1 tsp.	butter	5 mL

Slice salmon in 2'' (5 cm) strips and set aside. Blend onion with sour cream and mustard. In a separate bowl, whisk eggs with seasoning and water. Cook in butter in omelette pan. Arrange salmon strips over half the omelette; spread with half the cream sauce. Fold omelette, and slide out of pan. Spoon remaining sauce on top and serve. Serves 2.

STACKED CREPES FLORENTINE

Crepes

4	eggs	4
1 1/2 cups	cold water	375 mL
1 1/2 cups	cold milk	375 mL
2 cups	flour, sifted	500 mL
1/2 tsp.	salt	2 mL
4 tbsp.	butter	60 mL

Beat eggs well, add water and milk, and beat again. Add sifted flour and salt, blending until smooth. Melt butter and stir into mixture. Pour batter through a sieve. Refrigerate 2 hours before making crepes. When frying, grease pan occasionally with oil. Stack crepes when cool.

Filling

5 tbsp.	butter	75 mL
5 tbsp.	flour	75 mL
2 3/4 cups	hot milk	675 mL
1/2 tsp.	salt	2 mL
	pepper	
	nutmeg	
1 cup	Swiss cheese, grated	250 mL
1/4 cup	cream	50 mL
1/2 lb.	frozen chopped spinach	250 g
1/2 lb.	cream cheese	250 g
1	egg	1
10 oz.	cream of mushroom soup	284 mL
14 oz.	mushrooms, chopped	400 g

Melt butter, stir in flour, and slowly add milk and spices. Stir in cream with all except 2 tbsp. (30 mL) of the grated cheese. Cook the spinach and cool slightly; drain. Blend 3 tbsp. (45 mL) of sauce into spinach. Set aside. Combine remaining ingredients with several spoonfuls of white sauce. Place 1 crepe in the centre of a lightly greased baking dish. Spread with spinach sauce, cover with a crepe, then spread with cream cheese mixture. Continue alternating layers until crepes and fillings have been used up. Spread remaining cheese sauce on top, sprinkle with reserved cheese, dot with butter, and bake at 350°F (180°C) until bubbly and golden.

BROCCOLI AND CHEESE CREPES

16	entrée crepes (see above)	16

Filling

22 oz.	frozen broccoli	624 g
2 tbsp.	butter	30 mL
2 tbsp.	onion, chopped	30 mL
6 oz.	canned mushrooms	170 mL
2 tbsp.	flour	30 mL
1/2 cup	cream	125 mL
1/4 cup	pareve chicken bouillon	50 mL
2 tbsp.	Parmesan cheese, grated	30 mL
4 oz.	water chestnuts	114 mL
1 tsp.	salt	5 mL
1/8 tsp.	pepper	0.5 mL

Cook broccoli according to package directions. Drain well and set aside. Drain and chop canned vegetables. In a large skillet, sauté onions and mushrooms in melted butter until lightly browned. Stir in flour. Add cream and chicken bouillon. Cook, stirring, until thickened. Add remaining ingredients. Set aside while preparing sauce. When sauce is ready, divide filling between crepes and fold or roll up. Place crepes in a single layer in a greased, shallow baking dish. Pour sauce over all. Bake uncovered at 350°F (180°C) for 25 to 30 minutes until bubbly and lightly browned.

Sauce

½ cup	butter	125 mL
½ cup	flour	125 mL
1½ cups	cream	375 mL
2 cups	milk	500 mL
1½ cups	Parmesan cheese, grated	375 mL
2 tsp.	prepared mustard	10 mL
1 tsp.	salt	5 mL

Melt butter and stir in flour. Add cream and milk and stir until well blended. Stir in remaining ingredients until sauce thickens and cheese melts.

CHEESE BLINTZES

Batter

2	eggs	2
7 tbsp.	flour	105 mL
1 tbsp.	cornstarch	15 mL
½ tsp.	salt	2 mL
1 cup	water	250 mL

Break eggs into a bowl. Add flour, cornstarch, and salt, and whisk together until smooth. Slowly add water. Fry on one side in a crepe pan or small frying pan. Turn out onto a clean linen towel to cool. Yields 15 crepes.

Filling

1 lb.	dry cottage cheese	500 g
1 tsp.	salt	5 mL
1 tbsp.	sugar	15 mL
1	egg	1

Beat ingredients until smooth. Fill crepes on cooked side and fold into envelopes. Fry in butter on both sides until golden brown.

CHEESE BLINTZES

Batter

3	eggs	3
4 tbsp.	flour	60 mL
½ cup	water	125 mL
	pinch of salt	

Combine ingredients to make a thin batter. Pour 2 – 3 tbsp. (30 – 45 mL) into a greased frying pan, turning pan quickly so that batter covers whole area and makes a very thin pancake. Fry until brown on underside only.

Filling

1 lb.	dry cottage cheese	500 g
2	eggs	2
2 tbsp.	sugar	30 mL
	dash of cinnamon	

Mix ingredients together. Place a small amount of filling in the centre of each pancake on the cooked side. Roll, and fold ends under. Place blintzes in a well-greased baking dish, dot tops with butter, and sprinkle with additional cinnamon and sugar. Bake at 375°F (190°C) for 40 minutes until browned.

Variation
These blintzes may also be fried.

CHEESE BLINTZES

Batter

3	eggs	3
2 cups	water	500 mL
1½ cups	flour	375 mL
	pinch of salt	
½ tsp.	baking powder	2 mL

Beat eggs and water well. Add flour sifted with salt and baking powder. Beat until smooth. Heat a small frying pan and grease lightly with oil. Pour a little batter to coat pan thinly. Cook on one side. Turn out onto brown paper. If crepes start sizzling and frying unevenly, pan is too hot. Swing empty pan in the air a few times to cool it slightly.

overleaf:
Eggs Florentine (page 47)

Filling

1	egg	1
1 lb.	cream cheese	500 g
	salt	
	pepper	
	sugar	
	sour cream	

Mix all ingredients together, using enough sour cream to blend to a smooth consistency. Place a spoonful of filling on each blintz. Fold into envelope shape and pack closely in a well-greased pie dish. Dot with shortening and bake at 400°F (200°C) until golden brown. (These are crisper when fried.)

BLINTZ SOUFFLÉ

12	frozen cheese blintzes	12
1/4 lb.	margarine	125 g
6	eggs	6
1 cup	sour cream	250 mL
1/4 cup	sugar	50 mL
1 tsp.	vanilla	5 mL
1/2 tsp.	salt	2 mL

Lay blintzes out on a greased ovenproof pan. Melt margarine; cool. Combine with remaining ingredients, beating well. Pour over blintzes. Bake at 350°F (180°C) for 1 hour 10 minutes.

FLUFFLY BLINTZ SOUFFLÉ

18	blintzes	18
1/4 cup	butter, softened	50 mL
2 tbsp.	sugar	30 mL
3	eggs, separated	3
1 tsp.	salt	5 mL
3 tbsp.	orange juice	45 mL
1 cup	sour cream	250 mL
1 tsp.	vanilla	5 mL

Place blintzes in a single layer on a greased baking pan. Cream butter and sugar. Beat egg yolks and add together with salt and orange juice. Blend in sour cream and vanilla. Beat egg whites stiff, fold into batter, and pour over blintzes. Bake at 350°F (180°C) for 1 hour.

BREAD BLINTZES

1 loaf	fresh bread	1 loaf
1 lb.	cottage cheese	500 g
2	eggs	2
	salt	
2 tbsp.	sugar	30 mL
	raisins	

Remove crusts from bread and slice loaf as for sandwiches. Roll out each slice as thin as possible. Combine cheese with eggs, salt, sugar, and raisins. Place a generous spoonful of cheese mixture on each bread slice. Fold in edges and roll up. Dip in beaten eggs and fry in butter. Serve with sour cream.

CHEESE KNISHES

Dough

2 cups	flour	500 mL
2 tbsp.	sugar	30 mL
2 tsp.	baking powder	10 mL
	pinch of salt	
1/2 cup	margarine	125 mL
1/2 cup	sour cream	125 mL
1	egg	1

Sift dry ingredients together. Cut in margarine. Add sour cream and egg to make a soft dough. Roll out on a floured board, making the dough 3 times as long as it is wide. Place the filling along long side of dough. Roll up tightly as for a jelly roll. Cut with side of hand into 1" (2 cm) pieces. Tuck in top and bottom dough on each piece to make a flat round shape. Place on greased cookie sheets. Bake at 350°F (180°C) for 15 minutes on one side, turn knishes over, and bake 10 minutes more. Cool on cooling racks. Serve with sour cream and jam or preserves. Yields approximately 15.

Filling

2 1/4 lb.	creamed cottage cheese	1 kg
2	eggs, beaten	2
1 tsp.	salt	5 mL
2 tbsp.	sugar	30 mL
1 tbsp.	cream of wheat	15 mL

Variation

Divide dough in half. Roll each half out to fit a large ovenproof utility pan. Place one-half of dough on bottom of pan. Add ½ cup (125 mL) raisins to filling, and spread filling over dough in pan. Top with remaining dough. Cut a lattice square pattern in top dough, sprinkle with cinnamon and sugar, and bake at 350°F (180°C) for 1 hour.

CHEESE KNISHES

½ cup	butter	125 mL
½ cup	shortening	125 mL
2½ cups	flour	625 mL
½ tsp.	baking powder	2 mL
½ tsp.	salt	2 mL
1 tbsp.	sugar	15 mL
1 cup	sour cream	250 mL

Cut butter and shortening into dry ingredients as for pastry. Add sour cream, and work with hands until solid. Wrap in wax paper and refrigerate for a few hours or overnight. Divide dough into 6 parts. Roll each part thin into a rectangle. Place cheese filling 2'' (5 cm) inside, along length of dough. Fold over twice and seal ends. Mark off portions with a knife. Bake at 375°F (190°C) for 25 to 30 minutes until brown. May be frozen unbaked.

Filling

2 lb.	dry cottage cheese	1 kg
3	eggs	3
2 tbsp.	butter	30 mL
	salt	
	pepper	

VARENICKES WITH FRUIT

2 lb.	fruit	1 kg
1 cup	sugar	250 mL
3 cups	flour	750 mL
3	egg yolks	3
1 cup	water	250 mL
	salt	

Use plums, cherries, or blueberries. Wash fruit, cover with sugar, and let stand a few hours. Drain juice and boil to a syrup. If using cherries, crush a few pits and boil with the juice. Mix remaining ingredients to make the pastry. Roll out very thin. Cut into 3'' (7 cm) circles. Place a little drained fruit on each circle, moisten edges with slightly beaten egg white or water, fold over and press edges together with a fork. Drop into boiling salted water. Cook for 15 minutes. Drain, and serve on a hot plate with sugar, fruit syrup, or sour cream.

VARENICKES WITH CREAM CHEESE

4	eggs	4
2 cups	flour	500 mL
½ tsp.	salt	2 mL
	cold water	
1 lb.	cream cheese	500 g
2 tbsp.	sour cream	30 mL

Separate 2 of the eggs. Mix yolks with remaining 2 eggs, flour, salt, and enough cold water to make a stiff paste. Roll out very thin and cut into rounds about 3'' (7 cm) in diameter. Mix cream cheese, sour cream, egg whites, and a pinch of salt. Put a little of the mixture on each round of pastry. Fold over. Press edges together, moistening with a little water to seal well. Poach in boiling salted water for 15 minutes. Serve with sour cream.

COTTAGE CHEESE PANCAKES

4	eggs, separated	4
1 cup	creamed cottage cheese	250 mL
¼ cup	flour	50 mL
¼ tsp.	salt	1 mL

Beat egg yolks. Add cheese, flour, and salt. Beat well together. Fold in stiffly beaten egg whites. Drop by large spoonfuls onto a hot greased griddle or electric frying pan. Cook on both sides. Serve with sour cream.

NEW ORLEANS PANCAKES

4	eggs	4
1 cup	cottage cheese	250 mL
1 cup	sour cream	250 mL
3/4 cup	flour	175 mL
1 tbsp.	sugar	15 mL
1/4 tsp.	salt	1 mL

Beat eggs. Blend in cheese and sour cream. Add dry ingredients and beat very well. Drop onto a well-buttered griddle or electric frying pan and brown on both sides. Serve with sour cream, syrup or jam, or fruit.

SOUR CREAM CHEESE ROLLS

Dough

1/4 lb.	butter, softened	125 g
2 tbsp.	sugar	30 mL
2 cups	flour	500 mL
2 tsp.	baking powder	10 mL
1/4 tsp.	salt	1 mL
1/2 cup	sour cream	125 mL
1	egg	1

Cream butter and sugar. Add remaining ingredients and mix to form dough. Flour board lightly. Divide dough in half and roll 1/4'' (0.5 cm) thick. Place filling along edge; roll tightly, as for a jelly roll. Dot a little melted butter on each roll and place in a greased pan. Bake at 350°F (180°C) for 35 minutes until lightly browned. Cut while warm.

Filling

1 lb.	dry cottage cheese	500 g
1/2 cup	rice, cooked	125 mL
1	egg	1
1/4 tsp.	cinnamon	1 mL
1/4 cup	sugar	50 mL

Blend all ingredients well.

LINIVNIKIS OR MINICHKES

1/2 tsp.	baking soda	2 mL
1/2 cup	milk	125 mL
1 1/2 cups	sour cream	625 mL
1 lb.	dry cottage cheese	500 g
1/4 lb.	butter, melted	125 g
1 tbsp.	sugar	15 mL
1/2 tsp.	salt	2 mL
2 tsp.	baking powder	10 mL
3	eggs	3
2 cups	flour	500 mL

Dissolve baking soda in milk and 1/2 cup (125 mL) of the sour cream. Mix together with remaining ingredients, using enough flour to make a stiff batter. Heat a cookie sheet and grease generously. Drop batter onto sheet by spoonfuls, not too close together. Bake at 375°F (190°C) until medium brown. Remove from cookie sheet to a casserole. Pour remaining sour cream over pancakes, and bake until cream is absorbed. Serve with more sour cream.

CHEESE MUFFINS

2 cups	dry cottage cheese	500 mL
1/2 cup	creamed cottage cheese	125 mL
2	eggs	2
3 tbsp.	sugar	45 mL
1/2 cup	margarine, melted	125 mL
1 cup	flour	250 mL
2 tsp.	baking powder	10 mL
1/8 tsp.	salt	0.5 mL

Combine cheese, eggs, sugar, and margarine. Add dry ingredients and mix well. Bake in well-greased muffin tins at 400°F (200°C) for 20 to 25 minutes. Yields 12 muffins.

Variations
Omit creamed cottage cheese for a muffin slightly more dry. For cheese-rice muffins, add 1 cup (250 mL) cooked rice.

CHEESE AND RICE MUFFINS

1/2 lb.	dry cottage cheese	250 g
3/4 cup	rice, cooked	175 mL
1 tbsp.	butter, melted	15 mL
1 tbsp.	oil	15 mL
3 tbsp.	sugar	45 mL
3 tbsp.	sour cream	45 mL
3	eggs, beaten	3
3/4 cup	flour	175 mL
2 tsp.	baking powder	10 mL

Combine all ingredients, mixing well. Grease muffin tins and leave a dab of margarine in each cup. Place empty tins in a preheated 350°F (180°C) oven until sizzling. Pour batter into hot tins. Bake for 30 to 45 minutes. Yields 12 muffins.

CHEESE TUNA MUFFINS

7 oz.	canned tuna, drained	198 g
1 cup	Swiss cheese, grated	250 mL
1/2 cup	mayonnaise	125 mL
1 tbsp.	lemon juice	15 mL
1/4 tsp.	Worcestershire sauce	1 mL
1/8 tsp.	Tabasco sauce	0.5 mL
6	English muffins	6
	paprika	

Mix together tuna, 3/4 cup (175 mL) of the cheese, mayonnaise, lemon juice, Worcestershire and Tabasco sauce. Split muffins and toast lightly. Spread about 1 1/2 tbsp. (25 mL) tuna mixture on each muffin. Sprinkle with remaining cheese and paprika. Broil 3'' (8 cm) from heat for 2 to 3 minutes, until cheese is melted and bubbly. Makes 12 muffin halves.

CHEESE DELIGHT

6	eggs	6
1 lb.	cottage cheese	500 g
1 cup	flour	250 mL
1 lb.	Mozzarella cheese, grated	500 g
	salt	
	pepper	
1/2 lb.	Cheddar cheese, grated	250 g

Beat eggs, and combine with all ingredients except Cheddar cheese. Place in a large greased baking dish and sprinkle Cheddar cheese on top. Bake at 350°F (180°C) for 45 to 60 minutes.

Vegetables & Side Dishes

Side dishes are the accessories which embroider and enhance the main course of a meal.

Vegetable markets offer produce all year round in a palette of colours: the variegated greens of asparagus, beans, peas, broccoli and spinach, lightly steamed and served *au naturel*; baked in a casserole with a tangy cheese, crusted and bubbly brown; or folded into a velvety cream sauce scented with fresh herbs. Even the kitchen ingenue can perform culinary magic.

A standing ovation for the good Jewish wife of long ago who, not having enough carrots in the root cellar, decided it wouldn't hurt to throw a few fruits into the pot: carrots and prunes, carrots and pineapple, carrots and apricots, and carrots and apple. Tzimmes was born and nurtured and perfected.

In the sixteenth century Sir Francis Drake in England and Sir Walter Raleigh in Ireland developed a liking for a certain tuber-bearing plant which originated in South America. Its popularity rapidly spread, and Jewish cooks throughout Europe delighted in this plant called potato. Latkes, Tagachs, Kugels, Tzimmes, and all manner of potato delights were improvised and refined, and eventually emigrated to North America.

From their origins in the Mediterranean and the Orient, pasta and rice have become household staples the world over. Rice is as comfortable nestling alongside brisket and gravy as it is under a mound of exotic Chinese vegetables. And pasta is quickly graduating from its supporting role status, as Manicotti and Lasagne become the leading characters of a meal. Marco Polo has been credited with bringing noodles from China to Italy, but there is no question as to who created Lokshen Kugel, sweet or savoury.

Side dishes—made from one vegetable or a combination; grains; rice; or noodles—are the stuff that makes an ordinary meal into a banquet and, with the good fortune of leftovers, tomorrow's lunch.

SALMON-STUFFED ARTICHOKES

4	artichokes	4
	boiling water	
16 oz.	canned red salmon	500 g
1 cup	bread crumbs	250 mL
1/4 cup	celery, diced	50 mL
1 tbsp.	parsley, chopped	15 mL
1/2 cup	dry white wine	125 mL
3/4 cup	Italian dressing	175 mL
1	lemon, quartered	1

Trim artichokes by cutting off stems and sharp tips of leaves. Set in a pan of boiling salted water; reduce heat, cover, and simmer until tender, approximately 20 minutes. Drain well. Carefully spread leaves apart and remove the choke.

Drain and flake the salmon. Combine with bread crumbs, celery, and parsley. Fill the artichokes with this mixture, spooning salmon filling into centres and between leaves of artichokes. Arrange artichokes tightly together in a casserole. Sprinkle wine into centres of artichokes, and pour Italian dressing over all. Cover. Bake at 350°F (180°C) for 45 to 50 minutes, basting frequently with pan juices. Serve hot, warm, or cold, with a wedge of lemon. Serves 4.

BAKED ASPARAGUS AND CHEESE

10 3/4 oz.	cream of asparagus soup	284 mL
1 cup	Cheddar cheese, shredded	250 mL
2 tbsp.	pimento, diced	30 mL
1/2 tsp.	Worcestershire sauce	2 mL
1/3 cup	French-fried onion rings	75 mL
14 oz.	canned asparagus	398 mL

Combine soup, cheese, pimento, Worcestershire sauce, and half the onion rings in a 1 1/2 quart (1.5 L) casserole. Gently stir in drained asparagus. Bake at 350°F (180°C) for 30 minutes. Top with remaining onion rings and bake an additional 5 minutes.

CREAMED ASPARAGUS

1 tbsp.	butter	15 mL
1 small	onion, minced	1 small
1 tbsp.	flour	15 mL
1 cup	sour cream	250 mL
1/2 tsp.	salt	2 mL
	paprika	
14 oz.	canned asparagus	398 mL

Sauté onion in butter until golden brown, cover and steam for a few minutes. Add flour, stirring until well blended. Add sour cream and seasonings. Cook slowly, uncovered, until sauce is smooth but not too thick. Dilute with asparagus juice if necessary. Gently fold in drained asparagus. Transfer to a chafing dish and keep warm.

BAKED FRENCH-STYLE BEANS

48 oz.	French-style green beans	1.5 kg
1 large	onion, chopped	1 large
12 oz.	frozen mushrooms	340 g
20 oz.	cream of mushroom soup	568 mL
4 oz.	frozen onion rings	113 g

Cook beans in a small amount of boiling salted water; drain. Sauté onions and add mushrooms, cooking until tender. Combine with beans and undiluted mushroom soup. Pour into a greased casserole dish. Top with onion rings. Bake at 350°F (180°C) for 30 minutes until bubbly. Serves 12.

BEAN BAKE

14 oz.	canned lima beans	398 mL
28 oz.	baked beans	796 mL
14 oz.	canned red kidney beans	398 mL
2 cups	onion, chopped	500 mL
1 clove	garlic, crushed	1 clove
1 tbsp.	oil	15 mL
5 oz.	chili sauce	142 mL
1 tsp.	vinegar	5 mL
1/4 cup	brown sugar	50 mL

Drain lima beans. Combine all beans in a bowl. Sauté onion and garlic in oil; add chili sauce, vinegar, and sugar; mix well. Add to beans, then transfer to a utility pan. Sprinkle lightly with cinnamon and garnish with strips of beef or grated cheese. Bake at 350°F (180°C) for 1 hour. Serves 12 – 15.

LIMA BEAN TZIMMES

1 cup	dried lima beans	250 mL
4 cups	cold water	1 L
1 cup	sugar	250 mL
1/2 tsp.	salt	2 mL

Wash beans well. Cover with water and bring to a boil. Cook over low heat, adding water as required to keep beans covered. When beans are tender, add sugar and salt. Cook 15 minutes more. Cool. Serve cold as a side dish.

BROCCOLI AND CHEESE

1 bunch	broccoli	1 bunch
1 cup	Swiss cheese, grated	250 mL
1/3 cup	mayonnaise	75 mL
2 tbsp.	onion, grated	30 mL
1/4 tsp.	salt	1 mL
1/8 tsp.	pepper	0.5 mL
1/2 tsp.	dry mustard	2 mL

Parboil broccoli, drain, and arrange on an oven-proof dish. Combine remaining ingredients to make sauce. Spread over broccoli. Bake uncovered at 350°F (180°C) about 15 minutes, until broccoli is hot and cheese melted.

BROCCOLI CASSEROLE

24 oz.	frozen broccoli	680 g
1/4 cup	onion, chopped	50 mL
6 tbsp.	butter	90 mL
2 tbsp.	flour	30 mL
1/2 cup	water	125 mL
8 oz.	process cheese spread	250 g
3	eggs, well beaten	3
1/2 cup	salted cracker crumbs	125 mL

Parboil broccoli. Sauté onion in 4 tbsp. (60 mL) of the butter until soft. Stir in flour and water. Cook over low heat, stirring, until thick and boiling. Blend in cheese spread. Combine sauce, broccoli, and eggs. Mix gently until blended. Turn into a greased 1 1/2 quart (1.5 L) casserole, cover with crumbs, and dot with remaining butter. Bake at 325°F (160°C) for 30 minutes. Serves 8.

BROCCOLI BAKE

24 oz.	frozen broccoli	680 g
10 oz.	cream of mushroom soup	284 mL
1/2 cup	mayonnaise	125 mL
1 tbsp.	lemon juice	15 mL
1/2 cup	Cheddar cheese, grated	125 mL
2 oz.	pimento	56 mL
1 cup	cheese cracker crumbs	250 mL
1/4 cup	walnuts, chopped	50 mL

Cook broccoli and drain well. Arrange broccoli in a greased casserole. Combine soup, mayonnaise, lemon juice, and cheese in a saucepan and heat until warm. Spoon onto broccoli. Top with pimento, crumbs, and nuts. Bake at 350°F (180°C) for 25 minutes.

BROCCOLI PUDDING

12 oz.	frozen broccoli	340 g
2 cups	creamed cottage cheese	500 mL
3	eggs	3
1/4 cup	butter, diced	50 mL
1/4 lb.	hard cheese, grated	125 g

Thaw broccoli just enough to cut into chunks. Combine all ingredients. Add no seasoning. Pour into a well-greased 8" x 8" (2 L) pan. Bake at 325°F (160°C) for 1 hour or until set and brown on top. Serve hot.

HARVARD BEETS

2 lb.	fresh beets, boiled	1 kg
1/2 cup	sugar	125 mL

2 tbsp.	cornstarch	30 mL
1 tsp.	salt	5 mL
1/4 tsp.	pepper	1 mL
1 cup	cider vinegar	250 mL
1/4 cup	water	50 mL
1/4 cup	margarine	50 mL

Peel beets and dice or cut in julienne strips. Mix sugar, cornstarch, salt, and pepper in a large pot. Slowly stir in vinegar to dissolve. Add water and margarine. Cook, stirring, over medium heat until thick and clear. Reduce heat to low, add beets, cover and simmer 15 minutes.

SWEET AND SOUR RED CABBAGE

2 tbsp.	margarine	30 mL
1 small	onion, minced	1 small
1 tbsp.	flour	15 mL
1	red cabbage, shredded	1
3/4 cup	vinegar	175 mL
2/3 cup	brown sugar	150 mL
1	apple, diced	1
	salt	
	pepper	

Brown onion in margarine. Blend in flour, add remaining ingredients and simmer, covered, for 15 minutes.

PINEAPPLE CARROTS

32 oz.	frozen small carrots	1 kg
1/2 cup	sugar	125 mL
4 tsp.	cornstarch	20 mL
6 oz.	pineapple juice	175 mL
2 tbsp.	margarine	30 mL
2 tbsp.	fresh mint, chopped	30 mL

Cook carrots, covered, in boiling salted water in a large frying pan for 25 minutes until tender. Drain carrots and set aside. Mix sugar and cornstarch in same pan. Stir in pineapple juice. Cook, stirring constantly, until sauce thickens and boils, about 3 minutes. Stir in margarine until melted, then

add mint leaves. Place carrots in sauce. Heat slowly until bubbly. Spoon into a heated serving bowl. Garnish with several small sprigs of mint.

CARROT TZIMMES

8 large	carrots, peeled	8 large
1/2 cup	honey	125 mL
4 tbsp.	sugar	60 mL
4 tbsp.	oil	60 mL
	lemon rind, grated	
	dash of ginger	

Slice carrots and cook 10 minutes in boiling salted water just to cover. Add honey, sugar, and oil. Cook gently until liquid is absorbed and carrots slightly glazed, about 30 minutes. Sprinkle with lemon rind and ginger.

CARROT-APRICOT TZIMMES

3 lb.	carrots, sliced	1.5 kg
1 cup	brown sugar	250 mL
1 1/2 tbsp.	cornstarch	25 mL
1 tsp.	orange rind, grated	5 mL
1 cup	apricot juice	250 mL
2 tbsp.	margarine	30 mL
14 oz.	canned apricot halves	398 mL

Cook carrots until tender. Arrange cooked carrots in a greased baking dish. Drain apricots, reserving juice. Mix sugar, cornstarch, orange rind, and apricot juice, and cook until thick. Add margarine, stirring until it melts. Arrange drained apricot halves on top of carrots. Pour sauce over. Bake at 325°F (160°C) for 45 minutes.

CARROT AND PRUNE TZIMMES

2 lb.	carrots	1 kg
1	egg	1
1/2 cup	honey	125 mL

1/3 cup	brown sugar	75 mL
1/3 cup	oil	75 mL
1/2 cup	flour	125 mL
1/2 cup	prunes	125 mL

Parboil carrots, drain, and mash. Mix egg, honey, sugar, and oil. Blend in flour. Add carrots and prunes and bake in a well-greased pan at 350°F (180°C) for 1 hour. Serves 8 – 10. (Note: This tzimmes may also be made with raisins; substitute an equal amount of raisins for the prunes.)

CARROT RING

3/4 cup	shortening	175 mL
1/2 cup	brown sugar	125 mL
1	egg	1
1 1/2 cups	carrots, grated	375 mL
1 cup	flour	250 mL
1 tsp.	baking powder	5 mL
1/2 tsp.	salt	2 mL
1/2 tsp.	cinnamon	2 mL
1/2 tsp.	baking soda	2 mL
1 tsp.	lukewarm water	5 mL
1 tbsp.	lemon juice	15 mL

Cream shortening and sugar. Beat in egg and carrots. Add flour, baking powder, salt, and cinnamon. Dissolve baking soda in lukewarm water and add, together with lemon juice. Mix well. Bake in a greased mould at 350°F (180°C) for 45 to 55 minutes.

CARROT KUGEL

1 cup	carrots, grated	250 mL
1 cup	sweet potatoes, grated	250 mL
1 cup	potato, grated	250 mL
1 cup	tart apple, grated	250 mL
1 cup	raisins	250 mL
1 cup	brown sugar	250 mL
1 cup	flour	250 mL
1 tsp.	baking soda	5 mL
1/4 tsp.	nutmeg	1 mL
1/2 tsp.	cinnamon	2 mL
1/2 tsp.	salt	2 mL
1/2 cup	oil	125 mL

Grease a large loaf pan well, and line with greased heavy foil extending up over sides. Mix all ingredients together. Pour into pan and bake at 350° – 375°F (180° – 190°C) for 55 to 65 minutes. Serves 10.

SPICED CARROT MUFFINS

1 1/4 cups	flour	300 mL
3/4 cup	brown sugar	175 mL
1 tsp.	baking soda	5 mL
1 tsp.	baking powder	5 mL
1/2 tsp.	salt	2 mL
1/2 tsp.	cinnamon	2 mL
1/4 tsp.	allspice	1 mL
1/4 tsp.	nutmeg	1 mL
1/8 tsp.	ginger	0.5 mL
1	egg	1
1/3 cup	oil	75 mL
1/2 cup	buttermilk	125 mL
1/2 tsp.	vanilla	2 mL
1 1/2 cups	carrots, grated	375 mL
3/4 cup	walnuts, chopped	175 mL
3/4 cup	raisins	175 mL

Measure dry ingredients into a large bowl and stir until well mixed. In a smaller bowl, gently whisk the egg, oil, buttermilk, and vanilla. Add carrots, nuts, and raisins to liquid. Pour into dry ingredients, and stir until blended. Fill greased muffin tins three-quarters full. Bake at 350°F (180°C) for 25 to 30 minutes. Serve hot. Yields 12 muffins.

CHILI CORN BAKE

1	onion, chopped	1
1/2	green pepper, chopped	1/2
2 stalks	celery, chopped	2 stalks
12 oz.	canned corn	341 mL
14 oz.	canned red kidney beans	398 mL
10 oz.	canned mushrooms	284 mL
14 oz.	canned chili	398 mL

Sauté onion, green pepper, and celery. Drain the canned vegetables and add, together with the chili. Bake covered at 325°F (160°C) for 1 hour. Remove cover and bake a further 30 minutes.

CORN PUDDING

14 oz.	creamed corn	398 mL
2	eggs	2
1/4 cup	cream of wheat	50 mL
1 cup	milk	250 mL
4 tbsp.	butter, melted	60 mL

Mix all ingredients well and pour into a greased, ovenproof utility pan. Bake at 375°F (190°C) for 60 to 90 minutes until golden brown and set. (This recipe may be doubled.)

CAULIFLOWER PANCAKES

1 head	cauliflower	1 head
3	eggs	3
1/2 cup	bread crumbs	125 mL
	salt	
	pepper	
	oil for frying	

Boil cauliflower in salted water until tender. Drain, cool, and chop very small. Combine with remaining ingredients. Drop from a spoon into hot oil and fry until golden brown. Serves 4 – 6.

EGGPLANT PARMIGIANA

1	onion, chopped	1
2 cloves	garlic, minced	2 cloves
28 oz.	stewed tomatoes	796 mL
7 1/2 oz.	tomato paste	212 mL
1 tsp.	sugar	5 mL
1 tsp.	oregano or basil	5 mL
2 medium	eggplant, peeled	2 medium
2	eggs	2
1 tsp.	salt	5 mL
2/3 cup	bread crumbs	150 mL
1 lb.	Mozzarella cheese, sliced	500 g
1/2 cup	Parmesan cheese, grated	125 mL

Sauté onion and garlic in oil until soft. Stir in tomatoes, tomato paste, and sugar. Simmer 30 minutes. Mix in oregano. While sauce is simmering, prepare eggplant. Cut eggplant into 1/4" (0.5 cm) slices. Beat eggs and salt. Coat eggplant slices well on both sides by dipping first in egg and then in bread crumbs. Fry in hot oil in a skillet until golden on both sides. In 2, 9" x 12" (3 L) baking dishes, layer eggplant, sauce, and Mozzarella cheese, sprinkling Parmesan between each layer and on top. Repeat layers. Bake at 350°F (180°C) for 35 minutes. Serves 12.

ROSEMARY EGGPLANT CASSEROLE

4 tbsp.	margarine	60 mL
1 small	eggplant, cubed	1 small
1/2 tsp.	rosemary	2 mL
12 oz.	frozen whole carrots	340 g
12 oz.	frozen peas	340 g
1/4 tsp.	salt	1 mL

Cook eggplant in margarine with rosemary for 5 minutes. Steam carrots until almost cooked, and add to eggplant with frozen peas. Season, cover, and steam until heated through but not soft.

BAKED MUSHROOMS

1 clove	garlic, minced	1 clove
1	onion, grated	1
1 tbsp.	parsley, chopped	15 mL
1/8 tsp.	basil	0.5 mL
1 tsp.	salt	5 mL
1/4 tsp.	pepper	1 mL
1/3 cup	oil	75 mL
2 tbsp.	wine vinegar	30 mL
1 1/2 lb.	mushrooms, sliced	750 g
1/4 lb.	margarine	125 g
1/2 cup	bread crumbs	125 mL
1 tbsp.	Parmesan cheese, grated	15 mL

Combine garlic, onion, parsley, basil, salt, pepper, oil and vinegar in a large bowl. Add mushrooms and marinate 3 hours, basting often. Drain. Melt half the margarine, add mushrooms, and cook over high heat for 1 minute. Reduce heat to low and cook 10 minutes, stirring frequently. Grease a baking dish well and arrange mushrooms in it. Sprinkle bread crumbs and cheese on top; dot with remaining margarine. Broil until brown.

FRIED MUSHROOMS

1 lb.	fresh mushrooms	500 g
1/2 tsp.	salt	2 mL
3 tbsp.	flour	45 mL
2	egg yolks, beaten	2
1/2 cup	fine bread crumbs	125 mL
1/4 tsp.	fennel	1 mL

Peel mushrooms and trim, but do not remove stalks. Season with salt. Dip in flour, then egg yolk, then coat with bread crumbs. Fry in butter to a light golden colour. Drain. Place on a hot dish, sprinkle with chopped fennel, and serve hot with lemon wedges.

FRIED FARFEL AND MUSHROOMS

2 tbsp.	oil	30 mL
8 oz.	egg farfel	250 g
1 tsp.	salt	5 mL
1/4 tsp.	paprika	1 mL
1/4 tsp.	pepper	1 mL
3 cups	warm water	750 mL
1/4 cup	onion, grated	50 mL
10 oz.	canned mushrooms	284 mL

Fry farfel in oil until golden brown, turning constantly to prevent burning. Add seasoning, water, and onion. Reduce heat, cover tightly, and steam 30 minutes. Chop mushrooms and add. Mix well and cook another 5 minutes. Serve hot.

FALLAFEL

2 cups	canned chick peas	500 mL
1/2 tsp.	salt	2 mL
1/4 tsp.	hot pepper sauce	1 mL
1/4 tsp.	pepper	1 mL
2 cups	fine dry bread crumbs	500 mL
2	eggs, beaten	2
2 tbsp.	shortening, melted	30 mL
	oil for frying	

Drain and mash the chick peas. Combine with salt, hot pepper sauce, pepper, and crumbs. Stir thoroughly. Add eggs, then shortening. Shape into 1/2 – 3/4" (1.5 – 2 cm) balls and roll in crumbs. Fry balls a few at a time in deep hot oil for 2 to 3 minutes until golden brown. Drain on absorbent paper. Makes about 15 balls. Serve in pita bread with finely chopped salad and tahini sauce.

SCALLOPED ONIONS AND ALMONDS

4 cups	onion, sliced	1 L
1/2 cup	slivered almonds	125 mL
10 oz.	cream of mushroom soup	284 mL
	salt	
1/2 cup	corn flake crumbs	125 mL
1 tbsp.	butter	15 mL

Cook onions in boiling salted water until tender. Drain. Blanch almonds. Alternate layers of onion, almonds, and undiluted soup in a greased, shallow 1 quart (1 L) baking dish. Sprinkle each layer with salt. Combine crumbs with butter and sprinkle over onion mixture. Bake at 350°F (180°C) about 20 minutes, until mixture is thoroughly heated and crumbs are browned. Serves 6 – 8.

ONION-FILLED ONION SHELLS

6	Spanish onions	6
6 cloves	garlic	6 cloves
6 tbsp.	bread crumbs	90 mL
8 tbsp.	parsley, chopped	120 mL
	salt	
	pepper	
	olive oil	
	butter	

Simmer onions and garlic in boiling salted water until tender. Scoop out centres of blanched onions, reserving shells. Combine scooped out flesh and garlic. Chop very finely, and then pound together until smooth with bread crumbs, parsley, and salt and pepper to taste, adding enough oil to make a thick paste. Stuff onion shells. Place on a greased baking dish, sprinkle with bread crumbs, and dot with butter. Bake at 425°F (220°C) for 8 to 10 minutes until heated and golden. Serves 6.

SNOW PEAS AND TOMATOES

2 tbsp.	margarine	30 mL
1 small	onion, chopped	1 small
12 oz.	frozen snow peas	340 g
1 tbsp.	soy sauce	15 mL
1 tsp.	salt	5 mL
1/2 tsp.	oregano	2 mL
3 medium	tomatoes	3 medium

Melt margarine in a large frying pan over medium heat. Sauté onion for 1 minute. Add peas, soy sauce, salt, and oregano. Cook until peas are just tender, stirring occasionally. Cut tomatoes into wedges, add to peas, and cook 1 minute more.

CHEESE-BAKED POTATOES

5 large	baking potatoes	5 large
1/3 cup	milk	75 mL
1 tbsp.	butter	15 mL
1 tbsp.	onion, chopped	15 mL
1 tsp.	parsley, chopped	5 mL
1 cup	Cheddar cheese, grated	250 mL
	salt	
	pepper	

Bake potatoes at 450°F (230°C) for 45 to 50 minutes, until tender. Cool; cut in halves. Scoop pulp from shells and mash with milk until light and fluffy. Melt butter in a small frying pan. Cook onion 2 minutes until limp. Stir into potato mixture along with parsley, cheese, and seasoning. Pile mixture into 8 of the potato shells. Place stuffed potatoes on a baking sheet. Bake at 425°F (220°C) for 25 minutes. Serves 8. (Note: To freeze, place stuffed potatoes on a flat pan in freezer for 3 hours to firm potatoes, then wrap individually in airtight freezer wrap and store in freezer in a plastic bag. Heat in oven direct from freezer; do not thaw first.)

BABY POTATOES WITH CUCUMBER DRESSING

20 small	new potatoes	20 small
5	green onions, minced	5
1 medium	cucumber	1 medium
2 tbsp.	lemon juice	30 mL
1 tsp.	salt	5 mL
1/4 tsp.	paprika	1 mL
4 tbsp.	mayonnaise	60 mL

Cook potatoes with skins on. Drain, and dry a few seconds over heat. Cool slightly and peel. If potatoes are very small, leave them whole; if they are large, cut into thick slices. Mix with onions. Grate unpeeled cucumber finely, removing seeds. Place in a bowl with lemon juice, salt, paprika, and mayonnaise. Stir until blended. Pour dressing over potatoes and mix well. Keep at room temperature until ready to serve. Serves 6 – 8. (Note: If salad is prepared in advance and stored in refrigerator, let stand at room temperature 3 hours before serving.)

POTATO LATKES

6	potatoes	6
2	eggs	2
2 tbsp.	flour	30 mL
1 tsp.	salt	5 mL
	pepper	
1 small	onion, grated	1 small
1/4 tsp.	baking powder	1 mL
	oil for frying	

Grate peeled potatoes and place in colander. Rinse in cold water to wash off starch. Drain. Combine with remaining ingredients, mixing well. Drop by spoonfuls into at least ¼'' (0.5 cm) deep hot oil. Fry until brown on both sides, turning only once so that pancakes do not become soggy.

POTATO PATTIES

1 lb.	potatoes, peeled	500 g
	salt	
	pepper	
1 tsp.	baking powder	5 mL
4 sprigs	parsley, chopped	4 sprigs
	oil for frying	

Boil the potatoes, drain, and mash. Combine all ingredients. Form into patties and deep fry in oil until brown.

POTATO DUMPLINGS

2 lb.	potatoes	1 kg
¼ cup	onion, chopped	50 mL
	schmaltz or oil	
3 tbsp.	cornstarch	45 mL
4 tbsp.	flour	60 mL
2	egg yolks	2
	salt	
	pepper	
	nutmeg	
	parsley, chopped	

Boil, cool, and mash potatoes. Brown onion in schmaltz and add to potatoes with remaining ingredients, using just enough flour to make into a dough. Mix lightly with a wooden spoon. Turn onto a floured pastry board and, with floured hands, form into small balls. Drop dumplings gently into boiling salted water. They will rise to the top when cooked. Keep warm in an oven-proof dish. Just before serving, spoon on hot melted chicken fat and garnish with chopped parsley.

MASHED POTATO CASSEROLE

5 lb.	potatoes, peeled	2.5 kg
½ lb.	cream cheese	250 g
1 cup	sour cream	250 mL
2 tsp.	onion salt	10 mL
1 tsp.	salt	5 mL
	pinch of pepper	
2 tbsp.	butter	30 mL

Cook potatoes in salted water until tender. Drain, then mash until very smooth. Add remaining ingredients. Beat until light and fluffy. Cool slightly and place in a large greased casserole or souffle dish. Dot with more butter or buttered crumbs. Bake uncovered at 350°F (180°C) for 30 minutes until heated through. Serves 10 – 12. (Note: Before baking, casserole may be kept, covered, in refrigerator for up to 5 days or else frozen until needed.)

POTATO PIE

Dough

2 cups	flour	500 mL
2 tsp.	baking powder	10 mL
⅛ tsp.	salt	0.5 mL
2 tsp.	sugar	10 mL
3 tbsp.	shortening	45 mL
1	egg, beaten	1
½ cup	water	125 mL

Combine dry ingredients. Cut in shortening. Mix egg and water and add, stirring to form dough. Roll out on a lightly floured board. Line a 9'' or 10'' (1 or 1.5 L) pie plate.

Filling

6	potatoes	6
3	onions, chopped	3
	salt	
	pepper	
2	eggs, separated	2

Peel potatoes and boil until tender. Drain. Mash well. Fry onion to a golden brown. Add to potatoes with seasoning and egg yolks. Beat egg whites stiff, and fold into potato mixture. Pour into pie shell. Bake at 375°F (190°C) until crust is brown. Serve hot, cut into wedges. Serves 10 – 12.

POTATO TAGACHS (LITTLE PUDDINGS)

5 large	potatoes, boiled	5 large
4	eggs, separated	4
	salt	
	pepper	
	schmaltz or butter	
2	onions, diced	2

Mash potatoes well. Add beaten egg yolks, and beat until smooth. Season to taste. Fry onion in schmaltz and add. Beat egg whites stiff, then fold into potatoes. Bake in a well-greased bowl or individual cupcake tins at 400°F (200°C) for about 30 minutes until slightly browned.

POTATO KUGEL

6 large	potatoes	6 large
3	eggs	3
¼ cup	flour	50 mL
1 small	onion, grated	1 small
½ cup	shortening	125 mL
1 tsp.	baking powder	5 mL
1 tsp.	salt	5 mL
	dash of pepper	

Grate potatoes finely, drain off most of the water, and add remaining ingredients. Mix well. Pour into a well-greased, heated pudding dish or individual cupcake tins, and brush top lightly with oil. Bake at 400°F (200°C) for 1 hour until a brown crust has formed on top. Serve hot. Serves 4 – 6. (Note: For a pudding lighter in texture and colour, substitute 1 large cooked, mashed potato for 1 of the raw potatoes.)

POTATO MUFFINS

10 medium	potatoes	10 medium
1 tsp.	salt	5 mL
½ tsp.	pepper	2 mL
2 tbsp.	oil	30 mL
4	eggs	4
2	onions, chopped	2

Cook potatoes and mash with seasoning and oil. Beat eggs with a fork and add to potatoes. Sauté onions and add. Grease large muffin tins generously, and heat before filling. Bake at 400°F (200°C) for 40 minutes. Makes about 24 muffins. (Good for Passover.)

POTATO BOULANGÈRE

10 small	potatoes	10 small
8	pearl onions	8
8	mushrooms, sliced	8
½ cup	margarine	125 mL
	salt	
	pepper	
¼ tsp.	paprika	1 mL

Boil potatoes 30 minutes and onions 15 minutes. Drain. Combine all ingredients. Bake at 425°F (220°C) for 45 minutes. Stir once or twice while cooking. Serves 4 – 6.

PRUNE AND POTATO TZIMMES

½ lb.	boneless short ribs	250 g
1	onion, sliced	1
	water	
4	potatoes	4
1 small	sweet potato	1 small
½ cup	brown sugar	125 mL
½ lb.	prunes	250 g
2 tsp.	salt	10 mL
1½ tbsp.	flour	20 mL

Place meat and onion in a pot with water to cover. Simmer for 30 minutes. Add vegetables, sugar, prunes, and salt; cook over low heat for 1 hour longer. When ingredients are tender, make a paste of the flour and a little water, and add to the stew to thicken. The tzimmes should be thick and not soupy. Serves 4 as a side dish. (Note: The tzimmes is excellent served with chicken or other fowl, but is too rich to eat as a main course.)

POTATO CHEESE PUFFS

4 large	potatoes	4 large
1/2 cup	milk	125 mL
2	eggs, separated	2
3/4 cup	cheese, grated	175 mL
	salt	
	pepper	
1 1/2 tsp.	onion juice	7 mL
2 tbsp.	parsley, chopped	30 mL

Boil potatoes and mash while hot. Mix milk with egg yolks, and add to potatoes with cheese, salt, pepper, onion juice, and parsley. Whip until fluffy. Beat egg whites stiff; fold into potato mixture. Pile lightly into 8 mounds on a greased cookie sheet. Bake at 350°F (180°C) for 25 minutes.

MUSHROOM POTATO PUFFS

1 lb.	mushrooms, sliced	500 g
1	onion, diced	1
1 cup	celery, diced	250 mL
4 large	potatoes	4 large
2	eggs	2
1/2 cup	flour	125 mL
1 tsp.	salt	5 mL
1/2 tsp.	pepper	2 mL
	oil for frying	

Sauté mushrooms, onion, and celery until soft. Set aside to cool. Boil potatoes, drain, and mash until smooth. Add eggs, flour, and seasonings, and beat again until smooth. In wet palm of hand, shape a large spoonful of potato mixture into a round. Put a teaspoon (5 mL) of mushroom filling in centre and wrap potato mixture around to cover. Fry in oil until golden. Serves 6.

POTATO KNISHES

Dough

1 1/2 cups	flour	375 mL
1/2 tsp.	salt	2 mL
1/2 cup	shortening	125 mL
1	egg	1
1/3 cup	water	75 mL

Cut shortening into flour and salt as for pie crust. Add egg and stir in water to make a soft dough. Roll out on a lightly floured board, making a rectangle 3 times as long as it is wide. Place potato filling along long side edge. Roll up tightly as for a jelly roll. Cut into 1'' (2 cm) pieces with side of hand. Tuck in both sides of dough. Pour a thin layer of oil on a cookie sheet. Place knishes on cookie sheet, turning them over to oil both sides. Bake at 350°F (180°C) for 15 minutes, then turn knishes over and bake an additional 10 minutes. Cool on cooling racks.

Filling

5 lb.	potatoes	2.5 kg
2	onions	2
2	eggs	2
	salt	
	pepper	

Peel potatoes and boil in salted water until tender. Drain well. Dice onions and fry until golden. Mash potatoes with onion. Add eggs as necessary to give a fluffy consistency. Season to taste.

LIVER AND POTATO KNISHES

1 tbsp.	sugar	15 mL
3/4 cup	warm water	175 mL
1/2 tsp.	salt	2 mL
5 tbsp.	oil	75 mL
1 tbsp.	yeast	15 mL
2	eggs, beaten	2
3 1/2 cups	flour, sifted	875 mL
1	onion, diced	1
6	potatoes	6
1/2 lb.	liver	250 g
	salt	
	pepper	

Dissolve sugar in water, and add salt and 3 tbsp. (45 mL) of the oil. Add yeast, mix, and let stand 5 minutes. Add to eggs. Mix well into flour. Let stand in a warm place 3 to 4 hours until it rises. Roll out dough on a floured cloth as thin as possible. Fry onion in remaining oil. Boil potatoes, drain, and mash. Broil liver and chop. Combine onion, potatoes, and liver, and season to taste. Add more oil if required to hold mixture together. Place a row of filling along edge of dough. Roll as for jelly roll until filling no longer shows through the thin dough. Cut roll off from dough. Repeat filling and rolling until all the dough and filling is used up. Cut the long rolls into 1½'' (3 cm) pieces, pinching edges together so that filling is not exposed. Bake in a well-greased pan at 325°F (160°C) for 25 minutes.

Variation

For quick and easy knishes, use frozen puff pastry shells for the dough. Defrost shells slightly, until pliable. Roll out to 3'' x 8'' (7 x 20 cm). Lay filling down the long side, roll up as for jelly roll, saw through dough with side of hand, and pinch edges together. Dip in oil on oiled sheet. Bake at 375°F (190°C) for 15 to 20 minutes. May be frozen after baking.

PEROGY

Dough

1 cup	oil	250 mL
2½ cups	warm water	625 mL
7½ cups	flour	1875 mL
¼ tsp.	salt	1 mL

Mix all ingredients together. Perogy may be made immediately, or dough may be refrigerated up to 24 hours before making.

Filling

10 medium	potatoes	10 medium
6	cheese slices	6
2	onions, chopped	2
3 tbsp.	butter	45 mL
	salt	
	pepper	

Peel, boil, drain potatoes and mash with cheese. Fry onion. Add to potatoes together with butter, salt, and pepper. Roll dough; cut in circles with a glass. Place a spoon of filling in each centre, fold over, and pinch to seal. Boil 15 minutes in salted water. Rinse with cold water, drain, and dot with butter. Serve with fried onions and sour cream. Makes 11 – 12 dozen.

SWEET POTATOES

6	sweet potatoes	6
¼ cup	butter, melted	50 mL
½ cup	brown sugar	125 mL
2 tbsp.	lemon juice	30 mL

Cook potatoes until tender. Peel, cut in half lengthwise, and arrange in a shallow baking dish. Bring remaining ingredients to boil in saucepan. Pour over potatoes. Bake at 325°F (160°C) for 35 minutes, turning occasionally.

SPINACH CASSEROLE

36 oz.	frozen spinach, chopped	1 kg
½ lb.	cream cheese	250 g
10 oz.	mushroom soup	284 mL
2 oz.	French-fried onion rings	56 g
14 oz.	canned artichoke hearts	398 mL
	paprika	

Cook and drain spinach. Add cream cheese, mixing until melted. Blend in soup. Put half the spinach in a casserole. Top with onion rings. Add remaining spinach. Sauté artichoke hearts in butter and sprinkle with paprika. Arrange over spinach. Heat at 350°F (180°C) until soup bubbles. Serves 10 – 12.

SPINACH CREPES

Batter

4	eggs	4
¼ tsp.	salt	1 mL
2 cups	flour	500 mL
2¼ cups	milk	550 mL
¼ cup	butter, melted	50 mL

overleaf:
Carrot Strudel (page 87)

In a medium size mixing bowl, combine eggs and salt. Gradually add flour alternately with milk, beating until smooth. Beat in melted butter. Refrigerate batter at least 1 hour before cooking on upside-down crepe griddle or in crepe pan. Makes about 32 – 36 crepes. Freeze in packages of 8 – 12 for future use.

Filling (for 12 Crepes)

2/3 cup	cooked spinach	150 mL
1/2 cup	cottage cheese	125 mL
2	eggs, beaten	2
2 tbsp.	Parmesan cheese, grated	30 mL
	salt	
	pepper	
1 1/2 cups	Bechamel sauce	375 mL
1/2 lb.	Mozzarella cheese, sliced	250 g
3 tbsp.	butter	45 mL

Blend spinach, cheese, and eggs. Stir in Parmesan, and season to taste. Fill crepes, folding as for omelette. Arrange in a greased casserole. Pour Bechamel sauce (see page 152) over crepes, top with Mozzarella slices, and dot with butter. Bake at 375°F (190°C) for 15 to 20 minutes, then broil 2 minutes. Serves 8 – 12.

Variation

12 oz.	spinach, chopped	340 g
4	green onions, chopped	4
1/2 cup	Ricotta cheese	125 mL
1 cup	Mozzarella cheese, grated	250 mL
	pinch of nutmeg	
	salt	
	pepper	
1/4 cup	butter	50 mL
1/4 cup	Parmesan cheese	50 mL
2 tbsp.	lemon juice	30 mL

Combine spinach, green onions, Ricotta and Mozzarella cheese. Season to taste. Fill crepes; arrange in a greased casserole. Combine remaining ingredients, and spoon a little of this lemon-butter sauce over the crepes. Bake at 375°F (190°C) for 20 minutes, basting often with lemon-butter sauce.

SPINACH AND MUSHROOM CASSEROLE

1 lb.	fresh mushrooms	500 g
24 oz.	frozen spinach, thawed	675 g
1 tsp.	salt	5 mL
1/4 cup	onion, chopped	50 mL
1/4 cup	butter, melted	50 mL
1 cup	Cheddar cheese, grated	250 mL
	garlic salt	

Wash and dry mushrooms, and slice off stems. Sauté stems and caps until brown. Combine spinach with salt, onion, and butter, and spread onto the bottom of a 10" (1.5 L) casserole. Sprinkle with 1/4 cup (50 mL) of the grated cheese. Arrange mushrooms over spinach. Sprinkle with garlic salt. Cover with remaining cheese. Bake at 350°F (180°C) for 20 minutes.

Variation
French-style green beans may be used instead of spinach.

SPINACH CUSTARD

12 oz.	frozen spinach, chopped	340 g
1 cup	milk	250 mL
3	eggs	3
1 tbsp.	lemon juice	15 mL
1 1/4 tsp.	salt	6 mL
	dash of pepper	
1/8 tsp.	nutmeg	0.5 mL
1/2 clove	garlic, minced	1/2 clove
	dash of marjoram	

Thaw spinach and drain. Mix all ingredients together well. Pour into a 1 1/2 pint (750 mL) casserole dish and bake at 350°F (180°C) for 50 minutes.

SPINACH SOUFFLÉ

3 tbsp.	butter	45 mL
1/4 cup	flour	50 mL
1/2 tsp.	salt	2 mL

	dash of cayenne pepper	
1 cup	milk	250 mL
1/4 cup	Parmesan cheese, grated	50 mL
4	eggs, separated	4
12 oz.	frozen spinach, cooked	340 g

Melt butter and blend in flour and seasonings. Add milk. Cook over medium heat, stirring constantly, until thickened. Add cheese and stir until cheese melts. Remove from heat. Beat egg yolks until lemon coloured. Gradually add to mixture, blending well. Add spinach and mix well. Gently fold in stiffly beaten egg whites. Pour into a well-greased casserole, set in a shallow pan of hot water, and bake at 325°F (160°C) for 55 to 60 minutes.

STUFFED TOMATOES

8	tomatoes	8
	prepared mustard	
1 cup	rice, cooked	250 mL
2 oz.	cheese, grated	55 g

Halve the tomatoes. Scoop out pulp, reserving juice. Brush insides of tomato halves with mustard. Warm reserved juice with rice, and fill tomatoes. Sprinkle cheese over tops. Arrange in an ovenproof dish and bake at 375°F (190°C) for 20 minutes. Serves 4.

Variation
Any leftover vegetables, finely chopped, may be combined with rice.

TURNIP SOUFFLÉ

2 lb.	turnip	1 kg
2 cups	chicken bouillon	500 mL
5 tbsp.	margarine	75 mL
1 tbsp.	brown sugar	15 mL
	salt	
	pepper	
	pinch of mace	
1 tsp.	baking powder	5 mL
2	eggs, separated	2
1/2 cup	fine dry bread crumbs	125 mL

Peel turnip and cut into 1/2'' (1.5 cm) cubes. Boil in chicken bouillon until tender, approximately 25 minutes. Drain and mash. Stir in 2 tbsp. (30 mL) of the margarine together with brown sugar, seasonings, baking powder, and egg yolks. Beat egg whites until stiff, and fold into turnip mixture. Place in a 1 1/2 quart (1.5 L) casserole or soufflé dish. Fry bread crumbs in remaining margarine for 3 minutes and sprinkle over casserole. Bake, uncovered, at 375°F (190°C) for 25 minutes. Serve immediately. Serves 4. (Note: The soufflé may be prepared up to a day ahead before baking. Refrigerate before frying bread crumbs, which should be added just before baking.)

YELLOW TURNIP CASSEROLE

3 medium	turnips	3 medium
1 cup	apple sauce	250 mL
8 tbsp.	margarine	120 mL
4 tsp.	sugar	20 mL
3 tsp.	salt	15 mL
1/4 tsp.	pepper	1 mL
2	eggs	2
1 3/4 cups	soft bread crumbs	425 mL

Peel turnips and slice into strips, removing all traces of green. Cook in boiling salted water until tender. Drain and mash. Combine with remaining ingredients, except 3/4 cup (175 mL) of the crumbs and 2 tbsp. (30 mL) of the margarine. Mix well and pour into a greased 2 quart (2 L) casserole. Toss reserved crumbs in melted margarine and sprinkle over casserole. Cool slightly, then cover and refrigerate. Remove 1 hour before serving and bake at 350°F (180°C) at least 30 minutes. Serves 12. (Note: 2 chopped apples may be substituted for the apple sauce.)

ZUCCHINI CREOLE

6 medium	zucchini	6 medium
3 tbsp.	margarine	45 mL
3 tbsp.	flour	45 mL
2 cups	tomatoes, chopped	500 mL
1	green pepper, chopped	1

1 small	onion, chopped	1 small
1 tsp.	salt	5 mL
1 tbsp.	brown sugar	15 mL

Arrange unpeeled zucchini in a greased casserole. In a saucepan, melt the margarine. Stir in flour until blended. Add remaining ingredients. Cook 5 minutes, then pour over zucchini. Bake at 350°F (180°C) for 1 hour. Serves 6 – 8.

ZUCCHINI PIE

4 cups	zucchini, thinly sliced	1 L
1 cup	onion, chopped	250 mL
1 clove	garlic, chopped	1 clove
1/2 cup	parsley, chopped	125 mL
1/4 tsp.	basil	1 mL
1/4 tsp.	oregano	1 mL
1/2 tsp.	salt	2 mL
1/2 tsp.	pepper	2 mL
1/2 lb.	Mozzarella cheese, grated	250 g
2	eggs	2
14 oz.	frozen puff pastry	398 g
2 tsp.	prepared mustard	10 mL

Sauté zucchini, onions, and garlic in butter in a large saucepan until soft, about 10 minutes. Add herbs and seasonings. Beat eggs in a large bowl and add cheese. Pour in zucchini mixture. Preheat oven to 375°F (190°C). Line a 9'' x 12'' (3 L) ovenproof pan with pastry and spread with mustard. Pour zucchini-egg mixture over. Cook 18 to 20 minutes until done.

ZUCCHINI MEDLEY

1/4 cup	margarine	50 mL
4 cups	zucchini, sliced	1 L
1 1/2 cups	frozen corn	375 mL
1/2 cup	onion, chopped	125 mL
1/3 cup	green pepper, chopped	75 mL
1/2 tsp.	salt	2 mL
3/4 tsp.	dill weed	3 mL

Melt margarine in a large skillet. Add vegetables and sprinkle with salt. Cover and cook about 12 to 15 minutes, stirring occasionally. Sprinkle dill over top.

ZUCCHINI AND NOODLE CASSEROLE

3 tbsp.	margarine	45 mL
2 tbsp.	flour	30 mL
1 tsp.	salt	5 mL
1/8 tsp.	pepper	0.5 mL
2 cups	milk	500 mL
1 cup	Cheddar cheese, cubed	250 mL
1 cup	Swiss cheese, cubed	250 mL
8 oz.	wide egg noodles	250 g
1 1/2 lb.	zucchini, sliced	750 g
1/2 cup	bread crumbs	125 mL

Melt 2 tbsp. (30 mL) of the margarine and blend in flour, salt and pepper. Add milk gradually, stirring constantly over medium heat until thickened. Add all the cheese and stir until melted. Cook noodles as directed on package; drain. Spread half the noodles on the bottom of a greased 9'' (2 L) pan. Arrange half the zucchini slices over noodles, and pour on half the cheese sauce. Repeat layers. Toss bread crumbs in remaining margarine, melted. Sprinkle on top of casserole. Bake at 350°F (180°C) for 30 minutes until golden brown.

RATATOUILLE

1	eggplant, cubed	1
2	zucchini, thickly sliced	2
2 large	onions, cut in chunks	2 large
1	green pepper, cut in chunks	1
2	tomatoes, cut in chunks	2
1 tsp.	salt	5 mL
1/4 tsp.	pepper	1 mL
	dash of sugar	
1/8 tsp.	garlic powder	0.5 mL
1 tbsp.	parsley, chopped	15 mL
1/3 cup	Parmesan cheese, grated	75 mL
	black olives, pitted	

Fry eggplant, zucchini, and onions until soft. Add green pepper. Remove from heat and add tomatoes and seasonings. Turn out into a casserole. Top with Parmesan cheese and olives. Bake, covered, at 350°F (180°C) for 30 to 45 minutes until cheese browns.

CONTINENTAL ZUCCHINI

1 lb.	zucchini, cubed	500 g
12 oz.	canned corn, drained	340 mL
	garlic	
2 tbsp.	oil	30 mL
1 tsp.	salt	5 mL
1/4 tsp.	pepper	1 mL
1/2 cup	Mozzarella cheese, grated	125 mL

Stir together everything but cheese. Cover. Cook over medium heat, stirring occasionally, approximately 10 minutes until crisp. Stir in cheese. Serve when cheese melts.

GIVETCH

2	carrots, thinly sliced	2
2	potatoes, cubed	2
4	tomatoes, quartered	4
1	onion, sliced	1
1 small	cauliflower, broken up	1 small
1/2	green pepper, sliced	1/2
1/2	red pepper, sliced	1/2
6 oz.	frozen peas	170 g
1 cup	green beans, sliced	250 mL
1 stalk	celery, sliced	1 stalk
3	zucchini, sliced	3
1 cup	beef bouillon	250 mL
1/2 cup	olive oil	125 mL
1 clove	garlic, crushed	1 clove
2 tsp.	salt	10 mL
1/2	bay leaf, crushed	1/2
1/2 tsp.	seasoning salt	2 mL
1/4 tsp.	tarragon, basil, or oregano	1 mL

Combine all vegetables in a baking dish or casserole. Mix remaining ingredients in saucepan. Heat to boiling and pour over vegetables. Cover with foil. Bake at 350°F (180°C) until tender, about 1 hour. Serves 8 – 10.

CURRIED FRUIT

5 cups	fruit, sliced or pitted	1.25 L
3/4 cup	brown sugar	175 mL
1 1/2 tsp.	curry powder	7 mL
4 tbsp.	margarine	60 mL

Use any fruits—peaches, pears, cherries—and vary amount used according to taste. Cut margarine into sugar and curry powder until mixture resembles fine crumbs. Place fruit in baking dish, crumble mix onto fruit, and bake uncovered at 350°F (180°C) for 30 minutes.

CORN FRITTERS

2	eggs, beaten	2
1/2 cup	milk	125 mL
1 cup	flour	250 mL
1 tsp.	baking powder	5 mL
1 tsp.	salt	5 mL
1 cup	corn, drained	250 mL
1 tbsp.	butter, melted	15 mL
	oil for frying	

Combine eggs and milk. Sift together dry ingredients; add to egg mixture, stirring just to moisten. Fold in corn and butter. Drop by large spoonfuls into deep oil at 375°F (190°C), and fry until browned, turning once (1 to 2 minutes per side). Makes 15 – 20.

Variation

Apple Fritters

Prepare fritter batter as above, adding 1/4 cup (50 mL) sugar and an extra tsp. (5 mL) baking powder, reducing the amount of salt to taste, and using just enough flour to make a loose, but not thin, batter. Peel and core 4 apples. Roll them in additional flour, dip in fritter batter, and fry in deep oil for a few minutes. Set on a cookie sheet; place a dab of margarine in each centre, and bake at 400°F (200°C) for 20 minutes. Serves 4.

HARVEST FRUIT

12 oz.	mixed dried fruit	340 g
14 oz.	canned pineapple chunks	398 mL
21 oz.	cherry pie filling	590 g
1/2 cup	dry sherry	125 mL
1/4 cup	water	50 mL
1 1/2 tsp.	curry powder	7 mL

Soak dried fruit for 15 to 20 minutes, then drain well. Drain pineapple, discarding juice. Combine all ingredients in a baking dish. Bake at 350°F (180°C) for 1 hour. Serve warm with meat.

BAKED PINEAPPLES

2	pineapples	2
½ cup	brandy or rum	125 mL

Slit pineapples in half, cutting through green tops as well. Scoop out flesh, leaving a thick wall of fruit in the shell. Cut scooped flesh into cubes and marinate in brandy or rum for 3 to 4 hours. Refill shells and bake at 350°F (180°C) until pieces begin to get tender. After 30 minutes, cover with foil. Serve hot with duck or chicken. Serves 4.

RICE AND MUSHROOM RING

1 cup	rice, uncooked	250 mL
1 lb.	mushrooms, chopped	500 g
2 tbsp.	butter	30 mL
2 tsp.	onion, minced	10 mL
1 clove	garlic	1 clove

Steam rice. Sauté mushrooms in butter with onion and garlic. Remove garlic and mix mushrooms with steamed rice. Place in buttered ring mould, set in pan of hot water, and bake at 350°F (180°C) for 30 minutes.

BLINTZ SIDE DISH

3 large	onions, thinly sliced	3 large
½ lb.	mushrooms, thinly sliced	250 g
4	hard-boiled eggs, chopped	4
½ tsp.	salt	2 mL
¼ tsp.	pepper	1 mL
¼ tsp.	paprika	1 mL
	margarine	
15 large	blintz leaves	15 large

Sauté onion and mushrooms until soft. Add hard-boiled eggs and seasonings, and mix with enough margarine to bind. In a greased ovenproof utility pan, arrange 2 blintz leaves at the bottom and 2 halved leaves up the sides and overhanging the dish. Spread filling and repeat layering with blintz leaves until filling is finished. Top with blintz layer. Bring up overhanging pieces to cover entire dish. Bake at 350°F (180°C) for 40 minutes. Cut in squares and serve with sour cream as a milk dish, with gravy to accompany meat.

WINE RICE SIDE DISH

½ cup	currants	125 mL
⅓ cup	margarine	75 mL
2 cloves	garlic, sliced	2 cloves
1½ cups	dry white wine	375 mL
3 cups	water	750 mL
2 cups	rice, uncooked	500 mL
2 tsp.	salt	10 mL
	pepper	
¼ tsp.	nutmeg	1 mL
¼ tsp.	allspice	1 mL
2 tsp.	sugar	10 mL
⅔ cup	brazil nuts, chopped	150 mL

Bring currants to boil in water to cover. Let stand 5 minutes then drain thoroughly. Melt margarine with garlic. Simmer 5 minutes, remove garlic and add wine and water. Bring to a boil. Add rice and spices. Reduce heat and simmer, covered, until liquid has been absorbed. Stir in currants and nuts. Serves 6 – 8. May also be served as poultry stuffing.

FANCY RICE

½ cup	margarine	125 mL
1	onion, thinly sliced	1
1 cup	rice, uncooked	250 mL
2 cups	chicken bouillon	500 mL
1 tsp.	salt	5 mL

Melt margarine in heavy saucepan. Sauté onion until soft and golden, but not brown. Stir in rice.

Cook 2 minutes longer, stirring constantly. Add chicken bouillon and salt, and stir with a fork. Bring to a boil and lower heat. Cover and simmer 15 to 20 minutes until rice is tender and all liquid is absorbed.

Variations

Curried Rice
Add ¹/₂ cup (125 mL) raisins and 2 tsp. (10 mL) curry powder.

Orange Rice
Decrease bouillon to 1 cup (250 mL) and add 1 cup (250 mL) orange juice.

Rice in Wine
Decrease chicken bouillon to 1 cup (250 mL) and add 1 cup (250 mL) white wine.

GREEK PILAF

¹/₄ cup	butter	50 mL
¹/₂ cup	vermicelli noodles	125 mL
1 cup	rice, uncooked	250 mL
20 oz.	chicken bouillon	568 mL

Brown broken vermicelli in butter. Then add rice and continue to brown. Pour in hot chicken bouillon. Bring to boil. Cover tightly and simmer slowly about 25 minutes until tender.

ORIENTAL RICE

2 cups	rice, uncooked	500 mL
¹/₄ cup	oil	50 mL
1¹/₂ oz.	onion soup mix	42 g
3 tbsp.	soy sauce	45 mL
1	green pepper, sliced	1
8 oz.	water chestnuts	250 mL
8 oz.	bamboo shoots	250 mL
10 oz.	mushrooms	275 mL
3¹/₂ cups	liquid	875 mL
	salt	
	pepper	

If using canned vegetables, drain and reserve liquid, making up to 3¹/₂ cups (875 mL) with water. Combine all ingredients in a 2 quart (2 L) casserole. Cover and bake at 350°F (180°C) for 1 hour or until all liquid is absorbed. Serves 8 – 10.

Variation
Substitute sautéed celery for bamboo shoots. Add toasted almonds.

RIZ PROVENCALE

1 large	onion, thinly sliced	1 large
3 oz.	butter	80 g
14 oz.	rice, uncooked	400 mL
1 cup	dry white wine	250 mL
3¹/₄ cups	water	800 mL
3¹/₂ oz.	tomatoes	100 g
1 clove	garlic	1 clove
1 tbsp.	salt	15 mL
2 tbsp.	parsley, chopped	30 mL
1	bay leaf	1
2 oz.	Parmesan cheese, grated	50 g

In a large saucepan with a lid, sauté onion in 2 oz. (50 g) of the butter until tender. Add rice and wine. Cover and simmer slowly 10 minutes. Blanch tomatoes for 2 minutes, then run under cold water and peel. Cut into small pieces. Bring water to a rolling boil and add to rice with tomatoes, garlic, and salt. Simmer 10 minutes more. Add parsley and bay leaf. Adjust seasonings and cook an additional 5 minutes. Before serving stir in Parmesan and remaining butter.

RISSOTTO

1 cup	onion, chopped	250 mL
²/₃ cup	celery, chopped	150 mL
¹/₂ lb.	mushrooms, sliced	250 g
¹/₄ cup	oil	50 mL
2 cups	rice, uncooked	500 mL
5¹/₂ oz.	tomato paste	156 mL
1³/₄ cups	hot water	425 mL
2 tsp.	salt	10 mL
1 tsp.	Worcestershire sauce	5 mL
³/₄ tsp.	thyme	3 mL
¹/₄ tsp.	pepper	1 mL
3 cloves	garlic, chopped	3 cloves
1 cup	peas, cooked	250 mL

Sauté onion, celery, and mushrooms in oil until lightly browned. Remove vegetables from pan. In same pan, brown rice over low heat, stirring constantly. Return vegetables to pan and add all remaining ingredients, except peas. Cover, and simmer 1 hour until rice is tender. Stir in peas and cook another 10 minutes until heated through. Serves 6.

KASHA, RUSSIAN STYLE

1 cup	kasha (buckwheat groats)	250 mL
4 cups	boiling water	1 L
1/2 tsp.	salt	2 mL
1 tbsp.	instant minced onion	15 mL

Heat the kasha thoroughly in an extremely hot oven. Pour boiling water over hot grain and add seasonings. Bake at 375°F (190°C) for 1 hour. Mix occasionally. Serve with rich gravy or butter.

KASHA AND SHELLS

7 oz.	kasha (buckwheat groats)	200 g
1	egg, slightly beaten	1
1 tsp.	salt	5 mL
3 cups	boiling water	750 mL
1	onion, diced	1
3 tbsp.	oil	45 mL
1/2 cup	macaroni shells, cooked	125 mL

Combine kasha, egg, and salt in a large saucepan. Stir constantly over low heat until grain dries and separates. Add water. Cover and cook over low heat 10 to 15 minutes until all water is absorbed. Brown onion in hot oil. Add onion and shells to kasha. Season to taste. Serves 10.

KASHA KNISHES

1/2 lb.	kasha (buckwheat groats)	250 g
2	eggs	2
2 large	onions, minced	2 large
1 cup	flour	250 mL
1/2 tsp.	salt	2 mL
1 tbsp.	schmaltz or oil	15 mL
2 tbsp.	water	30 mL

Mix 1 egg with kasha. Place in a very hot oven to brown. When kernels are completely separated and dried, remove from oven and boil 10 minutes in the top of a double boiler until tender. Set aside. Fry onions in additional schmaltz until lightly browned. Set aside.

Thoroughly mix flour, salt, remaining egg, water and schmaltz to form a dough. Roll out on floured board as thin as possible. Spread fried onions over dough and then spread with cooked kasha. Roll as for jelly roll. Cut roll into 8 pieces. Bake at 350°F (180°C) for 30 minutes. Serve instead of potatoes with a main course.

Variation
Cut dough into rounds, fill, seal, and bake individually.

BARLEY PILAF

1 large	onion, diced	1 large
1/2 lb.	mushrooms, sliced	250 g
5 tbsp.	margarine	75 mL
1 cup	barley	250 mL
2 1/2 cups	bouillon	625 mL

Preheat oven to 350°F (180°C). Sauté onion and mushrooms in margarine until golden. Turn into greased casserole dish with barley. Pour bouillon over. Cover and bake for 30 to 40 minutes or until liquid is absorbed.

BARLEY CASSEROLE

1 lb.	pot barley	500 g
1/4 cup	margarine	50 mL
10 oz.	water chestnuts	284 mL
4 cups	beef bouillon	1 L
1 lb.	mushrooms, sliced	500 g
1 large	onion, chopped	1 large
1 cup	celery, sliced	250 mL
1 clove	garlic, minced	1 clove
1/2	green pepper, chopped	1/2
	salt	
	pepper	
1/8 tsp.	marjoram	0.5 mL

Brown barley in margarine. Drain water chestnuts and slice. Combine with barley and remaining ingredients in a casserole. Cover and bake at 350°F (180°C) for 1 hour. Add extra liquid if casserole becomes too dry. Serves 10 – 12.

FARFEL PILAF

3³/₄ cups	farfel	925 mL
2 tbsp.	schmaltz or oil	30 mL
1 cup	onion, chopped	250 mL
1 cup	mushrooms, sliced	250 mL
1¹/₂ cups	chicken bouillon	375 mL

Brown 2 cups (500 mL) of the farfel in schmaltz. Set aside. Sauté onions and mushrooms. Spread remaining farfel in the bottom of a greased casserole. Add vegetables and chicken bouillon. Cover. Bake at 350°F (180°C) for 30 minutes. Sprinkle with dry farfel.

CRACKED WHEAT PILAF

²/₃ cup	margarine	150 mL
3 cups	cracked wheat	750 mL
1	onion, chopped	1
6 cups	bouillon	1.5 L
	salt	
	pepper	

Sauté wheat in ¹/₂ cup (125 mL) of the margarine. Cook over low heat 5 minutes. Fry onion in remaining margarine and add to cracked wheat. Stir in bouillon and seasonings, cover, and bake at 350°F (180°C) for 30 minutes. Remove from oven to mix well. Cover and bake for another 10 minutes. Serves 6. May also be served as turkey, duck, or chicken dressing.

NOODLE RING

1 lb.	egg noodles	500 g
6	eggs, separated	6
1¹/₂ cups	milk	375 mL
3 tbsp.	butter, melted	45 mL
1 tsp.	salt	5 mL
¹/₄ tsp.	pepper	1 mL

Cook noodles according to package directions. Rinse and drain. Combine with egg yolks and other ingredients. Fold in stiffly beaten egg whites. Pour into 2 ring moulds, lightly greased. Set in a shallow pan of water and bake at 350°F (180°C) for 45 minutes. Or use 12 small individual moulds and bake for only 30 minutes. Invert onto serving plate. Fill centre with creamed tuna fish. Sprinkle with paprika or grated cheese. Serves 10 – 12.

NOODLE VEGETABLE CASSEROLE

1 large	onion, chopped	1 large
2 stalks	celery, chopped	2 stalks
1	green pepper, chopped	1
¹/₂ cup	milk	125 mL
8 oz.	egg noodles, cooked	250 g
10 oz.	condensed mushroom soup	284 mL
10 oz.	canned mushrooms	284 mL
1 cup	Cheddar cheese, grated	250 mL

Fry onion, celery, and green pepper. Add milk, noodles, soup, and partially drained mushrooms. Alternate layers of mixture and cheese in a greased 2 quart (2 L) casserole. Top with cheese. Bake at 350°F (180°C) for 1 hour.

NOODLE SOUFFLÉ

2¹/₂ cups	fine egg noodles	625 mL
¹/₄ cup	raisins	50 mL
3 tbsp.	fine bread crumbs	45 mL
¹/₂ cup	butter	125 mL
¹/₂ cup	sugar	125 mL
4	eggs, separated	4
1 tsp.	lemon rind, grated	5 mL
¹/₂ cup	sour cream	125 mL
2 cups	cottage cheese	500 mL
¹/₄ tsp.	salt	1 mL
¹/₄ cup	slivered almonds	50 mL

overleaf:
Salmon-Stuffed Artichokes (page 60)

overleaf:
Whole Baked Salmon in Wine Sauce (page 91)

Cook noodles in boiling salted water. Drain and set aside to cool. Wash raisins, drain, and set aside. Grease a large ovenproof dish and sprinkle bottom with bread crumbs. Cream butter; beat in sugar and egg yolks until light and fluffy. Add raisins, lemon rind, and sour cream, then mix in cottage cheese and cooked noodles. Lightly fold in egg whites beaten stiff but not dry. Pour into prepared baking dish. Blanch almonds and sprinkle over top. Bake at 350°F (180°C) about 45 minutes until top is slightly browned. Serve at once. Dust with vanilla sugar if desired. Serves 6. (Note: For previously cooked noodles, use 4½ cups (1.12 L).)

FRIED NOODLES

2 cups	fine egg noodles	500 mL
2 tbsp.	oil	30 mL
1 large	onion, diced	1 large
4 stalks	celery, diced	4 stalks
10 oz.	canned mushrooms	284 mL
½ cup	water	125 mL
4 tbsp.	soy sauce	60 mL
1 cup	bean sprouts	250 mL

Brown noodles in oil. Remove from pan and set aside. Brown onion and celery in same oil. Add mushrooms and juice, water, and soy sauce. Simmer 5 minutes. Add noodles and simmer another 10 minutes. Stir in bean sprouts. Serve when heated through.

APPLE KUGEL

Dough

1¼ cups	flour	300 mL
½ tsp.	baking powder	2 mL
¼ tsp.	salt	1 mL
1 tbsp.	sugar	15 mL
2 tbsp.	oil	30 mL
1	egg	1
4 tbsp.	warm water	60 mL

Sift dry ingredients together. Add oil and egg, and water to bind. Turn out on a floured board. Knead until smooth and spongy. Set in a bowl, sprinkle with flour, cover with plastic wrap, and chill 30 minutes.

Filling

3 lb.	apples, peeled and sliced	1.5 kg
½ cup	raisins	125 mL
1 tsp.	lemon juice	5 mL
¼ cup	sugar	50 mL
1 tsp.	cinnamon	5 mL
¼ tsp.	nutmeg	1 mL
1 tsp.	vanilla	5 mL

Combine ingredients in a bowl, sprinkling lemon juice over apples to prevent discoloration. Roll dough very thin. Brush with oil. Spread apple mixture along long end, and roll as for jelly roll. Place roll in a greased utility pan. Brush top with beaten egg. Bake at 350°F (180°C) until brown. Baste with orange juice if apples are not juicy enough.

YOM TOV LOKSHEN KUGEL

8 oz.	wide egg noodles (lokshen)	250 g
3 large	onions, diced	3 large
3 tbsp.	oil	45 mL
2 tbsp.	flour	30 mL
1 cup	chicken bouillon	250 mL
½ cup	canned mushrooms	125 mL
	salt	
	pepper	
2	eggs, beaten	2

Cook noodles and set aside. Brown onions in oil. Add flour, then slowly pour in chicken bouillon. Stir until thick. Add drained mushrooms. Pour mixture into noodles, stirring. Season to taste. Turn into a greased pan. Pour eggs over the top and sprinkle with paprika. Bake at 350°F (180°C) for 30 minutes.

CHEESE LOKSHEN KUGEL

12 oz.	wide egg noodles (lokshen)	360 g
1 lb.	cream cheese	500 g
3	eggs	3
½ cup	butter, melted	125 mL
½ cup	cream	125 mL
5 tbsp.	sugar	75 mL
2 tbsp.	sultana raisins	30 mL
⅛ tsp.	cinnamon	0.5 mL

Cook noodles in boiling salted water for 20 minutes. Drain and rinse under cold water. Combine remaining ingredients. Mix with cooked lokshen and place in a greased baking dish. Sprinkle with cinnamon and sugar. Dot with butter. Bake at 400°F (200°C) for 1½ hours.

CHEDDAR KUGEL

1 lb.	egg noodles	500 g
½ cup	margarine, melted	125 mL
4	eggs, beaten	4
2 cups	sour cream	500 mL
1 lb.	Cheddar cheese, grated	500 g
	salt	
	pepper	

Boil noodles according to package directions and drain. Melt 2 tbsp. (30 mL) of the margarine in a 9'' x 9'' (2 L) utility pan. Combine all ingredients in mixing bowl, seasoning to taste. Pour into utility pan and bake at 350°F (180°C) for 1 hour.

NOODLE KUGEL

12 oz.	wide egg noodles, cooked	360 g
4	eggs	4
4 cups	buttermilk	1 L
1 lb.	creamed cottage cheese	500 g
	salt	
	pepper	
1 tsp.	sugar	5 mL
	butter	

Spread drained noodles evenly across the bottom of a greased 8½'' x 12½'' (3 L) pan. Beat together remaining ingredients. Pour over noodles. Dot with approximately 2 tbsp. (30 mL) of butter. Bake at 400°F (200°C) for 1 hour. Serve with sour cream and frozen strawberries. Serves 16.

SWEET KUGEL

1½ lb.	wide egg noodles, cooked	750 g
6	eggs, separated	6
½ cup	butter, melted	125 mL
2 lb.	creamed cottage cheese	1 kg
⅓ cup	sugar	75 mL
1 tsp.	vanilla	5 mL
1 tsp.	salt	5 mL
2 cups	sour cream	500 mL
2 tsp.	flour	10 mL

Combine all ingredients except noodles. Mix half the mixture with the cooked noodles and turn into a greased utility pan. Pour remaining mixture on top. Bake at 325°F (160°C) for 1 hour. Sprinkle corn flake crumbs on top and serve.

MANICOTTI

1 lb.	Ricotta cheese	500 g
12 oz.	spinach, cooked	340 g
8 oz.	manicotti noodles	250 g
4 tbsp.	Parmesan cheese, grated	60 mL

Mix Ricotta and drained spinach. Stuff raw manicotti shells and pour tomato sauce or other spaghetti sauce over them. Sprinkle Parmesan over top. Bake according to package.

VEGETARIAN LASAGNE

1 medium	onion, chopped	1 medium
2 cloves	garlic, halved	2 cloves
2 tbsp.	olive oil	30 mL
28 oz.	canned tomatoes	796 mL
11 oz.	tomato paste	312 mL
½ cup	water	125 mL
7 tsp.	salt	35 mL
½ tsp.	oregano	2 mL

1/4 tsp.	thyme	1 mL
1/4 tsp.	basil	1 mL
1/8 tsp.	red pepper, crushed	0.5 mL
5 quarts	boiling water	5 L
1/2 lb.	curly-edged lasagne	250 g
1 lb.	cottage cheese	500 g
1 1/2 cups	Parmesan cheese, grated	375 mL
1/2 lb.	Mozzarella cheese, sliced	250 g

In a saucepan, sauté onion and garlic in oil until lightly browned. Discard garlic. Add tomatoes, tomato paste, water, 1 tsp. (5 mL) salt, herbs, and red pepper. Simmer covered for 1 hour. Add remaining salt to rapidly boiling water. Add lasagne gradually so that water does not go off the boil. Cook uncovered, stirring occasionally, until tender. Drain. Spread a small amount of sauce in a 4 quart (4 L) baking dish. Add a layer of lasagne. Dot with one-third of the cottage cheese and sprinkle with Parmesan. Repeat layers twice, ending with Parmesan. Top with Mozzarella slices. Bake uncovered at 375°F (190°C) for 30 to 40 minutes. Serves 8.

CARROT STRUDEL

14 oz.	puff pastry	396 g
1/2 cup	brown sugar	125 mL
1 cup	fresh bread crumbs	250 mL
1/4 tsp.	allspice	1 mL
1/2 tsp.	salt	2 mL
	dash of cloves	
1/2 tsp.	cinnamon	2 mL
1/2 cup	almonds, sliced	125 mL
3/4 cup	sultana raisins	175 mL
2 cups	carrots, grated	500 mL
2 tbsp.	lemon juice	30 mL
1 tsp.	lemon rind, grated	5 mL
1	egg yolk	1
1 tbsp.	water	15 mL

On a lightly floured board, roll out dough to a 15" (35 cm) square. Combine sugar with bread crumbs and seasonings, and sprinkle evenly over dough, leaving a 1" (2 cm) border on all sides. Distribute almonds, raisins, and carrots evenly over sugar mixture, and sprinkle with lemon juice and rind. Roll up as for a jelly roll. Place on a

cookie sheet lined with parchment paper. Mix egg yolk and water, and brush this glaze onto the roll. Bake at 325°F (160°C) for 45 minutes.

PEROGEN

Dough

1	egg, beaten	1
1/2 tsp.	salt	2 mL
	pinch of pepper	
1/2 tsp.	sugar	2 mL
2 tbsp.	schmaltz or oil	30 mL
1 cup	iced water	250 mL
	flour	
1 tsp.	baking powder	5 mL

Combine all ingredients, adding flour and baking powder last, to make a firm dough. Roll out and cut into squares. Place a little filling in each square. Fold over, dampening edges and pressing together to seal. Bake at 350°F (180°C) until golden brown. (Note: For a crisper pastry, refrigerate dough before rolling.)

Meat Filling

1 medium	onion, chopped	1 medium
1 lb.	steak, minced	500 g
	salt	
	pepper	
	schmaltz or oil	

Fry onion in schmaltz. Combine with meat, season and mix with enough schmaltz to bind.

KREPLACH

Dough

2 cups	flour	500 mL
3	eggs	3
1 tbsp.	water	15 mL

Combine ingredients into a stiff dough. Roll out thinly and cut into small squares. Dot with little balls of meat filling, press edges together well, and leave kreplach to dry for a little while. Cook in salted water for 15 to 20 minutes. Drain, and serve with soup.

Meat Filling

½ lb.	steak	250 g
1 small	onion, chopped	1 small
1	egg, hard-boiled	1
	salt	
	pepper	

Fry meat and onion. Mince together with hard-boiled egg. Season to taste. If too dry, add a little chicken fat or gravy.

KREPLACH

Dough

3 cups	flour	750 mL
3	eggs	3
½ cup	water	125 mL
¼ tsp.	salt	1 mL
1 tsp.	oil	5 mL

Knead all ingredients together until smooth. Roll out fairly thin on floured board. Cut into 2'' (5 cm) strips and then into squares. Place about 1 tsp. (5 mL) of meat filling on each square, fold into three-cornered shape, and press edges firmly together. Cook in boiling water until kreplach rise to the top. Remove from pot and pour a little oil over, shaking to coat. Serve with chicken soup, as a hot appetizer, or to accompany a meat dinner. Makes about 30.

Meat Filling

2 cups	cooked chicken or meat	500 mL
1	onion, sautéed	1
1	egg	1
	salt	
	pepper	

Mince meat and onion together. Mix with egg, and season to taste.

PIROZHKI

1	egg	1
¼ cup	water	50 mL
1 cup	flour	250 mL
	dash of salt	

Combine all ingredients well. Coat dough with oil, cover, and let stand 30 minutes. Roll out very thin and cut into rounds. Place 1 tsp. (5 mL) of filling on each round, fold over and crimp edges tightly to seal. Boil in salted water 10 to 12 minutes until pirozhki rise to the surface. Flip them once and remove with a slotted spoon to colander to drain. Immerse colander in cold water to rinse.

Fillings

- Chop ½ lb. (250 g) cooked salmon, 2 hard-boiled eggs, and a few mushrooms. Mix together with ½ cup (125 mL) cooked rice, and seasonings.

- Fry 1 chopped onion in fat until light brown. Combine with ground leftover meat.

- Fry chopped onion in butter; combine with diced potatoes.

- Combine chopped hard-boiled egg and ¾ cup (175 mL) cooked rice. Season to taste.

- Cook 1 lb. (500 g) drained sauerkraut in saucepan until almost dry. Fry 1 chopped onion in 2 tbsp. (30 mL) fat. Combine with sauerkraut.

- Mix fruit conserve and chopped nuts.

- Chop any dried fruits (prunes, apricots, apples), seasoning with nutmeg.

Variation

Wrap filling in phyllo dough and bake at 350°F (180°C) for 20 to 25 minutes.

Fish

Freshwater fish, saltwater fish, fish from the frozen Arctic or from warm gulf streams. This vast, unplanted food crop growing freely in the world's waters yields delicacies coveted by its harvesters.

Fish feeds mankind well. Rich in protein, vitamins and minerals, low in fat, and easily digestible, it has for good reason been dubbed "brain food."

The keynote is freshness. Fresh from the sea to the pan. Nothing whets the appetite more keenly than the aroma of fish frying over an open fire. A squeeze of lemon juice for punctuation, and there is a dish fit for a king.

Consider the humble herring. Cossetted with sour cream, marinated in wine, or embellished with onions and raisins, it has been elevated to gustatory heights which guarantee its place at every *simcha* table. The plate of herring is usually the first to be refilled at a Sunday brunch.

As far back as the Middle Ages, the poverty-stricken *shtetel* Jews of Eastern Europe created a delicious way to stretch their limited supply of fresh fish. Brought inland from the North Sea, pounded and mixed with bread crusts and eggs, then gently shaped into ovals, and cooked. The subtle amalgam was welcomed on the Sabbath table as Gefilte Fish (and the rich broth provided a chowder for another meal). Sweet, savoury, baked, fried, or restuffed into the skin, there seem to be as many recipes for Gefilte Fish as there are species of fish in the sea.

Many of today's huge fishing vessels carry their own processing equipment to enable them to pack their catch of tuna, salmon, and sardines at its unfaded peak. Hundreds of miles away and many months later, stored on the shelf till required, their contents baked into muffins or soufflés, folded into a thick creamy sauce, or tossed with crisp salad greens, these ordinary little cans have enhanced the reputation of many a hostess.

Fish interacts agreeably with the delicate flavour nuances of grapes, herbs, almonds, or butter, as well as with the more energetic characteristics of sweet pickles, ketchup, or onion. The results are indeed "a fine kettle of fish."

HALIBUT SOUFFLÉ

1½ lb.	halibut	750 g
1 small	onion	1 small
3 tbsp.	butter	45 mL
3 tbsp.	flour	45 mL
1½ cups	milk	375 mL
3	eggs, separated	3
	salt	
	pepper	
	cracker crumbs	
	paprika	

Boil halibut in water to cover with onion, salt, and pepper for 15 minutes. Cool, remove skin and bones, and flake with a fork. Melt butter in double boiler, add flour and milk, and cook until thick. Beat in egg yolks. Add fish and adjust seasonings. Beat egg whites stiff; fold into mixture. Pour into a greased casserole or soufflé dish, top with cracker crumbs and sprinkle with paprika. Bake at 350°F (180°C) for 30 minutes. Serve immediately. Serves 6.

CRISPY CRUSTY HALIBUT

4 (½")	halibut steaks	4 (1.25 cm)
2	eggs	2
1 tbsp.	lemon juice	15 mL
1 cup	corn flake crumbs	250 mL
½ cup	Parmesan cheese, grated	125 mL
½ tsp.	salt	2 mL
½ tsp.	dill weed	2 mL
2 tsp.	dried parsley flakes	10 mL
2 tsp.	butter, melted	10 mL

Wash steaks; dry with paper towel. Blend slightly beaten eggs and lemon juice. In a separate bowl, mix crumbs with cheese, salt, dill, and parsley. Moisten steaks with melted butter. Dip in egg, then in crumb mixture. Press mixture into steaks so coating will stick. Refrigerate for at least 1 hour, to set. Place steaks on buttered foil and broil 3" (7 cm) from heat for 5 minutes on each side. Serve with lemon wedges. Serves 4.

MARINATED LUNCHEON HERRING

4	salt herring	4
2 large	onions	2 large
4	bay leaves	4
2	peppercorns	2
¼ cup	water	50 mL
1 cup	vinegar	250 mL
¼ cup	oil	50 mL

Clean herring and soak in cold water overnight. Wash again with cold water and cut into serving-sized pieces. Slice onions. Prepare 2 pint-sized (500 mL) jars with 2 bay leaves, 1 peppercorn, and a few slices of onion in the bottom of each. Place a layer of herring in each jar, then a layer of onions. Repeat alternating layers until jars are almost full. Combine water and vinegar, and fill jars almost to the top. Top with oil and a slice of onion. Seal jars and refrigerate for 3 days before using. Makes 2 pints (1 L).

SOUR CREAM HERRING

6	Matjes herring	6
6	milt of herring	6
1 cup	vinegar	250 mL
3 oz.	mixed pickling spices	85 g
8 large	onions, sliced	8 large
1 cup	sour cream	250 mL

Skin the herring and clean inside. Soak overnight. Pound the milt thoroughly on a board, and place in a large jar with vinegar and spices. Slice each herring into 6 pieces, and pack into jar, with onion. Add sour cream. Let stand 3 days in refrigerator before serving. Keeps 1 to 2 weeks. Makes 2 – 3 pints (1 – 1.5 L).

PICKLED HERRING

3 large	salt herring	3 large
2 cups	water	500 mL
½ cup	white wine vinegar	125 mL

1 tsp.	mixed pickling spices	5 mL
	bay leaves	
	sugar	
4 large	onions, sliced	4 large
1	lemon, sliced	1

Soak herring for 24 hours. Change water as frequently as is convenient. Skin herring and cut into chunks. Boil water and vinegar, add pickling spices, bay leaves, and sugar. Cool. There should be enough liquid to cover the herring. Increase the quantities of water and vinegar if necessary, maintaining the proportions. Place herring in sterilized jars and cover with the liquid. Add the onion and lemon slices to each jar. Cover tightly and refrigerate. Let stand 3 to 4 days before eating. Will keep 1 or 2 weeks. (Note: If milter (male) herring is used, remove the milt (white organs) from inside the herring, mash through a strainer, and add to the vinegar and water mixture. This will make the liquid a creamy white and add excellent flavour.) Makes 2 pints (1 L).

DANISH PICKLED HERRING

6	herring	6
1 cup	sugar	250 mL
3/4 cup	oil	175 mL
1 cup	brown vinegar	250 mL
1 cup	tomato paste	250 mL
1 cup	apple, diced	250 mL
1/2 cup	raisins, washed	125 mL
1 cup	onion, chopped	250 mL
1 tsp.	prepared mustard	5 mL
1/4 tsp.	pepper	1 mL

Remove heads from herrings, clean, and soak 18 to 24 hours. Drain, fillet, and cut into small pieces. Mix sugar and oil well. Add vinegar and tomato paste, mixing very well. Stir in remaining ingredients. Pour over herrings and bottle. Makes 2 quarts (2 L).

Variation
Decrease oil to 1/4 cup (50 mL) and add 1/2 cup (125 mL) sweet wine.

BAKED SALMON

4	salmon steaks or fillets	4
	salt	
	pepper	
	garlic powder	
2 cups	milk	500 mL

Place salmon in an ovenproof utility pan. Sprinkle with seasonings. Place small pieces of butter on the salmon, then pour milk to top of fish. Bake at 375°F (190°C) for about 30 minutes. Serves 4.

BARBECUED SALMON

1 whole	fresh salmon	1 whole
1/4 lb.	lox	110 g
1 tbsp.	butter	15 mL
	salt	
	pepper	
1/2	lemon, sliced	1/2

Use fresh salmon — frozen salmon tends to be too dry. Salmon should be scaled, headed, finned, and cleaned.
   Wash salmon. Mash lox with butter. With a sharp knife, slash 3 slanted cuts across the back of the salmon. Pack the slits with lox mixture. Salt and pepper the fish, and place a few pieces of lemon in the cavity. Wrap the fish well in heavy-duty foil, sealing edges tightly. Barbecue. If the fish looks as if it is drying out, baste the top with lemon. Serves 4 – 6.

WHOLE BAKED SALMON IN WINE SAUCE

10 lb.	whole salmon	5 kg
3/4 cup	dry white wine	175 mL
1/4 tsp.	dried thyme	1 mL
8 leaves	fresh basil	8 leaves
3 sprigs	fresh tarragon	3 sprigs
2 sprigs	rosemary	2 sprigs
	celery leaves	
3	shallots, minced	3
2 slices	lemon, with peel	2 slices
	salt	

Thoroughly wash and clean the salmon. Place on paper towels to dry. Pour wine into a saucepan and add remaining ingredients, except salt. Simmer for 30 minutes uncovered, without boiling. Preheat oven to 375°F (190°C). Place fish lengthwise on a long sheet of foil, fold up the sides, and pour the wine mixture over the fish. Sprinkle with salt. Completely enclose the fish, crimping the foil to seal the edges tightly. Place the foil-wrapped fish in a large baking pan and transfer to oven. Bake until the fish flakes easily when tested with a fork (about 15 minutes per pound, or per 500 g).

White Wine Sauce

1/2 cup	butter	125 mL
2	shallots, minced	2
6 tbsp.	flour	90 mL
1 1/2 cups	wine	375 mL
1 1/2 cups	boiling water	375 mL
1/2 cup	whipping cream	125 mL
	salt	
	pepper	
2	egg yolks	2

While the salmon is baking, melt the butter in a saucepan and add the shallots. Cook until transparent but not brown. Stir in flour until well blended. Cook over low heat for 3 minutes. Let stand.

When fish is done, remove from oven and keep warm. Use a large spoon to dip out the juices. Make up to 5 cups (1.25 L) by adding equal amounts of wine and boiling water. Add gradually to the butter mixture in saucepan, stirring constantly over moderate heat, and cook until liquid is thickened and smooth. Add the cream; season with salt and pepper. Strain through a fine sieve. Just before serving, add some of the sauce to the lightly beaten egg yolk. Reheat sauce. Add egg yolk mixture and cook 2 minutes over low heat, but do not boil. Serve over salmon. Serves 6 – 8.

Note on substitutions

Instead of white wine, use equal parts of lemon juice and water. If fresh herbs are not available, the following are the equivalents for dried herbs: 1/2 tsp. (2 mL) basil; 1/4 tsp. (1 mL) tarragon; 1/4 tsp. (1 mL) rosemary. 1 small onion, finely minced, may be used instead of 3 shallots.

SWEET AND SOUR SALMON

3 lb.	salmon, filleted	1.5 kg
3	onions, sliced	3
1 tsp.	oil	5 mL
6 oz.	ketchup	160 mL
10 oz.	chili sauce	285 mL
9 oz.	sweet mixed pickles	250 mL
1 cup	pickle juice	250 mL
1/6 cup	vinegar	40 mL
2 tbsp.	brown sugar	35 mL
	salt	
	pepper	
1/2 tsp.	celery salt	2 mL
1 tsp.	mustard seed	5 mL
4	ginger snaps, crumbled	4

Salt the salmon, and cut in smallish chunks. Sauté 2 of the onions in the oil until slightly brown. Add remaining ingredients, and bring to a boil. Add fish and rest of onion rings. Cook slowly, about 30 minutes, until done. Refrigerate 24 hours before serving. Keeps in refrigerator for 2 weeks. Serves 6 – 8. (Note: Using 10 lb. (4.5 kg) salmon, while doubling quantities of the rest of the ingredients, more than triples the recipe.)

PICKLED SALMON

1	onion	1
3 lb.	salmon	1.4 kg
1 tbsp.	vinegar	15 mL
11 oz.	ketchup	310 mL
18 oz.	sweet mixed pickles	500 mL
	Tabasco sauce	
	pepper	

Slice onion rings into a pot. Skin and bone the salmon, and arrange over onion in pot; pour vinegar over. Add remaining ingredients. Bring to a boil and cook 20 minutes. Let cool in pot before placing carefully in serving dish. Serve cold. Best prepared 1 or 2 days in advance; keeps 10 days in refrigerator. Serves 6 – 8.

MARINATED PICKLED SALMON

2 lb.	salmon	1 kg
2	Spanish onions, sliced	2
½ cup	sugar	125 mL
¾ cup	vinegar	175 mL
½ cup	water	125 mL
1 tbsp.	salt	15 mL
	dash of pepper	
1 tsp.	pickling spice	5 mL

Wash salmon and place in pot on top of onions. Add remaining ingredients. Marinate in refrigerator overnight. Next day, simmer in same pot for 30 minutes. Cool in marinade. Serve chilled. Serves 4 – 6.

SALMON PATTIES

15½ oz.	canned pink salmon	440 g
2	eggs	2
1 tsp.	baking powder	5 mL
	salt	
	pepper	
2 tbsp.	flour	30 mL

Empty salmon can into bowl without draining. Remove bones, and mash. Add eggs, baking powder, salt and pepper. Beat well; add flour to make mixture the consistency of heavy pancake batter. Fry in part butter and part oil, dropping by the spoonful into frying pan. Cook until tops of patties are bubbly, turn, and cook until brown. Serves 4 – 6.

SALMON MUFFINS

4	soda biscuits	4
1 cup	milk	250 mL
2	eggs, separated	2
4 oz.	canned salmon, drained	110 g
	salt	
	pepper	
1 tbsp.	butter, melted	15 mL

Crush soda biscuits and soak in milk for at least an hour. Beat egg yolks well. Add to the salmon together with seasonings, milk and cracker crumbs, and melted butter. Beat egg whites until stiff. Add to salmon mixture. Spoon into well-greased muffin tins and bake at 325°F (160°C) for 1 hour. Serves 4.

SALMON CAKES

1 cup	canned salmon, drained	250 mL
1	egg, beaten	1
	salt	
	pepper	
1½ cups	mashed potatoes	375 mL
1 tbsp.	butter, melted	15 mL
½ tsp.	onion juice	2 mL
2 tbsp.	green pepper, minced	30 mL

Combine all ingredients and blend well. Form into cakes. Roll in finely sifted bread crumbs or crushed corn flakes. Sauté or deep fat fry. Drain and serve hot. Serves 4 – 5.

MUSHROOM SALMON LOAF

2 cups	canned salmon	500 mL
1½ cups	dry bread crumbs	375 mL
2	eggs, slightly beaten	2
½ cup	green pepper, minced	125 mL
10 oz.	cream of mushroom soup	284 mL

Drain and flake salmon. Combine with remaining ingredients and mix lightly. Pack firmly into a greased loaf pan. Bake at 350°F (180°C) for 1 hour or more. Serves 6.

SALMON AND ASPARAGUS BLINI

12	crepes	12
½ lb.	smoked salmon, sliced	250 g
14 oz.	canned asparagus spears	398 mL

Make small thin pancakes as for Salmon Blintzes. Place a thin slice of smoked salmon on each pancake. Arrange 2 asparagus spears on each, and roll up. Place in a buttered ovenproof dish, cover with strong cheese sauce, and bake at 350°F (180°C) for 20 to 25 minutes. Serves 5 – 8.

Cheese Sauce

2 tbsp.	butter	30 mL
1 tbsp.	flour	15 mL
1 cup	milk	250 mL
	salt	
	pepper	
1/8 tsp.	dry mustard	0.5 mL
	Worcestershire sauce	
3/4 cup	Cheddar cheese, grated	175 mL

Melt butter and blend in flour. Add milk; boil until thickened. Add seasonings, a dash of Worcestershire sauce, and cheese, and cook, stirring constantly, until cheese is melted.

SALMON BLINTZES

Blintzes

2	eggs	2
	salt	
	pepper	
1 cup	flour	250 mL
1 tsp.	baking powder	5 mL
1 1/4 cups	water	300 mL

Beat eggs with salt and pepper, stir in flour and baking powder, and mix well with enough water to make a smooth batter. Heat and grease a crepe pan. Pour a thin layer of batter into the pan. Fry on only one side until set and slight bubbles appear. Turn out onto a cloth to cool. There is sufficient batter for 12 – 15 thin pancakes.

Salmon Filling

7 3/4 oz.	canned red salmon	220 g
6	black olives, chopped	6
1	pickled cucumber, chopped	1
1	onion, chopped	1
1	hard-boiled egg, chopped	1
	salt	
	pepper	
2 cups	whipping cream	500 mL
1/4 cup	cheese, grated	50 mL

Mix drained salmon, olives, cucumber, onion, and egg together with a little cream to bind. Season to taste. Place a spoonful of the salmon mixture in each blintz, roll up, and place in a buttered baking dish. Cover with remaining cream, sprinkle with grated cheese, and bake until cheese melts. Serve hot. Serves 6 – 10.

SALMON RICE CASSEROLE

1 1/3 cups	quick-cooking rice	325 mL
1/2 tsp.	salt	2 mL
1 1/3 cups	boiling water	325 mL
10 oz.	cream of mushroom soup	284 mL
1/2 cup	milk	125 mL
7 3/4 oz.	canned salmon	220 g
	pepper	
2 tsp.	lemon juice	10 mL
1/2 cup	bread crumbs, buttered	125 mL

Add rice and salt to boiling water in a saucepan, mixing just to moisten rice. Cover and remove from heat. Let stand 5 minutes. Combine soup and milk in a saucepan. Heat, stirring occasionally. Drain and flake salmon. Mix with a dash of pepper, add to soup, and heat thoroughly. Stir in lemon juice, then add rice. Mix lightly and turn into a 1 quart (1 L) casserole. Sprinkle with bread crumbs and broil 2 or 3 minutes until lightly browned. Serves 4.

SALMON AND SPINACH MANICOTTI

15 1/2 oz.	canned pink salmon	439 g
20	manicotti shells	20
12 oz.	frozen spinach	340 g
1 cup	creamed cottage cheese	250 mL
1	egg, slightly beaten	1
1/2 cup	Parmesan cheese, grated	125 mL

Drain and mash salmon. Cook manicotti shells and spinach according to package directions. Chop spinach. Mix cottage cheese with egg, and add salmon and spinach. Fill the shells. Pour a small amount of Lemony Cream Sauce into a shallow 2 quart (2 L) casserole. Arrange stuffed shells over sauce. Add remaining sauce and sprinkle with Parmesan cheese. Bake at 350°F (180°C) for 35 to 40 minutes. Serves 4 as a main dish.

Lemony Cream Sauce

2 tbsp.	butter	30 mL
2½ tbsp.	flour	40 mL
1 tsp.	dill weed	5 mL
½ tsp.	salt	2 mL
¹/₁₆ tsp.	nutmeg	0.25 mL
2 cups	milk	500 mL
2 tbsp.	lemon juice	30 mL

Melt the butter in a saucepan and slowly add flour, stirring constantly. Add seasonings. Slowly add the milk and cook, stirring constantly, until the mixture boils and thickens. Remove from heat. Stir in lemon juice.

BAKED SOLE AU GRATIN

8	sole fillets	8
2 tbsp.	lemon juice	30 mL
	pepper	
1 tsp.	margarine	5 mL
12 oz.	frozen spinach, thawed	340 g
8 oz.	Swiss cheese, shredded	250 g
1 cup	sour cream	250 mL

Preheat oven to 350°F (180°C). Pat fillets dry and sprinkle with lemon juice and seasoning. Arrange half the fillets in a greased baking dish. Dot with margarine. Cover with half the spinach and a third of the cheese. Repeat layers. Bake until fish is tender and flakes easily, approximately 30 minutes. Spoon sour cream and remaining cheese mixture over the fish and bake for another 45 minutes. Serve hot. Garnish with a few sprigs of parsley. Serves 6 – 8. (Note: This recipe is excellent made with any kind of white fish if sole is not available.)

SOLE VERONIQUE

Stock

	bones and head of sole	
2	cloves	2
2	bay leaves	2
	sprig of parsley	
1 stalk	celery, sliced	1 stalk
1 small	onion, sliced	1 small
	salt	
	pepper	

Cover head and bones with water, then add rest of ingredients and season to taste. Simmer for 30 minutes.

Sole

4 large	sole fillets	4 large
	salt	
	pepper	
	lemon juice	
4	green onions	4
1 tbsp.	dry white wine	15 mL
	green grapes	

Season fillets, squeeze lemon juice over, and fold loosely in thirds. Chop the white portions of the green onions, and place in the bottom of a greased saucepan with folded fillets on top. Add wine and enough fish stock just to cover the sole. Poach for a few minutes until sole is cooked. While fish is cooking, peel and stone some grapes and warm slightly. Then prepare white sauce.

White Sauce

¼ cup	butter	50 mL
½ cup	flour	125 mL
1 cup	milk	250 mL
	gravy from fillets	
	cayenne pepper	

Melt butter, add flour, and stir over gentle heat for 1 to 2 minutes. Add milk and bring to boil, stirring constantly until sauce thickens. Reduce heat and cook for 2 minutes. Add gravy from fillets to achieve desired consistency; sauce may be thick or thin, according to preference. Season sauce to taste. Remove fillets to a hot serving dish; do not allow them to cool. Pour sauce over fillets and garnish attractively with the grapes. Serves 4.

BAKED SOLE AND MUSHROOMS

3 lb.	sole fillets	1.5 kg
	butter	
	salt	
	pepper	
	paprika	
1 1/2 lb.	mushrooms	750 g

Sauté the fillets 1 minute per side in hot butter. Transfer to a large baking dish and sprinkle with seasonings. Set aside 12 to 15 of the best-looking mushroom caps for garnishing, and slice their stems and remaining mushrooms. Sauté in butter for a few minutes. Spread mushrooms in a thick layer on top of sole.

Cream Sauce

5 tbsp.	flour	75 mL
6 tbsp.	butter	90 mL
1 1/2 cups	milk	375 mL
1/2 cup	sherry	125 mL
1 tbsp.	onion, grated	15 mL
1 tsp.	basil	5 mL
1 tsp.	parsley, chopped	5 mL
1/8 tsp.	cayenne pepper	0.5 mL
1 1/2 tsp.	chicken soup mix (pareve)	7 mL
1/2 lb.	cheese, grated	250 g
	salt	
	pepper	
	Tabasco sauce	

Combine all ingredients in the top of a double boiler, reserving some of the cheese. Season to taste. Cook until cheese melts. Spoon the sauce over mushrooms and fish, and sprinkle with reserved cheese and paprika. Garnish with the rest of the mushrooms, dot with butter, and brown at 350°F (180°C) for 30 minutes. Serves 4 – 6.

SOLE ROLLS IN CREAM SAUCE

6	sole fillets	6
1 small	fresh salmon cutlet	1 small
1/2 cup	water	125 mL
1 small	onion, chopped	1 small
	salt	

Cut salmon into 6 portions and wrap a fillet of sole around each. Set in water with the onion and a dash of salt, and poach about 15 minutes. While sole is cooking, prepare sauce.

Sauce

1/4 lb.	mushrooms, sliced	125 g
1 tbsp.	butter	15 mL
1 tsp.	onion, chopped	5 mL
1/2 tbsp.	vodka	10 mL
2 tsp.	tomato purée	10 mL
1/2 tbsp.	sherry	10 mL
2 tsp.	paprika	10 mL
	cayenne pepper	
	salt	
	pepper	
1/2 cup	fish stock	125 mL
1 cup	whipping cream	250 mL

Cook mushrooms over medium heat until soft. (Do not sauté.) Set aside. Melt the butter in a chafing dish. Add onion and fry until transparent. Stir in vodka. Flame briefly. When flames have died down, add purée, sherry, and seasonings, stirring continuously. Simmer a few minutes. Add stock from sole and cook, stirring rapidly all the time, for 5 to 10 minutes. Continue stirring while gradually adding the cream in a slow, thin stream. The consistency of the sauce should be smooth and rich. Add the mushrooms, reduce heat, and cook for a few more minutes, stirring gently.

Arrange the sole rolls on an oval serving platter and pour the sauce over. Serve immediately. Serves 4.

Variation

Add a dash of white wine to the sauce at the last minute to enhance the flavour.

SOLE SOUFFLÉ

8	sole fillets	8
	salt	
	pepper	
2 tbsp.	butter	30 mL
½ cup	cream	125 mL
1 tbsp.	cornstarch	15 mL
½ cup	Cheddar cheese, grated	125 mL
	cayenne pepper	
2	eggs, separated	2

Lay fillets in a greased ovenproof dish, and add salt, pepper, 1 tbsp. (15 mL) of the butter, and cream. Bake at 350°F (180°C) for 15 minutes. Melt remaining butter and add cornstarch. Stirring constantly, add the cheese, cayenne pepper and salt to taste. Mix until smooth and thick. Beat in yolks. Whip egg whites stiff and fold in. Pour over baked fish, return to oven, and brown. Serve immediately. Serves 5.

BAKED LAKE TROUT WITH CREOLE SAUCE

1	onion	1
1	green pepper	1
1	tomato	1
3 tbsp.	butter	45 mL
2 lb.	lake trout	1 kg
	salt	
	pepper	
2 oz.	cheese, grated	50 g

Chop onion, green pepper, and tomato, and fry in butter in a hot pan until soft. Sprinkle lake trout with salt and pepper and grated cheese. Combine with sauce. Bake at 350°F (180°C) for 20 to 30 minutes. Serves 3 – 4.

DEVILLED TUNA

⅓ cup	butter	75 mL
⅓ cup	flour	75 mL
½ tsp.	salt	2 mL
½ tsp.	chili powder	2 mL
	cayenne pepper	
1½ cups	milk	375 mL
2 tbsp.	Worcestershire sauce	30 mL
	dash of Tabasco sauce	
2 cups	flaked tuna, drained	500 mL
1 tbsp.	parsley, minced	15 mL
1½ cups	bread crumbs	375 mL

Melt butter. Combine flour with seasonings, and blend with butter. Add milk, stirring over low heat until smooth and thick. Add Worcestershire sauce, a dash of Tabasco, the tuna, and parsley. Pour into a casserole or individual ramekins and top with buttered crumbs. Brown under broiler, then heat through at 350°F (180°C) for about 20 minutes. Serves 6.

MANDARIN TUNA CASSEROLE

7 oz.	canned tuna, drained	198 g
10 oz.	mushroom soup	284 mL
¼ cup	water	50 mL
1 cup	celery, diced	250 mL
¼ cup	Spanish onion, diced	50 mL
½ cup	cashew nuts	125 mL
6 oz.	Chinese noodles	170 g
10 oz.	canned Mandarin oranges	284 mL

Mix all ingredients, except Mandarin oranges, with half the noodles. Place in a casserole. Spread remaining noodles on top. Bake at 350°F (180°C) for 20 minutes. Garnish with oranges. Serves 4.

TUNA CHOW MEIN CASSEROLE

10 oz.	cream of mushroom soup	284 mL
14 oz.	canned peas, drained	398 mL
½ cup	celery, diced	125 mL
½ cup	onion, chopped	125 mL
2 tbsp.	lemon juice	30 mL
10 oz.	mushrooms	284 mL
¼ cup	almonds	50 mL
14 oz.	canned tuna, drained	396 g
6 oz.	chow mein noodles	170 g

Combine all ingredients, using half the noodles. Turn into a buttered casserole and bake at 375°F (190°C) for 20 minutes. Fold in the rest of the noodles just before serving. Serve over patty shells. Serves 8.

CAPTAIN'S CASSEROLE

10 oz.	mushroom soup	284 mL
1/2 cup	milk	125 mL
2/3 cup	Cheddar cheese, grated	150 mL
1 1/3 cups	quick-cooking rice	325 mL
1/2 tsp.	oregano	2 mL
	pepper	
28 oz.	canned tomatoes	795 mL
1/2	onion, thinly sliced	1/2
14 oz.	canned tuna, drained	396 g
1/3 cup	stuffed olives, sliced	75 mL
1 cup	water	250 mL
1/2 cup	potato chips, crushed	125 mL

Heat soup, milk, and cheese until cheese is melted, stirring occasionally. Combine rice, oregano, and pepper in a greased 1 1/2 quart (1.5 L) baking dish. Drain tomatoes, reserving 1/2 cup (125 mL) juice. Slice tomatoes and arrange most of them on top of the rice. Add onion, tuna, and olives. Pour on juice and water; sprinkle with potato chips. Arrange remaining tomatoes on top. Bake at 375°F (190°C) for 25 to 30 minutes. Serves 8.

ITALIAN TUNA CASSEROLE

1/2 cup	onion, chopped	125 mL
2 cloves	garlic, chopped	2 cloves
15 1/2 oz.	canned tuna, drained	220 g
10 oz.	cream of celery soup	284 mL
1/2 cup	milk	125 mL
1/2 tsp.	oregano	2 mL
1/2 tsp.	basil	2 mL
2 tsp.	dried parsley	10 mL
8 oz.	noodles	250 g
3/4 cup	Mozzarella cheese, grated	175 mL
3/4 cup	Cheddar cheese, grated	175 mL
	processed cheese, sliced	

Sauté onion and garlic. Add tuna, cream of celery soup, milk, and seasonings. Simmer 5 minutes. Cook noodles in lots of boiling salted water. Drain. In a greased 3 quart (3 L) casserole, layer half the noodles, tuna filling, and mixed grated cheese. Repeat. Top with sliced processed cheese and bake at 350°F (180°C) for 30 minutes. Serves 8 – 10.

HOT TUNA PIZZA BURGERS

7 oz.	canned tuna	198 g
1/3 cup	mayonnaise	75 mL
1/2 tsp.	salt	2 mL
1/4 tsp.	oregano	1 mL
1 tbsp.	onion, grated	15 mL
1/4 cup	tomato paste	50 mL
1/4 cup	water	50 mL
1/3 cup	Parmesan cheese, grated	75 mL
4	hamburger buns	4

Drain tuna and break up with a fork. Blend together with mayonnaise, salt, oregano, and onion. Split buns and toast slightly. Spread mixture on bun halves. Blend tomato paste and water, and spoon over tuna mixture. Sprinkle with Parmesan cheese. Bake at 400°F (200°C) for 10 minutes. Serve immediately. Serves 6 – 8.

TUNA LASAGNE

20 oz.	canned tomatoes	568 mL
7 1/2 oz.	tomato sauce	210 mL
1 tsp.	salt	5 mL
1 tsp.	oregano	5 mL
1 tsp.	onion salt	5 mL
1/8 tsp.	pepper	0.5 mL
2 tbsp.	salad oil	30 mL
1 cup	onion, chopped	250 mL
1 clove	garlic, chopped	1 clove
7 oz.	canned tuna, drained	198 g
8 oz.	lasagne noodles	250 g
1/4 cup	Parmesan cheese, grated	50 mL
2 cups	creamed cottage cheese	500 mL
1/2 lb.	Mozzarella cheese, sliced	250 g

Heat tomatoes, tomato sauce, and seasonings in a saucepan. Fry the onion and garlic in oil until tender. Add to tomato mixture, then add the tuna. Simmer over low heat for 1 hour. Cook noodles in 3 quarts (3 L) of salted water until tender. Drain. Grease a medium-sized casserole dish and arrange ingredients in layers as follows: half the sauce, then Parmesan cheese, cottage cheese, noodles, and Mozzarella. Repeat the layers. Bake at 350°F (180°C) for 45 minutes. Serves 6.

GEFILTE FISH

2 1/2 lb.	white fish	1.2 kg
7 3/4 oz.	canned salmon, drained	220 g
3	eggs	3
3 tsp.	salt	15 mL
1 tsp.	pepper	5 mL
1 tbsp.	sugar	15 mL
3/4 cup	water	175 mL
1	onion, chopped	1

Grind fish. Add remaining ingredients and beat until fluffy.

For Boiled Gefilte Fish

	fish bones	
1	onion, fried	1
2	carrots, sliced	2
1 stalk	celery, sliced	1 stalk
	salt	
	pepper	
5 cups	water	1.25 L
1 tsp.	sugar	5 mL
	paprika	

Make a brine of fish bones, vegetables, salt, pepper, and water. Bring to a boil, and add sugar and a generous amount of paprika. Reduce heat to simmer. With dampened hands, form fish mixture into balls and drop into simmering brine. Cook for about 1 hour. Makes 25 – 30.

For Baked Gefilte Fish

Form fish mixture into balls, set in broth in an ovenproof dish, and bake uncovered at 350°F (180°C) for 45 minutes. Turn balls over, and cook the other side a further 45 minutes. Fish should appear slightly browned. Place gefilte fish in serving dish, pouring a little broth over the fish to keep moist until ready to serve.

For Fried Gefilte Fish

Form fish mixture into patties and fry in hot oil.

GEFILTE FISH

1 1/2 lb.	white fish	750 g
1 1/2 lb.	pickerel, carp, or pike	750 g
2 large	onions	2 large
1/4 cup	matzo meal	50 mL
3	eggs	3
1 1/2 tsp.	sugar	7 mL
1 1/2 tsp.	salt	7 mL
3 tsp.	pepper	15 mL
1 1/2 cups	cold water	375 mL

Grind fish and onions, and beat together with remaining ingredients, adding water slowly at the end. Refrigerate while you prepare broth in which to poach the fish.

Broth

2	onions, sliced	2
4	carrots, sliced	4
5 cups	water	1.25 L
	skin and bones of fish	
1 tbsp.	salt	15 mL
1 tsp.	pepper	5 mL

Combine ingredients in a large soup pot. Bring to boil. With wet hands, form fish mixture into balls, using approximately 1/4 cup (50 mL) fish mixture for each ball. Drop gently into boiling mixture. Cover the pot, reduce heat to medium for a slow boil, and simmer 2 hours. Carefully remove fish balls while hot, and place on a deep platter. Decorate with cooked carrots from the broth. Cool in refrigerator but do not freeze. Serve cold with beet horseradish. Serves 12 – 15.

TRADITIONAL GEFILTE FISH

3 lb.	white fish, ground	1.5 kg
3	eggs	3
	salt	
	pepper	
1/4 cup	matzo meal	50 mL
1/3 cup	sugar	75 mL
3/4 cup	water	175 mL
1 small	onion, grated	1 small
	fish bones and skin	
1	onion, sliced	1
1	potato, sliced	1
1	carrot, sliced	1

In a bowl combine the ground fish, eggs, salt, pepper, matzo meal, 1 tbsp. (15 mL) sugar, water, and grated onion. (You may add more or less matzo meal, depending on how far you want to stretch the fish.) In a roaster, place all the bones and the sliced vegetables. Cut the fish skin into pieces, make patties with the fish mixture and wrap in the skins, tucking the skin over and under. Place the wrapped patties on an oiled cookie sheet and broil until brown. Transfer patties to the roaster. Sprinkle with remaining sugar, and salt and pepper to taste. Fill roaster with water, bring to boil on top of stove, then bake at 350°F (180°C) for 1 hour. Serve warm. Serves 15 – 20. (Note: For colour, 1 beet may be sliced into the roasting pan with the other vegetables.)

BAKED GEFILTE FISH

2 1/2 lb.	whole white fish	1.2 kg
1 large	onion	1 large
2 slices	white bread	2 slices
1/2 tsp.	salt	2 mL
1/4 tsp.	pepper	1 mL
2	eggs	2
3 tbsp.	oil	45 mL
1 tsp.	sugar	5 mL
	paprika	

Have backbone of fish taken out. Remove all flesh from skin, leaving skin intact. Sauté onion.

Soak bread in water, remove from water, and squeeze out. Grind fish, sautéed onion, and bread. Mix together with salt, pepper, eggs, oil, and sugar. Line a cookie sheet with foil and grease well. Place opened up fish skin on sheet. Pile mixture onto bottom half of the skin and cover with top half. Oil top of skin, sprinkling with paprika. Bake at 325°F (160°C) for 45 to 60 minutes. Serves 8.

MOCK GEFILTE FISH

15 1/2 oz.	canned pink salmon	440 g
3 large	onions	3 large
3	carrots, sliced	3
2 tsp.	salt	10 mL
1/2 tsp.	pepper	2 mL
2 cups	water	500 mL
3	eggs, separated	3
4 tbsp.	matzo meal	60 mL

Drain salmon, reserving juice. Slice 2 of the onions, and combine with salmon juice, carrots, water, salt, and pepper. Simmer in a large shallow pan for 30 minutes. Remove skin and bones, and mash salmon. Grate remaining onion, and mix well with salmon, egg yolks, matzo meal, salt, pepper, and a little more water if required. Add beaten egg whites. Form into balls, wetting hands with cold water to facilitate handling. Place in pan, cover, and simmer about 40 minutes. Serves 4.

Variation
Canned tuna may be substituted for salmon.

STUFFED FISH WITH SOUR CREAM

3 lb.	cod or sole	1.5 kg
1/4 lb.	mushrooms, sliced	125 g
2	onions, chopped	2
3 tbsp.	butter	45 mL
1 tsp.	paprika	5 mL
2 cups	sour cream	500 mL
3/4 cup	bread crumbs	175 mL
	salt	

Wash and bone the fish. Lightly sauté mushrooms and onions with butter. Sprinkle with paprika. Add half the sour cream and simmer until tender. Mix in bread crumbs. Stuff fish with mixture. Place on the bottom of an ovenproof dish lined with foil; season, and bake at 400°F (200°C) for approximately 20 minutes, basting often with butter and remaining cream. Serves 6.

SEAFOOD SALAD

4 oz.	smoked black cod, cooked	125 g
4 oz.	halibut, cooked	125 g
7 oz.	canned white tuna	198 g
1/4 cup	celery, chopped	50 mL
1/4 cup	green onion, chopped	50 mL
2 tbsp.	fresh parsley, chopped	30 mL

Dressing

1/2 cup	mayonnaise	125 mL
1 tsp.	white pepper	5 mL
1/4 cup	lemon juice	50 mL
1 tbsp.	sandwich spread	15 mL

Remove bones and skin from cold fish and flake with a fork. Combine salad ingredients. Mix dressing ingredients together, and toss lightly with salad. Serves 4.

BAKED FISH IN PINEAPPLE SAUCE

1	green pepper, sliced	1
1	onion, chopped	1
2 tbsp.	salad oil	30 mL
1 tsp.	ginger	5 mL
1 tbsp.	brown sugar	15 mL
1 tbsp.	cornstarch	15 mL
1 tbsp.	soy sauce	15 mL
1/4 cup	vinegar	50 mL
2 1/2 cups	pineapple tidbits	625 mL
1 1/2 lb.	fish fillets	750 g

Sauté green pepper and onion in salad oil in skillet for 5 minutes. Add remaining ingredients, except fish. Cook, stirring, until thickened and blended. Arrange fish in a shallow baking dish, and sprinkle with a little salt and pepper. Pour on sauce. Bake at 350°F (180°C) for 30 minutes. Serves 4 – 6. (Note: 2 lb. (1 kg) of defrosted fish sticks may be used instead of the fillets.)

ROUMANIAN GEVATCH

2 lb.	whole white fish	1 kg
1/2 lb.	rice, uncooked	250 g
2 large	onions, chopped	2 large
28 oz.	tomatoes	796 mL
14 oz.	peas	398 mL
2	carrots, sliced	2
6 stalks	celery, sliced	6 stalks
5	potatoes, sliced	5
1/2 cup	oil	125 mL

Place rice in a 9" x 12" (2.5 L) ovenproof dish. Set fish in centre. Dot generously with butter and cover with vegetables and oil. Bake, covered, at 350°F (180°C) for 2 hours until all the vegetables are done. Baste occasionally. Serves 8.

SWEET AND SOUR FISH

2 lb.	white fish	1 kg
1	onion, sliced	1
1 cup	cider vinegar	250 mL
2 cups	water	500 mL
1 cup	brown sugar	250 mL
1/4 cup	raisins	50 mL
8 whole	allspice	8 whole
	cinnamon	
5	ginger snaps	5

Boil fish and onion in vinegar and water. Add sugar, raisins, allspice, and a dash of cinnamon. Cook 50 minutes. Add ginger snaps, and cook another 10 to 15 minutes. Cool. Refrigerate and serve cold. Gravy will jell. Serves 4 – 6.

Meat

Man is a meat-eater. But most nations of the world have a scarcity of meat for consumption. The most fascinating arrays of marinades, stuffings, and spicy fruit and vegetable combinations emanate from those countries where a little meat has to go a long way.

From the Middle East, boned Stuffed Leg of Lamb, redolent with nutmeg, mint, and aromatic herbs; and grape leaves (Dolmeh) stuffed with ground beef and rice. The Mediterranean countries offer ground beef, tomatoes, and herbs served with steaming bowls of pasta. From the Orient, meatballs with ginger and pineapple, and Beef with Peppers. And from generations of Jewish grandmothers, born-again *maicholim* like Sweet and Sour Tongue, Stuffed Kishkas, Kasha-stuffed Veal Breast, and Cholent.

Kosher cuts of beef are the kindest cuts of all. A brisket properly dressed and seasoned, or short ribs of beef in a tangy barbecue sauce, may be placed in the oven on low heat, left unattended for half a day, and courteously never over-cook. At the dinner hour they will present themselves as perfectly tender and saucy as if someone had held constant watch. A Tzimmes will even wait patiently for latecomers, and still provide leftovers as a side dish for the next day.

The true test of a cook's courage lies in what she can accomplish with a small amount of meat, or a less tender cut of beef, especially with the attitudes of a "steak and potatoes" family. A pinch of herbs, a few ounces of wine, some root vegetables, and meat simmering slowly in a covered pot on the back burner creates an aura of mouth-watering anticipation like nothing else does.

Over a hundred years ago it was said, "Kissing don't last—cookery do!"

MARINATED ROAST BEEF

Marinade

3 oz.	soy sauce	90 g
1 tbsp.	Worcestershire sauce	15 mL
1/4 cup	brown sugar	50 mL
1/4 cup	water	50 mL
1 tbsp.	lemon juice	15 mL
1/4 cup	bourbon, rye, or wine	50 mL

Mix all ingredients together in a large pan. Marinate the roast, covered, for several hours. Turn frequently. Roast in tightly covered pan without basting at 350°F (180°C) for 20 minutes per lb. (20 minutes per 500 g). Remove cover and cook an additional 40 minutes, basting frequently. An excellent marinade for rolled brisket, shoulder roast, or short ribs.

STUFFED BEEF OLIVES

1/2 lb.	beef (best cut)	250 g
	oil	
2	carrots, sliced	2
1	onion, sliced	1
1	parsnip, sliced	1
2	tomatoes, sliced	2

Cut beef into 4 thin slices and beat until very thin. Prepare stuffing. Lay beef flat, spread with stuffing, roll up, and close with toothpicks. Braise in oil with vegetables. Add a little water, cover, and simmer for 1 hour. Serve with rice or spaghetti. Serves 4.

Stuffing

2 tbsp.	schmaltz or oil	30 mL
2 cups	bread crumbs	500 mL
1 tbsp.	parsley, chopped	15 mL
	salt	
	pepper	
	dash of nutmeg	
2	eggs	2

Mix together schmaltz, bread crumbs, parsley, and seasoning. Blend with slightly beaten eggs.

STUFFED STEAK

2	eggs, beaten	2
4 slices	white bread	4 slices
1	onion, diced	1
1 stalk	celery, diced	1 stalk
	oil	
	salt	
	pepper	
4 (1/2'')	steaks, boned	4 (1 cm)
1/2 cup	water	125 mL

Soak bread in beaten eggs. Sauté onion and celery in oil until golden. Add to eggs. Season to taste and mix well. Pound steaks slightly. Place 2 tbsp. (30 mL) stuffing at end of each steak and roll up tightly. Secure with skewers or toothpicks. Brown in hot oil before transferring to an oven-proof dish. Spread a thin layer of additional sautéed onions over the steak rolls; add water and bake, covered, at 325°F (160°C) for 2 hours. Remove skewers, cut each roll diagonally in half, and serve. Serves 4 – 6.

STEAK À LA BORDELAISE

2 lb.	steak (best cut)	1 kg
	oil	
	salt	
	pepper	
1 tsp.	dry mustard	5 mL
3/4 cup	dry red wine	175 mL
3	chicken livers	3
1/4 lb.	fresh mushrooms	110 g
2 tbsp.	lemon juice	30 mL

In very hot oil, brown steak carefully on both sides, turning only once. Add salt and pepper to taste. Mix mustard with enough of the wine to make a thick paste and spread on steak. Simmer a few minutes in the oil, then pour in remainder of wine.

Clean chicken livers carefully. (It is very important to eliminate all traces of yellow-green bruising. Cut away part of the liver if necessary.) Broil livers until just done. Wash mushrooms and dry on a clean cloth. Fry quickly in oil, squeezing lemon juice on mushrooms while cooking. Cook for 5 minutes. Remove from oil and slice thinly. Add livers and mushrooms to steak and cook for 5 minutes only. (Total cooking time for medium done steak is approximately 10 minutes; 20 minutes for very well done steak.) Serves 4.

BEEF AND PEPPERS

1 lb.	lean beef round steak	500 g
1 1/2 tbsp.	paprika	20 mL

Pound steak to 1/4'' (0.5 cm) thickness. Cut into 1/2'' (1 cm) strips. Sprinkle with paprika and allow to stand for 10 minutes.

2 tbsp.	oil	30 mL
3 cloves	garlic, crushed	3 cloves
1 1/2 cups	beef bouillon	375 mL
1 cup	green onion, sliced	250 mL
2	green peppers, sliced	2
2 tbsp.	cornstarch	30 mL
1/4 cup	water	50 mL
1/4 cup	soy sauce	50 mL
2 large	tomatoes	2 large

In a large skillet, brown meat in oil. Add garlic and broth. Cover and simmer 25 minutes. Stir in onions and green pepper. Cover and cook 5 minutes more. Blend cornstarch, water, and soy sauce. Stir into meat mixture. Cook, stirring, until clear and thickened (approximately 2 minutes). Add tomatoes, cut in wedges, and toss gently. Serve over rice. Serves 4.

ORIENTAL BEEF AND VEGETABLES

1 1/2 lb.	beef steak	750 g
1 clove	garlic, minced	1 clove
1/2 cup	water	125 mL
1/3 cup	soy sauce	75 mL
1/4 cup	oil	50 mL
1	green pepper, sliced	1
1 cup	celery, thinly sliced	250 mL
2	onions, thinly sliced	2
2 cups	bok choy, thinly sliced	500 mL
10 oz.	water chestnuts	284 mL
10 oz.	canned mushrooms	284 mL
1 1/2 tbsp.	cornstarch	25 mL
10 oz.	tomato juice	284 mL

Chill meat in freezer until partially frozen. Cut across the grain into very thin slices. Place in bowl. Combine garlic, water, and soy sauce. Pour over meat and cover. Refrigerate 45 to 60 minutes. Drain meat, saving marinade, and pat dry. Drain canned vegetables and slice. Heat oil in a wok or skillet over direct high heat. Brown meat quickly, stirring constantly. Add vegetables. Stir fry just until vegetables are tender yet crisp (3 or 4 minutes). Combine cornstarch and tomato juice with remaining marinade. Stir until smooth and add to vegetables, stirring until mixture thickens. Serve with rice. Serves 4 – 6.

GERMAN STYLE SAUERBRATEN

4 lb.	beef rump or chuck	1.8 kg
2 tbsp.	flour	30 mL
1 1/2 tsp.	salt	7 mL
1/16 tsp.	pepper	0.25 mL
1/4 cup	vegetable oil	50 mL

Marinade

1 1/2 cups	vinegar	375 mL
1/2 cup	sweet red wine	125 mL
1 cup	water	250 mL
2 tbsp.	sugar	30 mL
2 tsp.	salt	10 mL
1/2 tsp.	peppercorns	2 mL
3	Spanish onions, sliced	3
1 tsp.	mustard seed	5 mL
12	whole cloves	12
5	bay leaves	5

Mix marinade ingredients in a narrow deep bowl. Wipe meat with a damp cloth and add. Refrigerate 2 days, turning meat frequently. Remove meat and wipe dry. Reserve marinade.

Combine flour with salt and pepper, and coat

meat. Brown slowly in oil in a dutch oven. Add ¾ cup (175 mL) marinade (including the onion, cloves, and whole peppercorns). Cover and simmer about 4 hours until meat is tender. Add more marinade if needed. Remove meat, and thicken broth with a little flour stirred to a smooth paste in cold water. Slice meat and serve over noodles, with the gravy. Serves 6.

SWEET AND SOUR POT ROAST

2½ lb.	pot roast	1.2 kg
½ lb.	brisket of beef	250 g
2 large	onions, sliced	2 large
1 clove	garlic, sliced	1 clove
½ cup	clear vegetable stock	125 mL
1	bay leaf	1
2 tbsp.	vinegar	30 mL
1 tbsp.	brown sugar	15 mL
2 tbsp.	ketchup	30 mL
⅓ cup	raisins	75 mL

In a heavy kettle or dutch oven, brown beef and brisket on all sides in beef suet or vegetable oil. Add onions and garlic, and brown. Add vegetable stock and bay leaf. Cover tightly and simmer 1 hour. Add vinegar and brown sugar, and more hot stock if needed. Cover and simmer another hour. Add ketchup and raisins. Cook, covered, for 30 minutes more. Serve with noodles or brown rice. Serves 6 – 8.

POT ROAST AND KASHA

5	onions, sliced	5
3½ lb.	chuck or end steak	1.6 kg
	salt	
	pepper	
	garlic powder	
½ cup	water	125 mL
12 oz.	kasha (buckwheat groats)	175 g

Place all ingredients except kasha in a large pot. Cook on low heat until tender, about 3 hours. Prepare kasha according to package instructions. To serve: pour meat, onions, and gravy over kasha. Serves 6 – 8.

ROAST BRISKET OF BEEF

5 lb.	lean brisket of beef	2.5 kg
2 tbsp.	vegetable oil	30 mL
3	onions	3
	salt	
	garlic	
1 tbsp.	flour	15 mL
1 cup	water	250 mL

Brown brisket well in oil on both sides. Slice onions onto the bottom of a roasting pan, and add brisket with water. Sprinkle meat with flour, salt and garlic to taste. Cover and roast at 325°F (160°C) for 3½ hours. Serves 6.

FLAUMEN TZIMMES (PRUNE TZIMMES)

2 lb.	brisket of beef	1 kg.
20	carrots	20
1	parsnip	1
1	turnip	1
½ lb.	pumpkin	250 g
¾ lb.	cabbage	375 g
1	potato or sweet potato	1
1 small	onion	1 small
	salt	
12	prunes	12
1 tbsp.	corn syrup	15 mL
1 tbsp.	flour	15 mL
2 tbsp.	sugar	30 mL

Place meat in a pot in enough boiling water to cover. Wash and scrape or peel vegetables. Cut carrots and parsnip in thin rounds, other vegetables in small pieces. Leave onion whole. Put all in pot with meat and boil for at least 4 hours. Add salt and washed or soaked prunes. Boil for another hour or more. To prevent burning, a little boiling water may have to be added as necessary, but there should be very little sauce left when cooking is done. To serve, remove meat and prunes, and discard superfluous fat. Mix syrup, flour, and sugar with vegetables and drippings. Place in vegetable dish, set prunes on top, and serve with the meat. Serves 4.

BRISKET AND PRUNE TZIMMES

1 lb.	prunes	500 g
3 lb.	brisket of beef	1.5 kg
	salt	
	pepper	
3	potatoes	3
3	sweet potatoes	3
2 tbsp.	lemon juice	30 mL
1/4 cup	sugar	50 mL
1/4 cup	honey	50 mL

Wash prunes. Place in a kettle with meat, season with salt and pepper and cover with boiling water. Cook slowly about 2 1/2 hours until meat is nearly tender. Add quartered potatoes, boil 10 minutes, then add lemon juice, sugar, and honey and boil 5 minutes longer. Bake at 350°F (180°C) about 1 hour until brown and tender, adding more water if necessary. Serves 4 – 6.

GANTZE TZIMMES

4 lb.	brisket of beef	2 kg
2	onions, diced	2
	vegetable oil	
1 cup	water	250 mL
1 1/2 tsp.	salt	7 mL
3/4 tsp.	pepper	3 mL
2	potatoes	2
4	sweet potatoes	4
4	carrots	4
1/2 cup	honey	125 mL
1/2 tsp.	cinnamon	2 mL
1/2 tsp.	allspice	2 mL

In a large dutch oven, brown meat and onion in oil. Add water and cook over low heat for 1 hour. More water may have to be added during cooking. Peel vegetables; quarter the potatoes and sweet potatoes, and slice the carrots thickly. Add to the meat with remaining ingredients, cover with water, and simmer at least 2 hours more until soft. Add water as necessary to prevent burning; but, when done, tzimmes should hold together and not be liquid. Serves 8.

BRISKET AND CARROT TZIMMES

2 large	sweet potatoes	2 large
12 – 15	carrots	12 – 15
1/2 cup	brown sugar	125 mL
	salt	
	pepper	
1 1/2 lb.	fat brisket of beef	750 g

Cut sweet potatoes in large chunks, and slice carrots thinly. Arrange in a dutch oven or roaster. Sprinkle with sugar and seasonings. Place brisket on top, fat side up. Cover and roast in 275°F (140°C) oven, or add a little water and cook over low flame on top of stove, for about 4 hours. Add more water during cooking if necessary. This is excellent prepared a day ahead and reheated. Serves 4.

BRISKET WITH PRUNES AND APRICOTS

3 lb.	brisket of beef	1.5 kg
1 1/2 oz.	dry onion soup mix	42 g
1/2 tsp.	Worcestershire sauce	2 mL
1 tbsp.	brandy	15 mL
1 tbsp.	lemon rind, grated	15 mL
2 tbsp.	brown sugar	30 mL
3/4 tsp.	ginger	3 mL
1/4 cup	honey	50 mL
2 tbsp.	lemon juice	30 mL
2 tbsp.	orange marmalade	30 mL
1 tsp.	pepper	5 mL
1/2 tsp.	cinnamon	2 mL
1 cup	dried apricots	250 mL
1 cup	dried prunes	250 mL
12 oz.	beer	360 mL

Place beef on a large square of foil. Sprinkle soup mix under and over meat. Wrap and seal, and bake at 350°F (180°C) for 4 hours. Combine remaining ingredients and bring to boil. Pour over meat in casserole. Cover and bake at 350°F (180°C) for 1 hour longer. Serves 4 – 6.

SAVORY SAKE BEEF BRISKET

4 lb.	brisket of beef	2 kg
1 1/2 cups	sake	375 mL
2 cups	onion, sliced	500 mL
1 cup	apple sauce	250 mL
1/4 cup	tomato paste	50 mL
1 1/2 tsp.	salt	7 mL
1/4 tsp.	pepper	1 mL
2	bay leaves	2
1/4 tsp.	thyme	1 mL

Place brisket in a large ovenproof glass or enamel pan. Combine remaining ingredients in a bowl and stir well. Pour over beef and marinate overnight in refrigerator, then for 2 to 4 hours at room temperature before cooking. Turn meat frequently so it absorbs flavour evenly. Cover pan with foil and bake at 325°F (160°C) for 2 1/2 to 3 hours. Turn meat twice during cooking. Remove meat from oven and allow to rest 15 minutes before slicing. Serves 6 – 8.

CRANBERRY BRISKET

3 1/2 lb.	rolled brisket of beef	1.5 kg
1 1/2 oz.	dry onion soup mix	42 g
14 oz.	jellied cranberry sauce	398 mL
1 cup	water	250 mL

Preheat oven to 350°F (180°C). Combine all ingredients and pour over brisket, using enough water to cover. Cover and bake for 3 hours. Slice while warm and return slices to pot to absorb juice. Reheat just before serving. Serves 6 – 8.

BARBECUE SAUCE BRISKET

4 lb.	point brisket of beef	2 kg
1 large	onion, chopped	1 large
3	carrots, chopped	3
3 stalks	celery, chopped	3 stalks
	salt	
	pepper	
1/4 cup	ketchup	50 mL
2 tbsp.	brown sugar	30 mL
1 tsp.	dry mustard	5 mL
1/4 tsp.	nutmeg	1 mL
1/2 cup	water	125 mL

Spread half the chopped vegetables in the bottom of a roasting pan. Place roast on vegetables. Sprinkle with salt and pepper, and add remaining vegetables. Combine the rest of the ingredients and pour over. Cover and roast at 300°F (150°C) for 1 1/2 hours. Remove meat, slice, and return to roasting pan. Cover and roast for another 2 to 3 hours. Serves 6 – 8.

CORNED BEEF OR TONGUE

5 lb.	brisket of beef, or tongue	2.5 kg
6 tbsp.	coarse salt	90 mL
3 tbsp.	brown sugar	45 mL
2 tsp.	saltpetre	10 mL
	dash of pepper	
3 cloves	garlic, chopped	3 cloves
4 tbsp.	pickling spices	60 mL

Wash brisket or tongue. Combine remaining ingredients and rub well into meat. Place in a rust-proof dish, uncovered. Set aside at room temperature for 1 day. Next day, cover dish and refrigerate for 10 days, turning meat every day. To cook: Cover with cold water and bring to a boil. Pour off liquid, again cover with cold water and bring to a boil. Simmer for 3 to 4 hours until tender. Sprinkle with paprika. Serve with glaze.

Corned Beef Glaze

1/2 cup	brown sugar	125 mL
1/4 cup	bread crumbs	50 mL
1/2 tsp.	dry mustard	2 mL
1/4 cup	orange juice	50 mL
1 tbsp.	orange rind, grated	15 mL
2 tbsp.	lemon juice	30 mL
2 tsp.	lemon rind, grated	10 mL
1 cup	sherry or cider	250 mL

Remove meat from boiling liquid. Combine glaze ingredients and spread over meat. Wrap meat in foil and bake at 350°F (180°C) for 30 minutes. Serves 6 – 8.

PICKLED BRISKET OR TONGUE

5 lb.	brisket of beef, or tongue	2.5 kg
3 cloves	garlic	3 cloves
5 tbsp.	coarse salt	75 mL
2 tsp.	saltpetre	10 mL
3 tbsp.	brown sugar	45 mL
3½ tbsp.	mixed pickling spices	55 mL
	garlic powder	
1 small	onion	1 small

Slice garlic cloves in half and place on the bottom of a roasting pan. Combine coarse salt, saltpetre, brown sugar, and 3 tbsp. (45 mL) mixed pickling spices. Rub over both sides of meat. Sprinkle garlic powder over meat. Place in roasting pan, cover, and refrigerate for 5 days, turning meat each day. Then wash off old spices and rinse out roasting pan with cold water. Return meat to roasting pan with enough cold water to cover. Add 2 tsp. (10 mL) mixed pickling spices and the whole onion. Cover and cook at medium heat on top of stove or in oven, until tender (approximately 3 hours). Check occasionally if additional water is needed. Serve hot or cold. Serves 6 – 8.

PASTRAMI

5 lb.	corned brisket of beef	2.5 kg
1 clove	garlic, minced	1 clove
3	bay leaves	3
4 small	hot red peppers	4 small
	liquid smoke	
1½ tsp.	pepper	7 mL
¾ tsp.	allspice	3 mL
¼ tsp.	coriander	1 mL

Simmer brisket, garlic, bay leaves, and red peppers in water to cover, for approximately 2½ hours until tender but still firm. Remove from liquid and cool. Brush lightly with liquid smoke. Mix seasonings and spread over meat. Bake uncovered at 375°F (190°C) for about 30 minutes. Serves 6 – 8.

MARINATED BRISKET

4 lb.	brisket of beef	2 kg
3 tbsp.	ketchup	45 mL
1 tsp.	dry mustard	5 mL
1 tsp.	pepper	5 mL
3 tbsp.	chili powder	45 mL
2 tbsp.	oil	30 mL
1 tsp.	salt	5 mL
	garlic	

Place brisket on double layer of foil. Combine remaining ingredients and spread over brisket on all sides. Wrap, and seal foil. Refrigerate 48 hours. Place foil-wrapped brisket in a utility pan and bake at 300°F (150°C) for 2½ to 3 hours, depending on size of brisket. Serves 6 – 8.

TRADITIONAL CHOLENT

2 cups	navy or lima beans	500 mL
3 lb.	brisket or short ribs	1.5 kg
3	onions, sliced	3
3 tbsp.	oil	45 mL
½ tsp.	pepper	2 mL
1 tsp.	paprika	5 mL
2 tsp.	salt	10 mL
2 cloves	garlic, minced	2 cloves
¾ cup	pearl barley	175 mL
6	potatoes, quartered	6

Soak beans overnight. When ready to use, wash them well. Brown meat and onions in oil in a heavy skillet. Rub meat with spices. Place all ingredients in a large ovenproof pot. Cover with water. Bring to boil, cover, and simmer on top of stove for a couple of hours. Ensure there is plenty of water, adding more as necessary during cooking. Place in a 250°F (130°C) oven for at least 8 hours. Check occasionally if more water is needed. Traditionally, this dish is cooked overnight and served at noon the next day. Serves 6 – 8.

CHOLENT

3 lb.	second-cut brisket	1.5 kg
5 lb.	potatoes	2.5 kg
	flour	
3	onions	3
	salt	
	pepper	
	paprika	
1/4 cup	ketchup	50 mL
1 cup	water	250 mL
28 oz.	kidney beans	796 mL

The brisket should be untrimmed, and with extra fat. Pare and quarter the potatoes. Place in a large roasting pan and sprinkle with enough flour to cover potatoes completely. Dice onions and toss over the potatoes. Sprinkle on seasonings. Mix ketchup and water, and add. Salt and pepper the meat and fat and place over potatoes. Cover and cook in a 250°F (130°C) oven for at least 8 hours. Check every few hours and add water if necessary. Add the undrained kidney beans 2 hours before serving. If there is too much liquid in pan, remove lid and roast uncovered until most of the liquid is absorbed. Serves 8.

DAY-BEFORE SHORT RIBS

2 1/2 lb.	short ribs	1.5 kg
1 1/2 cups	brown sugar	375 mL
1/2 cup	white wine	125 mL
1 1/4 cups	water	300 mL
1 tbsp.	corn syrup	15 mL
1 tbsp.	soy sauce	15 mL
	ketchup	

Cut ribs into 1'' x 1 1/2'' (2.5 x 3.5 cm) pieces, and roast covered at 350°F (180°C) for 1 1/2 hours or until fat dissolves. Combine brown sugar, wine, and 1 cup (250 mL) of water, and boil for 2 minutes. Add corn syrup, remaining water, soy sauce, and ketchup to taste. Add the ribs, which should be quite dry. Boil until sauce is thick, then simmer for another hour. May be stored in the refrigerator overnight and reheated next day. Serves 6.

BARBECUED SHORT RIBS

2 lb.	short ribs	1 kg
1 medium	onion	1 medium
2 tbsp.	vegetable oil	30 mL
1/4 cup	lemon juice	50 mL
2 tbsp.	vinegar	30 mL
1 tbsp.	Worcestershire sauce	15 mL
2 tbsp.	brown sugar	30 mL
1/2 cup	water	125 mL
1 cup	chili sauce	250 mL
	salt	
	pepper	

Cut short ribs into pieces. Roast in baking pan at 350°F (180°C) for 30 minutes. Chop onion and brown in oil. Add remaining ingredients. Cook over low heat on top of stove for 20 minutes. Pour over short ribs, cover, and bake at 350°F (180°C) for 1 hour. Serves 4.

SPICY BARBECUED RIBS

4 lb.	beef or veal ribs	2 kg
1 cup	ketchup	250 mL
3/4 cup	water	175 mL
3 tbsp.	vinegar	45 mL
2 tbsp.	Worcestershire sauce	30 mL
1 tsp.	salt	5 mL
1 tsp.	paprika	5 mL
1 tsp.	chili powder	5 mL
1/2 tsp.	pepper	2 mL

Broil ribs until brown. Combine remaining ingredients, bring just to a boil, and remove from heat. Pour over ribs in roasting pan. Cover and cook in oven at 350°F (180°C) for 1 1/2 to 2 hours. Baste frequently. Serves 4 – 6.

SHORT RIBS OF BEEF

3 lb.	beef short ribs	1.5 kg
2 1/2 cups	onion, thinly sliced	625 mL
1 1/2 cups	carrot, thinly sliced	375 mL
1	green pepper, sliced	1
	salt	

	pepper	
1 tsp.	tarragon	5 mL
1 tsp.	basil	5 mL
1/4 cup	jam or honey	50 mL
1 cup	ketchup	250 mL
1 cup	bouillon	250 mL
2 tbsp.	Worcestershire sauce	30 mL

Broil ribs until browned on all sides. Add a small amount of fat to a roasting pan, and sauté vegetables lightly. Lay ribs on bed of vegetables. Combine remaining ingredients and pour over ribs. Cover and bake slowly in oven or on top of stove for about 2 hours. Turn ribs occasionally and add more bouillon if desired. Serves 3 – 4.

FLEMISH STEAK

2 lb.	boneless beef chuck	1 kg
	flour	
	salt	
	pepper	
1/4 cup	oil	50 mL
6 small	onions, sliced	6 small
1 clove	garlic, chopped	1 clove
12 oz.	beer (flat)	340 mL
1 tbsp.	parsley, chopped	15 mL
1	bay leaf	1
1/4 tsp.	thyme	1 mL

Cut meat into 1'' (2.5 cm) cubes. Dredge in seasoned flour. Sauté onions and garlic in hot oil in a skillet until tender but not brown. Remove from skillet. Add meat and brown on all sides, adding more oil if necessary. Return onions and garlic to skillet with remaining ingredients. Cover and cook over low heat about 1 1/4 hours or longer, until meat is tender. Serves 4.

SOY SAUCE STEW

2 lb.	beef chuck	1 kg
1/4 cup	soy sauce	50 mL
2 cups	boiling water	500 mL
4	carrots, diced	4
2 cups	potato, diced	500 mL
2	onions, quartered	2
1 cup	celery, sliced	250 mL
1 clove	garlic, crushed	1 clove
1 tsp.	salt	5 mL
1/2 tsp.	seasoning salt	2 mL
1/8 tsp.	rosemary	0.5 mL
1/8 tsp.	thyme	0.5 mL
2 tbsp.	cornstarch	30 mL
2 tbsp.	water	30 mL
12 oz.	frozen vegetables	340 g

Sauté meat in soy sauce for 5 minutes. Add boiling water. Simmer for 30 to 45 minutes until beef is almost tender. Add vegetables, seasonings, and herbs. Cover and simmer for 20 to 30 minutes. Combine cornstarch and water and stir into stew. Bring to a boil, stirring until thick. Add frozen vegetables and heat through. Serves 4 – 6.

ESSECK FLEISCH (SWEET AND SOUR MEAT)

2 lb.	stewing meat	1 kg
2 medium	onions, diced	2 medium
1	green pepper, diced	1
3 tbsp.	honey	45 mL
2 tbsp.	lemon juice	30 mL
19 oz.	canned tomatoes	570 g

Brown meat and sauté onions. Place in roasting pan. Add remaining ingredients. Cover and bake at 325°F (160°C) for 3 hours or until tender. Check pan juices occasionally, adding water if necessary. Serves 4.

ESSECK FLEISCH

3 lb.	chuck	1.5 kg
	salt	
	pepper	
	garlic	
	paprika	
2	onions, diced	2
7 1/2 oz.	tomato sauce	210 mL
1/4 cup	lemon juice	50 mL
1 cup	brown sugar	250 mL

Cut meat into serving-sized pieces. Season well. Broil on both sides to remove excess fat. In a dutch oven or heavy aluminum pot, place the broiled meat, onion, tomato sauce, lemon juice and brown sugar to taste, and enough water barely to cover the meat. Cook slowly on top of stove or in oven for about 2 hours, until tender. Serves 4 – 6.

HUNGARIAN GOULASH

1 lb.	lean beef	500 g
1 lb.	lean veal	500 g
1 tbsp.	oil	15 mL
1 large	onion, diced	1 large
1 cup	tomatoes, drained	250 mL
1 clove	garlic	1 clove
1/2 cup	brown sugar	125 mL
	salt	
	pepper	
1 tbsp.	paprika	15 mL
8 small	potatoes	8 small

Cut meat into 1'' (2.5 cm) cubes. Roll in flour and brown in hot oil. Brown onions and add to meat with tomatoes, garlic, brown sugar, salt and pepper, and paprika. Simmer 1 hour or until almost tender. Add potatoes. Cook slowly, covered, until potatoes are done. Serves 4 – 6.

BEEF BOURGIGNONNE

3 lb.	stewing beef	1.5 kg
3 tbsp.	oil	45 mL
1 cup	onion, chopped	250 mL
1 cup	green pepper, chopped	250 mL
1 cup	celery, sliced	250 mL
1 clove	garlic, chopped	1 clove
8 oz.	tomato sauce	240 mL
1 1/2 tbsp.	salt	20 mL
1/8 tsp.	thyme	0.5 mL
2 tbsp.	parsley, chopped	30 mL
1 cup	red wine	250 mL
1 tbsp.	beef soup mix	15 mL
1/4 tsp.	pepper	1 mL
1	bay leaf	

2 cups	water	500 mL
2	potatoes, cut in pieces	2
4	carrots, halved	4
6	pearl onions	6
2 tbsp.	flour	30 mL
2 tbsp.	water	30 mL
1	tomato (for garnish)	1

Cut beef into cubes. In a dutch oven, brown well on all sides in hot oil. Remove meat and set aside. In same pot, sauté onion, green pepper, and celery until tender. Return beef to pot, add next 10 ingredients, and bring to boil. Reduce heat and simmer, covered, 1 1/4 hours. Add vegetables and cook 1 hour longer or until tender. Skim off fat. Make a smooth paste with the flour and water. Stir into beef stew and cook a few minutes until stew is thickened. Cut a tomato into 6 wedges; arrange skin side up on top of stew. Simmer, covered, 10 minutes. Serves 6 – 8.

HUNGARIAN VEAL STEAK

1 1/2 lb.	veal steak	750 g
1/4 cup	flour	50 mL
3 tbsp.	oil	45 mL
1 clove	garlic	1 clove
1/2 tsp.	salt	2 mL
2 tbsp.	onion, minced	30 mL
1 tbsp.	parsley	15 mL
1/4 tbsp.	paprika	4 mL
1/4 tsp.	celery salt	1 mL
1 cup	hot white wine	250 mL

Cut the steak into 1'' (2.5 cm) pieces and roll in flour. Heat the oil in a frying pan, add garlic and brown for 3 minutes. Discard garlic, add onion and veal, and brown well. Add remaining ingredients. Simmer for 1 hour. Serves 3 – 4.

VEAL CHOPS CASSEROLE

6	veal chops, pounded	6
1/4 cup	flour	50 mL
1	egg, beaten	1
1/2 cup	seasoned bread crumbs	125 mL

¼ cup	oil	50 mL
1 cup	rice, uncooked	250 mL
1	onion, sliced	1
1	green pepper, sliced	1
1	tomato, sliced	1
2½ cups	bouillon	625 mL

Wash and dry chops. Dip in flour, then egg, then seasoned crumbs. Brown on both sides in hot oil. Grease a large casserole and place rice at the bottom. Place veal chops on rice, then top with layers of onion, green pepper, and tomato. Pour bouillon over vegetables and cover. Bake at 350°F (180°C) for 1 hour. Serves 4 – 6.

VEAL CHOPS IN MUSHROOMS AND WINE

4	thick veal chops	4
3 tbsp.	flour	45 mL
¼ cup	oil	50 mL
1 cup	white wine	250 mL
¼ lb.	fresh mushrooms, sliced	125 mL
1	onion, grated	1
¼ cup	margarine	50 mL

Dredge chops in flour and sauté in oil until golden brown. Remove chops and place in casserole. Add wine to drippings and simmer to consistency of thin syrup. Pour this gravy over the chops. Melt margarine. Sauté mushrooms and onions slowly for 5 minutes. Pour around the chops. Cover casserole tightly and bake at 375°F (190°C) for 30 minutes. Serves 4.

KASHA-STUFFED VEAL BREAST

4 lb.	veal breast	2 kg
1 cup	kasha (buckwheat groats)	250 mL
2	onions	2
1	egg, beaten	1
1 clove	garlic, minced	1 clove
	salt	
	pepper	
	paprika	

Have the butcher make a pocket in the veal breast. Prepare kasha according to directions on package. Cool. Dice 1 onion and sauté in schmaltz. Add to kasha with well-beaten egg and salt and pepper to taste. Pack this stuffing into pocket of veal. Season roast to taste, arrange in roasting pan with sliced onion and minced garlic, and add sufficient water to bottom of pan to keep moist. Roast covered at 325 – 350°F (160 – 180°C) about 2½ hours. Serves 6 – 8.

VEAL BIRDS (MOCK DUCKS)

4	veal steaks, cut thin	4
1 clove	garlic	1 clove
	salt	
	seasoned pepper	
1 cup	bread stuffing	250 mL
1	egg, beaten	1
½ cup	bread crumbs	125 mL

Rub veal steaks well with garlic; pound to ¼" (0.5 cm) thickness. Season well. Spread bread stuffing thinly on the steaks. Roll up and tie securely. Dip rolls in egg, then bread crumbs, then again in egg. Fry in oil until golden brown on all sides. Roast slowly in oven at 300°F (150°C) for about 1 hour. Serves 4.

VEAL MARENGO

4 tbsp.	oil	60 mL
20	pearl onions	20
½ lb.	fresh mushrooms, halved	250 g
2 lb.	shoulder of veal	1 kg
	salt	
	pepper	
2 tbsp.	flour	30 mL
2 tbsp.	tomato paste	30 mL
1 clove	garlic, minced	1 clove
1 cup	dry white wine	250 mL
10 oz.	chicken soup	250 mL
1	bouquet garni	1
1 tsp.	thyme	5 mL
2 cups	cherry tomatoes	500 mL
1 tbsp.	fresh parsley, chopped	15 mL

Heat oil in a heavy casserole or saucepan. Sauté onions and mushrooms until brown, remove from pan and set aside. Cut veal into 1'' (2.5 cm) cubes. Brown them well, a few at a time, in the oil in the pan. Return browned veal to pan, season with salt and pepper, sprinkle with flour, and combine well. Stir in next 6 ingredients. Bring to a boil, reduce heat and simmer for 1 hour. Add mushrooms and onions, and cook over low heat for another 30 minutes or until heated through. Add cherry tomatoes, simmer 5 more minutes. Remove and discard bouquet garni, sprinkle parsley over veal and serve. Serves 4 – 6. (Note: Bouquet garni consists of 2 sprigs parsley, 1 bay leaf, and 1 celery leaf, tied together.)

VIENNA SCHNITZEL

4 large	veal cutlets	4 large
	salt	
	pepper	
	flour	
1	egg, beaten	1
1 tsp.	water	5 mL
1 cup	fresh bread crumbs	250 mL
1/4 cup	oil	50 mL

Beat cutlets very thin. Sprinkle with salt and pepper, and then lightly with flour. Dip in egg and water and then coat with bread crumbs, pressing crumbs onto meat with the side of a knife. Place meat on a wire rack and refrigerate for 2 hours, so that crust will adhere to cutlets. Heat oil, not too hot, in pan and gently fry cutlets until golden brown on both sides. Serve on a heated platter garnished with chopped hard-boiled egg, lemon slices, and anchovies. Serves 4.

SWEET AND SOUR VEAL SHORT RIBS

4 lb.	veal short ribs	2 kg
3/4 cup	vinegar	175 mL
1 1/2 cups	brown sugar	375 mL
1 1/8 cups	water	280 mL
1 tbsp.	cornstarch	15 mL
1 tbsp.	soy sauce	15 mL
1 tbsp.	ketchup	15 mL

Cut ribs into small pieces. Place on shallow cookie pans and roast, covered, at 375°F (190°C) for 1 1/2 to 2 hours, pouring off fat every 20 to 30 minutes, until most of the fat has cooked away. While ribs are baking, prepare sauce. Boil vinegar, sugar, and 1 cup (250 mL) of water about 5 minutes, until clear. Blend remaining ingredients with rest of water and add. Bring sauce to a boil. Transfer ribs to casserole, pour sauce over, cover and bake about 1 hour until tender. Serves 6 – 8.

VEAL SCALLOPINI

Marinade

1 tsp.	salt	5 mL
1 tsp.	paprika	5 mL
1/2 cup	oil	125 mL
1/4 cup	lemon juice	50 mL
1/2 clove	garlic	1/2 clove
1 tsp.	prepared mustard	5 mL
1/2 tsp.	sugar	2 mL

Shake ingredients well together.

2 1/3 lb.	veal, thinly sliced	1.2 kg
	flour	
1	onion, diced	1
1	green pepper, sliced	1
1/2 lb.	fresh mushrooms, sliced	250 g
1 cup	chicken bouillon	250 mL
	green olives, sliced	
1/2 cup	red wine	125 mL

Marinate veal 15 minutes or more. Brown marinated meat until golden, dredging first in flour if desired. Sauté onion and most of the green pepper with mushrooms until soft. Layer veal and mushroom mixture in a casserole. Pour remaining marinade and chicken bouillon over veal. (If dish is not to be used immediately, freeze at this stage.) Cover top with sliced green pepper and olives. Bake at 350°F (180°C) for 1 hour. Add red wine and bake another 30 minutes. Serves 6 – 8.

DRY RIBS

3 lb.	veal ribs, cut small	1.5 kg
1/4 cup	flour	50 mL
4 tsp.	seasoning salt	60 mL
1/4 tsp.	garlic powder	1 mL

Mix flour with seasonings, and dredge ribs. Place in a shallow roasting pan and bake at 325°F (160°C) for 2 1/2 hours. Drain off fat and loosen meat with spatula every 20 minutes. Serves 6 – 8. (Note: Lamb breast ribs are an excellent substitute for veal.)

MARINADE FOR SHISHKEBABS

1 1/2 cups	oil	375 mL
3/4 cup	soy sauce	175 mL
1/4 cup	Worcestershire sauce	50 mL
2 tbsp.	dry mustard	30 mL
2 1/4 tsp.	salt	11 mL
1 tbsp.	pepper	15 mL
1/2 cup	wine vinegar	125 mL
1 1/4 tsp.	parsley flakes	7 mL
2 cloves	garlic, crushed	2 cloves
1/3 cup	lemon juice	75 mL

Combine ingredients and use as marinade for beef or lamb cubes. Leftover marinade may be frozen and reused repeatedly until finished.

STUFFED LAMB

6 lb.	leg of lamb, boned	3 kg
12 oz.	frozen spinach	340 g
5 tbsp.	margarine	75 mL
1 1/2 cups	soft bread crumbs	375 mL
1/2 cup	fresh mint, chopped	125 mL
1 tsp.	salt	5 mL
1/4 tsp.	pepper	1 mL
1/8 tsp.	nutmeg	0.5 mL
2	tomatoes	2
2	onions, coarsely chopped	2
2	carrots, sliced	2
2 stalks	celery, chopped	2 stalks
1	bay leaf	1
2 tbsp.	flour	30 mL
2 cups	water	500 mL

Preheat oven to 325°F (160°C). Cook spinach, drain well and chop. Heat 4 tbsp. (60 mL) margarine in a skillet. Add bread crumbs and cook gently, stirring until lightly browned. Remove from heat. Add spinach, mint, salt, pepper, and nutmeg. Toss all together with a fork. Lay lamb out flat and spread spinach mixture over. Peel and dice the tomatoes. Melt remaining margarine in skillet. Add tomatoes and cook gently, stirring just until hot, about 2 minutes. Spread over spinach. Roll the lamb up around the stuffing and tie securely in several places. Put onions, carrots, celery, and bay leaf in the bottom of a shallow roasting pan. Set lamb on top. Roast 3 to 3 1/2 hours.

To make gravy: Chill drippings quickly by setting roasting pan in cold water. Remove 2 tbsp. (30 mL) fat to a saucepan; skim off remaining fat from cooking liquid, and discard. Heat fat in saucepan, sprinkle in flour, and stir to blend. Remove from heat, and add water and any cooking liquid left in roasting pan. Return to heat and bring to a boil, stirring constantly. Turn down heat; cook gently, stirring often, for 5 minutes. Taste, and adjust seasonings. Serves 8 – 10.

MANDARIN LAMB CHOPS

4	shoulder lamb chops	4
1 cup	rice, uncooked	250 mL
10 oz.	Mandarin oranges	284 mL
1 1/2 cups	beef bouillon	375 mL
1/2 tsp.	dried mint	2 mL
	salt	
	pepper	

Sear lamb chops briefly in their own fat. Place uncooked rice in a greased casserole. Set chops over rice and arrange oranges on top. Pour in bouillon. Sprinkle with mint, salt and pepper. Cover and bake at 350°F (180°C) for 45 minutes. Serves 4.

STUFFED LAMB CHOPS

2	lamb chops, thickly cut	2
1/2	green pepper, chopped	1/2
1/2	onion, diced	1/2
8	mushrooms, chopped	8
	salt	
	pepper	
	cayenne pepper	
3 oz.	rice, cooked	85 g
	oil	

Slit chops through middle to open like a book. Fry green pepper, onion, and mushrooms in oil, seasoning to taste. Mix with cooked rice. Stuff chops with mixture and close with toothpicks. Fry gently in oil. Serves 2.

SOSATIES (CURRIED LAMB KEBABS)

4 lb.	leg of lamb	2 kg
5 tsp.	salt	25 mL
1/2 tsp.	pepper	2 mL
2 large	onions, sliced	2 large
2 tbsp.	oil	30 mL
1 cup	water	250 mL
1 tbsp.	curry powder	15 mL
1/2 tbsp.	turmeric	7 mL
2 tbsp.	sugar	30 mL
1 tbsp.	cornstarch	15 mL
2 cups	vinegar	500 mL
1/2 cup	stewed apricots	125 mL
6	lemon or orange leaves	6

Remove meat from bone and cut into small cubes. Place in a bowl and sprinkle with 4 tsp. (20 mL) salt and the pepper. Fry onions in oil until light brown, then add water and simmer onions until tender. Combine curry powder, turmeric, sugar, cornstarch, 1 tsp. (5 mL) salt, and vinegar. Add onions and stir in the apricots. Cook for 3 minutes. Add crushed lemon or orange leaves and leave the sauce to cool. When cooled, pour over the meat to cover well. Marinate at least 24 to 72 hours. (Note: Chutney may be substituted for the apricots.)

Place the meat on thin wooden or wire skewers, using 6 pieces of meat per skewer. Broil or grill over coals or in a pan. Serve with well-heated sauce, rice, and chutney. (Note: Beef may be used instead of lamb. Lamb chops are excellent marinated in the sauce for 2 days and then barbecued or fried.)

PARTY MEAT SAUCE

5 lb.	ground beef	2.5 kg
5 large	onions, chopped	5 large
5 cloves	garlic, chopped	5 cloves
10 tsp.	chili powder	50 mL
10 tsp.	sugar	50 mL
4 tsp.	salt	20 mL
5 tbsp.	Worcestershire sauce	75 mL
9 cups	chicken soup	2.25 L
48 oz.	tomato juice	1.3 L
25 oz.	ketchup	710 mL
2 tbsp.	oregano	30 mL

Fry onions and garlic in oil. Add meat and brown thoroughly. Put in large pot, add all ingredients and simmer 1 to 1 1/2 hours. Makes a large quantity and freezes well.

SPAGHETTI MEAT SAUCE

2 lb.	ground beef	1 kg
1/2 cup	onion, minced	125 mL
1 clove	garlic, chopped	1 clove
1/2 cup	celery, diced	125 mL
1	green pepper, diced	1
1/4 cup	oil	50 mL
20 oz.	stewed tomatoes	568 mL
5 1/2 oz.	tomato paste	156 mL
1 cup	water	250 mL
3 tsp.	salt	15 mL
1/4 tsp.	pepper	1 mL
1 tsp.	Worcestershire sauce	5 mL
1 tbsp.	brown sugar	15 mL
2 tbsp.	vinegar	30 mL
1	bay leaf	1

Brown meat in oil with onion, garlic, celery, and green pepper. Add remaining ingredients, cover and simmer 1 1/2 to 2 hours. Serve over spaghetti or noodles. Serves 8.

overleaf:
Kasha-Stuffed Veal Breast (page 113)

overleaf:
Stuffed Lamb (page 115)

LASAGNE

Meat Sauce

1 cup	onion, chopped	250 mL
2 cloves	garlic, minced	2 cloves
1/4 cup	olive oil	50 mL
2 lb.	ground beef	1 kg
22 oz.	tomato sauce	624 g
11 oz.	tomato paste	312 mL
1/2 cup	water	125 mL
1/4 cup	parsley, chopped	50 mL
1 tbsp.	basil	15 mL
2	bay leaves	2
	salt	
	pepper	

Sauté onion and garlic in oil in a large pan. Add meat and brown. Add remaining ingredients. Stir well, bring to a boil, then reduce heat and simmer until sauce is very thick, about 3 to 4 hours.

To Assemble Lasagne

1 lb.	lasagne noodles	500 g
1 tbsp.	olive oil	15 mL
5 cups	meat sauce	1.25 L
2	hard-boiled eggs, grated	2

Add oil to boiling salted water. Carefully add noodles without breaking. Cook for 12 to 15 minutes. Drain and rinse in cold water. Line the bottom of a 13'' x 9'' (3 L) baking dish with a layer of cooked noodles. Spoon 1/3 cup (75 mL) meat sauce over noodles; sprinkle with some of the grated egg. Repeat until all the noodles, meat, and egg are used. Bake at 250°F (130°C) for 45 minutes. Serves 10 – 12.

SPAGHETTI BOLOGNAISE

1 large	onion, chopped	1 large
4 tbsp.	oil	60 mL
2 cloves	garlic, crushed	2 cloves
1 lb.	ground beef	500 g
1 lb.	tomatoes, skinned	500 g
5 1/2 oz.	tomato paste	156 mL
1 cup	tomato sauce	250 mL
1 tsp.	sugar	5 mL
	salt	
	pepper	
1/2 tsp.	rosemary	2 mL
1 tbsp.	parsley, chopped	15 mL
10 oz.	mushrooms, sliced	284 mL

Fry onion in oil until lightly browned. Add garlic, then meat. Stir until meat has lost its redness. Add remaining ingredients, except parsley and mushrooms. Simmer gently for 1 1/2 to 2 hours. Add mushrooms and parsley just before end of cooking. Serve with spaghetti. Serves 4.

DOLMEH (STUFFED GRAPE LEAVES)

1 large	onion, chopped	1 large
1/2 cup	oil	125 mL
1 lb.	lean ground beef	500 g
1/2 cup	rice	125 mL
2 tbsp.	green onion, chopped	30 mL
1/2 cup	leeks, chopped	125 mL
1 bunch	parsley, chopped	1 bunch
1 tsp.	dried mint	5 mL
3 tbsp.	dried dill weed	45 mL
1 tsp.	dried tarragon	5 mL
1/2 tsp.	salt	2 mL
1/4 tsp.	pepper	1 mL
1/4 cup	lemon juice	50 mL
4 tbsp.	sugar	60 mL
34 oz.	grape leaves	1 L
1 cup	water	250 mL

Filling

Sauté the onion in 1/4 cup (50 mL) of the oil until golden brown. Add ground beef, rice, green onion, leeks, herbs, salt, pepper, and half the lemon juice and sugar. Mix well.

To Prepare Dolmeh

Soak grape leaves overnight to remove salty taste. Drain, and spread out flat. Place a small amount of filling in the centre of each grape leaf, fold the edges over, and roll up. Arrange the stuffed grape leaves in a pan. In a small bowl mix remaining oil, lemon juice, and sugar. Add water. Pour this sauce over the dolmeh, cover, and simmer over very low heat until tender (about 45 minutes). Serves 4 – 6.

SWEET AND SOUR MEATBALLS

Meatballs

2 lb.	ground beef	1 kg
1 small	onion, grated	1 small
1/2 cup	bread crumbs	125 mL
2	eggs, beaten	2
	water	
	salt	
	pepper	

Combine ingredients lightly together and roll in hands to form small balls. Fry until evenly browned. Meatballs may be frozen until required. (Note: A grated raw potato and other seasonings are tasty additions to this meatball mixture.) Serves 6 – 8.

Sweet and Sour Sauce No. 1

2 tbsp.	vinegar	30 mL
2 tbsp.	lemon juice	30 mL
3/4 tbsp.	Worcestershire sauce	12 mL
1/2 cup	brown sugar	125 mL
1/2 cup	ketchup	125 mL
1/2 cup	chili sauce	125 mL
1/2 cup	beef bouillon	125 mL
1 cup	water	250 mL
	salt	
	pepper	
8	ginger snaps, crumbled	8

Combine all ingredients in a large saucepan, and cook over low heat for 30 minutes. Add fried meatballs, cover, and simmer for another hour.

Sweet and Sour Sauce No. 2

1 1/2 cups	brown sugar	375 mL
1 cup	pineapple juice	250 mL
3/4 cup	vinegar	175 mL
3 tbsp.	ketchup	45 mL
1 1/2 tbsp.	cornstarch	25 mL
	pineapple chunks	
	green pepper	

Combine brown sugar, juice, vinegar, and ketchup in a saucepan. Bring to a rolling boil. Mix cornstarch with water to a smooth paste, and add. Simmer for 5 minutes. Pour sauce over cooked meatballs. Cook for 30 to 45 minutes. Add pineapple chunks and chopped green pepper shortly before serving.

Sweet and Sour Sauce No. 3

10 oz.	condensed tomato soup	284 mL
2 tbsp.	lemon juice	30 mL
2 large	bay leaves	2 large
4	cloves	4
	brown sugar	

Heat ingredients together, adding brown sugar to taste. Boil 1 minute. Pour onto meatballs in an ovenproof dish; bake at 325°F (160°C) for 2 hours.

Sweet and Sour Sauce No. 4

1 cup	sugar	250 mL
10 oz.	condensed tomato soup	284 mL
1	onion, grated	1
1 tbsp.	oil	15 mL
10 oz.	water	284 mL
4 tbsp.	lemon juice	60 mL
	salt	
	pepper	

Caramelize the sugar by stirring in a hot frying pan until melted. Be careful not to burn. Brown onions slightly in oil. Combine all ingredients and bring to a boil. Drop meatballs into boiling sauce. Simmer slowly for 1 to 2 hours.

CHINESE MEATBALLS

1 lb.	ground beef	500 g
1/4 cup	green onion, minced	50 mL
1	egg	1
1/2 tsp.	ginger	2 mL

5 tbsp.	soy sauce	75 mL
4 tbsp.	cornstarch	60 mL
2¼ cups	oil	550 mL
1 cup	carrots, cooked	250 mL
13 oz.	canned pineapple chunks	365 mL
6 oz.	snow pea pods	170 g
¼ cup	water chestnuts, sliced	50 mL
3 tbsp.	sugar	45 mL
3 tbsp.	white vinegar	45 mL
	salt	
	pepper	

Combine first 4 ingredients with 2 tbsp. (30 mL) of the soy sauce and 2 tbsp. (30 mL) of the cornstarch and mix well. Shape in even round balls. Heat 2 cups (500 mL) oil in a deep heavy skillet. Fry balls quickly until well browned; drain and remove from pan. Drain carrots and pineapples, reserving liquid. Heat remaining oil in skillet. Add carrots, pineapple chunks, pea pods, and water chestnuts. Sauté about 3 minutes, then add meatballs. In a small saucepan mix sugar, vinegar, remaining soy sauce and cornstarch, reserved carrot water and pineapple syrup. Add water to make up to 1½ cups (375 mL). Bring to a boil, stirring, until thickened and clear. Adjust seasoning. Pour over meatballs and vegetables in skillet. Simmer 5 minutes and serve with rice. Serves 4.

CABBAGE ROLLS

1 lb.	ground beef	500 g
¼ cup	rice, uncooked	50 mL
1	egg	1
1	onion, grated	1
1	carrot, grated	1
¼ tsp.	salt	1 mL
10	cabbage leaves	10
¼ cup	lemon juice	50 mL
½ cup	brown sugar	125 mL
1 cup	tomato sauce	250 mL
	raisins	

Combine meat, rice, and egg; add onion, carrot, and salt. Blanch cabbage leaves by covering with boiling water for 2 to 3 minutes. Drain leaves. Place a ball of the meat mixture in the centre of each leaf and roll up, tucking in the ends securely. Set close together in a heavy frying pan; add remaining ingredients and enough water to cover. Cover tightly and cook over moderate heat for 30 minutes. Reduce heat and simmer 20 minutes more. Place in 350°F (180°C) oven, uncovered, for 20 minutes to brown on top. Turn rolls to brown on both sides. Add more hot water while baking if necessary. Serves 4 – 6.

FAST MEATBALLS AND CABBAGE

1	cabbage, sliced	1
12	meatballs	12
24 oz.	sweet and sour sauce	680 mL
20 oz.	condensed tomato soup	568 mL
1¾ cups	water	425 mL
½ cup	brown sugar	125 mL
4 tbsp.	lemon juice	60 mL

Place sliced cabbage on bottom of roaster. In a saucepan, combine ingredients for sauce; bring to a boil, and pour on top of cabbage. Drop meatballs in sauce and bake at 325°F (160°C) for 2 hours. Serves 2 – 3.

OLD-FASHIONED HAMBURGERS

3 lb.	ground beef	1.5 kg
2	eggs, beaten	2
1 medium	potato, grated	1 medium
1	onion, grated	1
	salt	
	pepper	
	garlic	
	paprika	
2 tbsp.	matzo meal	30 mL
½ cup	water	125 mL

Combine all ingredients and mix lightly but thoroughly. Form into patties. Brown well in hot oil. Cover frying pan and steam for 15 minutes. Just before serving, remove cover for patties to crisp. Serves 6 – 8.

HAMBURGER DELUXE

1 lb.	ground beef	500 g
1 tsp.	salt	5 mL
1/4 cup	ketchup	50 mL
	pepper	
1	potato, grated	1
1	Spanish onion, chopped	1
1/2 lb.	fresh mushrooms, sliced	250 g

Combine beef, salt, ketchup, pepper, and potato. Form into 4 flattened patties. Sauté onion and mushrooms. Spread a layer of mushrooms and onion on 2 of the patties, and top each with a plain patty. Pinch together all the way around. Fry both sides until done. Serves 2.

MARINATED HAMBURGERS

6 large	ground meat patties	6 large
3/4 cup	oil	175 mL
1/2 cup	ketchup	125 mL
1/4 cup	lemon juice	50 mL
1/8 tsp.	dry mustard	0.5 mL
1 clove	garlic, crushed	1 clove
3/4 tsp.	salt	3 mL
1/4 tsp.	pepper	1 mL

Combine seasonings with oil, ketchup, and lemon juice. Pour over patties in a shallow dish. Cover and refrigerate until 1 hour before cooking. Serves 6.

HAMBURGER CASSEROLE

2 lb.	ground beef	1 kg
2	onions, chopped	2
1	green pepper, chopped	1
1/2 lb.	fresh mushrooms, sliced	250 g
2 cups	elbow macaroni, cooked	500 mL
11 oz.	ketchup	313 mL
1 cup	chicken bouillon	250 mL

Brown meat in skillet. Add onions, green pepper, and mushrooms and cook until vegetables are soft. Add remaining ingredients. Mix thoroughly and pour into casserole. Bake at 350°F (180°C) for about 45 minutes until brown. Serves 6 – 8.

TACOS

1 lb.	ground beef	500 g
3 tbsp.	onion, minced	45 mL
7 1/2 oz.	tomato sauce	210 mL
1 tsp.	garlic salt	5 mL
1 tsp.	chili powder	5 mL
	dash of pepper	

Sauté onion and beef together until beef is browned. Add remaining ingredients. Reduce heat and simmer over low heat for 15 minutes. Serve in taco shells with chopped lettuce, tomatoes, and onions. Serves 6.

BOILED BEEF TONGUE

4 lb.	beef tongue	2 kg
6	peppercorns	6
4	whole cloves	4
1 tbsp.	vinegar	15 mL

Scrub tongue under running water. Place in a large pot; add seasonings and boiling water to cover. Boil 10 minutes, then simmer 3 to 5 hours, or until tender. Let stand in the water until cool enough to handle. Peel off outer skin and cut out membranous portions of roots.

TONGUE IN TOMATO SAUCE

3 lb.	tongue	1.5 kg
2 tbsp.	oil	30 mL
1	onion, diced	1
2 stalks	celery, diced	2 stalks
1/2	green pepper, diced	1/2
10 oz.	canned mushrooms	284 mL
1 clove	garlic, crushed	1 clove
14 oz.	stewed tomatoes	398 mL

Boil tongue; skin, and slice thin. Brown onions in oil. Add celery, green pepper, drained mushrooms, and garlic. Cook until softened, then add undrained tomatoes, mixing together well. Pour sauce over tongue in roaster. Bake at 400°F (200°C) for 1 hour. Serves 4 – 6.

TONGUE WITH GINGER SNAPS

4 lb.	pickled tongue	2 kg
1	onion, diced	1
1	green pepper, diced	1
½ lb.	fresh mushrooms, diced	250 g
½ cup	chili sauce	125 mL
½ cup	ketchup	125 mL
¼ cup	vinegar	50 mL
1 cup	water	250 mL
2 tbsp.	lemon juice	30 mL
½ cup	brown sugar	125 mL
	salt	
	pepper	
	garlic	
	seasoning salt	
6	ginger snaps	6

Slice tongue fairly thin. Sauté onion, green pepper, and mushrooms until soft. Add remaining ingredients, simmering for 30 minutes. Layer tongue and sauce in a casserole. Bake at 350°F (180°C) for 1½ to 2 hours. Sauce and tongue may be frozen separately; they keep perfectly for months. Serves 6 – 8.

SWEET AND SOUR TONGUE

4 lb.	pickled tongue	2 kg
2 tbsp.	oil	30 mL
1	onion, diced	1
2 tbsp.	potato flour	30 mL
⅓ cup	vinegar	75 mL
⅓ cup	honey	75 mL
½ tsp.	salt	2 mL
½ tsp.	ginger	2 mL
¼ cup	raisins	50 mL
¼ cup	almonds, sliced	50 mL
1	lemon, thinly sliced	1

Boil the tongue until soft. Drain, reserving 2 cups (500 mL) of the stock. Keep tongue warm while preparing sauce.

Brown onion in oil and add flour. Gradually add reserved stock, stirring until mixture boils. Stir in vinegar, honey, salt, ginger, and raisins. Cook over low heat 5 minutes. Add almonds and lemon. Cook 2 minutes. Slice tongue and serve with sauce. Serves 6.

VEGETABLE-TONGUE CASSEROLE

1	tongue	1
20 oz.	condensed tomato soup	568 mL
1	onion, sliced	1
2	carrots, diced	2
1	parsnip, sliced	1
4	potatoes, quartered	4
1	green pepper, diced	1
10 oz.	canned mushrooms	284 mL
14 oz.	canned peas	398 mL

Boil tongue until soft, and peel. Place in a roasting pan with undiluted tomato soup, onion, carrots, parsnip, potatoes, and green pepper. Cover. Roast at 350°F (180°C) for 30 minutes. Add undrained mushrooms and peas; reduce heat to 325°F (160°C), and roast uncovered for another hour.

BREADED SWEETBREADS

1 lb.	sweetbreads	500 g
1 cup	bread crumbs, browned	250 mL
¼ lb.	fresh mushrooms, sliced	120 g
1	onion, diced	1
2 tbsp.	margarine	30 mL
	salt	
	pepper	

Parboil sweetbreads for 15 minutes. Remove membranes, cut in serving-sized pieces, and roll in crumbs. Sauté vegetables in margarine. Add sweetbreads and seasonings; cook uncovered for 30 minutes, turning to brown evenly. Serves 3.

PETZAH (BRAWN)

1	cow's heel	1
4 cloves	garlic	4 cloves
2	bay leaves	2
3	peppercorns	3
	salt	
	pepper	
	ginger	
1 large	onion	1 large

Place all ingredients in a large saucepan. Cover with water, and boil until meat falls off bones. Add water continually to cover heel completely for first 5 or 6 hours. Adjust seasonings. Mince meat, garlic, and onion into gravy and pour into shallow serving dishes. Garnish with sliced hard-boiled eggs. Refrigerate to set. Serve with mustard. (Note: For softer Petzah, add extra liquid before setting.)

STUFFED KISHKAS

	beef casings	
3	onions	3
1/3 cup	schmaltz or oil	75 mL
1 cup	flour	250 mL
1/2 tsp.	salt	2 mL
1/4 tsp.	pepper	1 mL

Chop 1 onion. Combine chopped onion with schmaltz, flour, salt, and pepper to make the filling. Fasten one end of beef casing; stuff casing with filling, then fasten the other end. Plunge into boiling water, scraping the surface until clean. Place in a greased roasting pan, slice remaining onions on top, and bake slowly at 325°F (160°C) until well done and brown. Baste frequently with pan liquid.

Poultry

Tradition! Tradition! In every Jewish home on a Friday, the kitchen is redolent with the fragrance of chicken being prepared for the Sabbath meal. The aroma evokes memories of congenial family gatherings: golden chicken soup, afloat with homemade noodles; and a savoury roasted fowl surrounded by other traditional dishes.

From inauspicious beginnings in the jungles of Southeast Asia five thousand years ago, chickens have roamed the globe, completing the last leg of their conquest from Spain to the Americas with Columbus. Now held in the highest esteem by cooks the world over, chickens, like Jewish people, have absorbed the culinary customs of their environment. Provocative in their differences, like the Jewish people, they have retained that which they have in common.

In India, the chicken was curried; in France it was prepared with wine and herbs. In China, almonds and ginger were used to aesthetic perfection.

But a kosher chicken is in a class by itself. The equation of chicken plus imagination over a little time in the kitchen equals a banquet. Liver as an appetizer; feet prepared as Petzah—a side dish; fat combined with onion and coaxed into schmaltz and griben; back, neck, and wingtips, and—with luck—a few unhatched eggs, simmered with vegetables for soup; giblets for gravy; neck stuffed for Helzel; and even something out of nothing—the cavity filled with any number of delicious stuffings. As a gracious gesture, a wish bone is provided for an after-dinner game. And the meat of the chicken! The imagination is bedazzled with the infinite variations.

There is a bird for every size budget and every size family. Special occasion birds with international reputations, Rock Cornish hens may be shared by a family of two; and if there are four for dinner, Crispy Duck or Long Island duckling divides perfectly into quarters. The most popular and most economical member of the poultry family is the turkey. Brillat-Savarin, the French gastronome, wrote in 1800 that "the turkey is certainly one of the finest gifts made by the New World to the Old." He was right. Turkey is easy to prepare, has enough white meat and dark meat to appease all family arguments, and leaves the cook a good size carcass for turkey soup.

Poultry has no singular allegiance. An obliging family, it will happily hop into a pot with any combination of fruits, vegetables, herbs, spices, nuts, wines, or fruit juices. When the cupboard is bare, even a little salt and pepper will give the cook perfection—a beautiful golden bird.

GLAZED CHICKEN

2	fryers	2
	garlic powder	
	onion powder	
	paprika	
	salt	
	pepper	
2	onions, chopped	2
2 tbsp.	oil	30 mL
1 1/4 cups	apricot jam	300 mL
2 tbsp.	soy sauce	30 mL
1 tsp.	ginger	5 mL
1 tbsp.	prepared mustard	15 mL
1/4 cup	vinegar	50 mL

Cut chickens into eighths. Place in a large baking dish skin side down. Sprinkle with seasonings. Sauté onions in oil. Add remaining ingredients and simmer for 5 minutes. Pour over chicken. Bake at 325°F (160°C) for 1 hour. Turn skin side up. Bake 30 minutes or more, basting often. Serves 6 – 8.

Sauce Variation

Lemon Glazed Chicken

1 cup	apricot-pineapple preserve	250 mL
1/3 cup	prepared mustard	75 mL
2 tsp.	lemon rind, grated	10 mL
1/3 cup	lemon juice	75 mL
1	lemon, sliced	1

Combine all ingredients except lemon slices, heat, and pour over chicken. Bake at 375°F (190°C) for 30 minutes. Arrange lemon slices over chicken and bake 30 minutes more.

CURRIED CHICKEN

3 lb.	fryer, cut up	1.5 kg
4 tbsp.	margarine	60 mL
3/8 cup	honey	100 mL
1/4 cup	prepared mustard	50 mL
1 tsp.	salt	5 mL
1 1/4 tsp.	curry powder	6 mL

Melt margarine and mix with honey, mustard, salt, and curry powder. Roll chicken in this marinade and let stand for 1 hour. Bake uncovered, skin side up, at 375°F (190°C) for 1 to 1 1/2 hours until done. Serves 4.

SESAME CHICKEN

4 lb.	chicken thighs	2 kg
1 cup	flour	250 mL
1 cup	sesame seeds	250 mL
2 tbsp.	paprika	30 mL
1/2 tsp.	salt	2 mL
2	eggs, beaten	2
1/2 cup	chicken bouillon	125 mL

In a large bowl combine flour, sesame seeds, paprika, and salt. In a second bowl, beat eggs with chicken broth. Dip each piece of chicken first into the dry mixture, then into the liquid, then back into the dry. Place on a cookie sheet and bake at 350°F (180°C) for 45 to 60 minutes. Serves 4 – 6.

SESAME CHICKEN WITH BULGAR STUFFING

4 lb.	roasting chicken	2 kg
2 tbsp.	margarine	30 mL
2 small	onions, diced	2 small
1 cup	bulgar (medium)	250 mL
1 tsp.	cinnamon	5 mL
1 1/2 cups	chicken bouillon	375 mL
1/3 cup	dry apricots, chopped	75 mL
1/2 cup	dates, chopped	125 mL
	salt	
	pepper	
2 tbsp.	lemon juice	30 mL

Sauté onion in margarine over medium heat. Add bulgar and sauté 5 minutes. Stir in remaining ingredients. Bring to a boil then turn down heat, cover, and cook 5 minutes. Remove from heat and let stand at least 1 hour. Stuff chicken.

Glaze

2 tbsp.	margarine	30 mL
½ cup	honey	125 mL
6 tbsp.	sesame seeds	90 mL

In a small saucepan, stir margarine and honey over low heat until melted. Brush over chicken and roast at 350°F (180°C) for 1¼ hours, basting often. Sprinkle sesame seeds over chicken and return to oven for 15 minutes. Chicken becomes very dark and crusty. Serves 6.

LIME-BROILED CHICKEN

2	frying chickens	2
	salt	
	pepper	
½ cup	oil	125 mL
½ cup	lime juice	125 mL
2 tbsp.	onion, chopped	30 mL
½ tsp.	Tabasco sauce	2 mL
2 tsp.	tarragon	10 mL
1 tsp.	salt	5 mL

Preheat broiler. Sprinkle chicken with salt and pepper. In a separate bowl, combine remaining ingredients. Brush chicken with sauce and place skin side up on rack 6'' (15 cm) from broiler heat. Cook for 1 to 1¼ hours, turning and basting occasionally. For a richer flavour, marinate chicken in the sauce first for several hours.

CHICKEN WITH 40 CLOVES OF GARLIC

4 lb.	chicken, cut up	2 kg
4 bulbs	garlic	4 bulbs
½ cup	olive oil	125 mL
	salt	
	pepper	
1 tbsp.	mixed herbs	15 mL
6 small	potatoes	6 small
10	baby artichokes	10
1	bouquet garni	1
½ cup	flour	125 mL
	water	

Break garlic bulbs into cloves, but do not peel. Place chicken, garlic, and oil in a 4 to 6 quart (4 – 6 L) casserole, earthenware if possible. Season to taste with salt, pepper, and herbs. Peel potatoes and trim outer leaves from artichokes. Add potatoes and artichokes to casserole. Check that garlic cloves do not fall to bottom of casserole. Bury bouquet garni in the middle.

Mix flour with enough cold water to make a stiff dough. Roll out on a floured board, adding more flour if dough seems sticky. Cut into long strips about 1½'' (3 cm) wide, moisten the lip of the casserole and line with dough strips. Moisten inside lip of casserole cover, and place on top of casserole. Seal lid and casserole tightly with dough. Bake at 350°F (180°C) for 1½ hours. Serves 4. (Note: The mixed herbs should include rosemary, thyme, oregano, sage, and basil. The bouquet garni consists of 1 celery stalk with leaves, 2 sprigs of parsley, 2 bay leaves, and a sprig of fresh thyme.)

CHICKEN IN WINE

5 lb.	roasting chicken, cut up	2.5 kg
	flour	
½ cup	oil	125 mL
1 slice	salami, diced	1 slice
10 small	white onions	10 small
1 clove	garlic, chopped	1 clove
1 sprig	parsley	1 sprig
1	bay leaf	1
8	whole mushrooms	8
	salt	
	pepper	
¼ cup	cognac, warmed	50 mL
1 cup	dry red wine	250 mL

Preheat oven to 300°F (150°C). Dredge chicken with flour. Heat oil in a skillet, add chicken and brown on all sides. Transfer chicken to an oven-proof casserole and add the salami, onions, garlic, parsley, bay leaf, mushrooms, and salt and pepper. Pour cognac over chicken and ignite. When the flame dies, add wine. Cover, and bake for 2½ hours. Serves 6. (Note: The onions may be pickled or plain.)

CHICKEN CACCIATORI

2	fryers	2
6 tbsp.	oil	90 mL
1 cup	onion, minced	250 mL
3/4 cup	green pepper, minced	175 mL
4 cloves	garlic, minced	4 cloves
28 oz.	canned tomatoes	796 mL
1/2 tsp.	thyme	2 mL
7 1/2 oz.	tomato sauce	210 mL
1/2 cup	red wine	125 mL
3 3/4 tsp.	salt	18 mL
1/2 tsp.	pepper	2 mL
1/2 tsp.	allspice	2 mL
2	bay leaves	2
	cayenne pepper	

Cut chicken in serving-sized pieces. Heat oil in a large frying pan or dutch oven and fry chicken until golden brown on all sides. Add onion, green pepper, and garlic and brown lightly. Add remaining ingredients. Simmer uncovered for 30 to 40 minutes until chicken is tender. Serves 6.

APRICOT CHICKEN

6	baby chickens, halved	6
	salt	
	pepper	
	ginger	
32 oz.	canned apricots	1 L
1/3 cup	orange juice	75 mL
1 tsp.	orange rind, grated	5 mL
2 tbsp.	syrup	30 mL
1 tsp.	ginger	5 mL
1 tsp.	soy sauce	5 mL
1 tbsp.	lemon juice	15 mL

Sprinkle chicken with seasonings, rub with oil, and grill until brown and tender. Place in a large casserole with lid. Sieve apricots together with juice. Add remaining ingredients and bring to a boil. Pour over chicken and simmer for 10 minutes in oven with lid on. Remove cover and simmer another 10 to 15 minutes, ensuring that chicken is well coated with sauce. May be served hot or cold. Serves 6 – 8.

CHICKEN QUÉBECOIS

2	chicken breasts, boned	2
10 slices	apple	10 slices
	raisins	
2 tbsp.	maple syrup	30 mL
6 oz.	puff pastry	170 g
1	egg yolk, beaten	1

Peel and slice apples. Arrange slices on flattened chicken breasts. Top with raisins and maple syrup. Roll out puff pastry very thin. Divide in half. Wrap a chicken breast in each piece, pressing pastry ends firmly together. Place smooth side up on a greased baking pan. Glaze with beaten egg yolk. Bake at 350°F (180°C) for 20 minutes. Serve hot with Madeira Sauce. Serves 2.

Madeira Sauce

1 cup	brown gravy	250 mL
1/4 cup	Madeira wine	50 mL

JERUSALEM CHICKEN

4 lb.	chicken, cut up	2 kg
1 large	onion, chopped	1 large
1/2 lb.	mushrooms, sliced	250 g
1	green pepper, sliced	1
10	green olives, sliced	10
2 cups	dry white wine	500 mL

Combine all ingredients and bake in an open pan at 350°F (180°C) for 1 1/2 hours. Serves 6 – 8.

ALMOND GINGER CHICKEN

2 large	chicken breasts	2 large
3 tbsp.	oil	45 mL
1 cup	celery, sliced	250 mL
1 clove	garlic, chopped	1 clove
2 tbsp.	chicken bouillon mix	30 mL
1 1/2 cups	water	375 mL
1 tbsp.	soy sauce	15 mL
1 1/2 tbsp.	crystallized ginger	20 mL
6 oz.	frozen snow peas	170 g
2 tbsp.	cornstarch	30 mL
1/4 cup	slivered almonds	50 mL

Remove skin and bones from breasts. Slice meat into long thin strips. Heat oil in a large pan; add chicken and sauté for 5 minutes, stirring constantly. Stir in celery and garlic and sauté until chicken is tender, about 3 minutes. Stir in chicken bouillon, water, soy sauce, and ginger. Heat to boiling. Add pea pods and simmer for 5 minutes. Mix cornstarch with enough cold water to make a smooth paste. Pour into chicken mixture and stir over heat until mixture thickens. Spoon into serving dish, topping with toasted almonds. Serve with rice. Serves 6.

CHICKEN PIE WITH SWEET POTATO CRUST

3 cups	cooked chicken	750 mL
1 cup	cooked carrots	250 mL
6	pearl onions, cooked	6
1 tbsp.	parsley, chopped	15 mL
1 cup	water	250 mL
1 cup	chicken bouillon	250 mL
2 tbsp.	flour	30 mL
1 tsp.	salt	5 mL
1/8 tsp.	pepper	0.5 mL

Dice chicken and carrots, and arrange with onions and parsley in layers in a casserole. Combine water and chicken broth. Add slowly to flour, blending well. Cook until thickened, stirring constantly. Season, and pour over chicken and vegetables in casserole. Cover with sweet potato crust.

Sweet Potato Crust

1 cup	flour	250 mL
1 tsp.	baking powder	5 mL
1/2 tsp.	salt	2 mL
1 cup	cooked sweet potatoes	250 mL
1/3 cup	shortening, melted	75 mL
1	egg, beaten	1

Sift dry ingredients. Work in mashed potatoes, shortening, and egg. Roll to 1/4'' (6 mm) thickness, and cover chicken. Bake at 350°F (180°C) for 40 minutes until crust is golden brown. Serves 6 – 8.

CHICKEN WITH EGGPLANT

3 lb.	chicken, skinned	1.5 kg
6 small	onions	6 small
1 clove	garlic	1 clove
2 cups	peeled eggplant, diced	500 mL
2 cups	mushrooms, diced	500 mL
2	tomatoes, quartered	2
2	green peppers, diced	2
3/4 cup	chicken bouillon	175 mL
1	bay leaf	1
1 tsp.	mixed herbs	5 mL

Parboil onions 10 minutes. Rub chicken with garlic. Place in casserole with all ingredients. Cover and bake at 375°F (190°C) for 1 1/2 to 2 hours. Serves 4.

CHICKEN PAELLA

4 lb.	chicken	2 kg
2	bay leaves	2
2 stalks	celery	2 stalks
1	onion	1
1	carrot	1
2 tsp.	salt	10 mL
1 tsp.	pepper	5 mL
4 cups	rice, uncooked	1 L
1/2 tsp.	turmeric	2 mL
2 tbsp.	tarragon vinegar	30 mL
1/4 cup	oil	50 mL
1 tsp.	salt	5 mL
1/2 tsp.	dry mustard	2 mL
1/4 tsp.	seasoning salt	1 mL
1 large	onion, diced	1 large
1/3 cup	celery, diced	75 mL
1 clove	garlic, crushed	1 clove
1 cup	button mushrooms	250 mL
2 oz.	pimento, chopped	55 g
1/2 cup	cooked peas	125 mL
1/4 cup	soy sauce	50 mL
1 1/2	green peppers, chopped	1 1/2
1	peeled tomato, chopped	1

Boil chicken until tender with bay leaf, celery, onion, carrot, salt, and pepper. Remove chicken from bones and cool. Cut into bite-sized pieces. Cook rice in broth flavoured with turmeric, until almost done. Mix vinegar, oil, 1/8 tsp. (0.5 mL) salt, dry mustard, and seasoning salt. Immediately pour onto cooked rice. Let stand at room temperature until cool. Sauté diced onion, celery, garlic, and mushrooms. Remove from heat; add 2 1/2 cups (625 mL) chicken, and rice. Add pimento, peas, and soy sauce. Toss together lightly. Turn into a lightly greased casserole, cover with foil, and bake at 350°F (180°C) for 40 to 50 minutes. After baking, add green pepper and tomato. Serves 10 – 12.

Variation
Combine chicken and vegetables. Arrange rice on a serving platter and place chicken mixture in the middle.

SWEET AND SOUR CHICKEN

4 lb.	chicken, cut up	2 kg
3 tbsp.	flour	45 mL
1 tsp.	salt	5 mL
1/2 tsp.	pepper	2 mL
1/4 tsp.	garlic powder	1 mL
1/4 cup	oil	50 mL

Roll chicken in flour that has been seasoned with salt, pepper, and garlic powder. Brown slowly in oil.

Sweet and Sour Pineapple Sauce

2	onions, diced	2
15 oz.	canned pineapple chunks	450 mL
1/2 cup	ketchup	125 mL
1 tbsp.	lemon juice	15 mL

Drain pineapple, reserving juice. Combine onion, pineapple juice, ketchup, and lemon juice in a saucepan and simmer about 5 minutes. Put chicken in a casserole. Pour sauce over chicken and top with pineapple chunks. Bake at 375°F (190°C) for 20 to 25 minutes. Serve with rice. Serves 4 – 5.

Sweet and Sour Sauce with Peaches

1 cup	orange juice	250 mL
2 tbsp.	honey	30 mL
2 tbsp.	vinegar	30 mL
1 tbsp.	parsley, chopped	15 mL
1 1/2 cups	peaches	375 mL

Combine orange juice, honey, vinegar, and parsley. Add to chicken in casserole and bake at 350°F (180°C) for 45 minutes, until tender. Add drained peaches and bake 5 minutes more. Serves 4.

CHICKEN DELIGHT

2	fryers, cut up	2
8 oz.	French dressing	250 mL
1 1/2 oz.	onion soup mix	42 g
3 tbsp.	soy sauce	45 mL
10 oz.	canned mushrooms	284 mL
6 oz.	frozen pea pods	170 g
	green pepper strips	
2 cups	cherry tomatoes	500 mL
1 cup	dry wine	250 mL

Marinate chicken in dressing overnight. Combine onion soup powder with soy sauce and mushrooms, and pour over chicken. Bake, covered, at 350°F (180°C) for 1 hour. Add vegetables and wine. Return to oven for 15 minutes. Serve over rice. Serves 6 – 8.

LAZY CHICKEN

8 lb.	chicken, cut up	4 kg
1 1/4 lb.	onions	600 g
1 1/4 lb.	potatoes	600 g
1 lb.	carrots	500 g
6 cloves	garlic	6 cloves
2 tsp.	salt	10 mL
	pepper	
1 tsp.	thyme	5 mL
1 cup	dry white wine	250 mL
1 1/2 cups	chicken bouillon	375 mL
3 tbsp.	margarine	45 mL
	parsley, chopped	

Preheat oven to 500°F (260°C). Cut all vegetables into chunks. Pack vegetables and chicken tightly together in a large utility pan. (Pack every space to prevent drying out during cooking.) Sprinkle garlic and seasonings over. Pour wine and enough chicken bouillon into pan to half-cover chicken. Dot with margarine. Bake for 50 to 60 minutes. Baste often and add more stock if necessary. When ready, chicken has a rich crispy crust. Sprinkle with chopped parsley just before serving. Serves 8 – 12.

TANGY BARBECUED CHICKEN

2	fryers, cut in pieces	2
2 large	onions, diced	2 large
1/2 cup	ketchup	125 mL
1 cup	water	250 mL
1 tbsp.	Worcestershire sauce	15 mL
1 tbsp.	sugar	15 mL
1 tbsp.	vinegar	15 mL
1 tsp.	salt	5 mL
1 tsp.	dry mustard	5 mL
1/2 tsp.	chili powder	2 mL
	dash of Tabasco sauce	

Brown onion until golden. Add remaining ingredients and mix well. Pour over chicken in casserole. Bake at 350° (180°C), covered, for 1 1/2 hours. Remove lid and bake another 30 minutes. Serves 8.

FRIED CHICKEN

6 lb.	small chicken pieces	3 kg
1 1/2 cups	flour	375 mL
4 tsp.	dry mustard	20 mL
3 tsp.	poultry seasoning	15 mL
1 tsp.	nutmeg	5 mL
	oil	
1 tsp.	garlic powder	5 mL
1 tsp.	seasoning salt	5 mL
1 tsp.	paprika	5 mL

Pour oil in frying pan to a depth of 1/2 – 3/4'' (1 – 2 cm). Heat oil. Wash the chicken pieces. Combine flour, dry mustard, poultry seasoning, and nutmeg in a plastic bag. Shake each chicken piece in flour mixture to coat, and then fry on both sides in hot oil until well browned. Drain on paper towels. Sprinkle the chicken pieces on one side with garlic powder, and on both sides with seasoning salt and paprika. Place in a roasting pan and bake covered at 325°F (160°C) for 1 1/2 hours. (Note: To make this kosher for Passover, substitute cake meal for the flour.) Serves 8.

SWEET AND SOUR CHICKEN WINGS

30	chicken wings, halved	30
1 cup	water	250 mL
1 cup	soy sauce	250 mL
1 cup	sugar	250 mL
1/4 cup	pineapple juice	50 mL
1/4 cup	oil	50 mL
1 tsp.	garlic powder	5 mL
1 tsp.	ginger	5 mL

Combine all ingredients for sauce. Marinate chicken wings in sauce overnight. Coat a cookie sheet with a thin layer of liquid honey. Shaking off excess marinade first, place chicken pieces on honeyed pan. Bake at 350°F (180°C) for 1 1/2 hours. Serves 6.

STUFFED CHICKEN

1	chicken	1
2	carrots, sliced	2
1	parsnip, sliced	1
	water	
2	onions	2
1 lb.	ground veal	500 g
1	potato, grated	1
1/4 tsp.	salt	1 mL
1/4 tsp.	pepper	1 mL
1	egg	1
1 tbsp.	oil	15 mL

Cut chicken into 8 pieces. Place in a soup pot with carrot and parsnip and enough water to cover. Season to taste. Boil for 30 minutes. Remove chicken and strain stock, reserving 1 cup (250 mL). Dice 1 onion and mix with remaining ingredients. Slice a pocket in each piece of chicken; stuff with veal mixture. Slice remaining onion into roasting pan. Add stuffed chicken pieces and reserved stock, cover, and bake at 350°F (180°C) for 1 hour, until chicken is tender. Serves 4 – 6.

STUFFED CHICKEN THIGHS

8	chicken thighs	8
	salt	
	pepper	
¼ cup	onion, minced	50 mL
⅓ cup	carrot, grated	75 mL
½ cup	celery, minced	125 mL
⅛ tsp.	thyme	0.5 mL
½ tsp.	basil	2 mL
½ tsp.	garlic salt	2 mL
1	egg	1
¼ cup	soft bread crumbs	50 mL
⅓ cup	flour	75 mL
¼ cup	margarine	50 mL
⅓ cup	dry white wine	75 mL
1 cup	mushrooms, sliced	250 mL
1 cup	chicken bouillon	250 mL

Bone chicken thighs by cutting vertically on one skinless side, pushing meat away from bone and removing bone. Open thighs and pound flat. Season lightly with salt and pepper. Combine onion, carrot, celery, thyme, basil, and garlic salt. Mix in egg and bread crumbs. Fill thighs with mixture, close and secure with string. Dredge with ¼ cup (50 mL) of the flour. Melt margarine in a large skillet over medium heat. Brown thighs, then transfer to an ovenproof dish. Add wine. Bake at 350°F (180°C) for 50 to 60 minutes, until done. Remove drippings to a small saucepan or skillet, and heat. Sauté mushrooms 5 minutes. Blend in remaining flour and cook 1 minute. Slowly add chicken broth, stirring until smooth. Cook until thickened. Season to taste. Pour over chicken thighs on serving dish. Serves 3 – 4.

CHICKEN-NOODLE PATTIES

1	chicken	1
¼ cup	green pepper, diced	50 mL
2 oz.	pimento, chopped	60 mL
½ cup	onion, chopped	125 mL
2	eggs	2
1½ cups	cooked coil vermicelli	375 mL
½ cup	soft bread crumbs	125 mL
⅛ tsp.	celery salt	0.5 mL
	salt	
	pepper	
½ cup	fine dry bread crumbs	125 mL
3 tbsp.	oil	45 mL

Boil chicken with giblets until cooked. Reserve giblets and broth. Remove meat from bones, and dice. Combine 2½ cups (625 mL) diced chicken with all except last 2 ingredients, seasoning to taste. Mix well and shape into 8 patties. Coat with fine crumbs. Heat oil in a 10'' (25 cm) skillet and fry patties until golden brown. Serve hot with giblet gravy. Serves 6 – 8.

Giblet Gravy

	reserved giblets	
1½ cups	chicken bouillon	375 mL
2 tbsp.	margarine	30 mL
2 tbsp.	flour	30 mL
	salt	
	pepper	

Purée giblets, including livers, in broth until smooth. Melt margarine in a saucepan, stir in flour, and cook 1 to 2 minutes. Slowly add puréed mixture and simmer until thickened, stirring constantly. Add more water if a thinner sauce is desired. Season to taste with salt and pepper.

SCHMALTZ

1	chicken	1
1	onion, chopped	1
	salt	

Remove all fat from chicken, cut into small pieces, and place in a pan over low heat. Cook until almost all the fat turns to liquid, then add onion; cook until onion is brown, add salt, and cool. Strain, and refrigerate in a glass jar.

MOCK SCHMALTZ

| 1 cup | vegetable oil | 250 mL |
| 1 large | onion, diced | 1 large |

Boil onion and oil in a saucepan until the onion turns a caramel colour. Strain.

STUFFED HELZEL

	skin from chicken neck	
1	onion, diced	1
2 1/2 tbsp.	flour	40 mL
	pieces of chicken or beef fat	
	salt	
	pepper	
	water	

Combine onion, flour, salt, pepper, and tiny pieces of unrendered fat. Add enough water to make a paste. Let stand. Clean neck skin thoroughly and sew up one end. Fill the skin, leaving room for expansion, and sew up the other end. Cover with boiling water. Let stand for a while until neck shrinks, getting firmer and tighter. Remove from boiling water and cook in chicken soup for 1 hour.

CHICKEN LIVER SPAGHETTI SAUCE

3/4 cup	oil	175 mL
1/4 cup	margarine	50 mL
2 cups	onion, diced	500 mL
2 cloves	garlic, crushed	2 cloves
3/4 lb.	chicken livers, cut up	375 g
1/2 cup	parsley, chopped	125 mL
3 cups	tomatoes, chopped	750 mL
1/4 cup	dry red wine	50 mL
1 1/2 tsp.	salt	7 mL
1/2 tsp.	pepper	2 mL
2	green peppers, diced	2
	dash of Tabasco sauce	
	dash of cayenne pepper	

Sauté onion and garlic in oil and margarine. Add broiled livers and remaining ingredients, and bring to a boil. Cover and simmer 20 minutes. Stir occasionally. Serves 6.

CRISPY DUCK

3 lb.	duck	1.4 kg
1 tbsp.	dry sherry	15 mL
3 1/2 tsp.	salt	18 mL
2 1/2 tsp.	sugar	12 mL
2 tsp.	paprika	10 mL
6 slices	ginger	6 slices
4	cloves	4
	aniseed	
1	egg	1
2 tbsp.	flour	30 mL

Sprinkle duck with sherry and allow to stand for 15 minutes. Mix salt, sugar, and paprika. Rub over duck. Place duck in a large steamer with ginger, cloves, and aniseed, and steam for 1 to 1 1/2 hours until tender. Remove duck from steamer and allow to cool. Beat egg lightly, add flour and mix well. Coat duck with this mixture; deep fry until crisp, about 15 minutes. Serves 6. (Note: To improvise steamer, place pot in a slightly larger pot in which a small quantity of water has been placed.)

DUCK WITH ORANGE

4 lb.	duck	2 kg
	water	
	salt	
1 cup	white wine	250 mL
1 cup	bouillon	250 mL
	pinch of dry mustard	
1 tbsp.	tomato purée	15 mL
4	oranges	4
2 tbsp.	cranberries	30 mL

Put duck into a large roasting pan with very little salted water. Cook in oven at 350°F (180°C) for 1 hour. Pour off the gravy and fat and return duck to oven. Mix gravy and fat with wine, bouillon, mustard, tomato purée, and the juice of 2 oranges. Pour this sauce over duck. Baste duck well and cook in sauce for another 30 to 60 minutes.

Strain the gravy and mix with cranberries. Garnish duck with 4 orange halves, which have been warmed in the oven, and spread with some of the cranberries. Serves 4.

SWEET AND SOUR DUCK

5 lb.	duck	2.5 kg
1½ tsp.	salt	7 mL
¼ tsp.	pepper	1 mL
¼ cup	flour	50 mL
2 tbsp.	margarine	30 mL
1½ cups	onion, thinly sliced	375 mL
⅛ tsp.	cloves	0.5 mL
2 cups	chicken bouillon	500 mL
4 tbsp.	sugar	60 mL
1 tbsp.	water	15 mL
3 tbsp.	wine vinegar	45 mL
1 tbsp.	fresh mint, chopped	15 mL

Wash duck. Remove as much fat as possible; dry. Rub with a mixture of the salt, pepper, and flour. Melt margarine in a dutch oven or casserole. Add onion and the duck. Brown duck on all sides. Pour off fat. Add cloves and bouillon, cover, and cook over low heat for 2 hours or until tender, turning the duck frequently. Transfer duck to a pan and place in a 375°F (190°C) oven. Skim the fat off the gravy. In a small saucepan, combine sugar and water, and cook over low heat until browned. Stir into the gravy with the vinegar and mint. Cook over low heat 5 minutes. Carve the duck and serve sauce separately. Serves 4. (Note: ½ tsp. (2 mL) dried mint may be substituted for the fresh.)

ROAST STUFFED GOOSE

3 cloves	garlic, minced	3 cloves
5 tsp.	salt	25 mL
1¼ tsp.	pepper	6 mL
2 tsp.	paprika	10 mL
15 lb.	goose	7 kg
4 tbsp.	shortening	60 mL
½ lb.	fresh mushrooms, sliced	250 g
3	onions, chopped	3
¼ lb.	chicken livers, chopped	125 g
4 cups	buckwheat groats, cooked	1 L

Mix garlic, 4 tsp. (20 mL) of the salt, ¾ tsp. (3 mL) of the pepper, and paprika to a paste. Rub into goose, inside and out.

Melt shortening in a skillet. Sauté onions and mushrooms for 10 minutes, stirring frequently. Add the livers and sauté for 5 minutes longer. Add the buckwheat and remaining salt and pepper. Mix lightly and stuff the goose with the mixture.

Place goose in a roasting pan. Roast at 425°F (220°C) for 30 minutes. Pour off the fat. Prick the goose skin in several places with a fork. Reduce heat to 350°F (180°C) and roast for another 2½ hours, until goose is tender, crisp and brown. Pour off the fat frequently while roasting. Serves 10 – 15.

CHERRY BERRY TURKEY

3 lb.	turkey thighs or drumsticks	1.5 kg
⅓ cup	flour	75 mL
1 tsp.	salt	5 mL
1½ tsp.	paprika	7 mL
	pepper	
3 tbsp.	vegetable oil	45 mL
19 oz.	canned red cherries	540 mL
1 tsp.	soy sauce	5 mL
½ tsp.	ginger	2 mL
2 tbsp.	currants	30 mL
3 tbsp.	sherry	45 mL

Rinse turkey under cold water and pat dry. Mix flour, salt, paprika, and pepper. Shake turkey, a piece or two at a time, in flour mixture in a plastic bag to coat evenly. Brown on all sides in hot oil. Remove turkey from pan and drain off excess fat. Drain cherries, reserving juice, and pit if necessary. Combine cherry juice with soy sauce and ginger, and add to pan drippings. Heat, stirring to dissolve all brown from pan. Add cherries and currants and bring just to boiling point. Place turkey skin side down in a casserole and pour cherry mixture over it, ensuring that some fruit is on the meat. Bake, covered, at 375°F (190°C) for 1 hour. Turn turkey skin side up, baste with the juice in pan, drizzle with sherry and continue baking uncovered until fork tender, about 30 to 40 minutes. Serves 4 – 6.

overleaf:
Stuffed Chicken Thighs (page 134)

overleaf:
Chicken Paella (page 131)

POULTRY DRESSINGS & STUFFINGS

CREAM OF WHEAT STUFFING

2 cups	bread crumbs	500 mL
1/2 cup	flour	125 mL
1/2 cup	cream of wheat	125 mL
	salt	
	pepper	
1	onion, chopped	1
1 stalk	celery, chopped	1 stalk
1 tbsp.	parsley, chopped	15 mL
1 tbsp.	margarine, melted	15 mL
2	eggs, beaten	2
	water	

Combine all ingredients with enough water to make mixture fairly soft. Stuff chicken necks or any poultry. (Note: This mixture may be used for fish as well, substituting butter for margarine, if desired, and adding finely chopped gherkin.)

DRY POULTRY DRESSING

2 cups	dry bread crumbs	500 mL
1 cup	rolled oats	250 mL
1 medium	onion, grated	1 medium
1 1/2 tsp.	salt	7 mL
3/4 tsp.	pepper	3 mL
1/2 tsp.	poultry seasoning	2 mL
3/4 cup	schmaltz or shortening	175 mL
1/4 cup	hot water	50 mL

Combine dry ingredients. Rub in schmaltz. Stir in hot water to moisten. Stuff fowl.

BREAD STUFFING

5 cups	soft bread cubes	1.25 L
1 1/2 tsp.	salt	7 mL
1/4 tsp.	pepper	1 mL
1/2 tsp.	thyme	2 mL
1 tsp.	sage	5 mL

1/2 cup	onion, chopped	125 mL
1 1/2 cups	celery, chopped	375 mL
1/3 cup	margarine	75 mL
2/3 cup	hot water	150 mL

Mix bread crumbs with seasonings. Fry onion and celery in margarine until tender. Add to seasoned bread crumbs. Stir in hot water and mix lightly with a fork.

SPECIAL TURKEY DRESSING

4 cups	dry bread crumbs	1 L
4 tbsp.	cream of wheat	60 mL
2	onions, chopped	2
2 stalks	celery, chopped	2 stalks
1	carrot, grated	1
3 tbsp.	margarine, melted	45 mL
4	eggs	4
2 cups	water	500 mL
	salt	
	pepper	

Mix all ingredients well and stuff turkey.

EVERYDAY STUFFING

1	potato, minced	1
1	onion, minced	1
3 stalks	celery, minced	3 stalks
16 oz.	bread crumbs	454 g
4 tbsp.	margarine, melted	60 mL
	salt	
	pepper	
2	eggs, beaten	2

Mix potato, onion, and celery with just enough crumbs to bind together. Add margarine, salt and pepper, and then the eggs. Makes enough stuffing for an 8 lb. (4 kg) fowl.

CORN FLAKE STUFFING

3 tbsp.	shortening, melted	45 mL
12	salted crackers, crushed	12
2/3 cup	corn flakes	150 mL
3 tbsp.	oatmeal	45 mL
2 tbsp.	cream of wheat	30 mL
2 stalks	celery, diced	2 stalks
1 medium	onion, sliced	1 medium
1 tsp.	sugar	5 mL

Mix all together and stuff bird. (Note: The oatmeal must not be the instant kind.)

MASHED POTATO STUFFING

1/2 cup	onion, chopped	125 mL
1/3 cup	margarine	75 mL
4 cups	dry bread crumbs	1 L
1/3 cup	parsley, chopped	75 mL
1 1/2 cups	potato, mashed	375 mL
1/2 cup	bouillon	125 mL
1/2 tsp.	sage	2 mL
3/4 tsp.	thyme	3 mL
	salt	
	pepper	

Fry onion in margarine until slightly browned. Combine with remaining ingredients.

SESAME RICE STUFFING

1/3 cup	celery, chopped	75 mL
2 tbsp.	margarine	30 mL
3 tbsp.	sesame seeds, toasted	45 mL
1 tbsp.	onion flakes	15 mL
1 tbsp.	parsley flakes	15 mL
1/2 tsp.	salt	2 mL
	dash of thyme	
2 cups	long-grain rice, cooked	500 mL

Cook celery in margarine until tender but not brown. Add sesame seeds and seasonings. Combine with rice and toss lightly until mixed. Yields 2 cups (500 mL).

POTATO STUFFING

2 cups	hot potatoes, mashed	500 mL
1 cup	bread crumbs	250 mL
1/2 tsp.	salt	2 mL
1/2 tsp.	pepper	2 mL
1 tsp.	sage	5 mL
4 tbsp.	margarine	60 mL
1 large	onion, sliced	1 large
1 cup	celery, diced	250 mL
1 cup	mushrooms, chopped	250 mL

Mix potatoes, bread crumbs, and seasonings. Sauté onion and celery in margarine, add mushrooms, and mix together. Makes approximately 4 cups (1 L).

WILD RICE STUFFING

2 cups	wild rice	500 mL
4 cups	boiling water	1 L
1 tsp.	salt	5 mL
1	onion, chopped	1
1/2 cup	celery, chopped	125 mL
1/2 cup	water chestnuts, sliced	125 mL
	salt	
	pepper	

Wash wild rice several times until it is thoroughly clean. Drain. Stir slowly into boiling salted water. Cook without stirring, approximately 30 minutes, until nearly tender. Sauté onion and celery, and combine with wild rice and water chestnuts. Season to taste. Makes approximately 4 cups (1 L).

RICE AND RAISIN STUFFING

1 cup	rice, uncooked	250 mL
1 cup	seedless raisins	250 mL
1/2 cup	margarine, melted	125 mL
2 tbsp.	parsley, chopped	30 mL
	salt	
	pepper	

Boil rice until almost soft. Combine ingredients and season to taste.

Pickles, Jams & Sauces

Preserving food in ancient times was a necessity to guard against famine. Today, what a delight to bring the fruits of July to the tables of January. The sweet, tart aromas of jars of freshly-opened strawberry jam or orange marmalade, the shimmer of grape jelly, a basket of fresh rolls, and the setting for gratification is complete.

Piquancy, preserved in a glass jar. Sweet, sour, or spicy, pickles add spunk to a sandwich or a banquet. Crisp dills and pungent relishes flatter the mundane hot-dog and ground beef patty to gourmet heights. How impoverished the Thanksgiving turkey unadorned by Spiced Crabapples or Peaches. Sauerkraut, Watermelon Pickle, and Cucumber Relish fulfil the destiny of a corned beef brisket. Tiny white onions, gleaming like pearls through the cucumbers and carrots in a sealer of Sweet Mixed Pickles; ruby red Pickled Beets and delectable Pickled Eggs are condiments which add lustre to a buffet table.

Subtle sauces are, however, the epitome of meal enhancement. An eloquent Hollandaise enriches the enjoyment of fish or vegetables. The excitement a Barbecue or Creole Sauce adds to meat and poultry is immeasurable. Sweet and Sour Sauce is a savoury in which to dunk or simmer meaty tidbits. And luscious fruit sauces for puddings and cakes impart an elegance to the plainest dessert.

To gild the lily, to add variety and wit; that is the responsibility assumed by these piquant dining accessories.

PICKLES & RELISHES

PICKLED BEETS

1½ lb.	small beets	750 g
2 cups	water	500 mL
2 cups	vinegar	500 mL
1 tsp.	salt	5 mL
7 tbsp.	sugar	105 mL
1 tsp.	pickling spices	5 mL

Cook beets in salted water until just tender. Rinse in cold water and drain. Peel and slice beets and pack into hot sterilized jars. Tie pickling spices in a cheesecloth bag. Make a brine of the water, vinegar, salt, sugar, and pickling spices; bring to a boil and simmer 5 minutes. Pour hot liquid over the beets to cover completely. Seal the jars. Yields 2 – 3 pints (1 – 1.5 L).

FERMENTING BEETS

5 – 6	beets	5 – 6
8 cups	warm water	2 L
3 slices	rye bread	3 slices
1 tsp.	sugar	5 mL

Peel beets and grate into a ceramic pot. Add remaining ingredients. Cover. Leave in a cool room 3 to 4 days. Strain. The liquid will keep, refrigerated, in a tightly closed bottle for several weeks.

SPICED CRABAPPLES

	crabapples	
1½ cups	vinegar	375 mL
2½ cups	water	625 mL
6 cups	sugar	1.5 L
2 tsp.	whole cloves	10 mL
1 stick	cinnamon	1 stick

Sterilize jars. Wash crabapples, remove blossoms, and prick skins. Set aside. Tie cloves in a cheesecloth bag with cinnamon stick. Combine with remaining ingredients, bring to a boil, and boil 5 minutes. Put a few crabapples at a time in the syrup. Cook gently until apples are tender. Fill jars until syrup is used up. Yields 8 pints (4 L).

DILL PICKLES

	small cucumbers	
	fresh dill	
	alum	
	cream of tartar	
	garlic cloves	
2 quarts	water	2 L
1 quart	vinegar	1 L
½ cup	coarse salt	125 mL

Wipe cucumbers with a damp cloth but do not wash. In the bottom of each sterilized quart sealer, place a small piece of garlic and 1 tsp. (5 mL) each of alum and cream of tartar. Pack cucumbers tightly into jars, and top with a small amount of dill.

Combine remaining ingredients in a saucepan and heat to boiling. Let cool. Fill each sealer to the top with this brine. Seal tightly and store, inverted, in a dark place for 3 to 4 weeks before using.

PICKLED EGGS

12	eggs	12
3 cups	white vinegar	750 mL
1½ cups	water	375 mL
1½ tsp.	salt	7 mL
1 tsp.	peppercorns	5 mL
2 tsp.	mixed pickling spices	10 mL

Hard cook the eggs, drain, and cover with cold water. Tie pickling spices in a cheesecloth bag. Combine wth remaining ingredients in a saucepan and bring to boil. Simmer 10 minutes; cool. Remove shells from eggs and pack the eggs into sterilized jars. Pour cooled vinegar mixture over and seal. Yields approximately 3 pints (1.5 L).

SWEET MIXED PICKLES

1 lb.	cucumbers	500 g
2 heads	cauliflower	2 heads
2 cups	tiny onions	500 mL
4 cups	white or cider vinegar	1 L

2 cups	sugar	500 mL
1/2 cup	corn syrup	125 mL
1 tbsp.	mustard seed	15 mL
1 tbsp.	celery seed	15 mL
1 tsp.	whole cloves	5 mL
1/2 tsp.	turmeric	2 mL
2 tbsp.	coarse salt	30 mL

Cut cucumber into 1/2" (1.5 cm) slices. Break cauliflower into flowerettes. If onions are not tiny, cut into small pieces. Combine remaining ingredients and heat to boiling. Add vegetables, return to boil and boil gently for 2 minutes. Pack into hot sterilized jars. Seal. Yields 6 pints (3 L).

BREAD AND BUTTER PICKLES

3 lb.	small cucumbers	1.5 kg
3 cups	onion, thinly sliced	750 mL
1/2 cup	coarse salt	125 mL
4 cups	sugar	1 L
4 cups	white vinegar	1 L
2 tsp.	turmeric	10 mL
2 tsp.	mustard seed	10 mL
1 tsp.	celery seed	5 mL

Scrub cucumbers but do not peel. Slice thinly, about 1/8" (4 mm) thick. Combine cucumbers, onions, and salt. Cover and let stand for 12 hours (or add 2 trays of ice cubes and let stand 3 hours). Drain well. Combine remaining ingredients in a saucepan and bring to a boil. Add drained vegetables and return to full boil. Pack into hot sterilized jars, covering vegetables with hot liquid. Seal. Yields 6 pints (3 L).

PICKLED CARROTS

2 lb.	carrots	1 kg
4 cups	water	1 L
8 tsp.	salt	40 mL
1/2 cup	vinegar	125 mL
2 cloves	garlic, crushed	2 cloves
1 tsp.	dry mustard	5 mL
1 tsp.	white pepper	5 mL

1/4 cup	oil	50 mL
1 tsp.	sugar	5 mL
1 tsp.	oregano	5 mL
1/4 cup	green pepper, diced	50 mL

Clean carrots. Boil with water, 6 tsp. (30 mL) of the salt, and 1/4 cup (50 mL) vinegar until tender. Remove from liquid, cool, and slice into long quarters. Discard liquid. Combine remaining ingredients, including salt and vinegar, and bring to boil. Pour hot liquid over carrots. Seal in a jar or plastic container and store in refrigerator. Yields 4 pints (2 L).

PICKLED MUSHROOMS

1 cup	red wine vinegar	250 mL
2	whole cloves	2
1/2 cup	water	125 mL
5	peppercorns	5
1/2	bay leaf	1/2
2 tsp.	salt	10 mL
2 cloves	garlic, crushed	2 cloves
1 lb.	small fresh mushrooms	500 g
1 tbsp.	oil	15 mL

In a 2 quart (2 L) pot combine all except last 2 ingredients. Bring to a boil over high heat; drop mushrooms into liquid, reduce heat and simmer 10 minutes, uncovered. Stir occasionally. Cool to room temperature. Discard garlic and pour everything else into a 1 quart (1 L) jar. Slowly pour oil on top, cover jar with plastic wrap, and secure tightly. Keep in refrigerator at least 1 week before serving. Yields 1 quart (1 L).

PICKLED ONIONS

8 cups	tiny onions	2 L
1/2 cup	coarse salt	125 mL
3 cups	white vinegar	750 mL
3 cups	sugar	750 mL

Cover onions with cold water and peel. Sprinkle salt over peeled onions, cover, and let stand overnight. Drain and rinse with cold water. Combine vinegar and sugar. Bring to a boil and simmer 5 minutes. Add onions and simmer gently for 5 minutes more. Pack into hot sterilized jars, covering onions with hot liquid. Seal. Yields 4 pints (2 L).

SPICED PEACHES

30	peaches	30
10 cups	sugar	2.5 L
2 cups	cider vinegar	500 mL
4 sticks	cinnamon	4 sticks
60	whole cloves	60

Scald peaches and peel. Dissolve sugar and vinegar in oven at 300°F (150°C). Place a whole clove in both ends of each peach, slip into hot syrup and return to oven with cinnamon. Bake 3½ hours, basting every 30 minutes. Store in a cool place in a crock or sealers.

PICKLED PEARS

4 cups	vinegar	1 L
2 cups	water	500 mL
3 cups	sugar	750 mL
1 stick	cinnamon	1 stick
	small pears	

Boil vinegar, water, sugar, and cinnamon for 15 minutes. Add pears and cook slowly until pears appear clear and glazed. Place in sterilized sealers. Let syrup boil down until quite thick, pour over pears, and seal.

SAUERKRAUT

30 lb.	white cabbage, shredded	15 kg
¾ cup	coarse salt	175 mL
½ cup	sugar	125 mL
	water	
	caraway seed	

Mix salt and sugar. Put a layer of shredded cabbage in a pottery pickling crock. Rub the cabbage by hand with part of the salt and sugar mix, and pound with a wooden mallet until the juice comes out. Repeat in layers until all the salt and sugar mixture is used, pounding well until very juicy. Set a plate or board on top of cabbage and weigh it down with a large stone or other heavy object. Add cold water to 3'' (7.5 cm) above the plate. Cover with a clean cloth. Let stand in a cool place for 7 days. On the fourth day, remove the plate and weight and put a long clean stick or knife down to the bottom to create air holes for the gases to escape. Replace the plate, weight, and cloth. Repeat this procedure on the fifth and sixth days. On the seventh day pack in sterilized jars, adding caraway seed if desired. Store in cool place or refrigerator. 2 lb. (1 kg) cabbage yields 1 quart (1 L) sauerkraut.

TOMATO RELISH

6 quarts	ripe tomatoes	6 L
4 cups	onions, chopped	1 L
½ cup	coarse salt	125 mL
6 cups	celery, chopped	1.5 L
2 cups	green pepper, chopped	500 mL
2 cups	white vinegar	500 mL
2½ tbsp.	mustard seed	40 mL
¼ tsp.	cayenne pepper	1 mL
4 cups	sugar	1 L

Cover tomatoes and onions with salt. Let stand 8 to 10 hours. Drain. Combine with celery, green pepper, vinegar, mustard, and cayenne pepper. Cook for 10 minutes. Add sugar and boil 5 minutes longer. Store in refrigerator in sterilized jars. Yields 10 quarts (10 L).

WATERMELON PICKLE

4 lb.	watermelon rind	2 kg
1 tbsp.	lime (calcium oxide)	15 mL
8 cups	cold water	2 L
2 tbsp.	whole allspice	30 mL
2 tbsp.	whole cloves	30 mL
10 (2'')	cinnamon sticks	10 (5 cm)
4 cups	vinegar	1 L
4 cups	water	1 L
4 lb.	sugar	2 kg

Use watermelon rind with just a little of the pink. Cut into squares or fancy shapes. Dissolve lime in water and soak rind in this solution until firm. Drain. Cover rind with fresh water and cook 1 1/2 hours until tender, adding more water as needed. Drain. Tie spices in a cheesecloth bag and immerse in a kettle of vinegar, water, and sugar. Bring to boil, add rind, and cook 2 hours until rind is clear and transparent. Discard spice bag. Pack rind in clean, hot, sterile jars. Fill to tops with hot syrup and seal tightly. Yields 6 pints (3 L).

BEET CHOW-CHOW

4 cups	cabbage, chopped	1 L
1 cup	horseradish, chopped	250 mL
1 tsp.	pepper	5 mL
4 cups	cooked beets, chopped	1 L
1 tbsp.	salt	15 mL
1 cup	sugar	250 mL
	vinegar	

Combine all ingredients with enough vinegar to cover. Store in jars in refrigerator. Yields 5 pints (2.5 L).

CABBAGE AND PEPPER RELISH

2 heads	cabbage, shredded	2 heads
3	green peppers, chopped	3
2	red peppers, chopped	2
1/2 cup	salt	125 mL
4 cups	vinegar	1 L
3 cups	sugar	750 mL
1 tbsp.	celery seed	15 mL
2 tbsp.	mustard seed	30 mL

Mix cabbage, peppers, and salt. Let stand 24 hours. Strain water from cabbage. In a saucepan combine remaining ingredients and bring to boil. Cool, then strain over cabbage and peppers. Let stand 24 hours, stirring frequently. Pack in jars and seal tightly.

CORN RELISH

1	cauliflower	1
4 cups	cucumbers	1 L
3	green peppers	3
3	red peppers	3
8 cups	onion, diced	2 L
	boiling water	
	salt	
4 cups	vinegar	1 L
8 cups	sugar	2 L
3/4 cup	flour	175 mL
1/2 cup	dry mustard	125 mL
2 tbsp.	turmeric	30 mL
4 tbsp.	mustard seed	60 mL
1 tbsp.	celery seed	15 mL
15 oz.	canned corn, drained	425 mL

Grind cauliflower, cucumbers, and peppers. Mix in onions. Cover with boiling water and salt. Let stand overnight. Drain. Combine vinegar, sugar, flour, and spices. Bring to a boil. Add vegetables and corn. Yields 8 quarts (8 L).

CUCUMBER RELISH

9 medium	cucumbers	9 medium
5 medium	onions	5 medium
1/4 cup	coarse salt	50 mL
	boiling water	
2	red peppers, chopped	2
2 cups	vinegar	500 mL
1/2 cup	flour	125 mL
2 cups	sugar	500 mL
1 tbsp.	celery seed	15 mL
1 tbsp.	dry mustard	15 mL
1 tsp.	turmeric	5 mL

Grind cucumbers and onions together. Drain, reserving juice. Sprinkle with coarse salt and cover with boiling water. Let stand 4 hours. Drain. Add red peppers. Combine remaining ingredients and bring to a boil. Add vegetables, and cook 5 minutes. Pour into jars and seal. Yields 3 quarts (3 L).

RHUBARB RELISH

4 cups	rhubarb, chopped	1 L
2 cups	onion, sliced	500 mL
1 tsp.	salt	5 mL
½ tsp.	pepper	2 mL
2 tsp.	cinnamon	10 mL
½ tsp.	cloves	2 mL
1 tsp.	allspice	5 mL
3 cups	brown sugar	750 mL
2 cups	vinegar	500 mL

Mix all ingredients together in a saucepan. Simmer very slowly for 3 hours. Pour into clean jars. Yields 2 quarts (2 L).

JAMS & PRESERVES

FRUIT JAM

2½ cups	cantaloupe	625 mL
1	orange	1
1	lemon	1
2½ cups	peaches	625 mL
3½ cups	sugar	875 mL

Remove seeds and rind from cantaloupe and grind with orange and lemon. Dip peaches in boiling water for 30 seconds and plunge into cold water. Slip off skins, cut fruit in half and discard stones. Crush peaches and add to cantaloupe mixture. Cook, adding sugar when mixture comes to a boil. Continue cooking over moderate heat for 2 to 2½ hours. Pour into sterilized jars and seal. Yields 4 pints (2 L).

GRAPE JELLY

4 quarts	grapes	4 L
4	tart apples	4
¾ cup	water	175 mL
	sugar	

Cut up apples, core and all, and mix with washed grapes. Add water. Boil for 1½ hours. Strain in a jelly bag overnight. Measure out grape juice, return juice to heat and boil 20 minutes. Heat 1 cup (250 mL) sugar for each cup (250 mL) of grape juice. Add sugar to juice, bring to a boil, and pour out immediately into sterilized jars. Seal with paraffin. Store in a cool, dry place. Yields 4 pints (2 L).

ORANGE MARMALADE

3	bitter oranges	3
2	lemons	2
1	grapefruit	1
11 cups	water	2.75 L
8 cups	sugar	2 L

Wash fruit well, cut in quarters, and remove seeds. Squeeze out juice. Shred pulp and peel. Mix fruit and juice with water; soak 24 hours. Next day, boil mixture for 1 hour. Add sugar and boil approximately 30 minutes until slightly cooled juice falls cleanly from a spoon in a single sheet (test for jelly). Pour into sterilized jars and seal with wax. Yields 3 pints (1.5 L).

PEACH CONSERVE

4 lb.	peaches	2 kg
2 lb.	pears	1 kg
1	lemon	1
1	orange	1
14 oz.	pineapple, crushed	398 mL
5 lb.	sugar	2.5 kg

Peel peaches and pears. Chop with lemon and orange, removing all seeds, then add pineapple and sugar. Boil for 2 hours. Yields 6 pints (3 L).

STRAWBERRY JAM

5 cups	strawberries	1.25 L
½ cup	lemon juice	125 mL
5 cups	sugar	1.25 L

overleaf:
Pickles (pages 144–6)

Use only perfectly ripe strawberries in excellent condition. Hull, wash, and dry berries. Stand them in pan in which they are to be cooked, cover with sugar, and allow to stand overnight. Bring to a rolling boil and boil for exactly 8 minutes. (The timing is important.) Then add lemon juice. Bring to a boil again and boil for exactly 3 minutes. Remove from heat and cool in same pan. When completely cool, pour into sterilized glasses or jars and seal with paraffin. Yields 24 oz. (625 mL).

STRAWBERRY AND RHUBARB JAM

4 cups	strawberries, crushed	1 L
1 cup	rhubarb	250 mL
3 1/2 cups	sugar	875 mL

Cook strawberries and rhubarb about 15 minutes. Add hot sugar and cook 15 minutes longer. Seal with paraffin wax in sterilized jelly jars. Yields 2 pints (1 L).

SAUCES

ANISE FRUIT MARINADE

3/4 cup	sugar	175 mL
1 1/2 cups	water	375 mL
1 1/2 tbsp.	lemon juice	20 mL
1/4 tsp.	salt	1 mL
1 tbsp.	anise seed	15 mL

Combine ingredients in a saucepan and bring to a gentle boil. Cook for 15 minutes. Strain over cut up fruit in sterilized jars. Seal lids and refrigerate.

BLENDER HOLLANDAISE SAUCE

2	eggs	2
1/2 tsp.	salt	2 mL
1/2 cup	soft margarine	125 mL
1 slice	onion	1 slice
	dash of white pepper	
2 tbsp.	lemon juice	30 mL
1/2 cup	hot water	125 mL

Blend all ingredients until smooth, gradually adding the hot water last. Pour into top of double boiler. Cook over hot water, stirring constantly, to consistency of custard. Serve hot or cold over vegetables. Yields 1 1/2 cups (375 mL).

RED SEAFOOD COCKTAIL SAUCE

1 cup	ketchup	250 mL
1/4 cup	lemon juice	50 mL
1 tsp.	salt	5 mL
1 tsp.	Worcestershire sauce	5 mL
	dash of Tabasco sauce	
4 tsp.	prepared horseradish	20 mL

Combine all ingredients in a tightly covered jar and chill. Keeps for weeks in refrigerator. Yields 2 cups (500 mL).

SEAFOOD MAYONNAISE

1 cup	mayonnaise	250 mL
1 tbsp.	shallots, chopped	15 mL
1 tbsp.	onion, chopped	15 mL
1 tbsp.	chives, chopped	15 mL
1 tbsp.	water	15 mL
1 tbsp.	fresh parsley, chopped	15 mL
2	hard-boiled eggs, grated	2
	salt	
	pepper	

In blender, process mayonnaise and vegetables until vegetables are fine. Add eggs, and season to taste. Refrigerate until needed, up to 2 weeks.

BECHAMEL SAUCE

3 cups	milk	750 mL
2 tbsp.	onion, minced	30 mL
4 tbsp.	butter	60 mL
1/3 cup	flour	75 mL
1/2 tsp.	salt	2 mL
	dash of white pepper	

Bring milk and onion to a boil. Let stand 10 minutes, then strain. In a saucepan, melt the butter and stir in the flour with seasonings. Cook over low heat, stirring constantly, until the flour turns golden. Gradually add in milk and cook over low heat, stirring constantly, until sauce boils. Continue cooking for 20 minutes, stirring frequently. Yields approximately 2 cups (500 mL). (Note: For a richer sauce for desserts, add 1 egg yolk beaten with 4 tbsp. (60 mL) whipping cream, for each cup (250 mL) of sauce. Add a little of the hot sauce to the egg mixture first, before mixing it into the rest of the sauce.)

BARBECUE SAUCE AND MARINADE

1	onion, chopped	1
2 cloves	garlic, chopped	2 cloves
2 cups	ketchup	500 mL
1/2 cup	vinegar	125 mL
1 cup	oil	250 mL
2 tbsp.	Worcestershire sauce	30 mL
1/2 tsp.	salt	2 mL
1/2 tsp.	pepper	2 mL
1 tsp.	sugar	5 mL

Mix all ingredients well. Let stand overnight. Use as required as marinade and for basting.

BASIC GRAVY

2 tbsp.	fat drippings	30 mL
2 cups	water or bouillon	500 mL
2 tbsp.	cornstarch	30 mL
1/2 cup	cold water	125 mL

Measure fat into roasting pan. Stir in liquid. Cook over medium heat, stirring to loosen browned particles. Remove from heat. Mix cornstarch and water and stir into pan. Add seasonings. Stirring constantly, bring to a boil over medium heat. Boil 2 minutes. Yields 2 cups (500 mL).

CREOLE SAUCE

1 medium	onion, diced	1 medium
6 large	mushrooms, diced	6 large
28 oz.	canned tomatoes	796 mL
1/2	green pepper, diced	1/2
2 stalks	celery, diced	2 stalks
	salt	
	pepper	

Brown onion and mushrooms in a little oil then add remaining ingredients. Season to taste. Simmer 5 minutes or more. Serve over fish or meat.

MUSHROOM WINE SAUCE

2 tbsp.	margarine	30 mL
1/4 lb.	fresh mushrooms, sliced	125 g
2 tbsp.	onion, chopped	30 mL
1 clove	garlic, crushed	1 clove
2 tsp.	flour	10 mL
1/4 tsp.	salt	1 mL
	dash of pepper	
2 tbsp.	tomato paste	30 mL
1/2 cup	dry red wine	125 mL
1/4 cup	water	50 mL

Melt margarine over medium heat. Sauté mushrooms, onion, and garlic until onion is transparent. Remove from heat. Stir in flour, salt, pepper, and tomato paste. Blend in wine and water. Bring to a boil, stirring frequently. Cover, reduce heat, and simmer 20 minutes.

MUSHROOM SAUCE

1 lb.	fresh mushrooms	500 g
3 tbsp.	margarine	45 mL

2 tbsp.	flour	30 mL
1/2 tsp.	salt	2 mL
	pepper	
1/2 tsp.	sugar	1 mL
1/2 tsp.	lemon juice	2 mL
1/4 tsp.	browning sauce	1 mL
2 tbsp.	sherry	30 mL

Scrub mushrooms in cold water, but do not peel. Cut mushrooms into large chunks, leaving small ones whole. Melt margarine over low heat, add flour, and stir constantly while it browns. Add salt, pepper, sugar, and lemon juice and stir to a smooth paste. Add browning sauce and mushrooms; mix. Cover and simmer slowly 6 to 8 minutes. Remove from heat. For a thicker sauce, remove cover immediately. Add sherry just before serving over fish or meat.

ORANGE SAUCE

1 tbsp.	cornstarch	15 mL
1/2 cup	orange juice	125 mL
6 oz.	orange juice concentrate	180 mL
1/2 cup	orange liqueur	125 mL
2 tbsp.	brown sugar	30 mL

Mix cornstarch with orange juice, add to remaining ingredients, and cook over medium heat until thick. Simmer 5 to 10 minutes. Serve over duck or chicken.

SPANISH SAUCE

3 medium	onions, sliced	3 medium
6 stalks	celery, diced	6 stalks
1 lb.	fresh mushrooms, sliced	500 g
2	green peppers, diced	2
3 tbsp.	oil	45 mL
10 oz.	condensed tomato soup	284 mL
5 1/2 oz.	tomato paste	156 mL
7 1/2 oz.	tomato sauce	213 mL
9 oz.	pimento, diced	256 mL
1/2 cup	chili sauce	125 mL
1/2 cup	ketchup	125 mL
	dash of Tabasco sauce	

1 tsp.	sugar	5 mL
	seasoning salt	
	pepper	

Sauté onions, celery, mushrooms, and green peppers in oil. Combine remaining ingredients, seasoning to taste. Add sautéed vegetables and simmer 30 minutes. This sauce may be frozen.

SWEET AND SOUR SAUCE

1/2 cup	white vinegar	125 mL
1/2 cup	water	125 mL
1/4 cup	orange juice	50 mL
1 cup	crushed pineapple	250 mL
2/3 cup	sugar	150 mL
1 1/2 tbsp.	ketchup or chili sauce	20 mL
1 tbsp.	oil	15 mL
1 1/2	green peppers, chopped	1 1/2
1/2 tsp.	salt	2 mL
2 tbsp.	cornstarch	30 mL
2	tomatoes	2

In a large saucepan, combine all ingredients except cornstarch and tomatoes. Bring to a boil, stirring often. Make the cornstarch into a paste with some of the hot sauce. Peel and quarter the tomatoes, and add to sauce in pan together with cornstarch paste. Bring to a boil. Simmer covered for 10 minutes. Serve over steamed vegetables, sautéed chicken livers, or any meat you wish to make into a sweet and sour dish.

SWEET AND SOUR SAUCE

1/2 cup	white vinegar	125 mL
1 cup	brown sugar	250 mL
1 cup	water	250 mL
1 cup	tomato juice	250 mL
1/2 tsp.	soy sauce	2 mL
1 tbsp.	ketchup	15 mL
2 tbsp.	cornstarch	30 mL
2 tbsp.	cold water	30 mL

Bring vinegar, brown sugar, water, tomato juice, soy sauce, and ketchup to a boil. Take care not to burn the sugar. Combine cornstarch and cold water and pour into boiling sauce, stirring. Serve over ribs, meatballs, chicken wings.

TOASTED ALMOND SAUCE

½ cup	blanched almonds	125 mL
½ cup	butter, melted	125 mL
¾ cup	brown sugar	175 mL
1 cup	cream	250 mL
	pinch of salt	
2	egg yolks, slightly beaten	2
¼ tsp.	brandy flavouring	1 mL

Sauté almonds in butter. Transfer to the top of a double boiler and stir in brown sugar, cream, and salt. Cook over hot water, stirring constantly, until sugar dissolves. Stir a small amount of hot mixture into egg yolks mixed with brandy flavouring. Combine with remaining sauce and cook until thickened, stirring constantly. Serve hot or cold. If serving cold, dilute with 1 – 2 tbsp. (15 – 30 mL) of cream. Yields 2 cups (500 mL).

CHERRY SAUCE

15 oz.	canned red cherries	425 mL
½ cup	sugar	125 mL
2 tbsp.	cornstarch	30 mL

Pit and drain the cherries, reserving juice. Combine sugar and cornstarch. Gradually stir in cherry juice. Cook, stirring constantly, until thickened. Stir in the cherries. Simmer 5 to 10 minutes. Chill. Serve over cheesecake. Yields 2 cups (500 mL).

CRANBERRY SAUCE

¾ cup	sugar	175 mL
¾ cup	water	175 mL
12 oz.	cranberries	340 g
½ cup	walnuts, chopped	125 mL
1	orange, thinly sliced	1

Boil sugar and water. Add berries, stirring until berries pop. Stir in nuts and orange. Cool. Yields 2 cups (500 mL).

LEMON SAUCE

½ cup	sugar	125 mL
2 tbsp.	cornstarch	30 mL
1/16 tsp.	salt	0.25 mL
1 cup	boiling water	250 mL
1 tsp.	lemon rind, grated	5 mL
2 tbsp.	lemon juice	30 mL
2 tbsp.	butter	30 mL

Mix sugar, cornstarch, and salt. Moisten with a little cold water. Add the boiling water and lemon rind. Cook until thick, and raw starch flavour has disappeared. Remove from heat. Add lemon juice and butter. Strain if desired. (Note: 3 tbsp. (45 mL) flour may be substituted for the cornstarch.) Yields 2 cups (500 mL).

RUM SAUCE

¼ cup	orange juice	50 mL
3 tsp.	cornstarch	15 mL
1½ cups	brown sugar	375 mL
¼ cup	water	50 mL
¼ tsp.	cinnamon	1 mL
2 tbsp.	margarine	30 mL
2 tsp.	lemon juice	10 mL
1 tsp.	vanilla	5 mL
3 tbsp.	dark rum	45 mL

Mix orange juice and cornstarch together in the top of a double boiler. Combine remaining ingredients, except rum, and add. Bring to boil over hot water, stirring until thick. Lastly add rum. Yields 2 cups (500 mL).

Breads, Pancakes & Muffins

"Man doth not live by bread only . . ." (Deuteronomy 8:3). Especially when he can savour the delights of bagels, muffins, and Danish pastry! Bread has been sanctified in the Bible, venerated by poets, and vilified by dieters.

Since Biblical times, great significance has been placed on bread. Braiding the Challah to represent the twelve loaves on the Temple altar on the Sabbath. Sprinkling sesame seeds on the unbaked loaf to signify manna from the heavens. Bringing bread and salt to a family in a new home. In Judaism, a meal without bread is no meal at all.

Men love bread. "Here with a loaf of bread beneath the bough/ A flask of wine/ A book of verse/ And thou." Bread conjured up romantic notions for Omar Khayyam. And what is bachelors' fare? Bread, cheese, and kisses.

What is bread, but an uncomplicated fusion of flour, water and leaven, fortified at times with grains and honey, kneaded, and baked in the oven. Whether the dough is prepared with wholemeal, rye, or potato flour; whether the shape of the loaf is round, cylindrical, oblong, or unleavened; every nation of the world lays claim to its own version of the "staff of life."

To enhance perfection is to create Orange Cranberry Bread, Banana Nut Bread, or a loaf staunch with integrity and good health—spiced pumpkin and wholewheat. There are festive breads and symbolic breads. Rolls which are folded, braided and twisted, glazed, filled, and iced. Varieties of Hamantashen enough for ten Purims.

Let us "break bread"—an invitation of friendship.

BREADS & BUNS

WHITE BREAD

2 tbsp.	yeast	30 mL
1 ¼ cups	warm water	300 mL
1 cup	lukewarm milk	250 mL
3 tbsp.	sugar	45 mL
2 tsp.	salt	10 mL
2 tbsp.	shortening	30 mL
1 tbsp.	soft butter	15 mL
7 cups	flour	1.75 L

Dissolve the yeast in ⅓ cup (75 mL) of the warm water. Combine remaining water, milk, sugar, salt, shortening, and butter in a large bowl. Add the dissolved yeast and enough of the flour to make a soft sticky dough. Place remaining flour on a pastry board, turn the dough out on top of it, and knead until the dough is smooth and the flour absorbed. If dough is still sticky, add a little more flour. Place dough in a greased bowl and turn once so greased side is on top. Cover and let rise in a warm place for 1 hour, or until the dough doubles in bulk. Punch down, turn dough again, and let rise for 30 minutes or until almost double in bulk. Divide dough in half and let rest for 10 minutes. Shape each half into a loaf and place in a well-greased 9" x 5" (2 L) loaf pan. Cover and let rise in a warm spot 30 minutes. Bake in a pre-heated 425°F (220°C) oven for 25 minutes or until loaves sound hollow when tapped. Remove to racks to cool. Makes 2 loaves.

CLASSIC CHALLAH

3 tbsp.	yeast	45 mL
2 ¼ cups	lukewarm water	550 mL
1 tbsp.	salt	15 mL
½ cup	sugar	125 mL
⅓ cup	oil	75 mL
4	eggs	4
9 cups	flour	2.25 L

Dissolve yeast in water and let stand 10 minutes. Add salt, sugar, oil, and eggs. Add flour, 3 cups

(750 mL) at a time, beating well after each addition. Knead dough on a lightly floured board for approximately 7 minutes until smooth and elastic, adding more flour as necessary, possibly up to 1 cup (250 mL) more. Place in a large greased bowl, turning the dough once so the greased side is on top. Cover with a clean, damp towel and let stand in a warm place to rise for 1½ hours or until double in bulk. Punch down completely so there are no air pockets. Divide dough into 6; shape into ropes about 1" (2.5 cm) in diameter. Braid 3 ropes together to form a loaf. Repeat for second loaf. Place onto greased cookie sheets. Let rise again until double in size. Brush with glaze and sprinkle with sesame or poppy seeds. Bake at 350°F (180°C) for 30 minutes. Remove to racks to cool.

Glazes for Challah

1 egg yolk, on its own, mixed with a few drops of water, or mixed with 1 tsp. (5 mL) sugar. Or use a whole egg, on its own or mixed with 1½ tsp. (7 mL) sugar.

Traditionally the challah is topped with poppy seeds as a reminder of the manna of the desert.

CHALLAH

2 tbsp.	yeast	30 mL
2 ½ cups	warm water	625 mL
6 tbsp.	sugar	90 mL
2 tsp.	salt	10 mL
⅓ cup	oil	75 mL
4	eggs	4
8 ⅔ cups	flour	2.15 L
1	egg yolk	1
1 tsp.	cold water	5 mL
4 tsp.	poppy or sesame seeds	20 mL

Dissolve the yeast in warm water in a large bowl. Add the sugar, salt, oil, eggs, and 6 cups (1.5 L) of flour. Beat thoroughly with a wooden spoon. Gradually add more flour until the dough is too stiff to beat with a spoon. Place remaining flour on a pastry board, turn dough out on top of it and knead until dough is smooth and elastic and all the flour absorbed. If dough is still quite sticky, add a little more flour. Place dough in a large bowl, cover, and let rise in a warm place for 1½ hours or until triple in bulk. Punch dough down, and divide into 12 portions. On a lightly floured board, shape each portion into a rope about 1'' (2.5 cm) in diameter. Braid 3 ropes together. Repeat with remaining ropes. Place each braid in a well-greased 9'' x 5'' (2 L) loaf pan and let rise in a warm place for 45 minutes, until almost triple in bulk. Brush the tops of the risen dough with the egg yolk mixed with cold water, and sprinkle with poppy seeds or sesame seeds. Bake in a preheated 375°F (190°C) oven for 25 to 30 minutes until golden brown. Remove to racks to cool. Makes 4 loaves.

PUMPERNICKEL BREAD

2 tbsp.	yeast	30 mL
1 tsp.	sugar	5 mL
½ cup	lukewarm water	125 mL
1½ tbsp.	salt	25 mL
¼ cup	molasses	50 mL
1 cup	potatoes, mashed	250 mL
1 tbsp.	shortening	15 mL
2 cups	boiling water	500 mL
1¼ tbsp.	caramel colouring	18 mL
½ cup	yellow cornmeal	125 mL
4 cups	rye flour	1 L
2 tbsp.	caraway seeds	30 mL
5 cups	flour	1.25 L

Dissolve yeast with sugar in warm water. In a large mixing bowl combine the salt, molasses, mashed potatoes, and shortening. Pour boiling water over and stir to mix well. Cool. When lukewarm, add yeast mixture. Stir in colouring to desired colour. Combine cornmeal with rye flour, caraway seeds, and all but 1 cup (250 mL) of the white flour. Stir into the liquid mixture, beating well until it comes away from the sides of the bowl. Turn out and knead, adding enough reserved flour to form a soft dough. Cover and let rest 15 minutes. Knead another 15 minutes, add-

ing more flour if necessary. Place in a greased bowl, cover, and let rise until double in bulk. Punch down. Turn out and knead a few turns. Cover, let rest 10 minutes, then shape into 2 round loaves. Brush on corn or potato starch glaze, if desired (see below). Place on a greased baking sheet, cover with a tea towel, and let rise until double in size. Bake at 350°F (180°C) for 50 minutes. Cool on racks.

RYE BREAD

2 tbsp.	yeast	30 mL
2½ cups	lukewarm water	625 mL
¼ cup	honey	50 mL
1 tbsp.	salt	15 mL
2 tbsp.	shortening, melted	30 mL
2½ cups	rye flour	625 mL
2 tbsp.	caraway seeds	30 mL
6 cups	flour	1.5 L

Dissolve the yeast with the honey in lukewarm water. When yeast bubbles up, add salt and cooled shortening. Stir well. Beat in rye flour and caraway seeds. Add enough white flour to make a soft dough. Knead until smooth and elastic, adding more flour as necessary. Place in a greased bowl, cover, and let rise until at least double in bulk. Punch down. Knead for another 2 to 3 minutes. Return dough to bowl, cover, and let rest for 10 minutes. Shape into 2 loaves and place on a baking sheet sprinkled with cornmeal. Cover with a tea towel and let rise until doubled in size. With a sharp knife, make several crosswise cuts on the tops of the loaves. Let rise a few more minutes. Bake at 400°F (200°C) for 35 minutes. Potato or cornstarch glaze may be brushed on just before and after baking. Cool on racks.

Starch Glaze

5 tsp.	corn or potato starch	25 mL
7 tbsp.	boiling water	105 mL

Mix starch with boiling water. Cook until thick but soft enough to brush on bread.

CHEESE BREAD

1 tbsp.	yeast	15 mL
¼ cup	hot water	50 mL
2⅓ cups	flour	575 mL
2 tbsp.	sugar	30 mL
1 tsp.	salt	5 mL
¼ tsp.	baking soda	1 mL
1 cup	sour cream	250 mL
1	egg	1
1 cup	Cheddar cheese, grated	250 mL
½ tsp.	pepper	2 mL

Grease 2 empty 1 lb. (500 g) coffee cans. In the large bowl of an electric mixer, dissolve yeast in hot water. Add 1⅓ cups (325 mL) of the flour with sugar, salt, baking soda, sour cream, and egg. Blend 30 seconds at low speed, scraping the bowl constantly. Beat 2 minutes at high speed, scraping the bowl occasionally. Add remaining flour, cheese, and pepper and blend thoroughly for approximately 30 seconds at high speed. Divide the batter between the cans. Let rise in a warm place 50 minutes. Bake at 350°F (180°C) for 40 minutes or until golden brown. Remove immediately onto cooling racks.

ORANGE BREAD

1 cup	orange juice	250 mL
1 cup	boiling water	250 mL
1 tbsp.	yeast	15 mL
3 tbsp.	sugar	45 mL
6 cups	flour	1.5 L
1 tsp.	salt	5 mL
4 tbsp.	orange rind, grated	60 mL
1	egg yolk, beaten	1

Add orange juice to water and cool to lukewarm. Dissolve yeast in lukewarm liquid, then add 2 tbsp. (30 mL) of the sugar and half the flour. Beat hard and set aside to rise until dough has doubled in bulk. Add salt, remaining sugar, orange rind, and egg yolk. Mix well and add remainder of the flour to make a fairly stiff dough. Turn onto a floured board and knead well, then set into a greased bowl, cover, and let rise until light.

Punch down before shaping into 2 loaves. Place in well-greased loaf pans, cover, and let rise until double in bulk. Bake at 400°F (200°C) for 15 minutes. Reduce heat to 350°F (180°C) and continue baking for about 40 minutes longer.

PIZZA

Crust

1 tbsp.	yeast	15 mL
¼ cup	lukewarm water	50 mL
1 tbsp.	sugar	15 mL
1 tsp.	salt	5 mL
1 tbsp.	shortening	15 mL
1 cup	boiling water	250 mL
2¾ cups	flour	675 mL
3 tsp.	oil	15 mL
	Parmesan cheese, grated	

Soften yeast in lukewarm water for 10 minutes. Combine sugar, salt, shortening, and boiling water in a large bowl, stirring until sugar dissolves. Cool to lukewarm. Add 1½ cups (375 mL) of the flour and beat until smooth. Add enough of the remaining flour to make a dough just barely firm enough to handle. Knead until smooth on a lightly floured board. Divide into thirds. Knead each piece into a smooth ball. Flatten, then roll out to fit a greased 9'' (1 L) pie plate. Press around the edges to make a slight rim. Cover with a towel and let rise 15 minutes. Brush lightly with oil, sprinkle with Parmesan, and top with filling.

Filling

1 clove	garlic	1 clove
2 tbsp.	oil	30 mL
1	onion, sliced	1
½ cup	tomato paste	125 mL
2 cups	tomatoes, drained	500 mL
¼ tsp.	oregano	1 mL
½ tsp.	salt	2 mL
	dash of pepper	

Sauté garlic in oil until brown. Discard garlic. Add onions to oil and cook until golden brown. Stir in tomato paste, tomatoes, and seasonings. Simmer covered until thickened, about 1 hour. Spread filling over the 3 pizza crusts, sprinkle with Parmesan or Romano cheese, and top with 12 oz. (360 g) grated Mozzarella cheese. Bake at 425°F (220°C) for 20 to 25 minutes.

Variations
Add mushrooms, green pepper, anchovies, olives as desired.

PIZZA BREAD

1	French bread	1
2/3 cup	butter	170 mL
	garlic powder	
	oregano	
14 oz.	meatless spaghetti sauce	420 g
24 oz.	Mozzarella cheese slices	680 g
	Parmesan cheese, grated	

Cut bread diagonally in 1/2'' (1 cm) slices. Do not cut all the way through, but leave slices (approximately 18) joined at the bottom of the loaf. Beat butter with garlic powder and oregano until creamy. Apply generously to both sides of each slice. Cut cheese slices in half and place between bread slices. Spoon sauce between slices and sprinkle with Parmesan cheese. Sprinkle Parmesan over top of loaf. Wrap in foil. Bake at 350°F (180°C) for 30 to 45 minutes. Open foil on top and serve. Serves 9.

CELERY BREAD

1	French bread	1
1/2 cup	butter, softened	125 mL
1/4 tsp.	salt	1 mL
1/4 tsp.	paprika	1 mL
1/2 tsp.	celery seed	2 mL
	dash of cayenne pepper	

Cut bread diagonally in 1/2'' (1 cm) slices, leaving loaf joined at the bottom to retain loaf shape. Mix ingredients together and spread on both sides of slices. Wrap in foil and bake at 450°F (230°C) for 5 minutes.

ONION ROLLS

1 recipe	Challah dough	1 recipe
1	onion, chopped	1
1 tbsp.	poppy seed	15 mL
1 tsp.	caraway seed	5 mL
	coarse salt	

Divide dough into 36 pieces. On a lightly floured board, roll out each piece of dough 1/4'' (6 cm) thick. Combine onion with poppy and caraway seeds. Reserving a small amount of mixture to top rolls, sprinkle onion mixture on top of each piece of rolled dough. Work it slightly into dough with a rolling pin. Sprinkle with coarse salt and prick dough all over with a fork so that the salt is pushed into dough. Shape each piece into a ball and place on a greased baking pan. Flatten slightly. Brush buns with desired glaze for challah. Sprinkle with reserved filling. Cover with a clean towel and let rise in a warm place until double in size. Uncover and bake at 375°F (190°C) for 20 to 25 minutes until golden.

SWEET POTATO ROLLS

2	sweet potatoes, scrubbed	2
1	egg, lightly beaten	1
2 tbsp.	honey	30 mL
1 tbsp.	unsalted butter, softened	15 mL
2 tsp.	salt	10 mL
1/2 tsp.	pepper	2 mL
1 tbsp.	yeast	15 mL
3 1/2 cups	flour	875 mL
1	egg white, lightly beaten	1

Bring sweet potatoes to a boil in water to cover in a medium saucepan. Reduce heat, and simmer uncovered until fork tender, approximately 30 minutes. Drain, reserving 1/2 cup (125 mL) of liquid. Skin potatoes and mash by hand. Do not purée. Cool to room temperature and stir in egg, honey, butter, salt and pepper.

Heat reserved potato liquid to very warm. Dissolve yeast in liquid in a large bowl. Stir in mashed potato mixture and enough flour to make a soft dough. Knead on a lightly floured surface until smooth and elastic, about 10 minutes, adding flour to prevent sticking. Place dough in a large greased bowl, cover with plastic wrap, and let rise 1½ to 2 hours. Punch down. Knead 1 minute; let rest, covered, for 10 minutes. Divide dough into 24 equal pieces and shape into smooth balls. Place 2 each in greased muffin tins. Let rise at room temperature until doubled, approximately 1 hour. Brush rolls with egg white. Bake on centre rack of preheated 400°F (200°C) oven for about 20 minutes until golden and bottoms sound hollow when tapped. Remove from pan. Makes 12 rolls.

PITA BREAD

1 tbsp.	yeast	15 mL
½ tsp.	sugar	2 mL
1⅓ cups	lukewarm water	325 mL
2 tbsp.	olive oil	30 mL
2 tsp.	salt	10 mL
4 cups	flour	1 L

Dissolve yeast in lukewarm water with the sugar. When mixture is bubbly add the oil, salt, and flour. Mix well, turn out, and knead until smooth and elastic. Place in a greased bowl. Cover and let rise until double in bulk. Punch down. Knead a few times, then divide the dough into 6 pieces and shape each into a ball. Place the balls together and cover with the upturned bowl. Let them rest for 30 minutes. Working with 2 balls at a time, roll each ball into a circle about ⅛'' (3 mm) thick. Board and rolling pin need to be well floured so that the thin dough will not stick or tear. Place one round on top of the other on a baking sheet dusted with cornmeal. Bake on lower rack in a 500°F (260°C) oven for 5 minutes. Do not open door during this time. Move sheet to upper third of oven and bake 3 to 5 minutes longer. Remove from baking sheet and wrap in foil to prevent bread from hardening. Repeat with next 2 portions of dough until all 6 are baked. Bread will collapse but the two halves are easily parted. Cut pita across diameter and fill as desired.

BAGELS

1 tbsp.	yeast	15 mL
2 cups	lukewarm water	500 mL
¼ cup	sugar	50 mL
3 tbsp.	oil	45 mL
1 tbsp.	salt	15 mL
5 cups	flour	1.25 L
8 cups	boiling water	4 L
2 tbsp.	honey	30 mL

Dissolve yeast in warm water with 1 tsp. (5 mL) of the sugar. When it has bubbled up well, add remaining sugar, oil, salt, and enough flour to make a fairly firm dough. Turn out and knead well until dough is smooth and elastic. Place in a greased bowl, cover, and let rise until double in bulk. Punch down and let rise once more. Turn out on a floured board and knead 5 minutes. Let rest, covered, for 15 minutes. Roll into a rectangle about 12'' x 10'' (30 x 25 cm) and 1'' (2.5 cm) thick. Cut into 12 strips, each 10'' (25 cm) long. Loop each strip around back of hand and join the ends, rolling the join back and forth under or between palms to seal. Place rings on ungreased baking sheets and cover with a tea towel. Let stand 20 minutes in a warm place. Boil water with honey in a large wide-mouthed pot. Reduce heat to simmer. Gently slide in 2 or 3 bagels. Cook for 7 minutes, turning once. Remove and place on two or three thicknesses of tea towel and cool for 5 minutes. Place on an ungreased baking sheet. Glaze with beaten egg mixed with a little water, sprinkle with poppy or sesame seeds or coarse salt, and bake at 375°F (190°C) for 20 to 25 minutes until done.

AIR BUNS

1 tbsp.	yeast	15 mL
½ cup	lukewarm water	125 mL
½ cup	sugar	130 mL
1 tsp.	salt	5 mL
½ cup	shortening	125 mL
2 tbsp.	vinegar	30 mL
3½ cups	warm water	875 mL
10 cups	flour	2.5 L

Dissolve yeast in lukewarm water with 1 tsp. (5 mL) of the sugar. In a large bowl, combine remaining sugar, salt, shortening, vinegar, and warm water. Add yeast and enough flour so dough does not stick to hands. Place in a greased bowl, cover, and let rise 2 hours. Punch down. With greased hands, form dough into small balls, and set on greased pans; allow to rise, covered, for 3 hours. Bake at 400°F (200°C) for 20 minutes until golden. Brush with butter while still hot if a soft crust is desired. Yields 48.

CARAWAY BREAD STICKS

1 cup	lukewarm water	250 mL
1 tbsp.	yeast	15 mL
1 tbsp.	sugar	15 mL
1 1/2 tsp.	salt	7 mL
1/2 tsp.	nutmeg	2 mL
1 tbsp.	caraway seeds	15 mL
1 tbsp.	leaf sage, crumbled	15 mL
1/4 cup	shortening	50 mL
1	egg	1
3 1/4 cups	flour, sifted	800 mL

Dissolve yeast in warm water in a mixing bowl. Stir in remaining ingredients. Beat, then knead vigorously. Cover with a towel and refrigerate at least 2 hours, or overnight. Divide chilled dough into 36 parts. Roll into 6'' (15 cm) cigar-shaped strips and place 1'' (2.5 cm) apart on a greased baking sheet. Brush with melted shortening, sprinkle with coarse salt, and cover with a towel. Let rise until double in bulk, about 2 hours. Bake at 400°F (200°C) for 12 to 15 minutes until crisp and golden brown. Yields 36.

ICE KUFFLE

1 cup	shortening	250 mL
4	eggs	4
1 cup	sugar	250 mL
1 tbsp.	yeast	15 mL
1 cup	cream	250 mL
1/2 tsp.	salt	2 mL
5 cups	flour	1.25 L
2 tsp.	cinnamon	10 mL

Cream shortening. Beat eggs until thick and add with 2 tbsp. (30 mL) of the sugar. Dissolve yeast in cream and add to shortening mixture together with salt. Mix thoroughly. Add enough flour to make a dough stiff enough to knead. Turn onto a slightly floured board and knead lightly until smooth. Place in a bowl, cover, and set in a cold place about 3 or 4 hours. Sprinkle half the sugar over the board, set dough on sugar and roll out from left to right. Roll out again and fold; repeat 2 or 3 times. Roll to 1'' (2.5 cm) thickness and cut in strips 3'' x 1'' (7.5 x 2.5 cm). Twist, then roll in remaining sugar mixed with cinnamon. Place on a greased pan, let rise in a warm place for 30 minutes, and bake at 350°F (180°C) for 35 or 40 minutes.

DANISH KUFFLES

1 tbsp.	yeast	15 mL
1/2 cup	lukewarm milk	125 mL
1/4 cup	sugar	50 mL
3 cups	flour	750 mL
1/2 tsp.	salt	2 mL
1 cup	butter	250 mL
2	eggs	2
	melted butter	
	cinnamon	
	sugar	
	raisins	
	egg white	

Dissolve yeast in lukewarm milk and add 1 tsp. (5 mL) of the sugar. Cover and let stand 10 minutes. Sift flour, remaining sugar, and salt together into a large bowl. Cut in butter with a pastry cutter. Beat the eggs into yeast mixture. Add to dry ingredients and blend lightly. Cover and let stand overnight. The next day, refrigerate the dough for 1 hour before using.

Divide dough into 5 equal parts. Roll each part into a circle on a lightly floured board. Brush circles with melted butter and sprinkle with cinnamon mixed with sugar. Cut each circle into 8 wedges. At the wide end of each wedge put a row of raisins. Roll each wedge up tightly from the wide end to form a crescent shape. Place on a greased cookie sheet. Brush kuffles with egg white and sprinkle with cinnamon-sugar mixture. Cover with a clean linen cloth and let stand 15 to 20 minutes. Uncover and bake at 375°F (190°C) for 15 minutes or until golden brown. Yields 40 kuffles.

Variation
Refrigerate dough overnight, covered. Prepare circles and wedges as above, spread with soft butter, sprinkle with sugar and cinnamon, fill with raisins and nuts, and roll up. Dip tops of kuffles in cinnamon-sugar mixture or in sesame seeds. Bake as above.

DILL PUFFS

1 tbsp.	yeast	15 mL
1/4 cup	warm water	50 mL
1 cup	creamed cottage cheese	250 mL
2 tbsp.	sugar	30 mL
1 tbsp.	instant minced onion	15 mL
2 tsp.	dill weed	10 mL
1 tsp.	salt	5 mL
1/4 tsp.	baking soda	1 mL
1	egg	1
2 1/4 cups	flour	550 mL

Dissolve yeast in warm water in a large bowl. Heat cheese just until lukewarm and stir into yeast mixture. Stir in all remaining ingredients except flour. Mix well. Beat in flour gradually, scraping down sides of bowl until completely blended. Beat vigorously about 20 strokes. (Dough will be sticky and heavy.) Cover with a clean towel. Let rise in a warm place, away from drafts, for 1 hour or until double in bulk. Stir dough down. Divide evenly among 8 greased, 5 oz. (140 g) custard cups or muffin tins, cover with a towel, and let rise until double. Bake at 350°F (180°C) for 25 minutes or until puffs are golden brown. Remove from cups. Brush tops lightly with butter. Serve hot.

PUMKISHKIS

1/2 cup	butter	125 g
1/2 cup	oil	125 mL
3	eggs	3

1 tsp.	salt	5 mL
1/4 cup	sugar	50 mL
2 cups	sour cream	500 mL
2 lb.	dry cottage cheese	1 kg
2 tbsp.	yeast	30 mL
1/4 cup	lukewarm water	50 mL
6 cups	flour	1.5 L

Cream butter. Add oil, then eggs, salt, sugar, and sour cream. Combine creamed mixture with cottage cheese in a mixing bowl. Dissolve yeast in lukewarm water and add. Finally add flour, using enough to make the batter quite thick. Let rise 3 1/2 hours. Drop from a spoon onto greased cookie sheets. Bake at 450°F (230°C) for 25 minutes. Serve warm with sour cream. Yields 30.

PITTER BULKES (BUTTER BUNS)

5 cups	flour	1.25 L
1 tsp.	salt	5 mL
1 cup	sugar	250 mL
1 cup	butter	250 mL
1 cup	sour cream	250 mL
2 tbsp.	yeast	30 mL
1/2 cup	lukewarm water	125 mL
4	eggs	4

Sift flour, salt, and all except 2 tsp. (10 mL) of the sugar into a large bowl. Melt butter and add to sour cream; cool to lukewarm. Dissolve yeast in lukewarm water with reserved sugar. When it bubbles, make a well in the flour mixture, pour in yeast mixture and eggs, and blend with sour cream and butter. Beat well until mixture forms a ball, adding flour if necessary to prevent dough sticking to hands. Beat a few minutes. Brush with oil and let rise in a warm place until light. Knead well then let rise until double in bulk. Cut dough off with a knife a little at a time to form buns. Roll out slightly, cut in strips, and roll in cinnamon and sugar. Braid or make into twists and place close together on a well-greased pan. Let rise until light. Bake at 375°F (190°C) for 25 to 30 minutes. Let stand 5 or 10 minutes in pan, then remove to racks to cool. (Note: Buttermilk or sour milk may be used instead of sour cream.)

SOUR CREAM CRESCENT ROLLS

5 cups	flour	1.25 L
1 tbsp.	sugar	15 mL
1/4 tsp.	salt	1 mL
1 cup	butter	250 mL
1 tbsp.	yeast	15 mL
2	eggs	2
2 cups	sour cream	500 mL

Sift flour, and combine with sugar and salt. Rub butter and yeast into flour, add eggs and sour cream, and knead until smooth. Refrigerate overnight. Cut dough into 4 parts. Roll each part into a circle as for pie crust, and cut each circle into 8 wedges. Put a dab of jam on broad part of triangle, roll up and shape into a crescent. Let rise in pan until light and double in bulk. Bake at 350°F (180°C) for 15 to 20 minutes until golden brown.

CINNAMON BUNS

1/2 cup	sugar	125 mL
1 cup	milk	250 mL
1/2 tsp.	salt	2 mL
1/2 cup	margarine	125 mL
1 tbsp.	yeast	15 mL
3	eggs, slightly beaten	3
4 1/2 cups	flour	1.2 L
	oil	
	butter	
	golden brown sugar	
	pecan nuts	
	cinnamon	
	raisins	

Combine white sugar, milk, salt, and margarine in a saucepan. Place over low heat until margarine is melted. Cool to lukewarm. Sprinkle yeast over top, making sure it sinks below surface of liquid. Set aside 10 to 15 minutes. In a bowl combine eggs and flour. Add yeast mixture and blend thoroughly. Turn onto a lightly floured board and knead until bubbles appear beneath the surface of the dough, approximately 5 minutes. Return to bowl, brush with oil, cover with wax paper and then with a clean towel. Place in a warm place to rise until double in bulk.

Prepare 3 pie plates by dotting with pea-size pieces of butter. Sprinkle with brown sugar and arrange 8 to 10 whole pecans in each pan.

When dough has risen, remove it to a lightly floured board. Knead for 2 to 3 minutes. Divide dough into 2 parts. Roll each into a rectangle, brush with melted butter and sprinkle with brown sugar, cinnamon, and raisins. Roll tightly as for a jelly roll from the wide side, pulling dough back slightly with each turn to prevent air spaces when baked. Cut into 2" (5 cm) slices and place in prepared pans cut side up. Flatten slightly with palm of hand. Cover with a clean towel and let rise in a warm place until double in size. Bake at 350°F (180°C) for 25 to 30 minutes, until golden brown. Invert immediately onto cooling racks. Yields 15 – 18.

PECAN BUNS

2 cups	milk	500 mL
3/4 cup	sugar	175 mL
2 tsp.	salt	10 mL
6 tbsp.	sour cream	90 mL
1 cup	butter	250 g
8 cups	flour	2 L
1 tsp.	lemon rind, grated	5 mL
6	eggs, beaten	6
2 tbsp.	yeast	30 mL
	butter	
	brown sugar	
	pecan nuts	
	cinnamon	
	raisins	

Combine first 4 ingredients in a saucepan and bring to boil. Add butter, remove from heat and cool. In a large bowl, mix flour and lemon rind. Make a well in centre. Dissolve yeast in cooled milk mixture and pour into flour with eggs. Beat well. Let rise until doubled in bulk. Dot bottoms of 2 large utility pans with butter and sprinkle with brown sugar and pecans. Divide dough into 4 portions. On a lightly floured board, roll out each portion into a rectangle; brush with melted butter; and sprinkle on brown sugar, cinnamon, and raisins. Roll as for a jelly roll and slice into rounds. Set in prepared pans, cut side up; cover, and let rise until doubled in size. Bake at 325 – 350°F (160 – 180°C) for 40 minutes. Turn out of pan and let cool on racks. Yields 30 – 35.

Variation

Orange Bubble Bread

1 recipe	yeast dough	1 recipe
1 cup	raisins	250 mL
1 cup	orange juice	250 mL
1 tsp.	orange rind, grated	5 mL
1/2 cup	orange marmalade	125 mL
1/2 cup	sugar	125 mL
3 tbsp.	butter	45 mL
3/4 cup	coconut, toasted	175 mL

Make yeast dough as for Pecan Buns. After dough has risen, add raisins, and roll into 1'' (3 cm) balls. In a medium saucepan, combine orange juice, rind and marmalade with sugar and butter. Bring to a boil. Remove from heat and beat well. Spread 3/4 cup (175 mL) of this syrup onto the bottom of a greased and foil-lined angel food pan. Sprinkle with coconut. Dip balls in remaining syrup, roll in coconut, and arrange in 2 layers in pan. Bake at 350°F (180°C) for 40 to 45 minutes. Invert and brush with syrup.

DANISH PASTRY

1/2 tsp.	salt	2 mL
1/4 cup	sugar	50 mL
1 1/2 cups	butter	375 mL
1/2 cup	milk, scalded	125 mL
1 tbsp.	yeast	15 mL
1/4 cup	warm water	50 mL
1	egg, beaten	1
3 cups	flour	750 mL

Glaze

1	egg, beaten	1
1 tbsp.	water	15 mL

Add salt, sugar, and 1/4 cup (50 mL) of the butter to scalded milk. Cool to lukewarm. Dissolve yeast in warm water. Combine milk, yeast mixture, and egg. Stir in about half the flour. Beat until smooth, adding enough flour to make a soft dough. Turn out on a floured board and knead until smooth and elastic. Place in a greased bowl, grease surface of dough, and let stand in a warm place until double in bulk. Punch down and refrigerate 1 hour. Roll dough to a rectangle about 1/2'' (1 cm) thick; dot two-thirds of the dough with one-third of the remaining butter. Fold dough over in thirds, beginning with unbuttered portion, to make 3 layers. Repeat twice more, using up all the butter. Chill 30 minutes to overnight. Then let stand at room temperature until soft enough for rolling. On a lightly-floured board, roll the dough to a rectangle 1/4'' (0.5 cm) thick. Cut into squares (approximately 18) and place a spoonful of filling in the centre of each square. Fold corners towards centre, pressing gently so that filling does not spread. Place on a buttered pan 1 1/2'' (3 cm) apart, and let rise until doubled in bulk. Brush with glaze. Bake at 400°F (200°C) until brown (18 to 20 minutes). Frost with icing while still warm. Top with chopped nuts or dot with jelly, if desired.

FILLINGS

Almond Filling

2/3 cup	almonds, ground	150 mL
1/4 cup	sugar	50 mL
1	egg, beaten	1
	almond extract	

Combine all ingredients.

Apple Filling

1 lb.	apples	500 g
1 tsp.	lemon rind, grated	5 mL
1/3 cup	brown sugar	75 mL
	cinnamon or nutmeg	

Core and slice the apples, but do not peel. Place in a greased saucepan with the lemon rind, and cook over low heat until soft, stirring continually. Purée. Return purée to saucepan with the sugar and spices, and cook over low heat, stirring, until thick. Cool before using.

Apricot Filling

20	dried apricot halves	20
1/4 cup	apricot jam	50 mL
2 tbsp.	sugar	30 mL
1 tbsp.	apricot brandy	15 mL

Simmer the apricots in water to cover for 30 minutes, or until soft. Drain and mash the fruit. Stir in jam, sugar, and brandy. Chill.

Date Filling

1/2 cup	dates, chopped	125 mL
1/4 cup	sugar	50 mL
2 tbsp.	lemon or orange juice	30 mL

Combine ingredients in a saucepan and cook over medium heat until thick, stirring often. Cool before using.

Prune or Raisin Filling

Substitute chopped prunes or raisins for the dates above. It may be necessary to add 1 tbsp. (15 mL) cornstarch in 1/4 cup (50 mL) water to thicken and bind the filling.

Lemon Custard Filling

1/4 cup	butter	50 mL
3/4 cup	sugar	175 mL
4 tbsp.	lemon juice	60 mL
2 tsp.	lemon rind, grated	10 mL
2	egg yolks	2
2 tbsp.	cornstarch	30 mL
1/4 cup	water	50 mL

In the top of a double boiler, combine butter, sugar, lemon juice and rind. Stir over low heat until butter melts and sugar is dissolved. Add egg yolks and cornstarch dissolved in water. Cook, stirring constantly, until mixture thickens. Cool before using.

Fruit Fillings

Any flavour canned pie fillings may be used — blueberry, cherry, and so on.

CINNAMON TWISTS

1 cup	sour cream	250 mL
2 tbsp.	shortening	30 mL
3 tbsp.	sugar	45 mL
1/8 tsp.	baking soda	0.5 mL
1 tsp.	salt	5 mL
1	egg, unbeaten	1
1 tbsp.	yeast	15 mL
3 cups	flour, sifted	750 mL
2 tbsp.	soft butter	30 mL
1/3 cup	brown sugar	75 mL
1 tsp.	cinnamon	5 mL

In a large saucepan, bring sour cream to boiling. Remove from heat. Add shortening, sugar, baking soda, and salt and stir until well blended. Cool to lukewarm. Add egg and yeast, stirring until yeast is dissolved. Mix in flour with a spoon. Turn out onto a lightly floured board. Knead lightly a few seconds to form a smooth ball. Cover with a damp cloth and let stand 5 minutes to tighten up. Roll dough into a 6'' x 24'' (15 x 60 cm) rectangle 1/4'' (0.5 cm) thick. Spread soft butter over entire surface. Sprinkle half of dough lengthwise with mixture of cinnamon and brown sugar. Bring unsugared half of dough over sugared half, pressing top surface lightly to seal in filling. This makes the rectangle 3'' x 24'' (7.5 x 60 cm). With a sharp knife, cut dough into 24 strips 1'' (2.5 cm) wide. Holding each strip by the ends, twist in opposite directions to form a spiral stick. Place about 2'' (5 cm) apart on greased baking sheets, pressing both ends of sticks firmly and flatly to the baking sheet. Cover with a damp cloth and let rise in a warm place until very light, about 1 1/4 hours. Bake at 375°F (190°C) for 12 to 15 minutes. If desired, spread tops of warm baked sticks with thick white icing (icing sugar and milk). Makes 24 sticks.

YEASTED HAMANTASHEN DOUGH

½ cup	warm water	125 mL
2 tbsp.	yeast	30 mL
½ cup	warm milk	125 mL
½ cup	butter, melted	125 mL
2	eggs	2
½ cup	sugar	125 mL

Dissolve yeast in water. Stir in remaining ingredients and mix until smooth. Turn onto a floured board. Knead. Set in a greased bowl, covered with a damp cloth. Allow to rise 1½ hours. Punch down. Let rise another 30 minutes. Roll out and cut into squares. Place filling in the centre of each square. Fold into a triangle and allow to rise another 10 minutes. Brush with egg and milk glaze. Bake at 350°F (180°C) for 12 to 15 minutes.

HAMANTASHEN DOUGH

½ cup	butter	125 mL
1 cup	sugar	250 mL
1	egg	1
2 cups	flour	500 mL
2 tsp.	baking powder	10 mL
2 tbsp.	milk	30 mL
	vanilla or lemon extract	

Cream butter and sugar, and add egg. Sift flour and baking powder together and add a little to creamed mixture. Add milk, then remaining flour. Mix in flavouring. Roll dough out ⅛ – ¼" (2.5 – 5 mm) thick. Cut into rounds, dot each with a spoonful of filling (see below), form into triangles, and bake at 375°F (190°C) for 15 to 30 minutes until delicately browned.

HAMANTASHEN DOUGH

2 cups	flour	500 mL
2 tsp.	baking powder	10 mL
2 tbsp.	sugar	30 mL
	pinch of salt	
1 cup	butter	250 mL
1	egg	1
½ cup	orange juice	125 mL

Mix dry ingredients. Work in butter with fingers or a pastry blender. Add egg and orange juice and mix with a fork to form a soft ball. Roll dough out; cut into rounds or squares. Dot with a spoonful of filling (see below), and pinch up or fold over into triangular shape. Bake at 350°F (180°C) until golden brown, approximately 15 minutes.

CREAM CHEESE HAMANTASHEN DOUGH

1 cup	butter	250 mL
4 oz.	cream cheese	125 g
2 cups	flour, sifted	500 mL
4 tbsp.	berry sugar	60 mL

Cream butter well, add cheese, flour, and sugar and mix well. Cover with wax paper and refrigerate overnight. Roll out not very thin and cut into equal numbers of rounds and squares. Place a spoonful of apricot or other jam in the middle of each, or use traditional poppy seed filling. Pinch the rounds into triangles, and fold the squares over the triangle. Bake on a greased cookie sheet at 400°F (200°C) for 12 to 15 minutes until lightly browned.

HAMANTASHEN FILLINGS

Poppy Seed Filling

1 cup	poppy seed	250 mL
1 cup	milk	250 mL
1 oz.	butter	30 g
2 tbsp.	honey	30 mL
1	tart apple, grated	1

Bring poppy seed and milk to boil, add butter and honey, and boil until thick. Cool, then add grated apple.

overleaf:
Challah (page 156); Rye Bread (page 157);
Bagels (page 160); and other buns

Prune Filling

1 lb.	prunes, pitted	500 g
1 cup	sultana raisins	250 mL
1 tbsp.	lemon juice	15 mL
1 tsp.	lemon rind, grated	5 mL
1/2 cup	sugar	125 mL
1 tbsp.	honey	15 mL

Soak prunes overnight in cold water, or for 2 hours in hot water. Drain. Chop prunes and raisins. Mix all ingredients thoroughly.

Apricot Filling

1 lb.	dried apricots	450 g
1 cup	honey	250 mL
1 tbsp.	orange rind, grated	15 mL
3 tbsp.	orange juice	45 mL

Soak apricots overnight in water to cover. Drain, then purée. Combine with honey, orange rind and juice.

Prune and Date Filling

1 cup	prunes	250 mL
1 cup	raisins	250 mL
1 cup	dates	250 mL
1/2 cup	nuts	125 mL
1/2 cup	jam	125 mL
3 tbsp.	lemon juice	45 mL

Soak prunes in hot water for 2 hours; drain. Mince all ingredients and mix well.

SOOFGANIYOT (FILLED DOUGHNUTS)

2 1/2 cups	flour	625 mL
2 cups	hot milk	500 mL
1 oz.	yeast	28 g
1/4 cup	lukewarm milk	50 mL
6	egg yolks	6
2/3 cup	sugar	150 mL
1 tsp.	vanilla	5 mL
1 tsp.	lemon or orange rind, grated	5 mL
1/2 cup	butter	125 mL
	jam	

Sift 1 cup (250 mL) flour into the hot milk. Beat until smooth, then allow to cool. Dissolve yeast in lukewarm milk, add to flour mixture, and set aside for about 30 minutes. Mix egg yolks and sugar with vanilla and rind, and add to dough. Mix in remaining flour and butter. Knead. Set aside to rise until double in bulk, about 45 minutes. Roll out on a floured board to a thickness of 1/2'' (1 cm) and cut into rounds. Put a little jam in the centre of one round and cover with another round. Press edges together and allow to rise again in a warm place. Fry in hot oil. Drain on paper towels then dust with icing sugar.

YEASTED BOHEMIAN COFFEE CAKE

3 cups	flour	750 mL
1 tsp.	salt	5 mL
	cinnamon	
1/2 cup	butter	125 mL
3	egg yolks	3
3 tbsp.	sugar	45 mL
1 cup	cream	250 mL
1/4 cup	milk	50 mL
1 tbsp.	yeast	15 mL

Mix flour, salt, and cinnamon in a bowl. Cut in butter. Beat egg yolks with sugar and add, then blend in cream. Dissolve yeast in warm milk. Add to ingredients in bowl and mix well. Refrigerate overnight, covered, in a greased bowl. Next day, roll out chilled dough on a floured board. Spread with a thin layer of jam or other desired filling, and roll up as for a jelly roll. Place in a greased bundt pan and let rise 2 hours. Bake at 350°F (180°C) for 30 minutes.

APRICOT BREAD

2 cups	dried apricots	500 mL
1 cup	boiling water	250 mL
4 tbsp.	butter	60 mL
1 1/2 cups	sugar	375 mL
2	eggs, lightly beaten	2
3 cups	flour, sifted	750 mL

2 tsp.	baking soda	10 mL
1/2 tsp.	salt	2 mL
1 cup	pecan nuts, chopped	250 mL

With a pair of scissors, cut apricots into pieces. Cover with boiling water and let stand 15 minutes. Cream butter and beat in sugar. Add eggs, and the apricots with the water. Sift dry ingredients together. Stir into apricot batter with the pecans. Pour batter into a large, greased loaf pan. Bake at 325°F (160°C) for 1 hour (45 minutes for 2 small loaf pans).

BANANA NUT BREAD

1 1/2 cups	bananas, mashed	375 mL
1 tbsp.	honey	15 mL
1/4 cup	oil	50 mL
1	egg, beaten	1
1 tsp.	almond extract	5 mL
1 cup	flour	250 mL
1 tsp.	baking soda	5 mL
1 tsp.	baking powder	5 mL
1/2 cup	nuts, chopped	125 mL

Stir honey into bananas in a mixing bowl. Add oil, egg, and almond extract. Stir to mix well. Combine flour, baking soda, and baking powder and stir into banana mixture. Add nuts. Turn into a greased and floured 9" x 5" (2 L) loaf pan and bake at 350°F (180°C) for 40 minutes, until a toothpick inserted in the centre comes out clean.

BANANA LOAF

1/2 cup	oil	125 mL
1 cup	sugar	250 mL
2	eggs	2
1 cup	bananas, mashed	250 mL
1 tsp.	vanilla	5 mL
1 3/4 cups	flour	425 mL
2 tsp.	baking powder	10 mL
1/4 tsp.	salt	1 mL
1 tbsp.	vinegar	15 mL
1 tsp.	baking soda	5 mL
3 tbsp.	milk	45 mL

Beat oil, sugar, and eggs together well. Add mashed bananas and vanilla. Sift together flour, baking powder, and salt. Add. Mix remaining ingredients together and beat into batter until well blended. Bake in a 9" x 5" (2 L) loaf pan at 350°F (180°C) for 50 minutes.

BANANA BLUEBERRY BREAD

1/2 cup	blueberries	125 mL
1 1/2 cups	flour	375 mL
2/3 cup	sugar	150 mL
2 1/4 tsp.	baking powder	11 mL
1/2 tsp.	salt	2 mL
1/2 cup	rolled oats	125 mL
2	eggs, beaten	2
1/3 cup	shortening, melted	75 mL
1 cup	bananas, mashed	250 mL

Sprinkle blueberries with 2 tbsp. (30 mL) of the flour. Sift together remaining flour, sugar, baking powder, and salt, and stir in oats. Blend eggs, shortening, and banana. Add to dry ingredients, stirring just until combined. Fold in blueberries. Pour batter into a greased and floured 9" x 5" (2 L) loaf pan. Bake at 350°F (180°C) for 1 hour. Cool 10 minutes before removing from pan.

CHERRY LOAF

2/3 cup	shortening	150 mL
4	eggs	4
2 cups	sugar	500 mL
8 oz.	maraschino cherries	240 mL
	orange juice	
4 cups	flour	1 L
2 tsp.	baking powder	10 mL
1 tsp.	salt	5 mL
1 cup	nuts, coarsely chopped	250 mL

Cream shortening, eggs, and sugar. Drain cherries, reserving liquid and adding orange juice to make up to 1 cup (250 mL). Beat juice into creamed mixture. Add dry ingredients. Fold in cherries and nuts. Pour into 2 wax paper-lined, 9" x 5" (2 L) loaf pans and bake at 350°F (180°C) for 1 hour.

CRANBERRY BREAD

3 cups	flour	750 mL
1 1/3 cups	sugar	325 mL
1 3/4 tsp.	baking powder	8 mL
1 1/2 tsp.	salt	7 mL
3/4 tsp.	baking soda	3 mL
1 1/2 cups	cranberries, halved	375 mL
3/4 cup	nuts, chopped	175 mL
1 1/2 tsp.	orange peel	7 mL
2	eggs	2
1 1/3 cups	orange juice	325 mL
2 1/2 tbsp.	oil	35 mL

Sift dry ingredients together. Stir in cranberries with nuts and orange peel. Combine eggs, orange juice, and oil, and mix in. Bake in 2 well-greased 9'' x 5'' (2 L) loaf pans at 350°F (180°C) for 50 minutes. Remove from pans and cool.

DATE LOAF

1 cup	brown sugar	250 mL
2 cups	flour	500 mL
1/2 tbsp.	butter	10 mL
1	egg, beaten	1
1 cup	sour milk	250 mL
1 tsp.	baking soda	5 mL
1 cup	walnuts, chopped	250 mL
2 cups	dates, chopped	500 mL

Mix first 4 ingredients. Dissolve baking soda in a little sour milk, and add with rest of milk. Fold in walnuts and dates. Bake in a greased 9'' x 5'' (2 L) loaf pan at 350°F (180°C) for 55 minutes.

ORANGE CRANBERRY LOAF

2 large	oranges	2 large
1	egg	1
1/4 cup	oil	50 mL
1 3/4 cups	flour	425 mL
1 1/2 tsp.	baking powder	7 mL
1/2 tsp.	baking soda	2 mL
1 tsp.	salt	5 mL
1/4 tsp.	nutmeg	1 mL
1 cup	sugar	250 mL
1 cup	cranberries, chopped	250 mL
1/2 cup	walnuts	125 mL

Grate rind of 1 orange. Squeeze juice from both oranges and make up to 3/4 cup (175 mL) with water or more juice. Whisk juice and orange peel with egg and oil. Combine dry ingredients in a large bowl. Pour juice mixture into centre and stir just until all ingredients are moist. Fold in cranberries and nuts. Immediately turn into a greased 9'' x 5'' (2 L) pan and bake at 350°F (180°C) for 1 to 1 1/4 hours.

FRUIT BREAD

1 cup	sugar	250 mL
1 cup	butter	250 mL
5	eggs	5
1 tsp.	vanilla	5 mL
2 1/2 cups	flour	625 mL
1/2 tsp.	baking powder	2 mL
1 cup	sultana raisins	250 mL
1/4 cup	glacé cherries, chopped	50 mL
1/4 cup	glazed pineapple, chopped	50 mL

Cream butter and sugar. Beat in eggs and vanilla. Add flour and baking powder and stir in fruit. Pour into a long, greased loaf pan and bake at 350°F (180°C) for 55 to 60 minutes.

GINGER BREAD

3 cups	flour	750 mL
1 tbsp.	allspice	15 mL
1 tbsp.	ginger	15 mL
1 cup	sugar	250 mL
1/2 tsp.	salt	2 mL
1 cup	butter	250 mL
1 1/4 cups	syrup	300 mL
1 cup	milk	250 mL
2	eggs	2
3/4 cup	boiling water	175 mL
2 tsp.	baking soda	10 mL

Sift together dry ingredients. Melt butter in syrup and add. Beat in eggs and milk. Dissolve baking soda in boiling water and add to batter. Bake in greased loaf pan at 325°F (160°C) for 1 hour. Makes 2 small loaves or 1 large loaf.

HEALTHY PUMPKIN LOAF

2	eggs	2
½ cup	brown sugar	125 mL
½ cup	honey	125 mL
½ cup	oil	125 mL
3 tbsp.	water	45 mL
1 cup	canned pumpkin	250 mL
½ tsp.	cinnamon	2 mL
	cloves	
	allspice	
	nutmeg	
1 cup	wholewheat flour	250 mL
¾ cup	flour	175 mL
1 tsp.	baking soda	5 mL
¾ tsp.	salt	3 mL
¾ cup	dates and raisins	175 mL
¾ cup	nuts, chopped	175 mL

Beat eggs and sugar with honey. Add oil, water, and pumpkin. Sift dry ingredients and add with fruit and nuts. Pour into 2 greased and foil-lined 9'' x 5'' (2 L) loaf pans. Bake at 350°F (180°C) for 1 hour.

PUMPKIN LOAVES

2 cups	sugar	500 mL
¾ cup	butter	175 mL
2	eggs	2
14 oz.	canned pumpkin	398 mL
2 cups	flour	500 mL
½ tsp.	salt	2 mL
½ tsp.	baking powder	2 mL
1 tsp.	baking soda	5 mL
1 tsp.	cloves	5 mL
1 tsp.	cinnamon	5 mL
1 tsp.	nutmeg	5 mL

Cream together butter and sugar, then add eggs one at a time, beating well after each addition.

Beat in pumpkin well. Sift together dry ingredients, and add slowly. Pour batter into 3 greased and foil-lined 7'' x 3½'' x 2'' (1.5 L) loaf pans. Place pans on a large cookie sheet and bake at 350°F (180°C) for 50 to 55 minutes until a toothpick comes out clean. Let cool 10 minutes in pans before turning out onto racks.

PUMPKIN-RAISIN LOAF

4	eggs	4
3 cups	sugar	750 mL
1 cup	oil	250 mL
2 cups	canned pumpkin	500 mL
½ cup	water	125 mL
3½ cups	flour	875 mL
2 tsp.	baking soda	10 mL
1 tsp.	salt	5 mL
1 tsp.	cinnamon	5 mL
½ tsp.	cloves	2 mL
½ tsp.	allspice	2 mL
½ tsp.	nutmeg	2 mL
1 cup	raisins	250 mL

Beat eggs well with sugar and oil. Add pumpkin and water. Combine dry ingredients, add, and mix for 2 minutes. Stir in raisins. Pour into 3 well-greased loaf pans. Bake at 350°F (180°C) for 1 hour.

RAISIN LOAF

1 cup	raisins	250 mL
1 cup	cold water	250 mL
1 tsp.	baking soda	5 mL
2	eggs	2
1 cup	sugar	250 mL
½ cup	oil	125 mL
1¾ cups	flour	425 mL
1 tsp.	baking powder	5 mL
½ tsp.	cinnamon	2 mL
½ tsp.	allspice	2 mL
½ tsp.	nutmeg	2 mL
½ tsp.	salt	2 mL
1 tsp.	vanilla	5 mL

Bring raisins and water to a boil. Add baking soda; let cool. Beat eggs well with sugar and oil. Combine remaining ingredients and add alternately with vanilla and raisin mixture. Bake in a greased, long loaf pan at 350°F (180°C) for 1 hour.

ZUCCHINI BREAD

3	eggs, well beaten	3
³/₄ cup	oil	175 mL
1¹/₂ cups	honey	375 mL
2 cups	zucchini, grated	500 mL
2 tsp.	vanilla	10 mL

1 tsp.	salt	5 mL
3 cups	wholewheat flour	750 mL
1 tsp.	baking soda	5 mL
¹/₄ tsp.	baking powder	1 mL
1 tsp.	cinnamon	5 mL
	pinch of nutmeg	
	pinch of cloves	
	pinch of allspice	
¹/₂ cup	nuts, chopped	125 mL

Mix first 6 ingredients together in a large bowl. Combine remaining dry ingredients in a separate bowl, add to first mixture, and blend well. Pour into 2 greased 9" x 5" (2 L) loaf pans. Bake at 350°F (180°C) for 1 to 1¹/₄ hours.

PANCAKES & MUFFINS

TEA BISCUITS

4 cups	flour, sifted	1 L
¹/₂ cup	sugar	125 mL
1 tsp.	salt	5 mL
6 tsp.	baking powder	30 mL
¹/₂ cup	shortening, chilled	125 mL
1¹/₃ cups	milk	325 mL

Sift dry ingredients into a mixing bowl. Cut shortening into flour mixture, using a pastry blender or 2 knives. Add sufficient milk to make a slightly soft dough. Roll lightly on a floured board to ¹/₂" (1 cm) thickness and cut with a floured biscuit cutter. Arrange on an ungreased baking sheet. Bake at 450°F (230°C) for 12 to 15 minutes. Yields 28 – 30 biscuits.

Variations

Cheese Biscuits
Add ¹/₂ cup (125 mL) grated Cheddar or American cheese to dry ingredients.

Peach Biscuits
Add 1 cup (250 mL) peaches, chopped and drained, with 1 tsp. (5 mL) grated orange rind and 2 tbsp. (30 mL) sugar.

Maple Biscuits
Brush tops with maple syrup before baking.

WELSH CAKES

2 cups	flour	500 mL
¹/₃ cup	sugar	75 mL
2 tsp.	baking powder	10 mL
¹/₂ tsp.	salt	2 mL
¹/₂ cup	butter	125 mL
¹/₂ cup	milk	125 mL
1	egg	1
³/₄ cup	currants	175 mL

Preheat electric frypan to 360°F (180°C). Mix dry ingredients; blend in butter. Beat egg in milk and add, together with currants. Roll out to ¹/₂" – ³/₄" (1 – 2 cm) thickness and cut with a round cookie cutter to make approximately 16 biscuits. Fry 10 minutes on each side or until brown. Serve, split, with butter and honey or jam.

SCONES

3 cups	flour	750 mL
¹/₄ tsp.	salt	1 mL

1 cup	brown sugar	250 mL
2¾ tsp.	baking powder	13 mL
1 cup	margarine	250 mL
1	egg, separated	1
1 cup	milk	250 mL
1 cup	raisins	250 mL

Combine dry ingredients. Cut in margarine with a pastry cutter until pea-sized particles are formed. Mix in egg white and milk to combine. Add raisins. Spread on a lightly floured board, flattening slightly with a spoon. Spread the egg yolk over the top with palm of hand while flattening and evening off the batter to a height of ¾" (2 cm). Cut into diamond or triangle shapes. Bake on ungreased cookie sheets at 375°F (190°C) for 18 to 20 minutes. Yields 30.

RAISIN-ORANGE SCONES

2 cups	flour	500 mL
¼ cup	sugar	50 mL
1 tbsp.	baking powder	15 mL
1 tsp.	salt	5 mL
⅓ cup	shortening	75 mL
½ cup	raisins	125 mL
1 tsp.	orange peel	5 mL
2	eggs	2
½ cup	milk	125 mL

Combine flour, sugar, baking powder, and salt. Cut in shortening, then stir in raisins and orange peel. Separate 1 egg. Blend yolk with second egg and milk, and stir into mixture just until moist. Turn out on a floured board and knead 30 seconds. Roll or pat into 9" (22 cm) circles, ½" (1 cm) thick. Place on an ungreased cookie sheet and cut into 8 or 10 wedges. Brush with beaten egg white and sprinkle with extra sugar. Bake at 425°F (220°C) for 12 minutes. Yields 16 – 20.

CREAMY WAFFLES

1 tsp.	sugar	5 mL
3	eggs, separated	3
1 cup	cream	250 mL
¼ cup	butter, melted	50 mL
1½ cups	flour	375 mL
3 tsp.	baking powder	15 mL
½ tsp.	salt	2 mL

Mix sugar, egg yolks, cream, and butter in one bowl. Sift dry ingredients together and add. Fold in stiffly beaten egg whites. Bake in a waffle iron. (Note: Instead of cream, condensed milk may be used.)

BUTTERMILK HOTCAKES

1 cup	buttermilk	250 mL
1	egg	1
1 cup	flour	250 mL
½ tsp.	baking powder	2 mL
½ tsp.	baking soda	2 mL
½ tsp.	salt	2 mL
1 tbsp.	butter, melted	15 mL

Beat buttermilk and egg together slightly. Mix dry ingredients and add. Lightly stir in melted butter. Mixture must be lumpy. Grease griddle slightly before frying for first batch only. (This recipe may be doubled or tripled.)

SOUR CREAM PANCAKES

1¼ cups	sour cream	300 mL
1	egg, beaten	1
1 cup	flour	250 mL
½ tsp.	salt	2 mL
½ tsp.	baking soda	2 mL

Combine sour cream and egg. Sift dry ingredients and mix in. Do not beat. Heat pan and grease slightly. Drop batter onto hot pan by spoonfuls, turning to cook other side when bubbles appear on top of pancakes. Serve with stewed apples or cinnamon and sugar.

APPLE PANCAKES

2 cups	flour, sifted	500 mL
2 tbsp.	sugar	30 mL

4 tsp.	baking powder	20 mL
1 tsp.	salt	5 mL
2	eggs, separated	2
2 cups	milk	500 mL
2 tbsp.	butter, melted	30 mL
1 cup	apples, chopped	250 mL

Sift dry ingredients together. Beat egg yolks well and combine with milk. Pour into dry ingredients, mixing well. Stir in butter and apple. Beat egg whites until stiff and fold in. Let batter stand a few minutes before baking on a hot griddle. Use 1/3 cup (75 mL) batter for each pancake, and spread evenly with a spatula.

COFFEE CAKE MUFFINS

3 tbsp.	butter	45 mL
3/4 cup	sugar	175 mL
1	egg	1
	pinch of salt	
2 cups	flour	500 mL
3 tsp.	baking powder	15 mL
3/4 cup	milk	175 mL
1 cup	raisins	250 mL

Cream butter; add sugar and egg. Mix dry ingredients and add alternately with milk. Fold in raisins. Spoon into greased muffin tins, sprinkle with cinnamon and sugar, and bake at 375°F (190°C) for 20 minutes. Yields 12 muffins.

BANANA MUFFINS

1 cup	sugar	250 mL
1 tsp.	baking soda	5 mL
2 tsp.	baking powder	10 mL
2 cups	flour	500 mL
	pinch of salt	
1/2 cup	butter, melted	125 mL
2	eggs	2
4 tbsp.	milk	60 mL
3	bananas, mashed	3

Sift dry ingredients together. Add eggs, milk, and butter. Mix just until blended before adding banana. Fill paper muffin cups three-quarters full. Bake at 350°F (180°C) for 25 minutes.

Icing

1 1/2 cups	icing sugar	375 mL
2 tbsp.	butter, melted	30 mL
1 tsp.	vanilla	5 mL
1 1/4 tbsp.	milk	20 mL

Combine ingredients and spread over cooled muffins.

RAISIN MUFFINS

1 1/2 cups	raisins	375 mL
1 cup	water	250 mL
1/2 cup	brown sugar	125 mL
1/2 cup	butter	125 mL
1	egg, beaten	1
1 1/2 cups	flour	375 mL
1 tsp.	baking soda	5 mL
1/4 tsp.	mace	1 mL
1 tsp.	cinnamon	5 mL
1/4 tsp.	cloves	1 mL

Simmer raisins and water 20 minutes. Cool and drain, retaining 3/4 cup (175 mL) of the raisin water and discarding any excess. Cream butter and sugar. Beat in egg and raisin water and stir in raisins. Lastly add dry ingredients. Mix well. Bake in greased muffin tins at 350°F (180°C) for 10 to 15 minutes. Yields 16 large muffins.

OATMEAL MUFFINS

1 cup	oatmeal	250 mL
1/2 cup	brown sugar	125 mL
1 cup	flour	250 mL
1/2 tsp.	baking soda	2 mL
1 tsp.	baking powder	5 mL
1/2 tsp.	salt	2 mL
1 cup	sour cream	250 mL
1	egg	1
1/2 cup	shortening, melted	125 mL

Mix and sift dry ingredients. Combine remaining ingredients and add to first mixture. Stir only enough to moisten flour. Drop into greased muffin tins and bake at 400°F (200°C) for 15 to 20 minutes. Yields 12 muffins.

SPECIAL BRAN MUFFINS

½ cup	butter	125 mL
¾ cup	brown sugar	175 mL
1	egg, beaten	1
1 cup	flour	250 mL
1 tsp.	baking soda	5 mL
½ tsp.	salt	2 mL
1 cup	sour milk	250 mL
1½ cups	bran	375 mL

Cream butter and sugar. Beat in egg. Sift flour, baking soda, and salt together and add to creamed mixture alternately with sour milk. Add bran and mix well. Fill greased muffin tins two-thirds full. Bake at 375 – 400°F (190 – 200°C) for 20 to 25 minutes. Yields 12 – 14 muffins. (Note: Buttermilk may be substituted for the sour milk.)

Variation
For fruit muffins, add ½ cup (125 mL) raisins, ¼ tsp. (1 mL) cloves, and ½ tsp. (2 mL) cinnamon to batter; or ¾ cup (175 mL) sliced dates and ½ tsp. (2 mL) vanilla.

DATE BRAN MUFFINS

2 cups	bran	500 mL
4 cups	bran cereal	1 L
2 cups	boiling water	500 mL
3 cups	sugar	750 mL
1 cup	butter	250 mL
4	eggs, beaten	4
4 cups	buttermilk	1 L
5 cups	flour	1.25 L
3 tbsp.	baking soda	45 mL
2 tsp.	salt	10 mL
2 cups	dates, chopped	500 mL

Pour boiling water over bran and bran cereal; let stand to soften. Cream sugar and butter. Add eggs, buttermilk, and bran mixture. Sift dry ingredients together and add with dates. Bake in greased muffin tins at 375 – 400°F (190 – 200°C) for 15 to 20 minutes. This recipe makes over 10 dozen; make as many as needed at one time and store rest of batter in refrigerator up to 1 month. (Note: 2½ cups (625 mL) honey may be substituted for the sugar. Raisins may be used instead of, or in addition to, the dates.)

BLUEBERRY MUFFINS

¼ cup	soft butter	50 mL
¾ cup	sugar	175 mL
1	egg	1
1½ cups	cake flour	375 mL
½ tsp.	salt	2 mL
2 tsp.	baking powder	10 mL
½ cup	milk	125 mL
1 cup	blueberries	250 mL

Cream butter and sugar. Add egg, and mix well. Sift dry ingredients and add alternately with milk. Fold in blueberries. Fill greased muffin tins two-thirds full. Bake at 375°F (190°C) for 15 to 20 minutes. Yields 12 muffins. (Note: If using all-purpose flour, use slightly less than the amount given for cake flour. If frozen blueberries are used, they need not be thawed.)

Cakes & Tortes

The Sweet Table. In the centre, the cake of honour. Calligraphy in pink icing gives a tribute to the bride and groom or the Bar Mitzvah, says "Bon Voyage," "Welcome Home," "Happy Birthday," or simply "I Love You." Surrounded by an honour guard of cakes and tortes of every description: chiffon cakes and sponge cakes so light they seem to float; rich fudge cakes; fruit and nut cakes laced with brandies and liqueurs, ripened for months and brought out for special occasions; sinfulness masquerading as Chocolate Apricot Torte. Each creamy confection tempting and beckoning.

Cake has had a fascinating and sometimes violent history. Marie Antoinette proclaimed: "Let them eat cake!" and started a revolution. A celebrated court case in Vienna, to decide who really owned the recipe for the genuine and original Sachertorte, lasted seven years.

Over the centuries, recipes have spread across continents and oceans like smooth buttercream frosting. Treasured formulas were written on scraps of paper, or lovingly taught by mothers to daughters through the generations: honey cakes, carrot cakes, and apple cakes for the New Year, cheesecakes for Shavuot, and sponge cakes for the Sabbath.

American dairymen discovered the method for cream cheese, and the rest is cheesecake history. Cheesecake, the queen of cakes. Creamy-cool sensual perfection with strawberry, black cherry, or chocolate swirl topping. Sitting regally on a buttery crumb-crust throne. Cheesecake is always a command performance; a guest will rarely refuse it.

Cake baking has become a creative and artistic hobby with a delicious dual virtue: "You can have your cake and eat it, too." And with genius and inventiveness, Jewish homemakers have translated many of these confections into kosher-for-Passover use.

Cake is a symbol of prosperity, of something over and above "the daily bread," a gesture of goodwill. In the words of the song, "If I knew you were coming I'd've baked a cake/ And spread the welcome mat for you."

CAKES

APPLE CAKE

½ cup	butter	125 mL
2	eggs	2
⅔ cup	sugar	150 mL
2 cups	flour	500 mL
1 tsp.	baking powder	5 mL
½ tsp.	salt	2 mL
2½ tbsp.	water	35 mL
	tart jam	
10	apples, grated	10
½ cup	raisins	125 mL
½ cup	glazed fruit, chopped	125 mL
½ cup	coconut, shredded	125 mL
2 tsp.	cinnamon	10 mL

Cream together butter, eggs, and ½ cup (125 mL) sugar. Sift flour and baking powder together with salt. Fold into batter, stirring with water to lighten. Pour half the batter into a greased baking pan. Spread with jam, and sprinkle on fruit and coconut. Pour on remaining batter. Sprinkle with cinnamon and remaining sugar. Bake at 325°F (160°C) for 1 hour. (Note: Tart cranberry sauce may be substituted for tart jam.)

LATTICED APPLE CAKE

Batter

½ cup	butter	125 mL
2	eggs	2
2 cups	cake flour, sifted	500 mL
¾ cup	sugar	175 mL
2 tsp.	baking powder	10 mL
	pinch of salt	
1 tsp.	vanilla	5 mL

Cream butter. Add eggs and beat well. Add remaining ingredients; blend well. Pour three-quarters of the batter into a greased 8" square (2 L) utility pan. Cover with the filling. Lattice-strip remaining batter over filling, thus forming a pat-tern of squares. Dot each square with jam. Bake at 350°F (180°C) for 50 minutes.

Filling

9	apples, grated	9
¼ cup	sugar	50 mL
½ tsp.	cinnamon	2 mL
1 tsp.	lemon juice	5 mL

Combine ingredients.

BLUEBERRY CAKE

3 cups	blueberries	750 mL
2 tsp.	lemon juice	10 mL
2⅓ cups	sugar	575 mL
3 cups	flour	750 mL
3 tsp.	baking powder	15 mL
1 tsp.	salt	5 mL
1 cup	oil	250 mL
4	eggs	4
¼ cup	orange juice	50 mL
1 tbsp.	vanilla	15 mL

Mix blueberries and lemon juice with 5 tbsp. (75 mL) of the sugar, and set aside. Sift flour, remaining sugar, baking powder, and salt into a bowl. Make a well. Drop in remaining ingredients. Beat with a spatula or wooden spoon until smooth and shiny. Pour one-third of batter into a greased 10" (2 or 3 L) tube pan. Drain excess moisture off fruit, and spread half the blueberries over batter. Repeat, ending with last third of batter. Bake at 375°F (190°C) for 60 to 75 minutes or until done. If cake starts to get too brown, cover lightly with foil.

Variations

Peach Cake
Substitute sliced peaches for the blueberries.

Spiced Apple Cake
For the blueberries and lemon juice, substitute 4 cups (1 L) sliced apples and 3 tbsp. (45 mL) cinnamon.

APPLE LOAF

2	apples, grated	2
1/2 tsp.	vanilla	2 mL
1 cup	sugar	250 mL
1/4 cup	oil	50 mL
1	egg	1
1 tsp.	cinnamon	5 mL
1/8 tsp.	nutmeg	0.5 mL
1/8 tsp.	ginger	0.5 mL
1 cup	flour	250 mL
1 tsp.	baking soda	5 mL
	pinch of salt	

Stir first 5 ingredients together with a fork, adding them one at a time in the order given. Combine remaining dry ingredients and add to mixture, stirring just until moistened. Pour into a greased and floured loaf tin, and bake at 350°F (180°C) for 45 minutes.

SPECIAL APPLE AND PEAR CAKE

2	eggs	2
3/4 cup	sugar	175 mL
3/4 cup	flour	175 mL
2/3 cup	butter, softened	140 mL
2	apples	2
2	pears	2
1 1/2 tbsp.	light rum	20 mL
1 tbsp.	baking powder	15 mL

In a bowl, beat eggs well with sugar. Add flour and butter and mix well. Peel apples and pears, and slice thinly. Combine with remaining ingredients; stir into batter. Spoon batter into a well-buttered and sugared 9" (2 L) cake pan and bake in a preheated 325°F (160°C) oven for 45 to 50 minutes, until a cake tester comes out clean. Cool cake in pan on a rack for 30 minutes.

PAREVE BANANA CAKE

2 cups	flour, sifted	500 mL
1/2 tsp.	baking powder	2 mL
1/2 tsp.	salt	2 mL
3/4 tsp.	baking soda	3 mL
1/2 cup	shortening	125 mL
1 1/2 cups	sugar	375 mL
2	eggs	2
1 tsp.	vanilla	5 mL
1/4 cup	orange juice	50 mL
1 cup	bananas, mashed	250 mL

Sift first 4 ingredients together. In a large bowl, cream together shortening, sugar, eggs, and vanilla. Add juice. Blend in sifted dry ingredients alternately with bananas. Beat just to mix. Pour into a greased and floured 9" x 12" (3 L) pan. Bake at 350°F (180°C) for 40 to 50 minutes.

BANANA SPICE CAKE

1/2 cup	butter	125 mL
1 1/4 cups	sugar	300 mL
2	eggs	2
2 1/2 cups	cake flour	625 mL
2 1/2 tsp.	baking powder	12 mL
1/2 tsp.	salt	2 mL
1/4 tsp.	cloves	1 mL
1 1/4 tsp.	cinnamon	6 mL
1/2 tsp.	nutmeg	2 mL
1/2 tsp.	baking soda	2 mL
1/4 cup	milk	50 mL
1 1/4 cups	bananas, mashed	300 mL
1 tsp.	vanilla	5 mL

Cream butter and sugar; add eggs. Combine flour, baking powder, salt, and spices in a separate bowl. Dissolve baking soda in milk. Add bananas to creamed mixture, alternating with flour and milk. Lastly add vanilla. Mix well. Pour into a greased 9" x 11" (2 L) pan and bake at 350°F (180°C) for 30 minutes or until brown. Ice with maple-flavoured butter frosting (see p. 195); garnish with walnuts.

CARROT CAKE

2 cups	sugar	500 mL
1 1/2 cups	oil	375 mL
4	eggs	4

3 cups	carrots, shredded	750 mL
2 cups	flour	500 mL
2 tsp.	baking soda	10 mL
4 tsp.	cinnamon	20 mL
1 tsp.	salt	5 mL
½ cup	nuts	125 mL

Mix sugar and oil. Add eggs one at a time and beat in carrots. Sift dry ingredients and stir into mixture together with nuts. Pour into 3 layer pans. Bake at 350°F (180°C) for 25 to 30 minutes. Cool. Stack layers, spreading icing between layers and on top.

Icing

½ cup	butter	125 mL
2 cups	icing sugar	500 mL
8 oz.	cream cheese	250 g
2 tsp.	vanilla	10 mL
½ cup	nuts	125 mL

Beat first 4 ingredients until smooth and creamy. Fold in nuts. (Note: For the icing sugar, 1 or 2 cartons of prepared whip topping, mixed with the grated rind of 1 or 2 oranges, may be substituted.)

CARROT WALNUT CAKE

3	eggs, separated	3
1 cup	sugar	250 mL
½ cup	shortening	125 mL
1 tsp.	lemon juice	5 mL
1 cup	carrots, grated	250 mL
½ cup	walnuts, chopped	125 mL
1 cup	flour	250 mL
2 tsp.	baking powder	10 mL
⅛ tsp.	salt	0.5 mL

Beat egg yolks and sugar. Add shortening and lemon juice, beating until smooth. Mix in carrots and nuts. Gradually blend in flour, baking powder, and salt. Beat egg whites until stiff and fold into mixture. Pour into a greased tube pan and bake at 350°F (180°C) for 35 minutes, or until done. Invert tube pan on rack until cake is cool.

CARROT AND NUT CAKE

1½ cups	oil	375 mL
2 cups	sugar	500 mL
3	eggs	3
2 cups	carrots, shredded	500 mL
2 tsp.	vanilla	10 mL
1 cup	crushed pineapple	250 mL
2¼ cups	flour	550 mL
2 tsp.	cinnamon	10 mL
2 tsp.	baking soda	10 mL
1 tsp.	salt	5 mL
1 cup	coconut, shredded	250 mL
1 cup	walnuts, chopped	250 mL

Mix oil and sugar. Beat in eggs one at a time, then carrots and vanilla. Drain the pineapple well, discarding juice. Sift together flour, cinnamon, baking soda, and salt. Fold into carrot mixture with remaining ingredients, including pineapple. Mix thoroughly. Bake in a greased pan at 350°F (180°C) for 50 to 60 minutes. Ice when cool.

Icing

3 oz.	cream cheese	85 g
1 tbsp.	milk	15 mL
½ tsp.	vanilla	2 mL
⅓ cup	margarine, melted	75 mL
2 cups	icing sugar	500 mL
1 tsp.	lemon juice	5 mL

CARROT RAISIN CAKE

2 cups	flour	500 mL
1 tbsp.	cinnamon	15 mL
2 tsp.	baking soda	10 mL
2 tsp.	baking powder	10 mL
1 tsp.	salt	5 mL
¼ tsp.	nutmeg	1 mL
¼ tsp.	allspice	1 mL
7	prunes, chopped	7
¾ cup	pecan nuts, chopped	175 mL
¾ cup	golden raisins	175 mL
4	eggs	4
2 cups	sugar	500 mL
½ cup	oil	125 mL
5	carrots, shredded	5

Combine first 7 ingredients. Gently stir in prunes, pecan nuts, and raisins. In a separate bowl, beat eggs until light and foamy, then blend in sugar. Add oil and carrots. Fold into dry ingredients just until mixed. Turn into a greased and floured 12-cup (3 L) bundt pan. Bake at 350°F (180°C) for 50 to 55 minutes. (Note: For a heavier texture, substitute 1 cup (250 mL) wholewheat flour for half the regular flour, and brown sugar or part honey for the sugar.)

CHEESECAKE

½ cup	butter	125 mL
1 cup	flour	250 mL
¼ tsp.	salt	1 mL
¾ cup	icing sugar	175 mL
3	eggs, separated	3
¾ lb.	cottage cheese	375 g
	salt	
1 tbsp.	lemon juice	15 mL
1 tsp.	lemon rind, grated	5 mL
3 tsp.	sugar	15 mL

Cream butter. Sift flour, salt, and ½ cup (125 mL) of icing sugar, and add. Mix in 1 egg yolk. Pat dough into a 13" x 9" x 2" (4 L) utility pan. Bake at 325°F (160°C) for 15 minutes.

Combine cottage cheese, salt to taste, lemon juice and rind, sugar, and 2 egg yolks. Spread over baked crust and bake for 10 minutes. Beat egg whites stiff, gradually adding remaining ¼ cup (50 mL) of icing sugar. Spoon on top of cheesecake and bake at 250 – 275°F (130 – 140°C) for 10 to 15 minutes.

CHOCOLATE CHEESECAKE

Base

1 cup	flour	250 mL
½ cup	margarine	125 mL
½ cup	sugar	125 mL

Combine ingredients and cut with a pastry blender until crumbly. Press onto the bottom of an 8" or 9" (1.5 L) springform pan. Bake at 350°F (180°C) for 10 to 15 minutes. Cool.

Filling

5	eggs, separated	5
¾ cup	sugar	175 mL
1 cup	sour cream	250 mL
16 oz.	cream cheese	500 g
⅓ cup	cocoa	75 mL
2 tbsp.	liqueur	30 mL
3 tbsp.	flour	45 mL

In a blender, combine all ingredients except egg whites. Blend until creamy, up to 5 minutes. Beat egg whites stiff and fold into cheese batter. Pour onto cookie base. Bake at 350°F (180°C) for 45 minutes. Turn off the oven and leave cake in for 1 hour. Remove and let cool. Cover with whipped cream and shaved chocolate. Keep refrigerated.

PINEAPPLE CHEESECAKE

3 tbsp.	butter, melted	45 mL
7 oz.	chocolate wafers	200 g
8 oz.	cream cheese	250 g
1 cup	icing sugar	250 mL
17½ oz.	non-dairy whip topping	500 mL
14 oz.	crushed pineapple	398 mL
14 oz.	cherry pie filling	398 mL

Reserve 12 wafers and crush the rest. Mix crumbs with melted butter, and line the bottom of a 10" (3 L) springform pan. Line sides with reserved whole wafers. Beat cream cheese with icing sugar. Make whip topping as directed. Fold into cheese mixture, then fold in drained crushed pineapple. Pour into springform pan. Freeze until firm. (May be kept for 3 months in the freezer.) Before serving, top with cherry pie filling and remove sides of springform pan.

LEMON CHEESECAKE

36	chocolate wafers	36
⅓ cup	butter	75 mL
1 tsp.	lemon rind, grated	5 mL

Melt butter and mix with crushed wafers. Pat onto bottom and up the sides of a springform pan. Bake at 325°F (160°C) for 10 minutes.

Filling

2 lb.	cream cheese	1 kg
5	eggs, separated	5
5 tbsp.	cake flour	75 mL
1/4 cup	whipping cream	50 mL
1 1/3 cups	sugar	325 mL
6 tbsp.	lemon juice	90 mL
1 tbsp.	lemon rind, grated	15 mL

Beat the cheese, and add the rest of the ingredients except egg whites and 1 tbsp. (15 mL) sugar. Beat whites with reserved sugar until stiff; fold into cheese mixture. Pour onto crust and bake at 325°F (160°C) for 1 1/4 hours. Turn off heat and leave cake in oven for another hour.

SUNSHINE CHEESECAKE

6 oz.	graham wafers, crushed	175 g
1/2 cup	butter, melted	125 mL
1 lb.	cottage cheese	500 g
1 cup	sugar	250 mL
3	eggs	3
1 tsp.	vanilla	5 mL
	glacé cherries	
	canned pineapple cubes	

Prepare a crumb base using melted butter and graham wafer crumbs, and line a square or oblong baking dish. Blend cottage cheese and sugar; beat in eggs and vanilla. Pour into crumb-lined baking dish and bake at 350°F (180°C) for approximately 40 minutes. Decorate with red or green glacé cherries or canned pineapple cubes. (This quantity may be doubled, using 2 lb. (1 kg) cottage cheese with 4 eggs.)

SWIRL TOP CHEESECAKE

Crust

2 cups	graham wafer crumbs	500 mL
1/2 cup	sugar	125 mL
1/4 tsp.	cinnamon	1 mL
1/8 tsp.	nutmeg	0.5 mL
1/2 cup	butter, melted	125 mL

Combine dry ingredients. Stir in melted butter, and line the bottom of a springform pan.

Filling

1 oz.	unsweetened chocolate	28 g
1 lb.	cream cheese	500 g
1 cup	sugar	250 mL
6	eggs, separated	6
1 tbsp.	orange peel, grated	15 mL
1 tbsp.	orange juice	15 mL
1 tsp.	vanilla	5 mL
1 cup	whipping cream	250 mL

Melt chocolate. In a separate bowl, blend cheese and sugar. Add egg yolks, orange juice and peel, and vanilla. Beat egg whites and fold into cheese mixture, then fold in whipping cream. Spoon one-third of filling into crumb-lined pan. Trickle a little of the melted chocolate over the surface and swirl lightly into filling with the tip of a knife. Repeat twice. Bake at 300°F (150°C) for 1 hour. Then turn off heat and leave cake in oven for another hour.

CHEESE RIBBON CHOCOLATE CAKE

Filling

1/2 lb.	cream cheese, softened	250 g
1/4 cup	sugar	50 mL
1 tbsp.	cornstarch	15 mL
2 tbsp.	milk	30 mL
1 tsp.	vanilla	5 mL
1	egg	1

Cake

2 cups	flour	500 mL
2 cups	sugar	500 mL
1 tsp.	salt	5 mL
1 tsp.	baking powder	5 mL
1/2 tsp.	baking soda	2 mL
1 1/3 cups	milk	325 mL
1/2 cup	margarine	125 mL
1 tsp.	vanilla	5 mL

4 oz.	chocolate, melted	112 g
2	eggs	2

In a small bowl, combine ingredients for filling. Beat 2 minutes until creamy and set aside. Combine cake ingredients in separate bowl, beating 3 minutes at medium speed. Pour half of batter into a greased and lightly-floured 8'' square (2 L) utility pan. Spoon cream cheese mix over batter; spread to cover batter. Spoon remaining batter by teaspoonfuls over cream cheese layer. Bake at 350°F (180°C) for 50 to 60 minutes. Frost when cool.

Frosting

1/4 cup	margarine	50 mL
1/4 cup	milk	50 mL
1 tsp.	vanilla	5 mL
1 cup	chocolate chips	250 mL
2 cups	icing sugar	500 mL

Heat margarine and milk to boiling in a small saucepan. Remove from heat. Stir in vanilla and chocolate chips until smooth. Blend in icing sugar until smooth. If necessary, thin with milk to spreading consistency.

LEMON CHIFFON CAKE

2 1/4 cups	cake flour, sifted	550 mL
1 1/2 cups	sugar	375 mL
1 tbsp.	baking powder	15 mL
1 tsp.	salt	5 mL
1/2 cup	oil	125 mL
6	eggs, separated	6
3/4 cup	water	175 mL
1 tbsp.	lemon juice	15 mL
1 tsp.	lemon rind, grated	5 mL
1/2 tsp.	cream of tartar	2 mL

Sift together the flour, 1 cup (250 mL) sugar, baking powder, and salt. Make a well in centre of dry ingredients and add oil, then egg yolks, water, lemon juice, and rind. Beat until smooth and set aside. Whip egg whites until frothy, then beat in cream of tartar. Gradually add remaining sugar,

beating well after each addition. Beat until rounded peaks are formed. Slowly pour first mixture over entire surface of this meringue. Gently fold together until just blended. Do not stir. Pour batter into a 10'' (3 L) tube pan and bake at 325°F (160°C) for 55 minutes, then at 350°F (180°C) for 10 to 15 minutes or until cake surface springs back when lightly touched. Immediately invert pan, and remove cake when cool by gently easing out with a spatula. Frost with lemon frosting over entire cake.

Lemon Frosting

1/2 cup	butter	125 mL
2 tsp.	lemon rind, grated	10 mL
4 cups	icing sugar	1 L
3 tbsp.	lemon juice	45 mL

Cream butter and lemon rind until butter is softened. Add icing sugar gradually, stirring well after each addition. Blend in the lemon juice.

MARBLE CHIFFON CAKE

2 oz.	unsweetened chocolate	56 g
1/4 cup	hot water	50 mL
1/4 cup	sugar	50 mL
1/4 tsp.	baking soda	1 mL
2 cups	cake flour	500 mL
1 1/2 cups	sugar	375 mL
3 tsp.	baking powder	15 mL
1 tsp.	salt	5 mL
1/2 cup	oil	125 mL
7	eggs, separated	7
3/4 cup	water	175 mL
2 tsp.	vanilla	10 mL
1/2 tsp.	cream of tartar	1 mL

Melt chocolate. Add water, sugar, and baking soda; mix well and set aside to cool. Sift flour, sugar, baking powder, and salt together. Make a well in centre and add oil, egg yolks, water, and vanilla. In a separate bowl, beat egg whites with cream of tartar until very stiff. Pour batter over whites, and fold in carefully. Divide batter. Add chocolate mix to one half. Spoon white and chocolate mixtures alternately into a large, ungreased angel food pan. Run a knife gently through batter to marble. Bake at 325°F (160°C) for 55 minutes, then at 350°F (180°C) for 10 to 15 minutes. Invert pan until cold.

ORANGE CHIFFON CAKE

5	egg yolks	5
1½ cups	sugar	375 mL
½ cup	oil	125 mL
¾ cup	cold water	175 mL
1 tsp.	salt	5 mL
2¼ cups	cake flour, sifted	550 mL
3 tsp.	baking powder	15 mL
1 cup	egg whites (7 – 8 eggs)	250 mL
½ tsp.	cream of tartar	2 mL
3 tbsp.	orange rind, grated	45 mL

Leave eggs out at room temperature for several hours. Beat egg yolks, sugar, oil, water, and salt at medium speed in electric mixer for 10 minutes. Sift flour and baking powder; add to yolk mixture and beat for 5 minutes longer. Whip egg whites and cream of tartar until stiff. Slowly fold in yolk mixture over whites, together with orange rind. Pour batter into an ungreased tube pan. Bake at 325°F (160°C) for 55 minutes, then at 350°F (180°C) for 15 minutes. Invert pan (away from drafts). Do not remove cake from pan until cold.

Variations

Honey Chiffon
Use only ¾ cup (175 mL) sugar. Melt ¾ cup (175 mL) honey; add ½ tsp (2 mL) baking soda. When cool, add to yolk mixture and beat 5 minutes longer. Instead of orange rind, use rind of 1 lemon and juice of half a lemon.

Cherry Cordial Chiffon
For the water and 1 tbsp. (15 mL) rind, substitute ¼ cup (50 mL) maraschino cherry juice, ½ cup (125 mL) cold water, and 1 tsp. (5 mL) vanilla. Add ½ cup (125 mL) very finely chopped, well-drained maraschino cherries after egg whites.

Maple Pecan Chiffon
Use ¾ cup (175 mL) white sugar and ¾ cup (175 mL) brown sugar. Omit rind. Add 2 tsp. (10 mL) maple extract and 1 cup (250 mL) very finely chopped pecans after egg whites.

Coconut Chiffon
Omit rind. Add 1 tsp. (5 mL) vanilla, 1 tsp. (5 mL) almond extract, and ¾ cup (175 mL) finely shredded coconut after egg whites.

Chocolate Chiffon
Omit rind. Add 1 tsp. (5 mL) vanilla and 2 squares grated semi-sweet chocolate after egg whites.

Banana Chiffon
For the water, substitute 1 cup (250 mL) mashed bananas. Substitute 3 tbsp. (45 mL) lemon juice for the orange rind.

Pineapple Chiffon
Substitute pineapple juice for water. For the orange rind, substitute 2 tsp. (10 mL) lemon rind.

POPPY SEED CHIFFON CAKE

¾ cup	poppy seed	175 mL
1 cup	warm water	250 mL
7	eggs, separated	7
2 tsp.	vanilla	10 mL
½ cup	oil	125 mL
½ tsp.	baking soda	2 mL
2 cups	flour	500 mL
1 tsp.	salt	5 mL
3 tsp.	baking powder	15 mL
1½ cups	sugar	375 mL
½ tsp.	cream of tartar	2 mL

Soak poppy seeds in warm water for several hours. Do not drain. Add yolks, vanilla, oil, and baking soda to poppy seed mixture and mix well. Sift flour, salt, baking powder, and half the sugar several times. Make a well in centre, add poppy seed mixture, and beat for 5 to 6 minutes. Beat egg whites until very stiff, gradually adding remaining sugar, then cream of tartar. Fold batter into stiffened egg whites. Bake in an ungreased tube pan at 350°F (180°C) for 1¼ hours. Invert cake and cool completely before removing from pan.

CHIFFON HONEY CAKE

4	eggs	4
1 cup	sugar	250 mL
1 cup	oil	250 mL
1½ cups	honey	375 mL
3 cups	flour	750 mL
3 tsp.	baking powder	15 mL
½ tsp.	baking soda	2 mL
1 tsp.	cinnamon	5 mL
1 cup	cold coffee	250 mL

Beat eggs well, add sugar, and beat at high speed until light and creamy. Add oil and honey, beating at medium speed until well blended. Combine dry ingredients and add to mixture alternately with coffee. Pour into an ungreased 10'' (2 L) tube pan. Bake at 350°F (180°C) for 15 minutes. Reduce heat to 325°F (160°C) and bake for 1 hour. When cake is done, invert and cool completely before removing from pan.

ISRAELI CHOCOLATE CAKE

2 cups	flour	500 mL
1½ cups	sugar	375 mL
½ cup	cocoa	125 mL
½ tsp.	baking powder	2 mL
1 tsp.	baking soda	5 mL
¼ tsp.	salt	1 mL
2	eggs	2
¾ cup	oil	175 mL
½ cup	orange juice	125 mL
½ cup	water	125 mL

Combine dry ingredients in a large bowl. Make a well in the centre and add eggs, oil, juice, and water. Beat until well blended. Pour into a 13'' x 9'' (3 L) pan or 2 layer cake pans, greased and lightly floured. Bake at 350°F (180°C) for 25 to 30 minutes.

HONEY NUT CHIFFON CAKE

4	eggs	4
1 cup	sugar	250 mL
⅔ cup	oil	150 mL
1 cup	honey	250 mL
¾ cup	cold tea	175 mL
1 tsp.	baking soda	5 mL
½ cup	nuts, chopped	125 mL
2 tsp.	baking powder	10 mL
1½ tsp.	allspice	7 mL
3 cups	flour	750 mL
	pinch of salt	
1 cup	raisins	250 mL

Beat eggs and sugar until creamy. Add oil and honey, and beat well. Dissolve baking soda in tea. Mix dry ingredients together and add to egg mixture alternately with tea. Grease and flour an 8'' square (2 L) pan and 1 small loaf pan. Pour in batter. Bake at 325°F (160°C) for 1 hour.

CHOCOLATE CAKE

2 oz.	chocolate	56 g
½ cup	water	125 mL
⅓ cup	butter	75 mL
1½ cups	sugar	375 mL
3	eggs	3
1 tsp.	vanilla	5 mL
	pinch of salt	
2 cups	cake flour	500 mL
1 tsp.	baking soda	5 mL
1 cup	sour cream	250 mL

Melt chocolate in water, stirring constantly until well blended. Cool. Cream butter and sugar; add eggs one at a time, then vanilla. Sift dry ingredients together. Add alternately with chocolate liquid, mixing well. Grease and flour 2, 9'' (1 L) cake pans and line with wax paper. Bake at 350°F (180°C) for 1 hour.

PAREVE CHOCOLATE CAKE

2	eggs	2
2 cups	sugar	500 mL
1 cup	oil	250 mL
1 cup	cocoa	250 mL
2 tsp.	vanilla	10 mL
3 cups	flour	750 mL
2 tsp.	baking soda	10 mL

1 tsp.	salt	5 mL
1 cup	apple or orange juice	250 mL
1 cup	boiling water	250 mL

Beat eggs, sugar, and oil. Add cocoa and vanilla. Sift dry ingredients together and add to mixture alternately with juice and water. Grease and flour 2 round cake pans and line with wax paper. Pour in batter. Bake at 350°F (180°C) for 25 minutes.

CHOCOLATE DECK CAKE

1 cup	shortening	250 mL
2 cups	sugar	500 mL
3	eggs	3
3 cups	flour	750 mL
2 tsp.	baking powder	10 mL
1/4 tsp.	baking soda	1 mL
1/2 tsp.	salt	2 mL
1 cup	milk	250 mL
1 1/2 tsp.	vanilla	7 mL
3/4 cup	chocolate syrup	175 mL

Cream shortening and sugar. Beat in eggs one at a time. Sift dry ingredients together, and add. Blend in milk and vanilla. Beat chocolate syrup into one-third of batter. Grease a 9'' x 13'' (3.5 L) utility pan well, pour in white batter, then top with chocolate batter. Bake at 350°F (180°C) for 40 minutes. Put foil over pan, ensuring foil does not touch batter, and bake 25 minutes longer. Let cool completely before removing from pan.

NEVER-FAIL CHOCOLATE CAKE

2 cups	flour	500 mL
1 3/4 cups	sugar	425 mL
1/2 cup	cocoa	125 mL
1 tsp.	salt	5 mL
1 tsp.	baking soda	5 mL
2 tsp.	vanilla	10 mL
1/2 cup	shortening	125 mL
3/4 cup	water	175 mL
4	eggs	4

Combine all ingredients in a large mixing bowl. Beat at low speed until moistened, then at medium speed for 3 minutes. Scrape bowl occasionally. For a bundt pan, bake at 350°F (180°C) for 55 to 60 minutes; for 30 minutes for 2 round pans; and, for a glass pan, at 325°F (160°C) for 55 to 60 minutes.

Variation

Chocolate Banana Cake
Add 1 1/2 cups (375 mL) mashed bananas with 1/2 tsp. (2 mL) baking powder.

CHOCOLATE NUT FUDGE CAKE

3	eggs, separated	3
1/2 cup	milk	125 mL
1 tsp.	vanilla	5 mL
1 1/2 cups	sugar	375 mL
2 oz.	semi-sweet chocolate	56 g
1/3 cup	hot water	75 mL
1 3/4 cups	cake flour	425 mL
2 tsp.	baking powder	10 mL
1/2 tsp.	salt	2 mL
3/4 cup	nuts, chopped	175 mL
1/2 cup	oil	125 mL

Beat egg yolks until light; add milk and vanilla, then sugar. Melt chocolate, blend with hot water, and stir into first mixture. Sift together the flour, baking powder, and salt. Stir in nuts and add to chocolate mixture. Pour in oil. Beat egg whites dry, and fold gently into batter. Bake in an 8'' square (2 L) pan at 350°F (180°C) for 40 minutes. When cool, frost with soft fudge icing.

Soft Fudge Icing

2 oz.	semi-sweet chocolate	56 g
1 1/4 cups	milk	300 mL
1	egg	1
4 tbsp.	flour	60 mL
1 cup	sugar	250 mL
2 tbsp.	butter	30 mL
1 tsp.	vanilla	5 mL

Add chocolate to cold milk in the top of a double boiler and heat. When chocolate is melted, remove from heat, add egg and beat with an egg beater until smooth and blended. Sift flour with sugar; add in small amounts to the chocolate mixture, stirring until smooth. Return to double boiler and cook until thickened. Add butter and vanilla. Cool.

CHOCOLATE-FILLED BRAZIL NUT LOG

3	eggs, separated	3
1/2 cup	sugar	125 mL
1 cup	brazil nuts, toasted	250 mL
1/4 tsp.	salt	1 mL
1/2 tsp.	cream of tartar	2 mL
1/4 cup	flour, sifted	50 mL
4 tbsp.	cocoa	60 mL

Beat yolks until light and fluffy. Gradually add sugar, beating continuously. Blend in ground nuts. Beat egg whites and salt until stiff, gradually adding cream of tartar. Fold in egg-nut mixture, and lastly fold in flour and cocoa. Grease a 10'' x 14'' (25 x 35 cm) jelly roll pan; line with greased wax paper extending slightly beyond pan. Pour in mixture and bake at 350°F (180°C) for 8 to 10 minutes. Turn out onto a damp cloth that has been sprinkled with icing sugar. Spread with filling and roll up. For a white cake, omit the cocoa.

Filling

1 oz.	unsweetened chocolate	28 g
3/4 cup	milk	175 mL
5 tbsp.	cornstarch	75 mL
1/2 cup	sugar	125 mL
1 tbsp.	butter	15 mL
1/4 tsp.	vanilla	1 mL
1/2 cup	brazil nuts, chopped	125 mL

Melt chocolate with milk in the top of a double boiler. Beat until well blended. Sift cornstarch with sugar, add a small amount of chocolate mixture, and stir to moisten. Return all to double boiler. Stir until smooth and thick. Add butter, vanilla, and nuts and remove from heat.

Glaze

2 oz.	butter	56 g
2 tbsp.	cocoa	30 mL
1	egg white	1
1 1/2 cups	icing sugar	375 mL

Melt butter with cocoa and stir until smooth. Blend egg white with icing sugar and combine with cocoa mixture. Pour over cake. Decorate with nuts and cherries.

COCONUT CLOUD CAKE

3/4 cup	shortening	175 mL
1 1/2 cups	sugar	375 mL
3	eggs	3
3 cups	flour	750 mL
4 1/2 tsp.	baking powder	22 mL
3/4 tsp.	salt	3 mL
2 cups	milk	500 mL
1/2 tsp.	almond extract	2 mL
1 tsp.	vanilla	5 mL
1 cup	coconut, shredded	250 mL

Cream together shortening and sugar. Add eggs one at a time, beating after each. Sift together flour, baking powder, and salt. Add to creamed mixture alternately with milk, then add vanilla, almond extract, and coconut. Pour into 2 greased 9'' (1 L) layer pans. Bake at 375°F (190°C) for 25 minutes. Cool 5 minutes. Remove layers from pan and cool on wire rack.

Boiled Frosting

1 cup	sugar	250 mL
1/3 cup	water	75 mL
1 tsp.	vinegar	5 mL
2	egg whites	2
3/4 tsp.	vanilla	3 mL

Boil together sugar, water, and vinegar to 238°F (120°C) or until the syrup spins a long thread when dropped from the tip of a spoon. Beat 2 egg whites stiff. Gradually add syrup and beat constantly until frosting holds shape. Add vanilla.

SOUR CREAM COFFEE CAKE

1 cup	sour cream	250 mL
1 tsp.	baking soda	5 mL
½ cup	butter	125 mL
1 cup	sugar	250 mL
2	eggs	2
1 tsp.	vanilla	5 mL
2 cups	cake flour, sifted	500 mL
1 tsp.	baking powder	5 mL
½ tsp.	salt	2 mL

Topping

¼ cup	nuts, chopped	75 mL
½ cup	white or brown sugar	125 mL
1 tsp.	cinnamon	5 mL

Grease an 8'' (1.5 L) springform pan or 8'' square (2 L) ovenproof dish. Mix sour cream and baking soda, and let stand. Cream butter and add sugar gradually, beating until creamy. Add eggs one at a time, and beat until light and fluffy. Add vanilla. Sift together flour, salt, and baking powder. Fold sifted dry ingredients into butter mixture alternately with sour cream mixture. Pour half the batter into the greased pan. Sprinkle with one-third of the topping. Add rest of batter and sprinkle with remainder of topping. Bake at 350°F (180°C) for 40 to 45 minutes.

Topping Variation

¼ cup	brown sugar	75 mL
2 tbsp.	cocoa	30 mL
¼ cup	walnuts, chopped	75 mL
2 tbsp.	coconut, shredded	30 mL
	pinch of cinnamon	

SUGAR AND SPICE COFFEE CAKE

5 tbsp.	shortening	75 mL
¾ cup	sugar	175 mL
1	egg, beaten	1
1 tsp.	vanilla	5 mL
2 cups	flour, sifted	500 mL
1 tbsp.	baking powder	15 mL
¾ tsp.	salt	3 mL
¾ cup	milk	175 mL

Cream shortening and sugar until light and fluffy. Beat in egg and vanilla. Sift dry ingredients and add to creamed mixture alternately with milk. Pour half the batter into a greased square pan. Sprinkle with three-quarters of the filling. Add remaining batter and top with rest of filling. Bake at 350°F (180°C) for 40 minutes or until cake tests done.

Filling

½ cup	brown sugar	125 mL
2 tbsp.	flour	30 mL
2 tsp.	cinnamon	10 mL
2 tbsp.	butter	30 mL
½ cup	nuts, chopped	125 mL

Melt butter, and add to dry ingredients. Stir until moistened.

LIGHT FRUIT CAKE

1 cup	butter	250 mL
¼ tsp.	salt	1 mL
1½ cups	sugar	375 mL
6	eggs	6
3 cups	flour	750 mL
1 tsp.	baking powder	5 mL
¾ cup	orange juice or brandy	175 mL
1 tsp.	lemon extract	5 mL
1 cup	almonds, blanched	250 mL
1 cup	glazed cherries	250 mL
¾ cup	citron peel	175 mL
¼ cup	glazed pineapple	50 mL
2 cups	sultana raisins	500 mL

Cream butter, salt, and sugar until light. Add the eggs one at a time, beating well between each addition. Mix 1 cup (250 mL) of the flour with the fruit and nuts. Add remaining flour and baking powder to batter alternately with the orange juice. Add extract and, lastly, the fruit mixture. Grease a deep 8'' x 10'' (2 L) loaf pan, cover with heavy paper, and grease again. Pour in batter. Bake at 300°F (150°C) for 3 hours. A double recipe makes a three-tier wedding cake.

SUNSHINE FRUIT CAKE

1½ cups	butter	375 mL
2¾ cups	sugar	675 mL
9	eggs	9
½ tsp.	salt	2 mL
1 tsp.	nutmeg	5 mL
1 tsp.	vanilla	5 mL
5 cups	flour	1.25 L
2½ tsp.	baking powder	12 mL
1 lb.	glazed fruit, no peel	500 g
14 oz.	crushed pineapple	398 mL
4 rounds	glazed pineapple	4 rounds
1 lb.	glazed cherries	500 g
1½ cups	coconut, shredded	375 mL
¾ lb.	almonds, blanched	375 g
½ lb.	glazed apricots	250 g
3 lb.	sultana raisins	1.5 kg

Cream butter and sugar. Beat in eggs one at a time, then add salt, nutmeg, and vanilla. Dust fruit and nuts with some of the flour. Mix remaining flour and baking powder, and add to batter. Fold in fruit. Pour into 3 greased 9" x 5" (2 L) loaf pans. Bake at 300°F (150°C) for 2½ hours. (Smaller tin-foil pans require shorter baking time.)

TROPICAL FRUIT CAKE

3 cups	brazil nuts	750 mL
1 lb.	pitted dates	500 g
1 cup	maraschino cherries	250 mL
¾ cup	flour, sifted	175 mL
¾ cup	sugar	175 mL
½ tsp.	baking powder	2 mL
½ tsp.	salt	2 mL
3	eggs	3
1 tsp.	vanilla	5 mL

Mix nuts, dates, and drained cherries together in a large bowl. Sift dry ingredients over nuts and fruit, and mix with hands until coated. Beat eggs until foamy; add vanilla. Blend well with nut-fruit mixture. Spread evenly into a greased 9" x 5" (2 L) loaf pan that has been lined with wax paper. Bake at 300°F (150°C) for 1¾ hours. Cool before slicing. Yields 1, 3 lb. cake.

HONEY RAISIN CAKE

3	eggs	3
1 cup	sugar	250 mL
1 cup	oil	250 mL
1 cup	strong coffee	250 mL
1 tsp.	baking soda	5 mL
1 cup	honey	250 mL
3 cups	flour	750 mL
2 tsp.	baking powder	10 mL
½ tsp.	cinnamon	2 mL
¼ tsp.	allspice	1 mL
½ cup	raisins	125 mL
½ cup	maraschino cherries	125 mL

Beat eggs well. Add sugar and oil. Dissolve baking soda in coffee and add to batter. Add honey, and mix well. Beat in dry ingredients. Drain and chop the cherries, combine with raisins, and mix into batter. Pour into a greased bundt or tube pan and bake at 325°F (160°C) for 1 hour.

LECKACH

1¼ cups	brown sugar	300 mL
1 cup	honey	250 mL
4	eggs	4
¾ cup	oil	175 mL
3 cups	flour	750 mL
1 tsp.	baking powder	5 mL
1 tsp.	cinnamon	5 mL
1 tsp.	allspice	5 mL
1 tsp.	baking soda	5 mL
1 cup	cold strong coffee	250 mL

Beat brown sugar and honey together. Add eggs one at a time, beating after each addition. Add oil and beat well. Stir in remaining ingredients, pour into a greased 8" x 14" (3 L) pan, and bake at 325°F (160°C) for 1 hour.

SPICED HONEY CAKE

2½ cups	flour	625 mL
½ tsp.	baking soda	2 mL
½ tsp.	cinnamon	2 mL

3 tsp.	baking powder	15 mL
1 tsp.	allspice	5 mL
1 tsp.	ginger	5 mL
4	eggs	4
1 cup	sugar	250 mL
1/2 cup	oil	125 mL
1 cup	buckwheat honey	250 mL
1 cup	orange juice	250 mL

Grease a 10'' (2 L) tube pan. Combine dry ingredients and sift twice. Beat the eggs. Add sugar gradually, beating well. Mix oil, melted honey, and orange juice; add to egg mixture alternately with dry ingredients. Pour into prepared pan. Bake at 350°F (180°C) for 50 minutes or until cake tests done.

MOCHA CREAM CAKE

4	eggs, separated	4
1 tbsp.	very strong coffee	15 mL
1 cup	berry sugar	250 mL
1 cup	flour, sifted	250 mL
1 tsp.	baking powder	5 mL

Beat egg yolks, add coffee and sugar, and beat well. Add sifted flour and baking powder. Whip egg whites and fold into mixture. Pour into 2 greased, round baking pans. Bake at 325°F (160°C) for 15 minutes.

Filling

1 cup	whipping cream	250 mL
2 tsp.	very strong coffee	10 mL
5 tbsp.	icing sugar	75 mL

Whip all ingredients together. Pile between layers and on top of cake. Sprinkle with nuts.

LEMON POLKA DOT CAKE

1 cup	butter	250 mL
2 cups	sugar	500 mL
6	eggs	6
4 tbsp.	lemon rind, grated	60 mL

4 cups	flour	1 L
2 tsp.	baking soda	10 mL
2 tsp.	baking powder	10 mL
1/2 tsp.	salt	2 mL
2 cups	sour cream	500 mL
1 1/4 cups	chocolate chips	300 mL

Grease 2, 10'' (2 L) tube pans. Cream the butter at high speed in an electric mixer until light. Gradually add sugar, beating until creamy and light. Add eggs one at a time, beating well after each addition. Add lemon rind. Stop mixer. Sift dry ingredients together, then add all at once to creamed mixture. Pour sour cream on top. Mix with a spatula just to cover the flour, then mix at high speed for 2 minutes. Add chocolate chips and beat 1 minute at high speed. Pour batter into pans and bake at 350°F (180°C) for 55 minutes or until cake tests done. Cool on a cake rack for 10 minutes. Unmould onto wax paper and baste immediately with syrup.

Syrup

1 cup	sugar	250 mL
2 tbsp.	lemon juice	30 mL
4 tbsp.	orange juice or liqueur	60 mL

Bring to a boil over low heat.

VELVET ORANGE CAKE

1 2/3 cups	flour, sifted	400 mL
1 cup	sugar	250 mL
1/4 tsp.	salt	1 mL
1/2 tsp.	baking soda	2 mL
1/2 cup	butter	125 mL
1 tbsp.	orange rind, grated	15 mL
1/2 cup	orange juice	125 mL
1/2 tsp.	lemon extract	2 mL
1 tsp.	baking powder	5 mL
2	eggs	2

Sift flour, sugar, salt, and soda into a mixing bowl. Add softened butter, orange rind and juice, and lemon extract. Beat vigorously for 2 minutes by hand or at low speed with electric mixer. Stir in baking powder. Add unbeaten eggs and beat 2 minutes. Pour into a greased and lightly floured 8'' square (2 L) cake pan. Bake at 350°F (180°C) for 35 to 40 minutes. Let stand 5 minutes and turn out. Frost with orange icing (see p. 197) when cold.

PINEAPPLE CAKE

Filling

14 oz.	crushed pineapple	398 mL
1/3 cup	sugar	75 mL
2 tbsp.	cornstarch	30 mL
1 tbsp.	lemon juice	15 mL

Combine all ingredients in a saucepan and cook until thick. Cool.

Batter

1/4 cup	butter	50 mL
1 1/4 cups	flour	300 mL
1 tsp.	baking powder	5 mL
	pinch of salt	
2	egg yolks	2
3 tbsp.	milk	45 mL
1/2 tsp.	vanilla	2 mL

Mix all ingredients together and put on the bottom of a greased and lightly floured 8'' square (2 L) cake pan. Spread cooled filling over batter.

Topping

2	egg whites	2
	pinch of salt	
1 cup	coconut, shredded	250 mL

Beat egg whites with salt until stiff. Fold in coconut. Spread over pineapple filling. Bake at 350°F (180°C) for 30 to 40 minutes.

POPPY SEED CAKE

1 cup	poppy seed	250 mL
1 cup	milk	250 mL
1/2 cup	butter	125 mL
1 cup	sugar	250 mL
2	eggs, separated	2
2 cups	flour	500 mL
1/2 tsp.	salt	2 mL
2 tsp.	baking powder	10 mL
1 tsp.	orange rind, grated	5 mL

Soak poppy seeds in milk for 1 hour. Cream butter and sugar. Add beaten egg yolks, and mix until smooth. Sift dry ingredients together and add alternately with milk and poppy seed. Beat well. Add orange rind, and fold in stiffly beaten egg whites. Pour into a well-greased 8'' square (2 L) pan. Bake at 350°F (180°C) for 45 minutes. When cool, sprinkle with sifted icing sugar. (Note: 1/2 tsp. (2 mL) almond extract may be substituted for the orange rind.)

LEMON CREAM CHEESE POUND CAKE

1/2 lb.	cream cheese	250 g
1 cup	butter	250 mL
1 1/2 cups	sugar	375 mL
2 tbsp.	lemon juice	30 mL
1 1/2 tsp.	lemon rind, grated	7 mL
1 tsp.	vanilla	5 mL
2 1/4 cups	cake flour	550 mL
2 tsp.	baking powder	10 mL
1/4 tsp.	salt	1 mL

Cream together the cheese and butter. Add sugar a little at a time, beating well between each addition. Beat in lemon juice, rind, and vanilla. Sift flour, baking powder, and salt together and add to the cheese mixture a little at a time. Transfer the batter to a well-greased 2 1/2 quart (2.5 L) bundt or tube pan and bake at 325°F (160°C) for 1 1/4 hours, or until a cake tester inserted in the centre comes out clean. Let the cake cool in the pan on a rack for 10 minutes before removing. Sift icing sugar over the top before serving.

MOCHA POUND CAKE

1/3 cup	butter	75 mL
1/3 cup	shortening	75 mL

2 cups	cake flour, sifted	500 mL
1 1/4 cups	sugar	300 mL
1 tsp.	salt	5 mL
1/2 tsp.	cream of tartar	2 mL
1/4 tsp.	baking soda	1 mL
1 tbsp.	instant coffee	15 mL
1/2 cup	cold water	125 mL
1 tsp.	vanilla	5 mL
3	eggs	3
2 oz.	bitter chocolate	56 g

Cream butter and shortening. Add sifted dry ingredients, water, and vanilla. Beat at low speed until flour is dampened, then at medium speed until smooth (about 2 minutes). Add the eggs one at a time, beating between each addition. Add melted chocolate and beat 1 minute longer. Pour into a greased 9" x 5" (2 L) loaf pan, lined with wax paper. Bake at 325°F (160°C) for 80 minutes. Cool 10 minutes in pan before sprinkling with sifted icing sugar.

FLAMING CHERRY JUBILEE CAKE

2 tbsp.	butter	30 mL
3 tbsp.	light brown sugar	45 mL
14 oz.	pitted bing cherries	398 mL
3 tbsp.	soft butter	45 mL
2/3 cup	sugar	150 mL
1 cup	cake flour, sifted	250 mL
1 tsp.	baking powder	5 mL
1/4 tsp.	salt	1 mL
1/3 cup	milk	75 mL
1/2 tsp.	almond extract	2 mL
2	egg whites	2
1/4 cup	slivered almonds, toasted	50 mL
1/2 cup	whipped cream	125 mL
	red currant jelly	
	small sugar cubes	
	lemon extract	

In a 9" (1 L) layer cake pan, melt the 2 tbsp. (30 mL) butter. Remove from heat and sprinkle on brown sugar. Cover completely with drained cherries. In a small mixing bowl, beat soft butter until creamy. Gradually add sugar, beating until light and fluffy. Sift flour, baking powder, and salt, and beat in alternately with milk. Stir in almond extract. Whip egg whites until they form stiff peaks. Gently fold into the batter until well combined. Pour into cake pan over the cherries. Bake at 350°F (180°C) for 35 to 40 minutes or until a cake tester or toothpick comes out clean. Let stand in pan 5 minutes. Turn out onto serving platter and cool. Just before serving, sprinkle top with slivered almonds; garnish with swirls of whipped cream topped with dots of currant jelly. To flame: On top of cake, arrange sugar cubes dipped in lemon extract; light, and serve.

SOUR CREAM POUND CAKE

3 cups	sugar	750 mL
1 cup	butter	250 mL
6	eggs, separated	6
3 cups	flour	750 mL
1/4 tsp.	baking soda	1 mL
1/4 tsp.	salt	1 mL
1 cup	sour cream	250 mL
1 tsp.	vanilla	5 mL
1 tsp.	almond extract	5 mL
1/2 tsp.	lemon extract	2 mL

Cream butter and sugar. Add egg yolks one at a time, beating well after each addition. Sift dry ingredients; add alternately with sour cream. Add flavourings. Beat egg whites until stiff and fold in. Bake in a greased tube pan at 300°F (150°C) for 1 1/2 hours.

QUEEN ELIZABETH CAKE

1 cup	dates	250 mL
1 cup	boiling water	250 mL
1/2 tsp.	baking soda	2 mL
1/4 cup	butter	50 mL
1 cup	sugar	250 mL
1 tsp.	vanilla	5 mL
1 1/3 cups	flour	325 mL
1/2 tsp.	salt	2 mL
1/2 tsp.	baking powder	2 mL

Cook dates in water to a paste. Add soda; set aside. Cream butter and sugar slightly. Combine with date mixture, then add vanilla. Sift remaining dry ingredients together, and fold in. Turn into an 8" square (2 L) cake pan. Bake at 350°F (180°C) for 40 minutes. While cake is baking, prepare topping.

Topping

¾ cup	coconut, shredded	175 mL
4 tbsp.	butter	60 mL
6 tbsp.	brown sugar	90 mL
2 tbsp.	cream	30 mL

Combine all ingredients in a saucepan. Cook 3 minutes, stirring constantly. Spread on cake while warm. Place under broiler until brown and sizzly.

SPONGE CAKE

12	eggs, separated	12
2 cups	sugar	500 mL
2 tbsp.	lemon juice	30 mL
1 tsp.	lemon rind, grated	5 mL
1 tsp.	almond extract	5 mL
2 cups	flour	500 mL

Beat egg whites until stiff, adding sugar gradually. In another bowl, beat egg yolks. Add lemon juice and rind, and almond extract. Fold a third of the whites into yolks, then fold in a third of the flour. Repeat twice. Pour into a tube pan and bake at 350°F (180°C) for 1 hour. Invert onto rack and let cool completely before removing from pan.

COFFEE SPONGE CAKE

1 tbsp.	instant coffee	15 mL
1 cup	boiling water	250 mL
2 cups	cake flour, sifted	500 mL
3 tsp.	baking powder	15 mL
½ tsp.	salt	2 mL
6	eggs, separated	6
½ tsp.	cream of tartar	2 mL
2 cups	sugar	500 mL
1 tsp.	vanilla	5 mL
1 cup	pecan nuts, ground	250 mL

Dissolve instant coffee in boiling water. Cool. Sift flour with baking powder and salt; set aside. Beat egg whites with cream of tartar in a large bowl at high speed. Gradually add ½ cup (125 mL) sugar, 2 tbsp. (30 mL) at a time, until very stiff. Do not underbeat. In a separate bowl, beat egg yolks lightly. Add remainder of sugar, and vanilla. Beat at high speed until thick and lemon-coloured (about 4 to 5 minutes). Add dry ingredients alternately with cooled coffee to the egg yolk mixture, beginning and ending with dry ingredients and blending at low speed after each addition. Fold in nuts thoroughly. Fold batter one-quarter at a time into egg whites, folding 15 strokes after each addition. Pour into an ungreased tube pan. Bake at 350°F (180°C) for 60 to 75 minutes. Invert and cool.

Coffee Icing

2 tbsp.	butter	30 mL
2 cups	icing sugar, sifted	500 mL
1½ tsp.	instant coffee	7 mL
3 tbsp.	milk	45 mL

Cream butter. Blend in icing sugar and instant coffee, beating well. Add enough milk to make a spreading consistency.

MAGIC TOMATO SOUP CAKE

2 tbsp.	butter	30 mL
1 cup	sugar	250 mL
2 cups	cake flour	500 mL
1 tsp.	cloves	5 mL
1 tsp.	cinnamon	5 mL
1 tsp.	nutmeg	5 mL
¼ tsp.	salt	1 mL
10 oz.	condensed tomato soup	284 mL
1 tsp.	baking soda	5 mL

Cream butter and sugar well. Sift flour, measure, and re-sift 3 times with spices and salt. Dissolve baking soda in tomato soup. Add dry ingredients to creamed mixture alternately with soup. Pour into a greased 9" x 5" (2 L) loaf pan. Bake at 350°F (180°C) for 50 to 60 minutes.

Creamy Chocolate Frosting

3 oz.	cream cheese	100 g
3 tbsp.	milk	45 mL
3 cups	icing sugar, sifted	750 mL
2 oz.	unsweetened chocolate	56 g
1/2 tsp.	salt	2 mL
1 tsp.	vanilla	5 mL

Mash cheese. Add milk gradually, beating until blended. Gradually beat in icing sugar. When smooth, add melted chocolate, salt, and vanilla. Beat until smooth.

BUTTER-SPONGE CAKE

3	eggs	3
3/4 cup	sugar	175 mL
1/2 tsp.	vanilla	2 mL
1/2 tsp.	flavouring	2 mL
1 cup	flour, sifted	250 mL
1/4 cup	butter	50 mL
5 tbsp.	milk	75 mL
2 tsp.	baking powder	10 mL

Beat eggs and sugar until thick and creamy. Add flavourings and flour. Bring butter and milk to the boil and add to mixture. Lastly fold in baking powder. Bake at 325°F (160°C) for 15 minutes in 2 round pans or 25 minutes in 1 large pan.

CHERRY CUPCAKES

3	eggs	3
1/2 cup	shortening, melted	125 mL
3/4 cup	milk	175 mL
1 tsp.	vanilla	5 mL
1 1/2 cups	flour	375 mL
1 1/4 cups	sugar	300 mL
2 tsp.	baking powder	10 mL
	pinch of salt	
1 lb.	cherries	500 g

Mix eggs, shortening, milk, and vanilla together thoroughly. Sift dry ingredients together. Pit and chop the cherries. Combine with dry ingredients, then add to liquid mixture. Do not overmix. Fill paper muffin cups half full. Bake at 400°F (200°C) for 25 minutes. Makes 12 – 14.

FRUIT CUPCAKES

2 cups	flour	500 mL
1 tsp.	baking soda	5 mL
1 tsp.	salt	5 mL
1 tsp.	cinnamon	5 mL
1 tsp.	nutmeg	5 mL
1/2 cup	raisins	125 mL
1/2 cup	nutmeats, chopped	125 mL
1/2 cup	shortening	125 mL
1 cup	sugar	250 mL
1	egg	1
1 tbsp.	lemon rind, grated	15 mL
1 cup	apple sauce	250 mL

Sift flour, soda, salt, and spices. Combine raisins and nutmeats with flour mixture. Cream shortening. Add sugar, beating well. Break in egg and beat until mixture is fluffy. Stir in lemon rind and apple sauce. Add flour mixture and beat well. Fill greased muffin pans two-thirds full. Bake at 375°F (190°C) for 20 minutes. Makes 14 to 16 cupcakes.

ICINGS & FILLINGS

BUTTER FROSTING

½ cup	butter	125 mL
3 cups	icing sugar, sifted	750 mL
4 tbsp.	cream	60 mL
1 tsp.	vanilla	5 mL

Cream butter. Gradually add remaining ingredients and beat until well blended and fluffy.

Variations

Orange Frosting
Use orange juice instead of cream, and add 1 level tbsp. (15 mL) grated orange rind.

Mocha Frosting
Use strong coffee instead of cream, and sift 2 to 3 tbsp. (30 to 45 mL) cocoa with the icing sugar.

Lemon Frosting
Use half the amount of cream, substitute lemon juice to taste instead of vanilla, and add ½ tsp. (2 mL) grated lemon rind.

Pineapple Frosting
In place of cream, substitute ⅓ cup (75 mL) canned crushed pineapple and juice.

Toasted Coconut Topping
Spread desiccated coconut on a cookie sheet, and toast in a moderately hot oven until a delicate golden colour. Cool. Press thickly around sides and top of cake iced with butter frosting.

CONFECTIONER'S ICING

1 tbsp.	butter	15 mL
2 cups	icing sugar	500 mL
4 tbsp.	cream	60 mL
1 tsp.	vanilla	5 mL

Melt butter. Beat together with remaining ingredients until a smooth spreading consistency is obtained.

CREAM CHEESE FROSTING

3 oz.	cream cheese	75 g
1½ cups	icing sugar	375 mL
1 tsp.	vanilla	5 mL

Beat all ingredients together until fluffy.

SEVEN-MINUTE ICING

2	egg whites	2
1½ cups	sugar	375 mL
⅓ cup	water	75 mL
	pinch of salt	
¼ tsp.	cream of tartar	1 mL
1 tsp.	vanilla	5 mL

Combine egg whites, sugar, water, salt, and cream of tartar in the top of a double boiler. Beat constantly with rotary beater over boiling water for 7 minutes or until mixture holds a point when beater is lifted. Add vanilla, remove from heat, and continue beating until cool enough to spread.

Variation
Add ½ lb. (250 g) chopped marshmallows to hot icing, and beat until cool and smooth.

PAREVE CHOCOLATE ICING

1 cup	shortening	250 mL
3	eggs	3
2½ cups	icing sugar	625 mL
6 tbsp.	cocoa	90 mL
	pinch of salt	
1 tsp.	vanilla	5 mL

Cream shortening, then add eggs one at a time. Blend in remaining ingredients and beat very well.

PAREVE CHOCOLATE WHIP FROSTING

5 oz.	unsweetened chocolate	140 g
3 cups	icing sugar, sifted	750 mL
	pinch of salt	
2½ tbsp.	hot water	35 mL
3	egg yolks	3
½ cup	shortening	125 mL

Melt chocolate. Add sugar, salt, and water. Mix, then add egg yolks one at a time, beating well after each addition. Add shortening a little at a time, beating thoroughly.

CHOCOLATE CREAM FROSTING

3 oz.	unsweetened chocolate	85 g
3 oz.	cream cheese	85 g
¼ cup	milk	50 mL
3 cups	icing sugar, sifted	750 mL
	pinch of salt	
1 tsp.	vanilla	5 mL

Melt chocolate over boiling water. In a deep bowl, blend cream cheese and milk. Gradually add sifted icing sugar, salt, and vanilla. Beat in melted chocolate.

MINT CHOCOLATE ICING

2 oz.	unsweetened chocolate	56 g
3 tbsp.	butter	45 mL
1 cup	icing sugar	250 mL
1	egg	1
¼ cup	cream	50 mL
½ tsp.	peppermint extract	2 mL

Melt butter and chocolate. Beat all ingredients together, adding peppermint extract last. (If margarine is used instead of butter, more icing sugar will be required.)

FIVE-MINUTE CHOCOLATE ICING

| 2 oz. | chocolate | 56 g |
| 1⅓ cups | condensed milk | 325 mL |

Melt chocolate over boiling water, add condensed milk, and stir 5 minutes or until thickened.

CHOCOLATE BANANA ICING

¼ cup	butter	50 mL
½ cup	bananas, mashed	125 mL
⅔ cup	cocoa	150 mL
2½ cups	icing sugar	625 mL

Cream butter and mashed bananas. Gradually add cocoa and icing sugar. Beat until smooth.

MOCHA ICING

⅔ cup	butter	150 mL
1	egg yolk	1
1 tsp.	vanilla	5 mL
2½ cups	icing sugar	625 mL
	strong coffee	

Cream butter, add beaten egg yolk, and gradually add sugar, vanilla, and strong coffee to taste.

BROWNIES ICING

2 oz.	unsweetened chocolate	56 g
2 tbsp.	butter	30 mL
2 cups	icing sugar	500 mL
	pinch of salt	
½ tsp.	vanilla	2 mL
2	egg whites	2

Melt chocolate and butter. Beat in icing sugar, salt, and vanilla. Beat egg whites until stiff and fold in.

SOFT WHITE ICING

¾ cup	icing sugar	175 mL
3 tbsp.	milk	45 mL
1 tsp.	butter	5 mL
	almond or lemon extract	

Blend icing sugar, milk, butter, and a few drops of extract until smooth.

ANGEL FOOD TOPPING

3 cups	whipping cream	750 mL
6 tbsp.	cocoa	90 mL
6 tbsp.	sugar	90 mL
	pinch of salt	

Mix ingredients well. Refrigerate for a few hours and then beat until thick.

ORANGE ICING

2 tbsp.	butter	30 mL
¼ tsp.	lemon extract	1 mL
½ tsp.	orange rind, grated	2 mL
2 cups	icing sugar, sifted	500 mL
3 tbsp.	orange juice	45 mL

Cream butter until fluffy. Add lemon extract and orange rind. Add sifted icing sugar alternately with orange juice. Beat until creamy and smooth.

CREAMY ORANGE FILLING

5	eggs, separated	5
¾ cup	sugar	175 mL
1½ tbsp.	flour	20 mL
1 tbsp.	orange rind, grated	15 mL
3 tbsp.	lemon juice	45 mL
1½ cups	orange juice	375 mL
1½ tbsp.	butter, melted	20 mL
	pinch of salt	

Beat egg yolks slightly. Combine with the other ingredients, except egg whites, in the top of a double boiler. Cook over boiling water until thick, stirring constantly. Cool. Beat egg whites until stiff but not dry. Fold into filling. Chill overnight in refrigerator. Spread filling between layers of white cake and frost with whipped cream.

PINEAPPLE FILLING

1	pineapple, grated	1
½ cup	water	125 mL
½ cup	sugar	125 mL
½ tbsp.	custard powder	8 mL

Boil grated pineapple, water, and sugar to taste. Moisten custard powder with a little cold water and add to pineapple mixture. Stir until thick. Cool before using.

LEMON FILLING

2 oz.	butter	50 g
2 tbsp.	lemon juice	30 mL
½ cup	sugar	125 mL
2	eggs	2

Melt butter, juice, and sugar in the top of a double boiler. Slowly add well-beaten eggs. Stir until thick. Cool and bottle. Keeps in the refrigerator for months.

PASSION FRUIT FILLING

12	passion fruit	12
½ cup	butter	125 mL
1 cup	sugar	250 mL
2	eggs	2

Scoop out passion fruit pulp, and heat in the top of a double boiler. Add butter and sugar. Stir until butter is melted. Beat eggs well, and add. Cook until thick.

STABILIZED WHIPPED CREAM

½ tbsp.	unflavoured gelatine	3.5 g
3 tbsp.	water	45 mL
1 cup	whipping cream	250 mL
3 tbsp.	icing sugar	45 mL
1 tsp.	vanilla or brandy or rum	5 mL

In a heat-proof bowl, sprinkle gelatine over room-temperature water and let stand until water has been absorbed. Place bowl over boiling water and stir only until gelatine is dissolved. Do not boil. Cool to room temperature but do not let gelatine set. Beat chilled cream in a cold bowl to the consistency of soft custard. Continue beating while pouring in gelatine mixture in a steady stream. Beat until almost stiff. Add icing sugar and vanilla, or other flavourings, and beat until stiff. This stabilized cream may be made hours ahead of time and refrigerated. Yields 2½ to 3 cups (625 to 750 mL).

TORTES

APPLE TORTE

Apple Filling

3 lb.	apples	1.5 kg
1½ cups	brown sugar	375 mL
1 tsp.	water	5 mL
1 tbsp.	lemon juice	15 mL
14 oz.	crushed pineapple	398 mL

Peel, core, and cut up apples. Combine all ingredients and cook until thick, like apple sauce.

Dough

¾ cup	oil	175 mL
2	eggs	2
½ cup	sugar	125 mL
3 cups	flour	750 mL
2 tsp.	baking powder	10 mL
1 tbsp.	milk	15 mL
½ cup	brown sugar	125 mL
1 tsp.	cinnamon	5 mL
¼ cup	nuts, chopped	50 mL

Mix first 5 ingredients together. Divide dough into 4 portions. Put one layer of dough in an 8" x 12" (3 L) pan. Add one-third of apple filling. Repeat layers twice, and top with dough. Brush with milk. Combine brown sugar, cinnamon, and nuts; sprinkle over top. Bake at 350°F (180°C) for 1½ hours.

MEDITERRANEAN APPLE TORTE

1 lb.	phyllo leaves	454 g
1 lb.	butter, melted	450 g
1½ cups	sugar	375 mL
½ cup	Grand Marnier	125 mL
6	tart apples	6

Grease a 14" (3 L) flat pan. Place one phyllo sheet flat in pan and brush lightly with butter, using a pastry brush. Sprinkle with 1 tbsp. (15 mL) sugar, then a little Grand Marnier. Repeat 6 times. Peel apples and slice thinly onto dough. Brush apple layer with butter, sprinkle with ½ cup (125 mL) sugar, and Grand Marnier. Repeat layering of phyllo leaves, sugar, and Grand Marnier, ending with phyllo and butter. Pinch edges. Bake at 425°F (220°C) for 30 to 45 minutes until golden. Cover with aluminum foil if torte is becoming too dark. Serve hot.

CHOCOLATE APRICOT TORTE

1 cup	butter	250 mL
¾ cup	sugar	175 mL
1	egg	1
1 tsp.	vanilla	5 mL

¼ tsp.	baking soda	1 mL
3 cups	flour	750 mL
	pinch of salt	
19 oz.	apricot pie filling	540 mL

Cream butter and sugar. Mix in egg, vanilla, and dry ingredients. Divide dough into 5 portions and pat into 8" or 9" (1 L) layer pans. Bake at 375°F (190°C) for 15 minutes. Remove from pans, spread apricot pie filling between warm layers, and stack.

Icing

1½ oz.	semi-sweet chocolate	42 g
3 tbsp.	butter	45 mL
1	egg	1
5 tbsp.	icing sugar	90 mL
1 tsp.	vanilla	5 mL

Melt chocolate and butter; cool. Add egg, icing sugar, and vanilla, and beat with a spoon until smooth and glossy. Cover torte completely. Decorate with slivered almonds and refrigerate. This torte is best made a day or two before serving.

APRICOT MOCHA TORTE

Mocha Buttercream

4	egg yolks	4
⅔ cup	sugar	150 mL
1 tbsp.	instant coffee	15 mL
¼ cup	water	50 mL
1 cup	butter	250 mL

Beat egg yolks until thick and lemon-coloured, and set aside. In a medium saucepan, combine sugar, instant coffee, and water. Bring to boil, stirring until sugar and coffee dissolve. Cook over low heat without stirring until soft ball stage — 236°F (120°C) on a candy thermometer. Quickly pour hot syrup in a steady stream into egg yolks. Beat at high speed until smooth. Cool. Cream butter until fluffy. Beat into mocha mixture a spoonful at a time. Cover bowl and refrigerate 30 minutes or until cream is firm enough to spread evenly. While buttercream is in refrigerator, bake cake.

Cake

6	eggs, slightly beaten	6
1 cup	sugar	250 mL
1 cup	flour, sifted	250 mL
½ cup	butter, melted	125 mL
½ tsp.	vanilla	2 mL
½ tsp.	almond extract	2 mL

Combine eggs and sugar, stirring just until mixed. Set bowl over a large saucepan containing 2" (5 cm) hot water. (The water must not be boiling.) Heat egg and sugar mixture for 8 to 10 minutes until lukewarm, stirring occasionally. Remove from heat. Beat at high speed for about 15 minutes, until light and tripled in volume. Gently fold in flour, a third at a time. Gradually fold in cooled butter and flavourings. Pour into 2 greased and floured 9" (1 L) round pans. Bake at 350°F (180°C) for 25 to 30 minutes or until cake tests done. Cool in pan 10 minutes before removing to wire racks. While cake is cooling, prepare glaze.

Apricot Glaze

| ¾ cup | apricot preserves | 175 mL |
| 2 tbsp. | brandy | 30 mL |

Combine apricot preserves and brandy in a saucepan. Heat to boiling.

To Assemble Cake

Split layers in half. Place one layer on a platter. Spread thinly with apricot glaze. Top with second layer and spread with mocha buttercream. Add third layer, spreading with apricot glaze. Cover with last layer and ice with remaining buttercream. Decorate with apricot halves.

BANANA BUTTERSCOTCH TORTE

1 cup	butter	250 mL
1 cup	sugar	250 mL
1	egg	1
3 cups	flour	750 mL
1 tsp.	baking powder	5 mL

Cream butter. Add sugar and beat well. Beat in egg. Sift flour and baking powder, and add. Divide into 5 portions, pat into 9'' (1 L) layer pans, and bake at 350°F (180°C) for 10 to 15 minutes until golden.

Filling

9³/₄ oz.	butterscotch pudding mix	276 g
3	bananas	3
	lemon juice	

Cook puddings according to directions. Cool. Cut up bananas and soak in lemon juice. Stack shortbread layers, filling with pudding and bananas between each.

Topping

1 cup	whipping cream	250 mL
1 tbsp.	icing sugar	15 mL
	peanut brittle	

Whip cream, adding icing sugar gradually. Spread over top and sides of the torte. Sprinkle with crushed peanut brittle.

CHOCOLATE ALMOND TORTE

¹/₄ cup	shortening	50 mL
1 cup	sugar	250 mL
2	eggs, separated	2
2 oz.	unsweetened chocolate	56 g
1¹/₄ cups	flour, sifted	300 mL
¹/₂ tsp.	baking soda	2 mL
¹/₂ tsp.	baking powder	2 mL
¹/₂ tsp.	salt	2 mL
³/₄ cup	milk	175 mL
1 tsp.	vanilla	5 mL

Cream shortening and sugar. Beat egg yolks and blend with creamed mixture. Stir in melted chocolate. Combine flour, baking soda, baking powder, and salt; sift twice. Add to creamed mixture alternately with milk, and mix thoroughly. Add vanilla. Beat egg whites stiff and fold in. Spread batter into 2 greased 9'' (1 L) round pans and bake at 350°F (180°C) for 25 minutes. Cool.

Frosting

8 oz.	semi-sweet chocolate	250 g
1 cup	whipping cream	250 mL
¹/₂ cup	slivered almonds	125 mL

Melt chocolate in the top of a double boiler over hot water. Cool slightly. Whip cream until stiff and fold warm chocolate over it. Mixture should be smooth and dark. Spread thickly between the 2 cake layers, and frost cake completely. Decorate with roasted slivered almonds on sides and as a border on edge of top. Refrigerate.

CHOCOLATE CREAM TORTE

1 cup	butter	250 mL
¹/₂ cup	sugar	125 mL
2 cups	flour	500 mL
2	eggs	2
1 tsp.	baking powder	5 mL
2 tsp.	vanilla	10 mL

Cream butter and sugar. Blend in remaining ingredients to make dough. Divide into 6 portions and roll into circles 8'' (20 cm) in diameter. Bake at 350°F (180°C) for 10 minutes. Cool on wire rack.

Filling

3 oz.	chocolate pudding mix	90 g
1 cup	butter	250 mL
1 tsp.	vanilla	2 mL

Cook pudding according to package directions. Cool until cold. Beat butter until creamy. Fold in pudding one spoonful at a time. Add vanilla and beat well. Spread between layers.

FAMOUS NORMANDY TORTE

40	chocolate wafers	40
8 oz.	semi-sweet chocolate	250 g
1 cup	whipping cream	250 mL
¹/₂ tsp.	instant coffee	2 mL

overleaf:
Apricot Mocha Torte (page 199);
Chocolate-Filled Brazil Nut Log (page 187)

1 tbsp.	dark rum	15 mL
1 quart	dark chocolate ice cream	1 L
1 quart	Swiss mocha ice cream	1 L
8 oz.	Almond Roca	250 g

Crush wafers. Press half the crumbs into the bottom of an 8" or 9" (1.5 L) springform pan. Combine chocolate, cream, instant coffee, and rum in a saucepan and heat slowly until chocolate is melted. Spread a layer of chocolate ice cream over crumbs and spoon on a layer of sauce. Pat on the rest of the crumbs; then spoon another layer of sauce. Add a layer of mocha ice cream, then more sauce. Top with chopped Almond Roca. Freeze covered until needed. Cut in wedges and serve with extra sauce.

CINNAMON TORTE

1 1/2 cups	butter	375 mL
2 cups	sugar	500 mL
2	eggs	2
2 3/4 cups	flour	675 mL
2 tbsp.	cinnamon	30 mL

Beat butter and sugar until creamy. Beat in eggs. Sift flour and cinnamon together, and add. Cover dough and let stand for 15 minutes. Divide dough into 12 portions. Working dough with fingers or a knife, spread each portion on the back of a 9" (1 L) layer pan to within 1/8" (3 mm) of the edge. Bake at 375°F (190°C) for 12 to 15 minutes, until lightly brown. Immediately run a knife under each cake to loosen, and turn out onto foil or wax paper. (It is easiest to use 6 layer pans and bake the layers 3 at a time, preparing the next 3 while the first 3 are in the oven.)

Filling

4 cups	whipping cream	1 L
2 tbsp.	icing sugar	30 mL
1 tsp.	vanilla	5 mL
2 tbsp.	cocoa	30 mL

Whip cream with icing sugar and vanilla until stiff. Sandwich cake layers together with gener-

ous amounts of cream, reserving some for the top. Add cocoa to reserved cream, spread over top, and decorate with chocolate curls. (The cake layers may be prepared ahead of time and frozen until required.)

HUNGARIAN NUT TORTE

1 cup	butter	250 mL
1/2 cup	icing sugar	125 mL
1/4 lb.	almonds, ground	125 g
2 cups	flour	500 mL

Cream butter and icing sugar. Add almonds. Work in the flour with fingertips until mixture is completely blended. Pat dough into the bottoms of 4 greased, 8" (1 L) cake pans. Bake at 350°F (180°C) until lightly browned (about 15 minutes). Cool, and remove from pans.

Filling

1 lb.	walnuts, ground	500 g
1 cup	icing sugar	250 mL
1/2 cup	cream	125 mL
1 cup	whipping cream	250 mL

Make a paste of the walnuts, icing sugar, and just enough cream to moisten. Spread filling onto 3 of the cake layers. Stack them, and top with a plain layer. An hour before serving, cover top and sides of torte with whipped cream and decorate with chocolate swirls. Refrigerate until ready to serve.

FRUIT NUT TORTE

1 cup	canned fruit cocktail	250 mL
1	egg	1
3/4 cup	sugar	175 mL
1 cup	flour	250 mL
1 tsp.	baking soda	5 mL
1 tsp.	cinnamon	5 mL
1/4 tsp.	salt	1 mL
1/4 cup	brown sugar	50 mL
1/2 cup	walnuts, chopped	125 mL

Drain the fruit cocktail, reserving ¼ cup (50 mL) of the syrup. Beat egg, sugar, fruit cocktail and syrup together well. Stir in flour, baking soda, cinnamon, and salt; mix thoroughly. Turn into a greased 9" (1 L) springform pan. Combine walnuts and brown sugar and sprinkle evenly over the batter. Bake at 350°F (180°C) for 30 to 35 minutes. Pour hot icing over the cake as it comes out of the oven. Serve with whipped cream.

Hot Icing

¾ cup	sugar	175 mL
½ cup	evaporated milk	125 mL
⅓ cup	margarine	75 mL
½ tsp.	vanilla	2 mL

About 8 minutes before cake is done, combine sugar, evaporated milk, and margarine. Boil for 3 minutes, stirring. Remove from heat and add vanilla.

MARSHMALLOW TORTE

2 cups	vanilla wafer crumbs	500 mL
½ cup	butter	125 mL

Melt butter, mix with crumbs, and pat into the bottom of a springform pan to form crust.

Filling

3 oz.	unsweetened chocolate	84 g
½ cup	butter	125 mL
1½ cups	icing sugar	375 mL
3	eggs	3
½ cup	maple syrup	125 mL
1½ cups	whipping cream	375 mL
10 oz.	miniature marshmallows	283 g

Melt chocolate; cool. Cream butter and add icing sugar. Add eggs one at a time, beating well between each addition. Add chocolate. Place over a large bowl filled with ice cubes, and beat until fluffy. Pour over the wafer crust. Refrigerate. Whip syrup and cream until firm. Fold in marshmallows and pour over chocolate mixture. Decorate with chocolate shavings.

FROZEN LEMON MERINGUE TORTE

	lady fingers	
7	eggs, separated	7
1⅞ cups	sugar	450 mL
½ cup	lemon juice	125 mL
1½ tbsp.	lemon rind, grated	20 mL
2 cups	whipping cream	500 mL

Line the bottom and sides of a springform pan with lady fingers. (Either butter the pan or put a dab of butter on the lady fingers to hold them in place.) In the top of a double boiler, beat egg yolks with 1 cup (250 mL) sugar, lemon rind and juice. Cook until thick. Whip cream and fold into thickened lemon mixture. Pour into springform pan. Beat egg whites until stiff, adding remaining sugar. Spoon meringue over torte, covering right up to the edge of the lady fingers. Broil in oven until brown, about 5 minutes. Cover completely and freeze.

POPPY SEED TORTE

¾ cup	poppy seed	175 mL
¾ cup	milk	175 mL
¾ cup	butter	175 mL
1½ cups	sugar	375 mL
2 cups	cake flour	500 mL
2 tsp.	baking powder	10 mL
¼ tsp.	salt	1 mL
4	egg whites	4

Soak poppy seed in milk overnight. Cream butter, gradually adding sugar. Sift dry ingredients, and add to butter alternately with poppy seed and milk mixture. Beat egg whites stiff, and fold in. Bake in 3 paper-lined, 8" (1 L) round pans at 350°F (180°C) for 25 to 30 minutes. Remove from pans and cool.

Filling

½ cup	sugar	125 mL
1 tbsp.	cornstarch	15 mL
1½ cups	milk	375 mL

4	egg yolks, beaten	4
1 tsp.	vanilla	5 mL
1 tbsp.	rum extract	15 mL
1/4 cup	nuts, chopped	50 mL

Mix sugar and cornstarch in the top of a double boiler. Combine milk and egg yolks, and add. Stir constantly over medium heat until thick. Cool slightly, then add flavourings and nuts. Spread filling between poppy seed layers, then cover entire torte with chocolate icing.

SUPREME RUM TORTE

5 oz.	semi-sweet chocolate	140 g
2 oz.	bitter chocolate	60 g
1 cup	butter	250 mL
1/2 cup	icing sugar	125 mL
1/2 tsp.	vanilla	2 mL
	pinch of salt	
6	eggs, separated	6
1/4 cup	hot water	50 mL
3/4 cup	rum	150 mL
1 1/2 cups	milk	375 mL
22 oz.	vanilla wafers	625 g
1 cup	whipping cream	250 mL
	toasted almonds	
	shaved chocolate	

Melt semi-sweet and bitter chocolate in the top of a double boiler. Cool slightly. Cream together with butter and icing sugar. Add vanilla and salt. Beat in egg yolks one at a time, add hot water and 1 tbsp. (15 mL) of the rum, and beat well until creamy. Beat egg whites until stiff. Fold into chocolate mixture, and set aside. Pour milk and remaining rum into separate bowls. Working quickly, dip vanilla wafers first into milk then into rum, and line the bottom of an ungreased 9'' (1 L) springform pan. Pour one-third of the chocolate mixture over the wafer layer. Repeat dipped wafer and chocolate layering twice more (3 layers of chocolate filling). Top with a final layer of dipped wafers. Cover with plastic wrap and refrigerate overnight. Run a wet knife around inside of pan before releasing spring. Top with whipped cream and sprinkle with toasted almonds and shaved chocolate.

SHORTBREAD TORTE

1 cup	butter	250 mL
1 cup	sugar	250 mL
1	egg	1
3 cups	flour	750 mL
1 tsp.	baking powder	5 mL
6 oz.	chocolate pudding mix	170 g
1 cup	whipping cream	250 mL

Cream butter and sugar. Beat in egg, flour, and baking powder. Divide dough into 4 portions and press into 4 ungreased, 9'' (1 L) pans. Bake at 375°F (190°C) for 10 minutes, until very light brown. Remove layers from pans immediately. Prepare chocolate pudding according to package directions. While hot, spread onto shortbread layers, stacking them. Spread pudding over sides as well. Top with whipped cream. (The shortbread layers may be made ahead of time, but the final assembling should be done just before serving.)

Pies, Desserts & Cookies

"Promises and pie-crusts are made to be broken," but the promised taste-treat that is offered by a double-crust fresh fruit pie, warm from the oven, is always fulfilled.

In early culinary folklore, four-and-twenty blackbirds were baked in a pie and set before the King. Today, luscious fresh fruit, simmering with sugar and spice between two flaky crusts, has become symbolic of America. Apple Pie: a symphony of textures, yet honest and perfect in its simplicity.

Memories are made of cookies. From the time they are gummed by babies till they are dunked in tea to be more easily enjoyed, cookies are a happy food. They are easy to deal with, and require no special implements to prepare or to enjoy. Cookies say please or thank you, and are used as a bribe or a reward.

To many, dessert means chocolate. Chocolate is the crown-prince in the lexicon of sweets and, until the twentieth century, was considered an aphrodisiac. Imagine cloud-like Chocolate Mousse, sheltering a hint of liqueur; a gracious salver of assorted chocolate dainties, each cluster, square, bar, or drop a flavour enchantment. Chocolate Mint Surprise, Chocolate Jumbles, Chocolate Cookies, Crescents, Twists, Macaroons, and Meringues. Served with after-dinner coffee, with champagne or brandy, or with afternoon tea, they create an aura of congeniality.

No meal is really complete without dessert. Whether it is a simple Caramel Custard or a *tour de force* such as Pineapple Baked Alaska, dessert is the most eagerly anticipated course of all. The pot of gold at the end of the rainbow.

Jewish immigrants tucked their treasured recipes for dainties between the kitchen utensils in the huge wicker trunks which came with them on their journey to North America. Fluden, Pomerantzen, Komish, and Rugulach are just as much at home today on the sweet table as Sweet Dreams and fudge Brownies.

PIES

PIE CRUST

5 cups	flour	1.25 L
1 tbsp.	salt	15 mL
1 tsp.	baking powder	5 mL
3 tbsp.	brown sugar	45 mL
2 cups	shortening	500 mL
1	egg	1
1 tbsp.	vinegar	15 mL
	cold water	

Work shortening into dry ingredients with a pastry blender. Combine egg and vinegar in a measuring cup and add cold water to make up to 1 cup (250 mL). Mix. Add liquids to dry ingredients until flour just disappears. Divide dough into 8 equal portions. Wrap individually and freeze in a good quality freezer bag for future use. Each portion makes a single crust. Thaw pastry at least 2 hours before using, or remove from freezer and keep in refrigerator overnight. Pastry keeps in the freezer for months.

PAREVE FLAKY PASTRY

4 cups	flour	1 L
1/2 tsp.	salt	2 mL
1 1/2 cups	margarine	375 mL
1 tbsp.	lemon juice	15 mL
	iced water	

Mix flour and salt. Grate in one-third of the margarine. With a knife, stir in lemon juice and sufficient iced water to make a stiff dough. Roll out to a rectangle about 1/2'' (1 cm) thick. Divide remaining margarine into 3 and grate 1 part onto the pastry. Fold pastry in 3, turn, and roll into another oblong 1/2'' (1 cm) thick. Repeat twice with the other 2 parts of shortening, folding and rolling each time. Pastry may be kept in refrigerator until required.

GRAHAM WAFER CRUST

1 1/2 cups	graham wafer crumbs	375 mL
1/4 cup	sugar	50 mL
1/2 cup	butter, melted	125 mL

Roll the crumbs until fine with a rolling pin. Blend with the sugar and butter. Press evenly onto bottom and sides of a 9'' (1 L) pie plate. Chill 2 to 3 hours in the refrigerator before filling.

Variation

1 1/2 cups (375 mL) crumbs of any hard dry cookie may be used (chocolate, oatmeal, vanilla, dry cereal, ginger snap, for example).

MERINGUE SHELLS

4	egg whites	4
1/2 tsp.	cream of tartar	2 mL
1 cup	sugar	250 mL

Beat egg whites and cream of tartar until stiff. Add sugar very gradually, beating thoroughly after each addition, approximately 20 minutes in all. Grease cookie sheets well and spoon meringue to form 3'' (6 cm) shells, building up sides with back of spoon. Bake at 250°F (130°C) for 20 minutes then at 300°F (150°C) for 40 minutes.

TART SHELLS

3/4 cup	butter	175 mL
1/8 tsp.	salt	0.5 mL
1/3 cup	icing sugar	75 mL
1 1/2 cups	flour	375 mL

Cream butter. Sift dry ingredients and work into butter until well blended. Turn out on a floured board. Knead lightly, roll out, and cut to fit muffin tins or foil cups. Prick with a fork and bake at

350°F (180°C) until lightly browned, about 12 minutes. (Note: Do not roll too thin; pastry should be a little thicker than ordinary crust.) Makes 10 – 12 shells.

DUTCH APPLE PIE

1 (9'')	pie shell, unbaked	1 (1 L)
8	apples	8
1 cup	brown sugar	250 mL
½ cup	white sugar	125 mL
½ tsp.	cinnamon	2 mL
3 tbsp.	flour	45 mL
1 cup	cream or sour cream	250 mL

Peel, core, and quarter the apples. Mix sugars, cinnamon, and flour. Sprinkle half this mixure in the bottom of the pie shell. Arrange the apple quarters in rows on top. Mix cream with remainder of sugar-flour mixture and pour over apples. Bake at 450°F (230°C) for 10 minutes, then reduce heat to 325°F (160°C) and continue baking for another 45 minutes or until the apples are translucent and tender.

SWISS APPLE PIE

1 (9'')	pie shell, unbaked	1 (1 L)
2 cups	peeled apples, chopped	500 mL
¾ cup	sugar	175 mL
½ tsp.	nutmeg	2 mL
¾ tsp.	cinnamon	3 mL
¼ tsp.	salt	1 mL
2	eggs, slightly beaten	2
1 cup	milk, scalded	250 mL

Arrange apples in unbaked pie shell. Mix dry ingredients together and combine with eggs. Slowly add the milk, stirring until well blended. Pour mixture over the apples. Bake at 450°F (230°C) for 15 minutes, then reduce heat to 350°F (180°C) and bake for 35 minutes longer, until filling is set. Cool before serving. (Note: Apples may be ground instead of chopped. In this case, mix apples with liquid and pour all together into pie shell.)

CRANBERRY APPLE PIE

Orange Pastry

2 cups	flour, sifted	500 mL
¾ tsp.	baking powder	3 mL
1 tsp.	salt	5 mL
⅔ cup	shortening	150 mL
1 tsp.	orange rind, grated	5 mL
4 tbsp.	orange juice	60 mL

Cut shortening into dry ingredients. Add orange rind and juice and mix with a fork to bind. Chill. Roll out to line a 9'' (1 L) pie dish.

Filling

3 cups	peeled apples, sliced	750 mL
1 cup	cranberries, halved	250 mL
4 tbsp.	flour	60 mL
1 cup	sugar	250 mL
	salt	

Arrange apples and cranberries on crust. Mix flour, sugar, and salt; sprinkle over apples. Dot with shortening or butter. Make a lattice top with pastry offcuts. Bake at 450°F (230°C) for 10 minutes, then at 350°F (180°C) for 35 minutes.

HUNGARIAN APPLE PIE

6	peeled apples, cored	6
2¼ cups	flour, sifted	550 mL
¾ cup	butter	175 mL
2	eggs, separated	2
3 tbsp.	sour cream	45 mL
3 oz.	almonds, ground	90 g
3 oz.	sugar	90 g
	strawberry jam	

Stew the apples, seasoning with sugar, lemon juice, and cinnamon. Rub butter into flour. Mix to a dough with the egg yolks and sour cream; knead, and set aside in a cool place for 30 minutes. Divide in half. Roll out one-half to line a 9'' (1 L) springform pan or ovenproof dish. Bake crust at 400°F (200°C) for about 10 minutes.

Spread with strawberry jam and sprinkle with half the sugar and almonds. Whisk egg whites stiff, fold into stewed apples, and fill pie shell. Sprinkle remainder of sugar and almonds on top. Roll out second half of pastry and cover the pie. Slit top. Glaze with egg white, sprinkle with extra sugar, and bake at 400°F (200°C) for approximately 30 minutes. Serve cold, decorated with cream and glacé cherries.

BANANA MARSHMALLOW PIE

1 (9'')	graham wafer crust	1 (1 L)
4¾ oz.	vanilla pie filling	135 g
2	bananas	2
2 cups	miniature marshmallows	500 mL

Bake the graham wafer crust for 8 minutes at 375°F (190°C). Cook pie filling according to package directions. Cool about 5 minutes. Slice bananas into cooled crust and top with filling. Sprinkle marshmallows on top of pie. Broil until marshmallows turn a light brown, about 1 minute. Chill thoroughly.

BANANA CREAM PIE

1 (9'')	pie shell, baked	1 (1 L)
5 tbsp.	cake flour	75 mL
4 tbsp.	sugar	60 mL
¼ tsp.	salt	1 mL
½ cup	cold milk	125 mL
1½ cups	scalded milk	375 mL
3	eggs	3
2 tsp.	vanilla	10 mL
2	bananas, sliced	2

Combine flour, sugar, salt, cold and scalded milk in the top of a double boiler. Cook over boiling water until thick, beating constantly. Add eggs one at a time. Cook 3 to 4 minutes longer. Cool. Stir in vanilla. Line the pie shell with bananas; pour cream filling over. Garnish with whipped cream.

BUTTER TARTS

12	tart shells, unbaked	12
1 cup	raisins	250 mL
4 tbsp.	boiling water	60 mL
2 tbsp.	butter, melted	30 mL
¾ cup	brown sugar	175 mL
1	egg, well beaten	1
1 tsp.	vanilla or lemon juice	5 mL

For tart shells, use recipe for pastry on page 208. Pour boiling water over raisins. Drain. Mix butter, sugar, egg, and vanilla. Add raisins. Pour into tart shells. Bake at 400°F (200°C) for 15 minutes.

CHERRY PIE

	pastry for 2 pie crusts	
38 oz.	canned sour cherries	1.1 L
1 cup	sugar	250 mL
3 tbsp.	quick-cooking tapioca	45 mL
⅛ tsp.	salt	0.5 mL
¼ tsp.	almond extract	1 mL

With half the dough, line a 9'' (1 L) pie plate. Drain the cherries, reserving ⅔ cup (150 mL) of the juice and discarding remainder. Combine cherries and juice with the rest of the ingredients for the filling. Let stand 15 minutes. Spoon into pie crust, and roll out remaining dough to cover pie. Slit top. Bake at 450°F (230°C) for 10 minutes. Reduce temperature to 350°F (180°C) and bake 35 to 40 minutes.

CHOCOLATE MOCHA PIE

Crust

1 cup	flour	250 mL
¼ cup	golden brown sugar	50 mL
¼ tsp.	salt	1 mL
½ tsp.	baking powder	2 mL
⅜ cup	shortening	100 mL
¾ cup	walnuts, chopped	175 mL
1 oz.	unsweetened chocolate	28 g

1 tbsp.	water	15 mL
1 tsp.	vanilla	5 mL

Mix together flour, sugar, salt, and baking powder. Cut in shortening. Combine with walnuts and grated chocolate. Add water and vanilla and stir with a fork until well blended. Turn into a well-greased 9'' (1 L) pie plate, pressing pastry firmly against the bottom and sides of the plate. Bake at 375°F (190°C) for 12 to 15 minutes. Cool.

Filling

1/2 cup	soft butter	125 mL
3/4 cup	sugar	175 mL
1 oz.	unsweetened chocolate	28 g
2 tsp.	instant coffee	10 mL
2	eggs	2

In a small bowl, with electric mixer at medium speed, beat butter until creamy. Gradually add sugar, beating until light. Melt chocolate; cool, then blend into creamed butter together with instant coffee. Add 1 egg, beat 5 minutes; add second egg, and beat 5 minutes more. Turn filling into pie shell. Refrigerate, covered, overnight.

Topping

1 cup	whipping cream	250 mL
2 tbsp.	instant coffee	30 mL
1/2 cup	icing sugar	125 mL

Next day, combine cream with coffee and icing sugar in a large bowl. Refrigerate, covered, for 1 hour. Beat cream mixture until stiff. Spread over pie to decorate and garnish with chocolate curls. Refrigerate pie at least 2 hours before serving.

CHOCOLATE PIE

1 (9'')	pie shell, baked	1 (1 L)
3 oz.	unsweetened chocolate	84 g
2 1/2 cups	milk	625 mL
3/4 cup	sugar	175 mL

3 tbsp.	flour	45 mL
3 tbsp.	cornstarch	45 mL
2	egg yolks	2
1/2 tsp.	salt	2 mL
2 tsp.	butter	10 mL
1 tsp.	vanilla	5 mL

Heat chocolate with 2 cups (500 mL) of the milk in the top of a double boiler. Mix until smooth. Combine remaining milk with sugar, flour, cornstarch, egg yolk, and salt. Add gradually to hot mixture, stirring constantly. Cook until thick. Remove from heat and stir in butter and vanilla. Cool slightly. Pour into pie shell and refrigerate.

CHOCOLATE WHIP PIE

1 (9'')	graham wafer crust	1 (1 L)
2 tsp.	instant coffee	10 mL
3 tbsp.	hot water	45 mL
8 oz.	almond chocolate bar	250 g
16 oz.	prepared whip topping	500 g

In the top of a double boiler, melt chocolate with coffee and water. Cool. Fold in whipped topping and spoon into crust. Top with shaved chocolate.

DATE PIE

	pastry for 2 pie crusts	
1 cup	dates, chopped	250 mL
2 tbsp.	lemon juice	30 mL
1 tsp.	lemon rind, grated	5 mL
1 cup	water or juice	250 mL
1 tbsp.	flour	15 mL
1/2 cup	sugar	125 mL
2 tbsp.	butter	30 mL
1 tsp.	cinnamon or nutmeg	5 mL
1/4 cup	coconut	50 mL

Roll out pastry for top and bottom crusts. Line a 9'' (1 L) pie plate with pastry. Combine remaining ingredients for filling. Pour into pie shell, top with second crust, and slit top. Bake at 450°F (230°C) for 10 minutes and then at 425°F (220°C) for 30 minutes.

FRENCH PIE

Crust

3 cups	flour	750 mL
1 tsp.	salt	5 mL
½ tsp.	baking powder	2 mL
¾ cup	shortening	175 mL
½ cup	hot water	125 mL

Sift dry ingredients together. Cut in shortening, and add hot water to bind, mixing lightly. Chill. Roll out and line a 9'' (1 L) pie plate. Bake at 450°F (230°C) until brown.

Filling

¾ cup	sugar	175 mL
¾ cup	raisins	175 mL
¾ cup	walnuts, chopped	175 mL
3	egg yolks	3
¼ cup	butter	50 mL
2 tbsp.	milk	30 mL

Combine all ingredients. Cook in the top of a double boiler until thick. Pour into baked pie shell; chill until set.

LEMON PIE

Crust

1 cup	flour	250 mL
½ cup	shortening	125 mL
	pinch of salt	
¼ tsp.	baking powder	1 mL
3 tbsp.	cold water	45 mL

Cut shortening into flour. Add salt, baking powder, and water. Roll out on a floured board and line a 9'' (1 L) pie plate. Prick the bottom and bake at 400°F (200°C) for 15 minutes. Cool.

Filling

1 cup	sugar	250 mL
¼ cup	cornstarch	60 mL
¼ tsp.	salt	1 mL
1½ cups	boiling water	375 mL
2	egg yolks	2
2 tbsp.	lemon juice	30 mL
1 tsp.	lemon rind, grated	5 mL
1 tbsp.	butter	15 mL

Combine sugar, cornstarch, and salt. Add water gradually and cook in the top of a double boiler until smooth and thickened, stirring constantly. Cover and cook 15 minutes. Beat egg yolks and pour hot mixture over them gradually, stirring continually. Cook 5 minutes longer. Add lemon juice, grated rind, and butter. Remove from heat, mix well, and cool. Pour into pastry shell. Top with meringue.

Meringue

2	egg whites	2
¼ cup	sugar	50 mL

Beat egg whites until foamy. Gradually add sugar and beat until meringue forms peaks. Spread over pie and bake at 425°F (220°C) for 5 minutes.

LEMON CUSTARD PIE

1 (9'')	pie shell, unbaked	1 (1 L)
1 tbsp.	butter	15 mL
1 cup	sugar	250 mL
2 tbsp.	flour	30 mL
2 tbsp.	lemon juice	30 mL
1 tsp.	lemon rind, grated	5 mL
2	eggs, separated	2
1 cup	milk	250 mL

Cream butter. Add sugar, flour, lemon juice and rind. Beat egg yolks, add to mixture, then add milk. Lastly fold in stiffly beaten egg whites. Pour into pie shell. Bake at 350°F (180°C) until firm, about 30 minutes.

LEMON ALASKA

1 (9'')	pie shell, baked	1 (1 L)
⅓ cup	lemon juice	75 mL
1¼ cups	sugar	300 mL
4	eggs	4

2 cups	vanilla ice cream	500 mL
1 tsp.	lemon rind, grated	5 mL
	dash of salt	

Mix lemon juice and 1 cup (250 mL) of the sugar in the top of a double boiler. Separate 2 eggs. Beat yolks slightly with 2 whole eggs. Stir into lemon sugar. Cook until boiling, then chill. Spread softened vanilla ice cream into pie shell. Top with lemon mixture. Make meringue of the egg whites, remaining sugar, lemon rind, and salt. Spread over pie, sealing edges well. Freeze until ice cream hardens. Just before serving, bake at 500°F (250°C) for 3 minutes. (Note: Pie may be frozen without meringue topping, with meringue prepared and spread on just before baking.)

LEMON MERINGUE TARTS

12	meringue tart shells	12
4	egg yolks	4
1/3 cup	sugar	75 mL
1/4 tsp.	salt	1 mL
3 tbsp.	lemon juice	45 mL
1 tbsp.	lemon rind, grated	15 mL
1 cup	whipping cream	250 mL

Prepare meringue shells according to recipe on page 208. Combine egg yolks, sugar, salt, lemon juice and rind in the top of a double boiler. Bring to boil and simmer for 2 minutes; cool. Whip the cream and fold into the cooled lemon mixture. Spoon into meringue tarts. Chill. Garnish with fresh berries and extra whipped cream.

FROZEN MYSTERY PIE

Crust

1 cup	quick-cooking oatmeal	250 mL
1/3 cup	cake flour, sifted	75 mL
1/3 cup	brown sugar	75 mL
1/2 tsp.	salt	2 mL
1/3 cup	shortening, melted	75 mL

Combine dry ingredients and stir in melted shortening. If mixture seems dry add more melted shortening. Press into bottom and sides of a deep 9'' (1 L) pie plate. Bake at 375°F (190°C) about 15 minutes until golden. Chill.

Filling

32 large	white marshmallows	32 large
1 cup	milk	250 mL
2 tbsp.	instant coffee	30 mL
2	egg yolks	2
2 cups	whipped cream	500 mL
	vanilla, brandy, or rum extract	

Stir marshmallows, milk, and coffee together in a saucepan over low heat until marshmallows melt. Beat egg yolks slightly and stir in a little of the hot mixture. Pour egg mixture into saucepan and stir 2 or 3 minutes. Chill until thickened. Beat smooth and fold in the whipped cream, flavouring to taste. Pile into chilled crust. Freeze.

To serve: Garnish with sweetened whipped cream and grated chocolate. Defrost in refrigerator about 45 minutes. Before cutting, test with a toothpick to make sure filling is creamy.

LIME PIE

1 (10'')	graham wafer crust	1 (1.5 L)
6 oz.	lime gelatine	180 g
2 cups	boiling water	500 mL
1 tsp.	lime peel, shredded	5 mL
1/3 cup	lime juice	75 mL
1 quart	vanilla ice cream	1 L

Bake the graham crust and set aside to cool. Dissolve gelatine in water and stir in peel and lime juice. Add ice cream in spoonfuls, stirring until melted. Pour into baked graham crust. Chill.

IMPOSSIBLE PIE

4	eggs	4
1/2 cup	margarine	125 mL
1/2 cup	flour	125 mL
2 cups	milk	500 mL
1/2 cup	sugar	125 mL
1 cup	coconut, shredded	250 mL
1 tsp.	vanilla	5 mL
	nutmeg	

Mix all ingredients thoroughly. Pour into a greased 9'' (1 L) pie plate. Bake at 350°F (180°C) for 1 hour or until centre tests firm. The flour will settle to form the crust. The centre is an egg-custard filling. The coconut forms the topping.

BANANA PARFAIT PIE

1 (9'')	pie shell, baked	1 (1 L)
3 oz.	flavoured gelatine	85 g
1 1/4 cups	hot water	300 mL
2 cups	ice cream, any flavour	500 mL
2	bananas, sliced	2
1/2 cup	coconut, shredded	125 mL

Dissolve gelatine in hot water. Add ice cream by spoonfuls, stirring until melted. Chill 25 to 30 minutes until thickened but not set. Fold in bananas and coconut. Turn out into pie crust and chill until firm, between 15 and 35 minutes. Garnish with drained maraschino cherries, sliced bananas, whipped cream swirls, slivered sweet chocolate, toasted coconut, as desired.

FRESH PEACH PIE

	pastry for 2 pie crusts	
3/4 cup	sugar	175 mL
3 tbsp.	flour	45 mL
5 cups	peeled peaches, sliced	1.25 L
2 tbsp.	butter	30 mL

Combine sugar and flour, and pour over sliced peaches in a bowl. Toss to coat peaches evenly. Line a 9'' (1 L) pie plate with pastry. Add peaches. Dot with butter. Adjust top crust to cover, and seal the edges. Cut slits to allow steam to escape. Brush top with milk and sugar. Bake at 425°F (220°C) for 35 to 45 minutes.

BUTTERSCOTCH PEACH PIE

	pastry for 2 pie crusts	
28 oz.	canned peaches, sliced	796 mL
1/2 cup	brown sugar	125 mL
2 tbsp.	flour	30 mL
1/8 tsp.	salt	0.5 mL
1/4 cup	butter	50 mL
2 tsp.	lemon juice	10 mL

Drain peaches, reserving syrup. Arrange peaches in 9'' (1 L) pastry-lined pan. In a saucepan, combine sugar, flour, salt, and 1/4 cup (50 mL) of the peach syrup. Add butter; cook until thick. Remove from heat and stir in lemon juice. Pour butterscotch mixture over peaches. Cover with lattice top crust. Bake at 425°F (220°C) for 30 minutes.

PEACH NUT PIE

1 (9'')	pie shell, baked	1 (1 L)
10 large	marshmallows	10 large
1/4 cup	orange juice	50 mL
2 cups	peeled peaches, sliced	500 mL
1/3 cup	berry sugar	75 mL
1 cup	whipping cream	250 mL
1/2 cup	nuts	125 mL
1/4 cup	cherries, chopped	50 mL

Cut marshmallows and marinate in orange juice. Fill cooled pie shell with peaches; sprinkle with berry sugar. Whip the cream stiff. Fold in nuts and cherries and marshmallows in juice. Pour onto peaches. Refrigerate for several hours before serving.

STREUSEL CREAM PEACH PIE

1 (9'')	pie shell, unbaked	1 (1 L)
4 cups	peeled peaches, sliced	1 L
1/2 cup	sugar	125 mL
1	egg	1
2 tbsp.	cream	30 mL
1/4 cup	brown sugar	50 mL
1/2 cup	flour	125 mL
1/4 cup	butter	50 mL

Arrange peaches in pie shell and sprinkle with white sugar. Beat egg and cream together; pour over peaches. Mix brown sugar and flour, and blend in butter until crumbly. Sprinkle crumbs over fruit. Bake at 400°F (200°C) for 35 to 40 minutes until golden brown. Serve slightly warm, with cream. (Note: If using canned instead of fresh peaches, make sure they are well drained, and omit the sprinkling with sugar.)

Variation

Meringue Streusel

After pie has baked, beat 2 egg whites with 2 tbsp. (30 mL) sugar until stiff. Pile on top of pie, and return to oven for 30 minutes at 200°F (100°C).

PECAN PIE

1 (9'')	pie shell, unbaked	1 (1 L)
1/3 cup	butter	75 mL
3/4 cup	brown sugar	175 mL
3	eggs	3
1 cup	corn syrup	250 mL
1 cup	pecan nuts, broken	250 mL
1 tsp.	vanilla	5 mL
1/4 tsp.	salt	1 mL

Cream butter. Add sugar, and beat in eggs one at a time. Stir in remaining ingredients. Fill the pie shell and bake at 375°F (190°C) for 30 minutes.

PECAN TARTS

Crust

1 cup	flour	250 mL
1/2 cup	butter	125 mL
3 oz.	cream cheese	90 g

Combine all ingredients well. (If using a food processor, chill ingredients first; if mixing by hand, use ingredients at room temperature.) Press into bottom and sides of 12 small muffin tins.

Filling

2	eggs, beaten	2
1 1/4 cups	brown sugar	300 mL
2 tbsp.	butter, melted	30 mL
2 tsp.	vanilla	10 mL
	pinch of salt	
1 1/4 cups	pecan nuts, chopped	300 mL

Mix all ingredients together well. Fill unbaked tart shells and bake at 325°F (160°C) for 25 to 30 minutes.

ORANGE PECAN PIE

1 (9'')	pie shell, unbaked	1 (1 L)
1 cup	corn syrup	250 mL
4 tbsp.	butter, melted	60 mL
4 tbsp.	sugar	60 mL
1/4 cup	butter	50 mL
1 tbsp.	orange juice	15 mL
1 tbsp.	orange rind, grated	15 mL
3	eggs, well beaten	3
1 cup	pecan nuts, chopped	250 mL

Mix all ingredients, beating the eggs in well. Pour into unbaked pie shell and bake at 425°F (220°C) for 10 minutes. Reduce heat to 350°F (180°C) and continue baking until the filling is set, about 35 minues longer.

PINEAPPLE PIE

1 (9'')	pie shell, baked	1 (1 L)
2 1/2 tbsp.	cornstarch	40 mL
1/2 cup	water	125 mL
1 cup	pineapple juice	250 mL
3/4 cup	sugar	175 mL
1 cup	crushed pineapple	250 mL
3	egg whites	3
1/4 tsp.	salt	1 mL
17 1/2 oz.	prepared whip topping	500 mL

In a saucepan, blend cornstarch and water. Add pineapple juice and 1/2 cup (125 mL) of the sugar. Cook slowly until thickened, stirring constantly. Add drained pineapple. Cook a few minutes longer. Combine egg whites and salt, and beat until foamy. Add remaining sugar gradually, beating until stiff. Fold into pineapple mixture and pour into pastry shell. Cool. Spread with whipped cream topping.

PINEAPPLE TARTS

Crust

1 cup	flour	250 mL
1 tbsp.	cornstarch	15 mL
¼ cup	icing sugar	50 mL
½ cup	butter	125 mL
	pinch of salt	
1 tbsp.	cold water	15 mL

Mix dry ingredients. Blend in butter with a pastry blender. Work in cold water with hands. Roll out ¼" (5 mm) thick, and line 24 small muffin tins. Bake at 350°F (180°C) for 10 to 12 minutes.

Filling

2 tbsp.	sugar	30 mL
2 tbsp.	cornstarch	30 mL
1	egg yolk, beaten	1
1¼ cups	cold milk	300 mL
14 oz.	crushed pineapple	398 mL

In a saucepan, blend all ingredients, except pineapple, until smooth; cook until thick. Drain pineapple and add. Fill tarts, and leave to set. Top with a dab of whipped cream before serving.

FAVOURITE PUMPKIN PIE

1 (10")	pie shell, unbaked	1 (1.5 L)
1½ cups	canned pumpkin	375 mL
¾ cup	sugar	175 mL
½ tsp.	salt	2 mL
¾ tsp.	ginger	3 mL
1 tsp.	cinnamon	5 mL
½ tsp.	nutmeg	2 mL
½ tsp.	cloves	2 mL
3	eggs, slightly beaten	3
1¼ cups	milk	300 mL
6 oz.	evaporated milk	150 mL

Crimp edges of pie shell high. Thoroughly combine the pumpkin, sugar, salt, and spices. Blend in eggs, milk, and evaporated milk. Pour into pastry shell. Bake at 400°F (200°C) for 50 minutes or until a knife inserted halfway between centre and outside edge comes out clean. Cool. Serve plain or topped with whipping cream or ice cream.

PUMPKIN ICE CREAM PIE

Crust

1½ cups	ginger snaps, crushed	375 mL
1 tbsp.	sugar	15 mL
¼ cup	butter, melted	50 mL

Combine ingredients. Press firmly onto the bottom and sides of a 9" (1 L) pie plate. Bake at 300°F (150°C) for 12 to 15 minutes. Cool, then chill.

Filling

2 cups	vanilla ice cream	500 mL
1 cup	pumpkin, cooked	250 mL
¾ cup	sugar	175 mL
½ tsp.	ginger	2 mL
½ tsp.	cinnamon	2 mL
¼ tsp.	nutmeg	1 mL
½ tsp.	salt	2 mL
1 cup	whipping cream	250 mL
½ tsp.	vanilla	2 mL

Spread softened ice cream over bottom of crust. Freeze 15 minutes. In a large bowl combine pumpkin, sugar, spices, and salt. Whip the cream and vanilla until soft peaks form. Fold in pumpkin mixture, then pour on top of the ice cream, swirling the top with a spatula. Freeze. If desired, garnish with pecan nut halves.

RAISIN PIE

	pastry for 2 pie crusts	
2 cups	sultana raisins	500 mL
1¼ cups	boiling water	300 mL
½ cup	orange juice	125 mL
½ cup	brown sugar	125 mL
2 tbsp.	cornstarch	30 mL
1 tsp.	cinnamon	5 mL
1 tsp.	orange rind, grated	5 mL

1/8 tsp.	salt	0.5 mL
1/4 cup	cold water	50 mL
1 tbsp.	vinegar	15 mL
2 tbsp.	butter	30 mL

Roll out half the pastry to line a 9'' (1 L) pie plate. Boil raisins in a covered pot with water and orange juice for 5 minutes. Combine brown sugar, cornstarch, cinnamon, orange rind, and salt with the cold water. Add to raisins. Bring to a boil, stirring constantly until clear and thickened. Remove from heat; add vinegar and butter. Cool slightly before pouring into pastry-lined pie plate. Cover with pastry top. Cut slits for steam to escape, and bake at 425°F (220°C) for 25 minutes or until done. Serve warm.

RASPBERRY PIE

	pastry for 2 pie crusts	
28 oz.	canned raspberries	796 mL
1/2 cup	raspberry juice	125 mL
1/4 cup	sugar	50 mL
1 tbsp.	quick-cooking tapioca	15 mL

Roll out half the pastry and line a 9'' (1 L) pie plate. Drain the raspberries, and combine with remaining ingredients. Pour into pie shell. Cover with latticed pastry top and bake at 425°F (220°C) for 15 minutes. Reduce heat to 325°F (160°C) and bake 30 minutes longer.

Variation
Use canned loganberries instead of raspberries.

RHUBARB PIE

	pastry for 2 pie crusts	
2 tbsp.	flour	30 mL
1 cup	sugar	250 mL
2	eggs	2
1 tbsp.	soft butter	15 mL
1 tsp.	lemon rind, grated	5 mL
1 tsp.	nutmeg	5 mL
4 1/2 cups	rhubarb	1.12 L

Roll out half the pastry and line a pie plate. Mix flour and sugar. Sprinkle 1/4 cup (50 mL) of the mixture in the bottom of the pie shell. Beat eggs with remaining flour and sugar, butter, lemon rind, and nutmeg. In a large bowl, cut the rhubarb into 1/2'' (1 cm) chunks. Pour mixture over rhubarb. Toss well and pour into pie shell. Cover with a lattice top. Bake on the bottom oven rack at 425°F (220°C) for 15 minutes. Reduce heat to 325°F (160°C) and bake a further 30 minutes. If edges become too dark, cover with foil.

STRAWBERRY PIE

1 (9'')	flaky pastry crust, unbaked	1 (1 L)
	strawberry jam	
6	eggs	6
4 cups	milk	1 L
2/3 cup	sugar	150 mL
1 tsp.	vanilla	5 mL

Spread pie shell generously with strawberry jam. Combine eggs and sugar. Add milk slowly, stirring constantly. Add vanilla. Strain and pour over jam. Bake at 325°F (160°C) for 30 minutes. Cool.

Topping

	strawberry jam	
1 cup	whipping cream	250 mL
1/2 tsp.	vanilla	2 mL

Cover the custard completely with jam. Whip the cream, flavouring with vanilla. Spread over jam. Chill before serving. (Note: Any flavour berry jam may be used to vary the taste of this pie.)

PINK VELVET COMPANY PIE

16	graham wafers, crushed	16
4 tbsp.	butter, melted	60 mL
3 oz.	strawberry gelatine	85 g
1/2 cup	hot water	125 mL
1/4 cup	lemon juice	50 mL
1/4 cup	sugar	50 mL
13 1/2 oz.	evaporated milk	385 mL
1 tsp.	lemon rind, grated	5 mL

Mix wafer crumbs with butter and line a greased 9'' (1 L) pie plate, reserving ¼ cup (50 mL) of the mixture for topping. Dissolve jelly powder in hot water and add lemon juice and sugar. Set aside to cool slightly. Whip evaporated milk to a stiff froth. Add jelly mixture and stir in lemon rind. Pour into crust and top with reserved crumbs. Chill 4 hours.

YOGURT CREAM CHEESE PIE

1 (9'')	graham wafer crust	1 (1 L)
½ lb.	cream cheese, softened	250 g
⅔ cup	yogurt	150 mL
¼ cup	skim milk powder	50 mL
⅓ cup	honey	75 mL

Beat all ingredients together well. Pour into prepared graham crust. Freeze. Thaw about 30 minutes before serving, topped with fresh berries.

MINCEMEAT

2 cups	currants	500 mL
2 cups	raisins	500 mL
2 cups	brown sugar	500 mL
2 cups	apples, chopped	500 mL
1 cup	shortening	250 mL
1 cup	glazed fruits	250 mL
1 cup	almonds, chopped	250 mL
1 cup	brandy or fruit juice	250 mL
1 tsp.	nutmeg	5 mL
1 tsp.	ginger	5 mL
½ tsp.	cloves	2 mL
1 tsp.	cinnamon	5 mL
¼ cup	lemon juice	50 mL
1 tbsp.	lemon rind, grated	15 mL

Mix all ingredients together well and pack in jars. Seal. Allow to mellow for at least 2 weeks.

ALMOND FILLING

1	egg, beaten	1
1 tbsp.	butter, melted	15 mL
2 tbsp.	almonds, ground	30 mL
1 tbsp.	sugar	15 mL

Mix ingredients to a smooth paste. Bake in unbaked tart shells at 400°F (200°C) for 15 minutes. Fills 1 large or 4 mini shells.

CONFECTIONER'S CUSTARD

1 cup	flour	250 mL
½ cup	butter	125 mL
½ cup	sugar	125 mL
1 cup	milk	250 mL
2	eggs, beaten	2

Cook flour, butter, and sugar over gentle heat, stirring constantly to a thick paste. Remove from heat. Add milk and eggs. Return to stove and cook, stirring until thick. (It may be necessary to add a little more flour.) Use as filling for baked tart shells, eclairs, cream puffs.

PAREVE CONFECTIONER'S CUSTARD

6	egg yolks	6
9 tbsp.	sugar	135 mL
2 cups	orange juice	500 mL
9 tbsp.	flour	135 mL
2 tsp.	rum	10 mL

Beat yolks with sugar. Pour into the top of a double boiler with orange juice. Add flour. Cook, stirring constantly, until very thick. Flavour with rum. (Note: ½ tsp. (2 mL) rum essence may be substituted for the rum.)

overleaf:
Amaretto Mousse (page 225);
Lime Pie (page 213)

DESSERTS

APPLE DUMPLINGS

2 cups	flour	500 mL
4 tsp.	baking powder	20 mL
1/2 tsp.	salt	2 mL
1/4 cup	shortening	50 mL
2/3 cup	milk	150 mL
6	apples	6
6 tbsp.	sugar	90 mL
	nutmeg or cinnamon	

Sift together flour, baking powder, and salt. Blend in shortening. Stir in milk to form dough. Divide into 6, and roll each portion out to a thin sheet. Peel and core the apples; place an apple on each sheet. Fill centre with sugar and sprinkle with spice. Draw dough up around apple and seal. Steam dumplings or bake at 350°F (180°C) for 30 minutes, or until apples are tender. Serves 6.

APPLE KIPPURS

Filling

6	apples	6
1 cup	sugar	250 mL
2 tbsp.	lemon juice	30 mL
1 tsp.	lemon rind, grated	5 mL

Peel, core, and slice the apples. Cook with remaining ingredients to consistency of jam. Cool.

Dough

1 cup	butter	250 mL
1 cup	whipping cream, soured	250 mL
1	egg, separated	1
2 1/2 cups	flour	625 mL
1 tsp.	baking powder	5 mL
1 cup	crushed nuts or coconut	250 mL

Blend butter, cream, and yolk. Stir in flour and baking powder. Chill dough overnight. Next day, roll out to 1/4" (0.5 cm) thickness; cut into small rectangles. Place a little bit of filling at one end of each rectangle and roll up. Seal ends with a fork. Dip in slightly beaten egg white, then in crushed nuts. Bake at 450°F (230°C) for 15 minutes or until brown. Serves 6. (Note: To sour the whipping cream, add 1 tsp. (5 mL) vinegar.)

APPLE FRITTERS

1 1/2 cups	flour	375 mL
3/4 tsp.	salt	3 mL
2	eggs	2
2 tsp.	baking powder	10 mL
3/4 cup	milk	175 mL
1 tbsp.	sugar	15 mL
6 medium	apples	6 medium
1 tbsp.	lemon juice	15 mL
	oil for frying	

Mix first 6 ingredients for batter together and beat until smooth. Set aside for a few minutes. Peel and core the apples and cut into 1/2" (1 cm) rounds. Sprinkle with lemon juice. Dip apples in batter, taking care to coat well. Deep fry on both sides in hot oil until brown. Drain on paper towels, sprinkle with cinnamon and sugar, and serve. Yields 25 – 35.

STRUDEL (STRETCHED DOUGH)

3 cups	flour, sifted	750 mL
1/4 tsp.	salt	1 mL
2	eggs	2
3 tbsp.	oil	45 mL
1/4 cup	lukewarm water	50 mL

Sift together flour and salt. Combine the eggs, oil, and water, and work them into the flour, mixing until the dough leaves the side of the bowl. Knead about 10 minutes, until dough is smooth. Place a warm bowl over the dough, and let stand for 20 minutes.

Cover a large working surface with a clean tablecloth. (A kitchen table 24 – 30'' (60 – 75 cm) square is about right; you should be able to walk easily around the table.) Sprinkle the cloth with flour and roll out the dough as thin as possible, taking care not to tear it. Now begin the stretching process. Flour knuckles, form hands into fists, and place them under the pastry. Carefully and gently pull the dough toward you with the backs of your hands. Change position around the table from time to time so that the dough is stretched in all directions without strain. Continue stretching until the dough is transparent and as thin as tissue paper. Cut away any thick edges. Brush with oil or melted shortening. Place filling down the length of one side, about 2'' (5 cm) in from the edge. Turn this 2'' (5 cm) flap over the filling and lift the cloth to continue to roll the dough over and over as for a jelly roll.

Cut rolled strudel across the middle into 2 loaves. Place loaves on a well-greased baking pan, brush tops with oil, and bake at 400°F (200°C) for approximately 35 minutes, until crisp and brown. Cut into slices. Each strudel will yield 20 slices.

Apple Filling

3 lb.	tart apples	1.5 kg
1¼ cups	bread crumbs	300 mL
½ cup	raisins	125 mL
½ cup	walnuts	125 mL
	sugar	
	cinnamon	

Peel and dice the apples and spread over dough, together with bread crumbs, raisins, and walnuts. Top with a sprinkling of sugar and cinnamon mixture.

Filling Variations

Cherry

8 cups	cherries	2 L
½ cup	bread crumbs	125 mL
1 tsp.	lemon rind, grated	5 mL
1 cup	sugar	250 mL
½ tsp.	cinnamon	2 mL
¾ cup	nuts, chopped	175 mL

Wash and pit the cherries. Combine with remaining ingredients. (Note: If using canned cherries, drain them first.)

Cheese

1½ lb.	dry cottage cheese	750 g
1	egg	1
1	egg yolk	1
½ tsp.	lemon rind, grated	2 mL
½ cup	sugar	125 mL
1 tsp.	vanilla	5 mL

Work cheese through a sieve or ricer. Mix remaining ingredients in with cheese. Serve cheese strudel warm with sour cream.

Almond

2 cups	almonds, chopped	500 mL
1 cup	sugar	250 mL
¾ cup	bread crumbs	175 mL
1 tsp.	lemon rind, grated	5 mL
2 tbsp.	lemon juice	30 mL
1½ cups	maraschino cherries	375 mL
¾ lb.	Turkish delight	375 g

Combine almonds, sugar, bread crumbs, lemon rind and juice. Drain the cherries, and stir into mixture with chopped Turkish delight. (Note: For added colour, use green and red maraschino cherries. 1 cup (250 mL) shredded coconut may be added to the filling.)

BANANA PATTIES

4	bananas, mashed	4
12 tbsp.	flour	180 mL
2	eggs, beaten	2
3 tbsp.	honey	45 mL
1½ tsp.	cinnamon	7 mL
¼ tsp.	nutmeg or mace	1 mL

Mix all ingredients together. Drop by heaping spoonfuls onto a greased frying pan. Fry on both sides until browned and crisp. Serves 3 – 5.

BANANA FRITTERS

5	ripe bananas	5
	lemon juice	
2 tbsp.	icing sugar	30 mL
1/2 cup	flour	125 mL
2 tsp.	sugar	10 mL
1/2 tsp.	baking powder	2 mL
1/4 tsp.	salt	1 mL
1	egg, separated	1
1/2 cup	milk	125 mL
2 tsp.	butter, melted	10 mL
	oil for frying	

Slice bananas diagonally into thick chunks. Sprinkle lemon juice over slices to prevent discolouring, and dust with icing sugar. Combine remaining dry ingredients. Beat egg yolk and milk and stir into dry ingredients with butter. Fold in beaten egg white. Dip banana slices in batter and deep fry in hot oil for about 2 minutes. Drain on paper towels. Serve hot with liqueur sauce. Serves 6 – 8.

Liqueur Sauce

1/4 cup	sugar	50 mL
1 tbsp.	cornstarch	15 mL
	salt	
3/4 cup	water	175 mL
1 tbsp.	butter	15 mL
3 tbsp.	Cointreau	45 mL

Mix dry ingredients in the top of a double boiler. Add water and cook until transparent. Stir in butter and liqueur to taste. Serve hot.

CREAM PUFFS

1 cup	water	250 mL
1/2 cup	butter	125 mL
1 cup	flour, sifted	250 mL
4	eggs	4
1/4 tsp.	salt	1 mL

Boil water and butter in a saucepan. Stir in flour all at once. Stir vigorously over low heat until mixture leaves sides of pan and forms a ball, about 1 minute. Remove from heat. Beat in eggs thoroughly, one at a time. Add salt. Beat until smooth and velvety. Drop from a spoon onto an ungreased baking sheet, forming 8 mounds 3'' (8 cm) apart. Bake at 400°F (200°C) for 45 to 50 minutes until puffed, golden brown, and dry. Cool slowly, away from drafts. Cut off tops with a sharp knife and scoop out any filaments of soft dough. Fill with whipped cream or rich custard, then replace tops. Dust with icing sugar. Serve immediately or refrigerate. Yields 8 large puffs.

Variations
Fill with peppermint ice cream; top with chocolate sauce. Fill with burnt almond ice cream; top with butterscotch sauce.

FRUIT COMPOTE

8 oz.	dried peaches	250 g
8 oz.	prunes	250 g
8 oz.	dried apricots	250 g
2 large	oranges	2 large
1 cup	light brown sugar	250 mL
	pinch of salt	
1	vanilla bean	1
1	cinnamon stick	1
	Cointreau	

Wash dried fruit and place in a large saucepan. Slice oranges, discarding top and bottom slices and any seeds. Add to fruit in saucepan. Barely cover fruit with cold water; bring to a boil. Add sugar, salt, vanilla bean, and cinnamon stick. Simmer for 30 minutes until fruit is tender. Add Cointreau to taste. Chill. Serve plain or with cream, whipped cream, or ice cream.

GRAPES WITH HONEY CREAM

1 cup	sour cream	250 mL
3 tbsp.	Drambuie	45 mL
1/3 cup	honey	75 mL
3 tsp.	lemon juice	15 mL
24 oz.	seedless green grapes	700 g

Combine sour cream, Drambuie, honey, and lemon juice. Just before serving, pour cream mixture over grapes. Toss gently. Serve in glass bowls. Serves 4 – 6.

YOGURT FRUIT TOPPING

1 cup	plain yogurt	250 mL
2 tbsp.	honey	30 mL
¼ cup	walnuts, chopped	50 mL
¼ tsp.	cinnamon	1 mL
¼ tsp.	lemon rind, grated	1 mL

Mix all ingredients together. This is a sauce for fresh fruit salad. Serve salad and sauce separately, spooning sauce over individual servings.

BAKED PINEAPPLE WHIP

4	egg whites	4
1 cup	crushed pineapple	250 mL
½ cup	icing sugar	125 mL
1 tsp.	vanilla	5 mL

Beat egg whites until stiff. Drain pineapple, and fold into egg whites together with remaining ingredients. Bake in a soufflé dish at 300°F (150°C) for 20 minutes. Serves 4.

PINEAPPLE BAKED ALASKA

3	pineapples	3
½ cup	Grand Marnier	125 mL
1⅛ cups	sugar	280 mL
6	egg whites	6
	pinch of salt	
1 tsp.	vanilla	5 mL
1½ pints	hard ice cream	750 mL
	ice cubes	

Cut the pineapples lengthwise in half, right through the green tops. Cut out the hard cores and discard. Leaving shells intact, scoop out the flesh and cut into bite-sized cubes. Place cubes in a bowl, pour Grand Marnier over, and dust with 2 tbsp. (30 mL) of the sugar. Mix well. Cover, and chill for a few hours. Wrap foil around green tops, and chill pineapple shells as well.

Fill a large roasting pan with coarsely crushed ice cubes. Set pineapple shells carefully into the ice, and partly fill with liqueur-soaked pineapple cubes. Beat egg whites with salt until stiff but not dry. Add remaining sugar by spoonfuls, beating until meringue is stiff. With the last spoon of sugar, add vanilla. Place a scoop of ice cream in each pineapple shell. Cover completely with the meringue, taking care to touch the edges of the pineapple shells all around, to prevent shrinking. Bake at 500°F (250°C) for 5 minutes until meringue is barely tinged with colour. Remove from oven immediately and remove foil from tops. Serve each shell on an individual plate. (The meringue may be sprinkled with sugar, chopped nuts, or candied fruits before baking.) Serves 6.

PINEAPPLE "ROMANOFF"

1	pineapple	1
¼ cup	rum	50 mL
¼ cup	brandy	50 mL
1 cup	whipping cream	250 mL
3 tbsp.	sugar	45 mL
	kirsch	
	chocolate vermicelli	
	glacé cherries or walnuts	

Cut pineapple lengthwise in half. Scoop the pineapple flesh out of the shells and dice. Soak the pieces in a mixture of rum and brandy. Drain, and replace the fruit in the shells. Whip the cream with sugar and flavour with kirsch, to taste. Heap on top of the pineapple halves. Garnish with chocolate vermicelli and glacé cherries or walnuts. Serve on a bed of crushed ice. Serves 2.

BRANDIED PRUNE FRITTERS

16 oz.	prunes	500 g
4 oz.	blanched almonds	125 g
2	eggs	2
4 tbsp.	sugar	60 mL

2 tbsp.	brandy	30 mL
	pinch of salt	
	flour	
4 tbsp.	oil	60 mL
2 oz.	bitter chocolate, grated	56 g

Boil and stone the prunes. Replace the pits with nuts. In a separate bowl, beat eggs and sugar. Add brandy, salt, and enough flour to make a thick, flowing batter. Heat oil in a frying pan. Coat each prune with batter and fry until golden brown. Sprinkle hot fritters with bitter chocolate and serve warm. Serves 4.

MARINATED STRAWBERRIES

4 cups	strawberries	1 L
1 cup	marmalade	250 mL
1/4 cup	Grand Marnier	50 mL
1/2 cup	orange juice	125 mL
1 tbsp.	lemon juice	15 mL
1 tbsp.	orange rind, grated	15 mL

Wash and hull the strawberries. Heat together marmalade and Grand Marnier. Add juices and rind, and pour over the berries. Refrigerate for at least 1 hour. Serves 4 – 6.

STRAWBERRIES ROMANOFF

8 cups	strawberries	2 L
1/2 cup	berry sugar	125 mL
3 tbsp.	Cointreau	45 mL
3 tbsp.	rum	45 mL
3 tbsp.	vodka	45 mL
1 cup	whipping cream, chilled	250 mL
	pinch of salt	
1 tbsp.	kirsch	15 mL
1 tbsp.	raspberry liqueur	15 mL
1 pint	vanilla ice cream	500 mL

Wash and hull the strawberries, and drain. Place in a deep mixing bowl and sprinkle with sugar. Combine the Cointreau, rum, and vodka. Pour onto strawberries and mix, being careful not to crush berries. Cover bowl tightly to preserve the aroma of the liqueurs. Chill 2 to 3 hours. Whip cream and salt until stiff. Add remaining liqueurs. With the same beater, in a separate bowl, whip softened ice cream at low speed until as smooth as the cream. Combine cream and ice cream. Serve the marinated strawberries topped with creamed mixture. Serves 8 – 10.

STRAWBERRY WHIP

3 oz.	lemon gelatine	85 g
1 cup	hot water	250 mL
10 oz.	frozen strawberries	300 g
1 cup	whipping cream	250 mL

Dissolve gelatine in hot water in a blender. Beat for 15 seconds. Add partially thawed berries and beat 5 seconds. Refrigerate 10 minutes or until mixture starts to thicken. Add 3/4 cup (175 mL) of the cream, unwhipped. Blend for 2 seconds. Pour into cups and top with remaining cream, whipped. Refrigerate until set.

AMARETTO MOUSSE

5	eggs, separated	5
1/2 cup	sugar	125 mL
	pinch of salt	
1 tsp.	vanilla	5 mL
1 cup	milk	250 mL
3 oz.	gelatine	85 g
1/4 cup	cold water	50 mL
2 cups	whipping cream	500 mL
3 oz.	Amaretto	90 mL
	Almond Roca	

Beat egg yolks with sugar until light. Add salt. Bring vanilla and milk to a boil. Lighten egg mixture with a small amount of the hot milk, then pour into the rest of the milk in the saucepan, stirring until well mixed. Heat until mixture starts to thicken. Soften gelatine in cold water and heat until gelatine is dissolved. Cook 2 to 3 minutes. Add to thickened eggs, stirring until mixed. Add Amaretto. Cool in refrigerator until thickened to the consistency of unbeaten egg whites. Whip the cream. Beat egg whites until stiff. Fold whipped cream into Amaretto mixture, then fold in egg whites. Refrigerate overnight. Serve sprinkled with crushed Almond Roca. Serves 8 – 10.

FROZEN FRUIT MOUSSE

8 oz.	cream cheese	250 g
³/₄ cup	sugar	175 mL
14 oz.	pineapple tidbits	398 mL
10 oz.	frozen strawberries	300 g
2	bananas	2
¹/₂ cup	nuts, chopped	125 mL
17¹/₂ oz.	prepared whip topping	500 g

Beat cheese and sugar. In a separate bowl, combine drained pineapple, frozen strawberries, sliced bananas, nuts, and whip topping. Fold the fruit and cheese mixtures together. Freeze in a greased bundt pan. Unmould in hot water. Serves 8.

FROZEN STRAWBERRY MOUSSE

4 cups	fresh strawberries	1 L
3	egg whites	3
2 cups	whipping cream	500 mL
¹/₈ tsp.	salt	0.5 mL
1 cup	sugar	250 mL
2 tbsp.	lemon juice	30 mL

Mash strawberries. Beat egg whites stiff and fold into strawberries. Whip cream, adding salt, sugar, and lemon juice. Fold into berry mixture. Pour into a greased 2 quart (2 L) mould or individual moulds. Freeze 12 hours. Unmould, and garnish with whole strawberries. Serves 8.

CHOCOLATE MOUSSE

6 oz.	semi-sweet chocolate chips	175 g
2 tsp.	strong coffee	10 mL
4	eggs, separated	4
1 tsp.	vanilla or liqueur	5 mL
2 cups	whipping cream	500 mL

Melt chocolate in coffee, beating until smooth. Beat in egg yolks, one at a time, and flavouring. Beat egg whites stiff; whip the cream stiff. Fold egg whites and three-quarters of the cream into the chocolate. Turn into individual dishes or a large bowl, and decorate with remaining whipped cream. Refrigerate 2 to 3 hours before serving. Serves 8 – 10.

KAHLÚA MOUSSE

4 cups	non-dairy whip topping	1 L
3 tsp.	instant coffee	15 mL
5 tsp.	cocoa	25 mL
6 tsp.	sugar	30 mL
6 oz.	Kahlúa	180 mL

Whip the topping until stiff. Blend in dry ingredients, then fold in liqueur. Chill. Serves 8.

SUNSHINE MOUSSE

1 cup	orange juice	250 mL
¹/₂ cup	lemon juice	125 mL
1 tsp.	orange rind, grated	5 mL
3 tbsp.	cornstarch	45 mL
	cold water	
3	eggs, separated	3
1 cup	sugar	250 mL

In a saucepan, bring orange and lemon juice and orange rind to a boil. Mix cornstarch with cold water to a thin paste. Add to boiling juice and stir constantly until it thickens. Place pot in cold water to cool. Beat egg yolks with sugar until very thick and creamy. Gradually add cooled orange mixture, beating continuously. Beat egg whites stiff, and fold in. Set in individual dishes or a large glass bowl in refrigerator. Decorate with crystallized orange and lemon slices. Serves 6.

CHOCOLATE RUM MOUSSE

6 oz.	unsweetened chocolate	170 g
1 tsp.	instant coffee	5 mL
1¹/₂ cups	sugar	375 mL
6	eggs, separated	6

| 1 tsp. | rum | 5 mL |
| 1/2 cup | almonds, ground | 125 mL |

Melt broken up chocolate with instant coffee and sugar in the top of a double boiler. When sugar is completely dissolved, remove from stove and immediately immerse the top of the double boiler in cold water. Beat in egg yolks one at a time. When completely cooled, beat in rum and stir in almonds. Refrigerate 10 minutes to ensure mixture is cold before folding in stiffly beaten egg whites. Turn into individual serving dishes or a large glass bowl and refrigerate until set. Decorate with glacé cherries and bitter chocolate vermicelli. Serves 6.

PINEAPPLE CUSTARD DELIGHT

2	eggs	2
1 tbsp.	butter	15 mL
2 cups	milk	500 mL
2 tbsp.	cornstarch	30 mL
3 tbsp.	sugar	45 mL
1 tsp.	vanilla	5 mL
14 oz.	pineapple chunks	398 mL
12 1/2 oz.	graham wafers	350 g
1/2 cup	whipping cream	125 mL

Combine eggs, butter, milk, cornstarch, sugar, and vanilla in a saucepan. Heat over medium heat, stirring constantly, until mixture thickens. Cool. Drain the pineapple, reserving juice. Line a 7" x 11" (3 L) glass baking dish with unbroken wafers. Pour in half the custard. Top with half the pineapple chunks, and sprinkle with a little pineapple juice. Repeat layers. Top with a final layer of wafers, and sprinkle with juice. Cover with whipped cream. Chill for 24 hours.

CHOCOLATE FREEZE

6 oz.	unsweetened chocolate	200 g
4	eggs, separated	4
8 oz.	non-dairy whip topping	250 mL
1/2 tsp.	sugar	2 mL

peppermint extract or liqueur
pecan nuts

Melt chocolate in the top of a double boiler. Beat in egg yolks one at a time. Fold in stiffly beaten whites. Beat topping until thick, adding sugar and peppermint extract. Fold together with chocolate mixture. Add nuts. Freeze. Serves 6.

CHOCOLATE ICE CREAM RING

6 oz.	unsweetened chocolate	200 g
1 cup	walnuts, chopped	250 mL
2 1/2 cups	Rice Krispies	625 mL
1 quart	ice cream	1 L

Chill a ring mould in the freezer for 10 minutes. Melt chocolate in the top of a double boiler. Add walnuts and Rice Krispies and mix until coated with chocolate. Press mixture around the sides of the ring mould. Refrigerate for 25 minutes. Fill ring with ice cream, unmould onto serving dish, and freeze until serving time. Pour chocolate sauce over individual servings. Serves 6.

BANANA SPLIT DESSERT

Crust

1 3/4 cups	graham wafer crumbs	425 mL
1/3 cup	butter, melted	75 mL
4 tbsp.	brown sugar	60 mL

Mix all ingredients together and pack into a springform pan, reserving a couple of spoonfuls of crumbs for garnish.

Filling

4	bananas	4
2 quarts	Neapolitan ice cream	2 L
	crushed nuts	

Slice bananas and layer on crust. Spread partially softened ice cream on top. Sprinkle with nuts. Freeze.

Fudge Sauce

1 cup	chocolate chips	250 mL
1/2 cup	butter	125 mL
2 cups	berry sugar	500 mL
1 1/2 cups	evaporated milk	375 mL
17 1/2 oz.	prepared whip topping	500 mL

Melt chips and butter over low heat. Add sugar and milk, and cook until thick and smooth, approximately 20 minutes. Cool completely. Pour sauce over ice cream. Cover with whip topping and sprinkle with reserved crumbs. Cover and freeze. Serves 8 – 10.

PAREVE ICE CREAM

6	eggs, separated	6
3/4 cup	sugar	175 mL
	flavourings	

Beat egg yolks. Gradually add 1/2 cup (125 mL) sugar, and beat until thick and creamy. Slowly add flavouring, beating until thoroughly blended. Whip egg whites with remaining sugar until stiff. Fold into yolk mixture. Freeze in ice trays or a suitable container. Serves 4.

Flavourings

1/2 cup (125 mL) liquidized peaches.

2 oz. (60 g) chocolate melted with 1/2 tsp. (2 mL) vanilla.

6 oz. (170 mL) orange juice (not frozen).

10 oz. (280 g) frozen raspberries.

10 oz. (280 g) frozen strawberries.

FROZEN ORANGE MOUSSE GRAND MARNIER

8	oranges	8
6	egg yolks	6
3/4 cup	sugar	175 mL
2 3/4 cups	whipping cream	675 mL
3 oz.	Grand Marnier	90 mL

Clean oranges well. Cut off tops, and scoop out and discard pulp. Refrigerate shells. Beat egg yolks and sugar until thick and lemon coloured. Fold in stiffly whipped cream and liqueur. Fill orange shells with mixture and freeze at least 2 hours. Garnish with powdered cocoa or shaved chocolate. Serves 8.

FAVOURITE ICE CREAM

2 cups	whipping cream	500 mL
10 1/2 oz.	condensed milk	300 mL
2 tsp.	vanilla	10 mL
2	egg yolks, beaten	2
1 1/2 cups	fruit, chopped	375 mL

Whip the cream and fold in condensed milk, vanilla, and egg yolks. Fold in fruit. Pour into a container and freeze 6 to 10 hours. Serves 4 – 6.

BANANA-PINEAPPLE FREEZE

3 cups	crushed pineapple	750 mL
1 1/2 cups	icing sugar	375 mL
3 cups	bananas, mashed	750 mL
1 cup	orange juice	250 mL
3/4 cup	lemon juice	175 mL
3	egg whites	3

Mix drained pineapple and icing sugar. In a separate bowl, mix bananas with juices. Combine pineapple and banana mixtures. Freeze slightly in a utility pan. Beat egg whites until stiff, add fruit slush, and beat very well with an electric mixer. Return to pan and freeze, covered, until required. Remove from freezer about 10 minutes before serving, to soften slightly.

PEACH TRIFLE

2 cups	milk	500 mL
4	egg yolks	4
1/3 cup	sugar	75 mL
1 tsp.	vanilla	5 mL

10¾ oz.	frozen pound cake	300 g
¼ cup	peach preserves	50 mL
⅔ cup	brandy	150 mL
16 oz.	canned sliced peaches	450 mL

Scald milk in a medium saucepan. Beat egg yolks and sugar with a wire whisk until light and fluffy. Gradually beat in scalded milk and return to saucepan. Cook over medium heat, stirring constantly, until mixture thickens. Remove from heat. Add vanilla, mix well, and cool. Cut frozen pound cake into ½'' (1 cm) slices. Spread one side of each slice with peach preserves and line the bottom and sides of a glass serving bowl with slices, plain side out. Sprinkle with half the brandy. Pour half of the cooled custard into the cake-lined dish. Arrange remaining cake slices, preserves side up, on top of custard. Sprinkle with remaining brandy and pour on remaining custard. Chill several hours. Just before serving, top with drained peach slices, and garnish with whipped cream and slivers of crystallized ginger. Serves 6 – 8.

AMARETTO TRIFLE

4 cups	milk	1 L
8	egg yolks	8
1 cup	sugar	250 mL
1 tbsp.	cornstarch	15 mL
1½ tsp.	vanilla	7 mL
1 cup	Amaretto	250 mL
2 tbsp.	butter	30 mL
6 oz.	lady fingers	180 g
½ cup	raspberry preserves	125 mL

Heat milk to scalding in a medium saucepan. With a wire whisk, beat egg yolks, sugar, and cornstarch in a medium-sized bowl until light and fluffy. Gradually beat in scalded milk. Pour back into saucepan. Cook over medium heat, stirring constantly, until custard boils and thickens. Remove from heat. Stir in vanilla, 2 tbsp. (30 mL) Amaretto, and butter. Chill several hours. Spread flat sides of half the lady fingers with preserves and sandwich together with plain lady fingers. Cut each in half lengthwise. Line the bottom and sides of a large glass serving bowl with lady

fingers, cut side out. Sprinkle liberally with Amaretto. Pour in half the custard. Layer remaining lady fingers and custard in bowl, sprinkling lady fingers with remaining Amaretto. Chill several hours or overnight. Decorate with whipped cream, candied cherries, angelica, and slivered almonds. Serves 8 – 10.

HOLIDAY PEACH TRIFLE

3⅛ oz.	vanilla pudding mix	90 g
2½ cups	milk	625 mL
32 oz.	canned sliced peaches	900 mL
20 oz.	frozen raspberries	600 g
⅓ cup	dry sherry	75 mL
1 (8'')	round sponge cake	1 (20 cm)
¾ cup	raspberry jam	175 mL
½ cup	almonds, sliced	125 mL
½ cup	whipping cream	125 mL
1½ tbsp.	sugar	25 mL

Prepare pudding as directed on package, using the 2½ cups (625 mL) milk. Cool to room temperature. Drain peaches and thawed raspberries separately, reserving 2 tbsp. (30 mL) syrup from each. Set aside a few peach slices and a few berries for garnishing. Mix reserved syrup with sherry. Slice cake into 3 layers. Place 1 layer in a straight-sided 8'' (2 L) glass bowl. Spread with ¼ cup (50 mL) raspberry jam. Pour one-third of the sherry mixture over cake, and top with one-third each of the almonds, pudding, peach slices, and raspberries, arranged in layers. Repeat layers twice. Beat cream and sugar until stiff, and garnish trifle. Serves 8.

MARSALA TRIFLE

	lady fingers	
1 cup	Marsala	250 mL
17½ oz.	frozen vanilla pudding	500 g
6 oz.	blackberry jam	170 g
2 cups	whipped cream	500 mL
½ cup	pecan nuts, chopped	125 mL

Line a glass bowl with lady fingers. Sprinkle with Marsala. Spoon half the vanilla pudding, jam, and cream into the dish in layers. Repeat layers, end-ing with cream. Sprinkle with pecans. Chill at least 2 hours. Serves 6. (Note: Prepared whip topping may be substituted for whipped cream.)

APPLE AND RAISIN PUDDING

Dough

1 1/2 cups	flour	375 mL
1/4 tsp.	salt	1 mL
2 tsp.	baking powder	10 mL
3 tbsp.	butter	45 mL
2/3 cup	milk	150 mL
3	apples, diced	3
1/2 cup	raisins	125 mL
1/3 cup	brown sugar	75 mL
3 tsp.	cinnamon	15 mL
1/2 tsp.	lemon juice	2 mL

Mix flour, salt, and baking powder. Cut in butter, add milk, and stir to bind. Roll dough into a rectangle and place in a greased, ovenproof dish. Arrange apples and raisins on dough; sprinkle generously with brown sugar, cinnamon, and lemon juice. Bake at 350°F (180°C) for 1 hour. Serve with syrup.

Syrup

1 cup	brown sugar	250 mL
1 cup	hot water	250 mL
1 tbsp.	butter	15 mL

Bring all ingredients to a boil and cook for a few minutes. Pour over pudding.

CARAMEL CUSTARD

1 1/2 cups	sugar	375 mL
4 cups	milk	1 L
6	eggs	6
1/8 tsp.	salt	0.5 mL
1 tsp.	vanilla	5 mL

Place 1 cup (250 mL) sugar in a heavy pan, and cook over low heat without stirring until the sugar forms a light brown syrup. Then stir to blend. Coat the bottom of a cool 1 1/2 quart (1.5 L) casserole with syrup. Set aside.

In the top of a double boiler, heat milk over medium heat until bubbles form around edge of saucepan. In a large bowl, beat eggs slightly with rotary beater. Add remaining sugar, salt, and va-nilla. Gradually pour in hot milk, stirring con-stantly. Pour into casserole.

Set casserole in a shallow pan. Pour hot water into outer pan to a depth of 1/2" (1 cm). Bake at 250°F (130°C) for 1 hour, then reduce heat to 225°F (110°C) for 30 minutes or until a knife inserted in centre comes out clean. Cool, and refrigerate overnight. Turn out on a shallow serv-ing dish. Shake gently to release. The caramel is the sauce. Serves 8.

BAKED LEMON PUDDING

3 tbsp.	flour	45 mL
1 cup	sugar	250 mL
3 tbsp.	soft butter	45 mL
3	eggs, separated	3
1 tbsp.	lemon rind, grated	15 mL
3 tbsp.	lemon juice	45 mL
1 1/2 cups	milk	375 mL
1/4 tsp.	salt	1 mL

Cream flour, 1/2 cup (125 mL) sugar, and butter until smooth. Stir in beaten egg yolks, lemon rind, juice, and milk. Beat salt and egg whites until stiff, then beat in remaining sugar. Fold into lemon mixture. Fill a greased pan two-thirds full and set in a shallow roasting pan. Pour boiling water into outer pan to a depth of 1/2" (1 cm). Bake at 350°F (180°C) for 45 minutes or until done. Chill thoroughly. Serve with whipping cream or lemon sauce.

STEAM PUDDING

1/2 cup	butter	125 mL
1 cup	brown sugar	250 mL
2	eggs	2

2 cups	carrots, grated	500 mL
1 cup	bread crumbs	250 mL
1/2 tsp.	salt	2 mL
1 tsp.	baking soda	5 mL
1 tsp.	allspice	5 mL
1 tsp.	cinnamon	5 mL
1 cup	currants	250 mL
4 oz.	mixed peel	115 g
1/2 cup	nuts, chopped	125 mL
1 cup	raisins	250 mL

Cream butter and sugar. Beat in eggs. Add carrots, crumbs, salt, baking soda, and spices. Mix thoroughly. Fold in fruits and nuts. Place in a greased bowl, cover with cheesecloth, and steam for 3 hours. Serve hot with lemon sauce. Serves 8.

BAKED TAPIOCA APPLES

4 tbsp.	tapioca	60 mL
1 cup	cold water	250 mL
1 cup	sugar	250 mL
1 cup	milk	250 mL
7	apples	7
	cinnamon	
	pinch of salt	

Combine tapioca and water; let stand overnight. Chop 1 apple finely, and cook slowly with tapioca, sugar, milk, cinnamon, and salt for 20 minutes. Wash and core remaining 6 apples, peel halfway, and place in a baking pan. Fill cavities with cooked tapioca mixture. Add 2 cups (500 mL) water to the pan and bake at 375°F (190°C) for 15 minutes. Serves 6.

CREPES SUZETTE

1/2 cup	flour	125 mL
1 tbsp.	sugar	15 mL
1/8 tsp.	salt	0.5 mL
2	eggs, beaten	2
2/3 cup	milk	150 mL
1 tbsp.	butter, melted	15 mL
1/4 tsp.	lemon rind, grated	1 mL

Sift flour, sugar, and salt together into a bowl. Make a well, and add remaining ingredients, stirring well. Let stand for a few hours. Pour spoonfuls into a hot, greased crepe pan. Fry until set; turn and fry other side. Remove to a clean tea towel until required. Combine sauce ingredients in a chafing dish, and stir until well mixed. Fold crepes in 4. Place in sauce in chafing dish and simmer slowly, spooning sauce over crepes continually. Serve directly from chafing dish. Makes 8 crepes.

Sauce

6 tbsp.	butter	90 mL
3 tbsp.	sugar	45 mL
1/2 tsp.	lemon rind, grated	2 mL
1 1/2 tsp.	lemon juice	7 mL
1/3 cup	orange juice	75 mL
2 tbsp.	brandy	30 mL
2 tbsp.	Cointreau	30 mL

NORMANDY OMELETTE

4	apples	4
8 tbsp.	butter	120 mL
1 tbsp.	calvados or brandy	15 mL
7	eggs	7
1 tsp.	sugar	5 mL
	pinch of salt	

Peel and core the apples. Slice, and fry lightly in butter flavoured with a few drops of calvados. When done, remove from pan and keep hot. Beat eggs well, adding salt and sugar to taste. Pour into a hot buttered frying pan. Cook without stirring until edges are light brown. Flip over, arrange apples on top of omelette, and fold in half. Place on an ovenproof platter, sprinkle with sugar, and bake at 425°F (220°C) for a few minutes. Pour a little heated calvados over the omelette and ignite just before serving. Serves 4.

SQUARES & BARS

ALMOND SQUARES

1 cup	butter	250 mL
2 cups	flour	500 mL
3/4 cup	sugar	175 mL
3/4 tsp.	cinnamon	3 mL
	pinch of salt	
1	egg, separated	1
1 cup	almonds, sliced	250 mL
1/2 cup	icing sugar	125 mL

Blend together butter, flour, sugar, cinnamon, and salt. Add egg yolk and mix well. Press dough onto a large, greased cookie sheet. Beat egg white with icing sugar, and spread over dough. Sprinkle on almonds, pressing almonds down slightly. Bake at 350°F (180°C) for 25 to 30 minutes until light golden brown. Remove from oven and immediately slice into squares.

CHOCOLATE NUT SQUARES

Base

1/2 cup	butter	125 mL
1/4 cup	sugar	50 mL
1/4 cup	brown sugar	50 mL
1 tsp.	vanilla	5 mL
1	egg yolk	1
1/2 cup	flour	125 mL
1/2 cup	rolled oats	125 mL

Cream butter and white and brown sugar. Stir in remaining ingredients. Press into a greased 8" square (2 L) pan and bake at 350°F (180°C) for 20 minutes.

Topping

6 oz.	milk chocolate	176 g
1 tsp.	butter	5 mL
1/4 cup	nuts, crushed	50 mL

Melt chocolate with butter. Spread onto semi-cooled crust and sprinkle with crushed nuts. Cut into small squares while warm. Store covered in refrigerator.

APRICOT BARS

1 1/3 cups	flour	325 mL
1/4 cup	sugar	50 mL
1/2 cup	butter	125 mL
12 oz.	dried apricots	340 g
1/2 cup	water	125 mL
2	eggs	2
1 cup	brown sugar	250 mL
1 tsp.	vanilla	5 mL
1/3 tsp.	baking powder	2 mL
1/4 tsp.	salt	1 mL
1/4 cup	icing sugar	50 mL

Sift together white sugar and 1 cup (250 mL) flour. Cut in butter. Pat into an ungreased 8" square (2 L) pan. Bake at 350°F (180°C) for 15 to 20 minutes, until golden brown. Cool.

Wash apricots and cut into slivers. Cook in water over low heat for 5 minutes. Drain and cool. Beat eggs lightly. Gradually add brown sugar, beating until thick. Add vanilla. Sift remaining dry ingredients. Stir into egg mixture until all ingredients are moistened. Fold in cooled apricots with a wooden spoon, cutting through quickly to distribute apricots through batter. Pour onto cooled base. Bake at 350°F (180°C) for 35 minutes or until done. Cool. Cut into squares, and dust with icing sugar.

CHERRY SLICE

Base

1 3/4 cups	flour	425 mL
1 cup	butter	250 mL
2 tbsp.	sugar	30 mL

Blend ingredients together as for pie crust. Pat into a 9" x 11" (2 L) baking pan. Bake at 350°F (180°C) for 10 minutes.

Topping

2	eggs	2
1 cup	brown sugar	250 mL
½ tsp.	baking powder	2 mL
2 tbsp.	flour	30 mL
¼ cup	coconut, shredded	50 mL
1 tsp.	vanilla	5 mL
1 cup	walnuts, chopped	250 mL
1 cup	cherries, chopped	250 mL

Combine all ingredients well. Spread over pastry. Bake at 350°F (180°C) for 30 minutes. Cut into squares.

BROWNIES

2 oz.	unsweetened chocolate	58 g
½ cup	butter	125 mL
1 cup	sugar	250 mL
½ cup	flour	125 mL
2	eggs	2
1 tsp.	vanilla	5 mL
½ cup	nuts, chopped	125 mL

Melt chocolate in the top of a double boiler. Cream together butter and sugar. Add flour, then chocolate, eggs, vanilla, and nuts. Stir well. Pour into a greased 12" x 7½" (3 L) utility pan. Bake at 325°F (160°C) for 25 minutes.

Icing

2 oz.	unsweetened chocolate	58 g
2 cups	sugar	500 mL
1 cup	milk	250 mL
2 tbsp.	butter	30 mL
1 tsp.	vanilla	5 mL

Melt chocolate with sugar and milk in the top of a double boiler. Boil until soft ball stage for candy. Stir in butter and vanilla. Cool 20 minutes, then whip mixture until it lightens in colour. Pour onto brownies. Cut in squares.

ALMOND BROWNIES

1½ cups	graham wafer crumbs	375 mL
14 oz.	condensed milk	395 g
¾ cup	semi-sweet chocolate chips	175 mL
¾ cup	sweet chocolate chips	175 mL
1 cup	almonds, sliced	250 mL

Combine ingredients in the order given. Spread in a foil-lined, greased 9" square (2.5 L) pan. Bake at 350°F (180°C) for 25 to 30 minutes until medium brown in colour. Cut in squares when cool.

CREAM CHEESE BROWNIES

4 oz.	sweet chocolate	120 g
5 tbsp.	butter	75 mL
3 oz.	cream cheese	85 mL
1 cup	sugar	250 mL
3	eggs	3
⅗ cup	flour	140 mL
1½ tsp.	vanilla	7 mL
½ tsp.	baking powder	2 mL
¼ tsp.	salt	1 mL
½ cup	nuts, chopped	125 mL
¼ tsp.	almond extract	1 mL

Melt chocolate and 3 tbsp. (45 mL) butter over very low heat, stirring constantly. Cool. Cream remaining butter with cheese. Gradually add ¼ cup (50 mL) sugar, beating until light and fluffy. Stir in 1 egg, 1 tbsp. (15 mL) flour, and ½ tsp. (2 mL) vanilla. In a separate bowl, beat remaining eggs until fluffy and light. Gradually add remaining sugar, beating until thickened. Fold in baking powder, salt, and remaining flour. Blend in cooled chocolate mixture. Stir in nuts, almond extract, and remaining vanilla.

Set aside 1 cup (250 mL) chocolate batter. Spread remaining batter in a greased 9" square (2.5 L) pan. Pour cheese mixture over top. Spoon reserved chocolate batter onto cheese; swirl together with a spatula to marble. Bake at 350°F (180°C) for 30 to 40 minutes. Cool. Cut in squares. Cover and store in refrigerator.

DOUBLE CHOCOLATE WALNUT BROWNIES

1 cup	butter	250 mL
4 oz.	unsweetened chocolate	112 g
2 cups	sugar	500 mL
3	eggs	3
1 tsp.	vanilla	5 mL
1 cup	flour	250 mL
1½ cups	walnuts, chopped	375 mL
6 oz.	semi-sweet chocolate chips	170 g

Melt butter and chocolate. Beat in sugar gradually. Add eggs one at a time, beating well after each addition. Stir in vanilla. Sift flour, and add with 1 cup (250 mL) of the walnuts. Spread on the bottom of a greased 9" x 13" (3 L) pan. Combine remaining walnuts with chocolate chips and press lightly into batter. Bake at 350°F (180°C) for 35 minutes. Cool completely on a wire rack before cutting into bars.

CHOCOLATE WALNUT CREAMS

3/4 cup	butter	175 mL
1/4 cup	sugar	50 mL
5 tbsp.	cocoa	75 mL
1	egg, slightly beaten	1
1 tsp.	vanilla	5 mL
2 cups	graham wafer crumbs	500 mL
1 cup	coconut, shredded	250 mL
1 cup	walnuts, chopped	250 mL
2 cups	icing sugar	500 mL
3½ tbsp.	vanilla pudding mix	55 mL
3 tbsp.	milk	45 mL
4 oz.	semi-sweet chocolate	112 g

Melt ½ cup (125 mL) of the butter in the top of a double boiler. Stir in sugar, cocoa, egg, and vanilla. Cook over simmering water for 3 minutes or until thick, stirring constantly. Pour onto graham wafer crumbs, coconut, and walnuts in a large bowl. Stir well. Pat evenly into a 9" square (2.5 L) pan. Blend icing sugar with 3 tbsp. (45 mL) butter in a medium bowl. Beat in instant pudding

powder and milk until thick and smooth. Spread over crumb layer. Set for 20 minutes.

Melt chocolate with remaining butter in top of double boiler, then spread on top of filling. Chill several hours. Cut into 36 squares.

CHOCOLATE HALFWAY SQUARES

1 cup	butter	250 mL
1/2 cup	sugar	125 mL
1½ cups	brown sugar	375 mL
2	eggs, separated	2
1 tbsp.	cold water	15 mL
1 tsp.	vanilla	5 mL
2 cups	flour, sifted	500 mL
1/4 tsp.	salt	1 mL
1 tsp.	baking powder	5 mL
1/4 tsp.	baking soda	1 mL
7 oz.	semi-sweet chocolate	200 g

Cream butter and sugar until light. Add ½ cup (125 mL) brown sugar, beating until light. Add slightly beaten egg yolks, water, and vanilla. Blend thoroughly. Sift dry ingredients together 3 times and add. Mix well. Spread evenly in a greased 8" (2 L) baking dish. Grate chocolate over batter. Beat egg whites until stiff, then gradually beat in remaining brown sugar. Spread meringue smoothly on top of chocolate. Bake at 375°F (190°C) for 25 minutes. Cut into squares when cool.

COCONUT WALNUT SLICE

1 cup	flour	250 mL
1/2 cup	butter	125 mL
1/2 cup	coconut, shredded	125 mL
1½ cups	brown sugar	375 mL
1 cup	walnuts	250 mL
1/2 tsp.	salt	2 mL
1 tsp.	vanilla	5 mL
2	eggs	2

Crumb flour and butter. Pack into a buttered 8" square (2 L) pan. Blend together coconut, brown sugar, walnuts, and salt. Stir in vanilla. Add eggs one at a time, and mix well. Pour filling into crumb-lined pan. Bake at 350°F (180°C) for 30 minutes or until quite brown. Spread with butter icing. Cut into squares.

DATE SQUARES

Dough

1 cup	brown sugar	250 mL
1 tsp.	baking soda	5 mL
2 cups	oatmeal	500 mL
2 cups	flour	500 mL
	pinch of salt	
1 cup	butter	250 mL

Combine dry ingredients. Cut in butter until crumbly. Press half this mixture onto the bottom of a lightly greased baking pan. Spread date filling over dough, and top with remaining crumb dough. Bake at 325°F (160°C) for 35 to 40 minutes. Cool, then cut into squares.

Filling

2 cups	dates, chopped	500 mL
1/4 cup	sugar	50 mL
1/2 cup	water	125 mL

Combine ingredients in a saucepan. Cover, and cook until thick.

CURRANT SQUARES

Dough

3 cups	flour	750 mL
1 tsp.	salt	5 mL
2 tbsp.	sugar	30 mL
1 1/2 cups	shortening	375 mL
3/4 cup	ice water	175 mL
1 tsp.	baking powder	5 mL

Mix flour, salt, and sugar together. Cut in shortening as for pie crust. Dissolve baking powder in water; stir into flour mixture to form pastry. Divide into 2 parts, one slightly larger than the other. Roll out the larger piece to line a 9" x 13" (3 L) baking pan.

Filling

2 cups	currants	500 mL
1 cup	sugar	250 mL
1/8 tsp.	cinnamon	0.5 mL
2 tsp.	cornstarch	10 mL
1 cup	water	250 mL
1 tbsp.	lemon juice	15 mL
1 cup	walnuts, chopped	250 mL

In a large saucepan, combine currants, sugar, and cinnamon. Dissolve cornstarch in water and lemon juice, and add to saucepan. Stirring often, cook over low heat until thick, about 30 minutes. Cool. Spread filling over pie crust. Roll out remaining dough to cover filling. Sprinkle with walnuts. Bake at 375°F (190°C) for 50 to 60 minutes. Cut into squares.

DATE MERINGUE SQUARES

2 cups	dates, chopped	500 mL
1/2 tsp.	lemon juice	2 mL
1/2 cup	water	125 mL
2	eggs, separated	2
1/4 cup	butter	50 mL
3/4 cup	brown sugar	175 mL
1/2 tsp.	vanilla	2 mL
1 1/2 cups	flour	375 mL
1 tsp.	baking powder	5 mL
1/4 tsp.	salt	1 mL
1/4 cup	icing sugar	50 mL
3 tbsp.	almonds, slivered	45 mL

Combine dates, lemon juice, and water in a saucepan, and cook over medium heat to a smooth paste. Set aside to cool. Beat egg yolks until thick and light. Cream butter and brown sugar, and blend with yolks. Add vanilla. Sift flour, baking powder, and salt together; fold in. Spread into a greased 9" square (2.5 L) baking pan. Cover with date mixture. Beat egg whites with a pinch of salt until stiff, gradually adding icing sugar to make a stiff meringue. Spread over date filling. Top with slivered almonds. Bake at 300°F (150°C) for 50 minutes. Cool in pan and cut into squares.

DATE STICKS

2	eggs	2
1 cup	icing sugar	250 mL
3 tbsp.	flour, sifted	45 mL
1 tsp.	baking powder	5 mL
1 tsp.	vanilla	5 mL
1 cup	dates, chopped	250 mL
1 cup	walnuts, chopped	250 mL

Beat eggs. Add dry ingredients, then vanilla. Fold in dates and walnuts. Turn into a well-greased baking pan and bake at 400°F (200°C) for 20 minutes. Cut into narrow strips when cool.

FLUDEN

4	eggs	4
1 cup	sugar	250 mL
1 cup	oil	250 mL
1 tsp.	vanilla	5 mL
	pinch of salt	
2 tsp.	baking powder	10 mL
4 cups	flour	1 L

Beat eggs well, then beat in sugar. Mix in remaining ingredients, using enough flour to make a soft dough. Divide dough in half and roll out. Line a greased 9'' square (2.5 L) baking pan with first half of rolled dough; spread filling over base, dot with butter, and cover with remaining dough. Mark in squares. Bake at 350°F (180°C) for 1 hour. Cut into squares when cool.

Apple Filling

8	apples, grated	8
1 cup	sugar	250 mL
1/8 tsp.	ginger	0.5 mL
	pinch of salt	
3/4 tsp.	cinnamon	3 mL
1 tbsp.	lemon juice	15 mL
2 tbsp.	bread crumbs	30 mL

Drain apples. Combine with remaining ingredients and mix well. Sprinkle cinnamon and nuts over top layer of dough before baking.

Poppy Seed Filling

1 lb.	poppy seed	500 g
1/2 cup	sugar	125 mL
1/2 cup	walnuts, ground	125 mL
1	egg	1
1 tbsp.	lemon juice	15 mL
3/4 cup	honey, melted	175 mL

Soak seeds overnight. Drain, and grind. Mix with remaining ingredients. After baking fluden, spread additional melted honey on top and sprinkle with additional nuts.

LEMON SQUARES

1 cup	butter, melted	250 mL
2 1/4 cups	flour	560 mL
1 cup	icing sugar	250 mL
4	eggs	4
2 cups	sugar	500 mL
1 tsp.	baking powder	5 mL
6 tbsp.	lemon juice	90 mL

Combine butter, 2 cups (500 mL) flour, and icing sugar. Pack into a buttered 9'' x 13'' (3 L) pan. Bake at 350°F (180°C) for 20 minutes. Beat together eggs, sugar, baking powder, remaining flour, and lemon juice. Pour lemon mixture over crust. Bake for 30 to 35 minutes. When cool, sprinkle with icing sugar and cut into squares.

JAM FLUDEN

2 cups	flour	500 mL
1/4 tsp.	salt	1 mL
1 tsp.	baking powder	5 mL
2 tbsp.	sugar	30 mL

overleaf:
Cranberry Apple Pie (page 209);
Apple Strudel (page 221)

1 cup	shortening	250 mL
1	egg	1
1 tsp.	vanilla	5 mL
½ cup	orange juice	125 mL
	jam	
	candied fruits	

Mix dry ingredients, and cut in shortening. Add egg, vanilla, and orange juice. Refrigerate 1 hour.

Divide dough into 3. Roll each portion out to fit an 8'' square (2 L) utility pan. Arrange dough in layers in pan, spreading jam and fruit between layers. Bake at 325°F (160°C) for 1 hour. Cut into squares when cool. (Note: This makes an easily handled and rich dough that is very good for hamantashen.)

MILLE FEUILLES DESSERT

18	graham wafers (unbroken)	18
8 oz.	vanilla instant pudding mix	230 g
2 cups	whipping cream	500 mL
2⅛ cups	icing sugar	530 mL
4 tbsp.	milk	60 mL
½ tsp.	vanilla	2 mL
2 oz.	semi-sweet chocolate	56 g

Arrange wafers closely together in a 9'' x 13'' (3 L) pan. Fill spaces with broken wafers. Prepare pudding as directed and pour over wafers. Refrigerate until set. Whip the cream with 2 tbsp. (30 mL) icing sugar, and spread carefully over pudding. Top with remaining wafers. Blend remaining icing sugar, milk, and vanilla and spread on top of wafers. Melt chocolate in the top of a double boiler. Drizzle parallel lines of chocolate over icing about 1'' (2 cm) apart down length of pan. Use a toothpick to make a decorative pattern through the chocolate lines. Cut into rectangles. Do not freeze; will keep 3 days in refrigerator.

NANAIMO BARS

½ cup	butter	125 mL
¼ cup	sugar	50 mL
5 tbsp.	cocoa	75 mL
1 tsp.	vanilla	5 mL
1	egg	1
2 cups	graham wafer crumbs	500 mL
1 cup	coconut, shredded	250 mL
½ cup	nuts, chopped	125 mL

Blend butter, sugar, cocoa, vanilla, and egg in the top of a double boiler. Heat over boiling water until butter is soft and mixture resembles custard. Combine remaining ingredients and add, mixing well. Pack evenly into a 9'' square (2.5 L) pan. Spread with icing.

Icing

¼ cup	butter	50 mL
3 tbsp.	milk	45 mL
2 tbsp.	custard powder	30 mL
2 cups	icing sugar, sifted	500 mL

Cream butter. Add milk and custard powder, then blend in icing sugar. Spread over base; let stand 15 minutes before adding topping.

Topping

4 oz.	semi-sweet chocolate	112 g
1 tsp.	butter	5 mL

Melt chocolate and butter. Spread on top of custard icing. Refrigerate until set, then cut into bars.

PINEAPPLE SQUARES

½ cup	butter	125 mL
2	eggs	2
½ cup	sugar	125 mL
1½ cups	flour	375 mL
1½ tsp.	baking powder	7 mL
	pinch of salt	
2 tsp.	vanilla	10 mL
1 tsp.	almond extract	5 mL
2 cups	miniature marshmallows	500 mL
14 oz.	crushed pineapple	398 mL
3	egg whites	3
1 cup	icing sugar	250 mL
	pecan nuts	

Combine butter, eggs, sugar, flour, 1 tsp. (5 mL) baking powder, salt, 1 tsp. (5 mL) vanilla, and almond extract. Mix well. Spread into a buttered 9'' square (2.5 L) pan. Bake at 300°F (150°C) for 10 minutes. Spread marshmallows and drained pineapple over base. Beat egg whites until stiff. Gradually beat in icing sugar, remaining baking powder and vanilla. Spread this meringue over pineapple filling and sprinkle with pecans. Bake for 45 minutes. Cut into squares.

CRUNCHY PEANUT MALLOW SLICE

12 oz.	semi-sweet chocolate chips	350 g
3/4 cup	crunchy peanut butter	175 mL
3 cups	miniature marshmallows	750 mL

Melt chocolate chips with peanut butter over boiling water in a double boiler. Stir until well blended, then fold in marshmallows. Press into a greased 8'' square (2 L) pan. Chill until firm. Cut into squares. (Note: Butterscotch chips may be substituted for the chocolate chips.)

RAISIN SQUARES

1 1/4 cups	butter	300 mL
3 1/2 cups	flour	875 mL
2 cups	brown sugar	500 mL
3	eggs, separated	3
1 cup	milk	250 mL
1 tsp.	salt	5 mL
1 tsp.	vanilla	5 mL
3 tsp.	baking powder	15 mL
1 cup	raisins	250 mL

Mix 1 cup (250 mL) of the butter and 2 cups (500 mL) flour to a crumbly dough. Pat into a greased utility pan. Bake at 350°F (180°C) for 15 minutes until light brown.

Cream remaining butter, gradually adding half the sugar. Mix in egg yolks, milk, salt, and vanilla. Fold in remaining flour with baking powder and raisins. Spread over base. Bake 20 minutes. Beat egg whites; add remaining sugar and vanilla to taste, beating to a stiff meringue. Spread on top of cake. Return to oven to brown. Cut into squares.

RASPBERRY SQUARES

1 cup	flour	250 mL
1 tsp.	baking powder	5 mL
1 3/4 cups	sugar	425 mL
2	eggs	2
2/3 cup	butter	150 mL
2 tbsp.	milk	30 mL
1 cup	raspberry jam	250 mL
2 cups	coconut, shredded	500 mL
	vanilla	

Combine flour, baking powder, and 1 cup (250 mL) of the sugar. Mix in 1 egg, all except 2 tbsp. (30 mL) of the butter, and the milk. Press into a lightly greased 8'' square (2 L) pan. Spread jam over base. Beat remaining egg until frothy. Melt the rest of the butter and add together with remaining sugar, coconut, and vanilla. Stir to combine well. Spread onto jam layer. Bake at 350°F (180°C) for 30 minutes until lightly browned. Cut into squares. (Note: For variation, any flavour of jam may be used.)

TOFFEE BARS

1 cup	butter	250 mL
1 cup	brown sugar	250 mL
1	egg yolk	1
1 cup	flour	250 mL
7 oz.	milk chocolate or chips	200 g
1/2 cup	walnuts, chopped	125 mL

Cream butter. Add sugar and egg yolk, and stir in flour. Press into the bottom of an 11'' x 15'' (2 L) baking sheet. Bake at 350°F (180°C) for 15 to 20 minutes. Spread melted chocolate on top and sprinkle with nuts. Cut into bars.

COCONUT TOFFEE BARS

1/2 cup	butter	125 mL
1 1/2 cups	brown sugar	375 mL
1 1/8 cups	flour	280 mL
2	eggs	2
1 tsp.	vanilla	5 mL

1 tsp.	baking powder	5 mL
1/2 tsp.	salt	2 mL
1 cup	coconut, shredded	250 mL
1 cup	almonds, chopped	250 mL

Cream together butter and 1/2 cup (125 mL) brown sugar. Stir in 1 cup (250 mL) flour and mix well. Press into the bottom of a 9'' square (2.5 L) pan. Bake at 350°F (180°C) for 10 minutes.

Beat eggs well. Add remaining 1 cup (250 mL) sugar and vanilla. Mix thoroughly. Combine baking powder and salt with remaining flour; stir into mixture. Fold in coconut and chopped nuts. Spread over base. Bake for 25 minutes until topping is golden brown. Cool slightly, then cut into bars.

WALNUT RAISIN SLICE

1 1/8 cups	flour	280 mL
1/2 cup	butter	125 mL
2 tbsp.	sugar	30 mL
3	eggs	3
1 1/2 cups	brown sugar	375 mL
1 tsp.	baking powder	5 mL
1/2 tsp.	salt	2 mL
1 tsp.	vanilla	5 mL
1 cup	raisins	250 mL
1/2 cup	walnuts, chopped	125 mL

Mix together 1 cup (250 mL) flour, the butter, and sugar. Press into an 8'' square (2 L) pan. Bake at 300°F (150°C) for 20 minutes. Beat eggs. Stir in remaining ingredients. Pour onto crust. Bake at 325°F (160°C) for 35 minutes. Cool, then spread on icing. Cut into squares.

Icing

3 tbsp.	soft butter	45 mL
3 tbsp.	icing sugar	45 mL
1	egg	1
1 oz.	chocolate, melted	28 g
1 tsp.	vanilla	5 mL

Beat ingredients together well.

COOKIES & DAINTIES

BEETLE BISCUITS

1 cup	butter	250 mL
1 cup	sugar	250 mL
1 tsp.	vanilla	5 mL
1 1/2 cups	flour	375 mL
1 tsp.	baking powder	5 mL

Melt and slowly brown the butter. When cool, add sugar and vanilla. Refrigerate until set. Add flour and baking powder and mix well. Scoop dough by spoonfuls onto baking sheets, easing dough gently out of spoon so that shape is retained. Allow to harden. Bake at 350°F (180°C) for 20 minutes. Cool. Dip one tip of each cookie in chocolate icing glaze to look like a beetle's back. Yields 50.

Chocolate Icing Glaze

3 oz.	semi-sweet chocolate	85 g
1 tbsp.	butter	15 mL
3 tbsp.	water	45 mL

Melt chocolate and butter, and thin with water. Use while warm, before icing sets.

ALMOND MERINGUES

3	egg whites	3
6 tbsp.	brown sugar	90 mL
4 1/2 oz.	whole almonds	130 g

Beat egg whites until stiff. Beat in brown sugar gradually until batter forms peaks. Carefully fold in nuts. Drop by spoonfuls onto an ungreased cookie sheet. Bake at 275°F (140°C) for 25 minutes. Turn off oven and leave meringues for 4 hours or overnight. Store in an open container. Yields 24.

BRAZIL-DATE DAINTY

3	egg whites	3
3 tbsp.	sugar	45 mL
30	brazil nuts	30
30	dates, pitted	30
1 cup	coconut, shredded	250 mL

Beat egg whites with sugar until stiff. Place a nut inside each date. Roll in egg white, then in coconut. Bake at 325°F (160°C) until lightly browned. Yields 30.

CANDY WARSHT

3¼ oz.	chocolate pudding mix	92 g
¾ cup	condensed milk	175 mL
⅛ tsp.	salt	0.5 mL
¼ tsp.	vanilla	1 mL
1 cup	nuts, chopped	250 mL

Mix pudding, condensed milk, and salt. Cook 2 minutes in the top of a double boiler until thick. Remove from heat, add vanilla and nuts, and mix well. Cool slightly. Turn out onto wax paper and roll up to make a log. Refrigerate until firm. Slice.

CARAMEL CRUNCHIES

24	graham wafers	24
1 cup	butter	250 mL
¾ cup	brown sugar	175 mL
¼ tsp.	vanilla	1 mL
2 cups	almonds, slivered	500 mL

Line a cookie sheet with graham wafers. Combine butter and brown sugar in a saucepan and heat until bubbly. Add vanilla. Pour over graham wafers and sprinkle with slivered almonds. Bake at 350°F (180°C) for 8 minutes. Cool and slice.

CHOCOLATE JUMBLES

4 cups	semi-sweet chocolate chips	1 L
½ cup	butter	125 mL
8 oz.	unsweetened chocolate	224 g
8	eggs	8
3 cups	sugar	750 mL
2 tsp.	vanilla	10 mL
8 tsp.	instant coffee	40 mL
1 tsp.	baking powder	5 mL
1 cup	flour	250 mL
9 cups	walnuts	2.25 L

Melt half the chocolate chips with the butter and unsweetened chocolate in the top of a double boiler. Beat together eggs, sugar, vanilla, and coffee until light and fluffy. Stir into chocolate mixture. Mix in remaining ingredients, including chocolate chips. Drop by spoonfuls onto ungreased cookie sheets. Bake at 350°F (180°C) for 5 minutes. Yields 90 medium-sized cookies.

CORN FLAKE COOKIES

1 cup	butter	250 mL
1 cup	brown sugar	250 mL
1	egg	1
1¼ cups	oatmeal	300 mL
½ cup	corn flakes, crushed	125 mL
1½ cups	flour	375 mL
½ tsp.	baking soda	2 mL
	pinch of salt	
½ cup	walnuts	125 mL

Cream together butter, sugar, and egg. Stir in remaining ingredients. Drop by spoonfuls onto a greased cookie sheets. Bake at 350°F (180°C) for 10 to 12 minutes. Yields 60.

COCONUT ICEBOX COOKIES

1 cup	butter	250 mL
1 cup	sugar	250 mL
1	egg	1

2¹/₂ cups	flour	625 mL
¹/₂ tsp.	baking soda	2 mL
	pinch of salt	
2¹/₂ cups	coconut, shredded	625 mL
1	egg yolk	1
3 tbsp.	milk	45 mL
¹/₄ cup	nuts, ground	50 mL

Cream together butter and sugar. Beat in egg. Add dry ingredients, stirring in coconut last. Form into 5 rolls. Wrap in wax paper and refrigerate overnight. Slice into cookies, brush tops with a mixture of egg yolk and milk, and sprinkle with ground nuts. Bake on a lightly greased cookie sheet at 350°F (180°C) for 10 to 12 minutes.

DATE NUT COOKIES

3	egg whites	3
1 cup	sugar	250 mL
1 tbsp.	flour	15 mL
1 cup	dates, chopped	250 mL
1 cup	coconut, shredded	250 mL
¹/₂ cup	filberts	125 mL
1 tsp.	vanilla	5 mL
¹/₂ tsp.	almond extract	2 mL
2 tsp.	orange rind, grated	10 mL
	semi-sweet chocolate chips	

Beat egg whites until stiff. Gradually beat in sugar. Combine remaining ingredients and fold into egg whites. Drop by spoonfuls onto greased cookie sheets. Bake at 350°F (180°C) for 12 to 15 minutes. Yields 36.

KAFFLES

1 cup	icing sugar	250 mL
¹/₂ tbsp.	lemon juice	10 mL
1 tsp.	vanilla	5 mL
¹/₂ tsp.	cinnamon	2 mL
1 cup	almonds, ground	250 mL
¹/₄ cup	coconut (angel flake)	50 mL
3	egg whites	3

Combine icing sugar, lemon juice, vanilla, cinna- mon, almonds, and coconut. Beat egg whites until stiff and fold into first mixture, combining well. With wet hands, form the mixture a tea- spoonful at a time into crescent shapes. Place on greased and floured cookie sheets. Let stand, covered, for 30 minutes at room temperature. Bake at 325°F (160°C) for 15 minutes. Yields 36.

HORSESHOES

1 cup	butter	250 mL
³/₄ cup	icing sugar	175 mL
2 cups	cake flour	500 mL
1 cup	pecan nuts, chopped	250 mL

Cream together butter and icing sugar. Stir in flour and nuts. Form into horseshoe shapes and place on lightly greased cookie sheets. Bake at 350°F (180°C) for 15 to 20 minutes, until barely golden. Dip in icing sugar while still hot. Cool on rack. Cookies will be delicate and should be handled gently. Yields 60.

CRUNCHY KOMISH BROIT

3	eggs, beaten	3
1 cup	sugar	250 mL
1 cup	oil	250 mL
1 tsp.	vanilla	5 mL
³/₄ cup	coconut, shredded	175 mL
³/₄ cup	almonds, sliced	175 mL
³/₄ cup	chocolate chips	175 mL
¹/₄ tsp.	salt	1 mL
¹/₂ tsp.	baking powder	2 mL
¹/₂ tsp.	baking soda	2 mL
3 cups	flour	750 mL

Beat eggs, sugar, oil, and vanilla. Add coconut, nuts, and chocolate chips. Sift together dry ingre- dients and add, using more flour if necessary, to make a stiff dough. Refrigerate dough for 15 minutes to facilitate handling. Shape into 3 rolls, each approximately 3'' x 6'' (8 x 15 cm); bake at 350°F (180°C) for 30 to 40 minutes. Cut into ¹/₂'' (1 cm) slices and return to oven to dry at 200°F (100°C) for 10 minutes.

Variations

Sprinkle slices on both sides with cinnamon and sugar before returning to oven to dry.

Cocoa Komish Broit

Add 1 tsp. (5 mL) cocoa and 1 tsp. (5 mL) cinnamon to dry ingredients.

Alternatively, prepare regular komish broit dough, above. Cut dough in half. Add 1 tsp. (5 mL) cocoa to one-half of dough. Form each half into a ball, press one on top of the other, and cut this into 3 equal parts. Stretch and roll each portion of this mixed dough into a log shape and bake as above, sprinkling slices with a mixture of cinnamon and sugar before drying.

FILBERT MACAROONS

3	egg whites	3
³/₄ tsp.	cream of tartar	3 mL
1 cup	sugar	250 mL
	pinch of salt	
1 tsp.	vanilla	5 mL
1 cup	corn flakes, crushed	250 mL
1 cup	coconut, shredded	250 mL
³/₄ cup	filberts, whole	175 mL

Beat egg whites with cream of tartar until stiff. Gradually add sugar, salt, and vanilla. Fold in corn flakes and coconut. Roll filberts in mixture and place on greased cookie sheets. Bake at 300°F (150°C) for 15 to 20 minutes. Yields 36.

MARSHMALLOW ROLL

4 oz.	unsweetened chocolate	112 g
1 tsp.	butter	5 mL
1 cup	icing sugar	250 mL
1	egg	1
1 tsp.	vanilla	5 mL
1 cup	walnuts, chopped	250 mL
25 – 30	marshmallows	25 – 30

Melt chocolate and butter in the top of a double boiler. Mix together icing sugar, egg, and vanilla, and stir into chocolate mixture. Add chopped walnuts. Pour over marshmallows in a large bowl. Stir quickly, coating marshmallows before chocolate mixture thickens. Divide into 2, place on a long strip of wax paper, and shape into logs by rolling as tightly as possible as for a jelly roll. Chill overnight before slicing. Keeps indefinitely in refrigerator. (Note: Pecan nuts may be substituted for the walnuts.)

SWEET DREAMS

1 cup	butter	250 mL
2 cups	icing sugar	500 mL
1 ¼ cups	flour	300 mL
³/₄ cup	cornstarch	175 mL
3 tbsp.	orange juice	45 mL
	orange rind, grated	

Cream butter and ½ cup (125 mL) icing sugar until light and fluffy. Beat in flour and cornstarch. Mix well. Wrap dough, and refrigerate at least 2 hours. Preheat oven to 325°F (160°C). Roll dough into 1'' (2.5 cm) balls. Bake on ungreased cookie sheets for 8 to 10 minutes until golden. Cool slightly. Remove to wire racks to cool completely. Mix remaining icing sugar with orange juice and rind. When cookies are cool, place wax paper under racks before spooning on glaze. Let dry on racks. Yields 40.

MINT SURPRISE COOKIES

1 cup	butter	250 mL
1 cup	sugar	250 mL
½ cup	brown sugar	125 mL
2	eggs	2
2 tbsp.	water	30 mL
1 tsp.	vanilla	5 mL
3 cups	flour, sifted	750 mL
1 tsp.	baking soda	5 mL
½ tsp.	salt	2 mL
9 oz.	chocolate mints	255 g
	walnut halves	

Cream butter, gradually adding white and brown sugar. Blend in unbeaten eggs, water, and vanilla. Beat well. Sift together flour, baking soda, and salt, and add. Mix thoroughly. Cover and refrigerate at least 2 hours. Using approximately 1 tbsp. (15 mL) of chilled dough at a time, enclose each chocolate mint in dough. Place on greased baking sheets 2'' (5 cm) apart. Top each cookie with a walnut half. Bake at 375°F (190°C) for 15 minutes. Yields 50.

NUT COOKIES

4	eggs	4
	pinch of salt	
¾ cup	sugar	175 mL
½ cup	oil	125 mL
¾ cup	nuts, chopped	175 mL
2½ cups	flour	625 mL
2 tsp.	baking powder	10 mL
½ tbsp.	lemon juice	10 mL
1 tsp.	lemon rind, grated	5 mL
1 tsp.	vanilla	5 mL
½ tsp.	cinnamon	2 mL
2 tbsp.	coconut	30 mL

Beat together eggs and salt. Beat in sugar, then oil. Stir in remaining ingredients. Drop by spoonfuls onto ungreased cookie sheets. Bake at 375°F (190°C) for 20 minutes. Yields 50.

OATMEAL CHOCOLATE CHIP COOKIES

1 cup	shortening	250 mL
½ cup	brown sugar	125 mL
½ cup	sugar	125 mL
2	eggs	2
1½ cups	wholewheat flour	375 mL
1 tsp.	baking soda	5 mL
½ tsp.	salt	2 mL
2 cups	oatmeal	500 mL
12 oz.	semi-sweet chocolate chips	350 g

Cream shortening and sugars. Add eggs and mix well. Combine flour, baking soda, and salt. Add to creamed mixture, beating thoroughly. Add oatmeal and chocolate chips, and mix thoroughly. Drop by spoonfuls onto greased cookie sheets. Bake at 350°F (180°C) for 15 minutes. Yields 80.

NUT CRESCENTS

2	egg whites	2
1 tsp.	vinegar	5 mL
1 cup	icing sugar	250 mL
½ cup	baking filberts, crushed	125 mL

Beat egg whites. Add vinegar and icing sugar. Fold in filberts, mixing well. Oil hands and form nut mixture into crescents. Bake on a greased cookie sheet at 300°F (150°C) for 15 to 20 minutes. Remove from pan immediately. Yields 30.

BANANA OATMEAL COOKIES

1½ cups	flour, sifted	375 mL
½ tsp.	baking soda	2 mL
1 tsp.	salt	5 mL
¼ tsp.	nutmeg	1 mL
¾ tsp.	cinnamon	3 mL
¾ cup	shortening	175 mL
1 cup	sugar	250 mL
1	egg	1
1 cup	bananas, mashed	250 mL
1¾ cups	rolled oats	425 mL
½ cup	nuts, chopped	125 mL
¼ cup	raisins	50 mL

Sift together flour, baking soda, salt, and spices; set aside. Cream shortening. Gradually add sugar, creaming well. Beat in egg. Stir in bananas, oats, nuts, and raisins. Add flour mixture and mix thoroughly. Drop by spoonfuls onto greased cookie sheets. Bake at 375°F (190°C) for 12 to 15 minutes. Remove at once. Yields 80.

POPPY SEED OATMEAL COOKIES

½ cup	butter	125 mL
½ cup	oil	125 mL
1 cup	brown sugar	250 mL
⅓ cup	sugar	75 mL
1	egg	1

½ cup	poppy seed	125 mL
2 cups	oatmeal	500 mL
2½ cups	flour	625 mL
¼ tsp.	salt	1 mL
1 tsp.	baking powder	5 mL
¼ cup	milk	50 mL
1 tsp.	vanilla	5 mL

Cream butter. Add oil, sugars, and egg. Beat until light. Stir in remaining ingredients, adding milk and vanilla last. Roll dough out on a floured board or pastry cloth. Cut into desired shapes and bake on greased cookie sheets at 350°F (180°C) for 10 minutes, until light brown. Yields 80.

RAISIN OATMEAL COOKIES

1 cup	raisins	250 mL
½ cup	shortening	125 mL
1 cup	sugar	250 mL
2	eggs, beaten	2
¼ cup	milk	50 mL
1⅔ cups	oatmeal	400 mL
1½ cups	flour	375 mL
1 tsp.	baking soda	5 mL
½ tsp.	salt	2 mL
1 tsp.	cinnamon	5 mL

Rinse raisins in hot water; drain. Cream shortening and sugar. Add eggs and milk, then stir in oatmeal and raisins. Sift dry ingredients together and add. Mix well. Drop by spoonfuls onto greased cookie sheets and bake at 350°F (180°C) for 12 minutes. Yields 48.

ORANGE ICEBOX COOKIES

1 cup	shortening	250 mL
½ cup	brown sugar	125 mL
½ cup	sugar	125 mL
1	egg	1
3 tbsp.	orange juice	45 mL
2 tsp.	orange rind, grated	10 mL

2 cups	flour	500 mL
¼ tsp.	salt	1 mL
¼ tsp.	baking soda	1 mL
½ cup	nuts, chopped	125 mL

Cream shortening with sugars. Add egg, orange juice, and rind. Mix well. Sift dry ingredients together and add to creamed mixture. Fold in nuts. Form into a roll 2'' (5 cm) in diameter. Wrap in wax paper and chill thoroughly. Cut into slices ⅛'' (0.5 cm) thick. Bake at 350°F (180°C) for 12 minutes. Yields 96.

Variation

Spiced Icebox Cookies
Prepare as for orange cookies, omitting orange juice and rind, using slightly less flour, and adding ¼ tsp. (1 mL) each of mace, nutmeg, and cloves, and 1 tsp. (5 mL) cinnamon. Chopped glazed fruit may be added as well.

PEANUT COOKIES

3	eggs	3
¾ cup	oil	175 mL
¾ cup	sugar	175 mL
2½ cups	flour	625 mL
	pinch of salt	
2 tsp.	baking powder	10 mL
¾ cup	peanuts, ground	175 mL
1 tsp.	vanilla	5 mL

Beat together eggs, oil, and sugar. Sift in dry ingredients and mix well. Add peanuts and vanilla. Roll into 1½'' (3.5 cm) balls, pressing with a fork to flatten slightly. Bake on ungreased cookie sheets at 350°F (180°C) for 12 to 15 minutes. Yields 60.

PEANUT BUTTER COOKIES

2 cups	brown sugar	500 mL
1 cup	butter	250 mL
2 tbsp.	peanut butter	30 mL
2	eggs, beaten	2

4 cups	flour	1 L
1 tsp.	baking soda	5 mL
1 tsp.	cream of tartar	5 mL

Cream together sugar and butter. Add peanut butter and eggs. Sift in dry ingredients, and mix well. Form into rolls and wrap in wax paper. Refrigerate overnight. Slice into 1/4'' (0.5 cm) rounds, and bake on ungreased cookie sheets at 350°F (180°C) for 10 minutes. Yields 100.

PEANUT BUTTER MACAROONS

2	egg whites	2
3/4 cup	sugar	175 mL
1/4 tsp.	almond extract	1 mL
1/3 cup	peanut butter	75 mL
2 cups	Rice Krispies	500 mL

Beat egg whites until stiff. Fold in sugar, almond extract, and peanut butter. Add Rice Krispies, stirring just to combine. Drop by spoonfuls onto greased cookie sheets. Bake at 375°F (190°C) for 20 minutes. Yields 60.

POPPY SEED COOKIES

1/3 cup	poppy seed	75 mL
1/2 cup	shortening	125 mL
1/2 cup	sugar	125 mL
2	eggs	2
1 tsp.	lemon juice	5 mL
2 1/2 cups	flour	625 mL
2 tsp.	baking powder	10 mL
1 tsp.	salt	5 mL

Scald poppy seed; drain. Cream together shortening, sugar, eggs, and lemon juice. Stir in poppy seed. Sift dry ingredients together and add. Mix well. Chill dough. Roll out on a floured board and cut into desired shapes. Bake on a greased cookie sheet at 350°F (180°C) for 15 minutes, until golden brown. (Note: For crispy cookies, roll the dough thin.)

Variation

Substitute vanilla for the lemon juice. Sprinkle rolled dough with cinnamon and sugar before cutting into cookies.

FREEZER RAISIN COOKIES

1/2 cup	butter	125 mL
1	egg	1
2 tsp.	vanilla	10 mL
1 cup	flour	250 mL
1 tsp.	baking powder	5 mL
1/4 tsp.	salt	1 mL
3/4 cup	raisins	175 mL
1 cup	coconut, shredded	250 mL
1 cup	walnuts, chopped	250 mL

Beat butter with egg and vanilla until smooth. Combine flour, baking powder, and salt. Gradually add dry ingredients to butter mixture and beat until blended. Fold in raisins, coconut, and walnuts. Form dough into 2 rolls and wrap in wax paper. Freeze until firm enough to slice easily, about 2 hours. (Frozen dough will keep up to 1 month.) Cut rolls into 3/4'' (2 cm) slices. Place on a lightly greased baking sheet. Bake at 350°F (180°C) for 12 minutes or until golden. Cool on rack. Yields 24. (Note: Chopped pitted dates may be substituted for the raisins.)

ROLY POLY

4	eggs	4
1 cup	sugar	250 mL
1 cup	oil	250 mL
1 tsp.	vanilla	5 mL
2 tsp.	baking powder	10 mL
1/3 tsp.	salt	1.5 mL
4 cups	flour	1 L
	jam	
	nuts, chopped	
	jelly fruit drops	

Mix eggs with sugar. Stir in oil and vanilla. Sift in baking powder and salt with the flour, using just enough flour to form a soft dough. Divide into 6.

Roll each portion out on a floured board. Spread with jam and sprinkle with chopped nuts and jelly fruit drops. Roll as for a jelly roll, first turning in sides. Bake on a greased pan at 375°F (190°C) for 30 minutes. Brush top with melted butter, cool on rack, then slice.

RUGULACH

1 cup	butter	250 mL
1 cup	cottage cheese	250 mL
2 cups	flour	500 mL
1/4 cup	butter, melted	50 mL
	jam	
2 tbsp.	cinnamon	30 mL
1/2 cup	brown sugar	125 mL
3/4 cup	raisins	175 mL
3/4 cup	nuts, chopped	175 mL

Cream butter and cheese. Blend in flour. Chill. Divide dough into quarters and, on a floured board, roll each piece out to approximately 1/4'' (0.5 cm) thickness. Spread with melted butter and jam, and sprinkle liberally with mixed cinnamon and brown sugar, raisins, and nuts. Cut into wedges. Starting at wide end, roll each wedge up and shape into a crescent. Dip in a mixture of white sugar and cinnamon before placing on greased cookie sheets. Bake at 400°F (200°C) for 15 minutes until browned.

Variations

Do not dip crescents into cinnamon and sugar. Rather, bake on ungreased cookie sheets and sprinkle with berry sugar when cool.

For turnovers, cut dough into large squares, fill with jam, and fold over to make a triangle.

SESAME CRESCENTS

6 tbsp.	oil	90 mL
6 tbsp.	sugar	90 mL
6 tbsp.	flour	90 mL
2	eggs	2
2 1/2 cups	sesame seeds	625 mL

Mix ingredients together well. Refrigerate 1 hour. With wet hands, form dough into crescent shapes, a spoonful at a time. Place on ungreased foil-covered cookie sheets. Bake at 350°F (180°C) for 15 to 20 minutes. Cool slightly before removing from pan. Yields 36.

SESAME COOKIES

1/4 cup	liquid honey	50 mL
1/4 cup	butter	50 mL
1/4 cup	tahini (sesame paste)	50 mL
1 tsp.	almond extract	5 mL
1 1/2 cups	wholewheat flour	375 mL
1/2 cup	sesame seeds, toasted	125 mL
1 tsp.	baking powder	5 mL
1/2 tsp.	salt	2 mL

Beat together the honey, butter, tahini, and almond extract. Mix dry ingredients, and add to butter mixture. Shape into 1 1/2'' (3.5 cm) balls and place on a greased cookie sheet. Flatten with a fork. Bake for 12 minutes, until lightly browned. Yields 18 – 24.

SOUR CREAM SPICE COOKIES

1 cup	shortening	250 mL
2 cups	sugar	500 mL
4	eggs	4
1 tsp.	vanilla	5 mL
1 cup	sour cream	250 mL
5 cups	flour	1.25 L
1 tsp.	baking soda	5 mL
1 tsp.	baking powder	5 mL
1 tsp.	salt	5 mL
1 tsp.	cinnamon	5 mL
1/2 tsp.	cloves	2 mL
1/2 tsp.	nutmeg	2 mL

Cream shortening and sugar. Beat in eggs and vanilla. Combine dry ingredients and add to mixture alternately with sour cream, blending well. Drop by spoonfuls onto greased cookie sheets. Bake at 350°F (180°C) for 12 to 15 minutes. Yields 60.

SHORTBREAD

1 cup	butter	250 mL
1/2 cup	icing sugar	125 mL
1/2 cup	cornstarch	125 mL
1 1/2 cups	flour	375 mL

Cream butter. Add remaining ingredients. Knead dough on a floured board for 3 minutes. Roll a spoonful of dough at a time into a smooth ball. Place on a lightly greased cookie sheet and flatten with a fork dipped in flour. Bake at 300°F (150°C) for 20 to 30 minutes. Yields 24.

SHORTBREAD CRESCENTS

1 cup	sweet butter	250 mL
1/2 cup	salted butter	125 mL
2 2/3 cups	flour	650 mL
2/3 cup	icing sugar	150 mL
2 cups	almonds, ground	500 mL
2	egg yolks	2

Cream butter. Add dry ingredients, then mix in egg yolks. Cover, and refrigerate 2 hours. Roll out; cut dough into horseshoe shapes. Bake on ungreased cookie sheets at 350°F (180°C) for 10 to 14 minutes. While warm, dust with a mixture of icing sugar and vanilla sugar. Dust again, lightly, just before serving. (Note: Makes a large quantity, and freezes well. This recipe may not be doubled. Nor is it recommended to substitute margarine for the butter.)

SUGAR COOKIES

1/2 cup	shortening	125 mL
1 cup	sugar	250 mL
1 tsp.	lemon rind, grated	5 mL
1	egg	1
2 tbsp.	milk	30 mL
1 tsp.	vanilla	5 mL
2 cups	flour	500 mL
1 tsp.	baking powder	5 mL
1/2 tsp.	baking soda	2 mL
1/4 tsp.	salt	1 mL

Cream together shortening, sugar, and lemon rind. Stir in egg, milk, and vanilla. Sift dry ingredients together and add. Mix well. Chill dough 15 minutes. Roll out on a floured board and cut into desired shapes. Bake on a greased cookie sheet at 350°F (180°C) for 8 to 10 minutes.

SWEDISH COOKIES

1/2 cup	butter	125 mL
1/4 cup	brown sugar	50 mL
1	egg, separated	1
1 cup	flour	250 mL
1/2 cup	nuts, chopped	125 mL
1/2 cup	jam	125 mL

Cream butter. Gradually add sugar, then slightly beaten egg yolk. Stir in flour. Form into small balls. Dip in egg white, then in chopped nuts. Make a small dent in the middle of each ball. Place on a greased cookie sheet and bake at 350°F (180°C) for 5 minutes. Dent each ball again. Bake for 15 minutes longer. Fill cavities with jam while still hot. Yields 24. (Note: Coconut may be substituted for the chopped nuts.)

TAIGLACH

8	eggs	8
4 1/2 cups	flour	1.12 L
2 tsp.	baking powder	10 mL
2 cups	honey	500 mL
1 tsp.	ginger	5 mL
1 cup	sugar	250 mL
1/2 cup	walnuts, chopped	125 mL

Mix eggs, flour, and baking powder thoroughly. Knead well. Dough should be soft, but stiff enough to roll. With very lightly floured hands, roll bits of dough into long ropes 1/2'' (1.5 cm) in diameter. Slice in 1/2'' (1.5 cm) lengths. Preheat oven to 350°F (180°C). Bring honey, ginger, and sugar to a boil in a shallow, broad-bottomed pan. Drop in pieces of raw dough while syrup is boiling. Immediately place pan in oven. Do not open oven for 15 to 20 minutes. By this time, each piece of dough will be coated with syrup. Bake for 1 hour, stirring every 10 minutes to prevent taiglach from sticking together. Pieces are done when they are brown and remain firm and crisp when tested in cold water. Pour onto a moistened board, and flatten. Sprinkle with nuts and cut into squares. Makes 40 pieces. Will keep indefinitely.

CHERRY TAIGLACH

2	eggs, well beaten	2
3/4 cup	flour	175 mL
	pinch of salt	
1 cup	honey	250 mL
1 tsp.	sugar	5 mL
1 1/2 tbsp.	ginger	25 mL
1 cup	walnuts, chopped	250 mL
10	maraschino cherries	10

Thoroughly mix eggs, flour, and salt. Roll out onto a lightly floured board; cut into 1/2'' (1.5 cm) squares. Boil together honey, sugar, and ginger. Drop squares into lightly boiling syrup. Cover and boil lightly for 20 minutes. Raise heat and boil for 10 minutes more. During the last 2 minutes, stir in walnuts and quartered cherries. Spoon into paper cups. Cool.

FRUIT-FILLED TAIGLACH

9	eggs, separated	9
2 1/2 tbsp.	oil	40 mL
2 1/2 tbsp.	brandy	40 mL
5 cups	flour	1.25 L
1/2 cup	prunes, chopped	125 mL
1/2 cup	raisins, chopped	125 mL
4 cups	sugar	1 L
4 cups	syrup	1 L
4 cups	water	1 L
1 tbsp.	ginger	15 mL

Beat 7 egg whites well. Mix in 9 beaten yolks. Add oil, brandy, and enough flour to make a stiff dough. Roll onto a floured board and cut in desired shapes. Fill with prunes and raisins, folding or rolling dough to seal. Bring sugar, syrup, and water to a boil. Drop in taiglach. Cover and boil 25 minutes without lifting lid. Continue boiling, stirring occasionally, until taiglach turn brown. Add ginger just before removing from heat. Turn out onto a wet board to cool.

SWEETS & TREATS

ALMOND TREATS

2 cups	almonds, slivered	500 mL
3/4 cup	sugar	175 mL
3 tbsp.	flour	45 mL
3	egg whites	3
2 1/2 tbsp.	butter, melted	40 mL

Combine almonds, sugar, and flour. Add egg whites and butter. Mix well. Refrigerate 1 1/2 hours. Drop batter by spoonfuls onto a greased cookie sheet, and flatten cookies with a fork dipped in milk. Let stand, covered, at room temperature for 30 minutes. Bake at 350°F (180°C) for 8 to 10 minutes until golden brown. As cookies are removed from oven, lift each cookie off with a spatula and roll around a rolling pin to shape. Cool.

ALMOND DROPS

1/2 cup	shortening	125 mL
1/2 cup	butter	125 mL
1/2 cup	sugar	125 mL
1/2 cup	brown sugar	125 mL
1	egg, beaten	1
2 tsp.	cream of tartar	10 mL
1 tsp.	baking soda	5 mL
2 cups	flour	500 mL

1 tsp.	almond extract	5 mL
1/2 tsp.	salt	2 mL
	almonds, blanched	

Cream shortening, butter, and sugars. Add egg. Sift in dry ingredients, then add extract. Mix well. Roll into small balls. Place on a greased cookie sheet, and press half a blanched almond on top of each. Bake at 400°F (200°C) for 10 minutes.

BITTER SWEETS

1/2 cup	seedless raisins	125 mL
1/2 cup	dates, pitted	125 mL
1/4 cup	nuts	50 mL
1/4 cup	maraschino cherries	50 mL
6 oz.	sweet chocolate	168 g

Chop fruits and nuts very fine. Mix thoroughly and press into balls. Melt chocolate over hot water in the top of a double boiler. Dip fruit balls in melted chocolate. Set on wax paper to cool. (Note: Unsweetened or semi-sweet chocolate may be used instead of sweet chocolate.)

CHERRY FLIPS

12 oz.	maraschino cherries	340 mL
1/2 cup	butter	125 mL
1/2 cup	icing sugar	125 mL
1	egg yolk	1
1 cup	flour	250 mL
	pinch of salt	
1 tsp.	almond extract	5 mL
1 cup	nuts, chopped	250 mL

Drain cherries, reserving syrup. Cream butter until very light, then add 1/4 cup (50 mL) icing sugar and egg yolk. Work in flour and salt with hands until flour is absorbed and dough is light and rich. Pinch off dough in pieces the size of a walnut. Press flat in palm and wrap around a cherry. Place balls on a greased cookie sheet and bake at 325°F (160°C) until light brown. Cool. Combine cherry juice and enough icing sugar to make a thin icing. Dip cookies in icing, then roll in nuts.

DATE NUT ROLLS

1 cup	sugar	250 mL
3/4 cup	flour	175 mL
1 tsp.	baking powder	5 mL
1/2 tsp.	salt	2 mL
1 cup	dates, chopped	250 mL
1 cup	walnuts, chopped	250 mL
2	eggs	2
1/2 cup	icing sugar	125 mL

Mix first 4 ingredients together. Stir in dates and nuts. Beat eggs and add. Pour onto a greased cookie pan and bake at 350°F (180°C) for 20 minutes. Cut into 1'' (2.5 cm) squares. While hot, lift squares out of pan, form into balls, and roll in icing sugar.

CHOCOLATE SNOW BALLS

4 oz.	unsweetened chocolate	112 g
10 1/2 oz.	condensed milk	300 mL
28	graham wafers, crushed	28
1/2 cup	coconut, shredded	125 mL

Melt chocolate; stir in milk. Add wafer crumbs until mixture forms a stiff, cookie-like dough. Shape into walnut-sized balls and roll in coconut. Refrigerate 15 minutes.

FRUIT TREATS

2	egg whites	2
1 cup	icing sugar	250 mL
1 cup	walnuts, chopped	250 mL
1 cup	coconut, shredded	250 mL
1 tbsp.	orange rind, grated	15 mL
1 tsp.	lemon juice	5 mL
1 cup	dates, chopped	250 mL
1/4 cup	cherries, chopped	50 mL
	almonds, ground	

Beat egg whites until stiff. Fold in remaining ingredients. Form into balls the size of a walnut. Roll in ground almonds or walnuts and bake on a greased cookie sheet at 325°F (160°C) for 20 minutes.

CHOW MEIN CHOCOLATE BALLS

12 oz.	semi-sweet chocolate chips	350 g
6 oz.	butterscotch chips	175 g
1 cup	peanuts	250 mL
2 cups	chow mein noodles	500 mL
1 tsp.	oil	5 mL

Melt chocolate and butterscotch chips in the top of a double boiler. Stir in peanuts and noodles. Cool 10 minutes. Add oil, and mix well. Drop by spoonfuls onto wax paper. Refrigerate until set.

CREAM CHEESE DAINTIES

1/2 lb.	cream cheese	250 g
1/3 cup	sugar	75 mL
10	glacé cherries	10
1 slice	glazed pineapple	1 slice
1/2 cup	coconut, shredded	125 mL
	pinch of salt	

Blend cream cheese and sugar. Chop cherries and pineapple, and stir into cream cheese with coconut and salt. Mix well. Form into balls the size of a walnut and roll in coating.

Graham Crumb Coating

12	graham wafers, crushed	12
1 tbsp.	sugar	15 mL
	pinch of salt	
1 tbsp.	butter	15 mL

Mix dry ingredients. Cut in butter as for pastry. Roll cream cheese balls in crumbs until well coated. Refrigerate several hours before serving.

MARSHMALLOW COCONUT BALLS

1 cup	marshmallows	250 mL
1 cup	dates, chopped	250 mL
3/4 cup	nuts, chopped	175 mL
1/2 cup	coconut, shredded	125 mL

Melt marshmallows in the top of a double boiler. Add dates and nuts. Mix well. Drop by spoonfuls into coconut. Roll into balls. Refrigerate.

PECAN SNOW BALLS

7/8 cup	flour	200 mL
1/4 tsp.	salt	1 mL
8 tbsp.	butter	120 mL
1 tbsp.	sugar	15 mL
1 tsp.	vanilla	5 mL
1 cup	pecan nuts, chopped	250 mL

Sift together flour and salt, and set aside. Cream butter. Blend in sugar, vanilla, and pecan nuts. Work in the flour mixture. Form dough into small balls. Bake on an ungreased cookie sheet at 325°F (160°C) for 15 minutes. While hot, coat with icing sugar.

FUDGE

12 oz.	semi-sweet chocolate	340 g
1/4 cup	butter	50 mL
10 1/2 oz.	condensed milk	300 mL
1 tsp.	vanilla	5 mL
1/2 cup	raisins	125 mL

Melt chocolate with butter and condensed milk in the top of a double boiler. Add vanilla and raisins. Mix well. Pour into a greased 8'' square (2 L) utility pan. Refrigerate until set, then cut into squares. Store in refrigerator.

CARROT HALVA

5 cups	carrots, grated	1.25 L
4 cups	milk	1 L
1 cup	cream	250 mL
1/2 cup	sugar	125 mL
1 cup	brown sugar	250 mL
1 tbsp.	molasses	15 mL
1/2 cup	slivered almonds	125 mL
1/4 cup	butter	50 mL
1/4 tsp.	saffron	1 mL
1/4 tsp.	nutmeg	1 mL
1/2 tsp.	cardamom seeds	2 mL

Combine carrots, milk, and cream in a heavy saucepan. Bring to a boil, stirring constantly. Reduce heat and simmer, stirring occasionally, for approximately 1 hour, until mixture is reduced by half and coats a spoon. Add sugars and molasses, and cook 10 minutes more. Simmer over very low heat, adding toasted almonds, butter, saffron, and nutmeg. Cook until mixture draws away from sides of pan. Stir in cardamom seeds. Mound on a platter or bowl and decorate with toasted almonds.

HONEY CANDY

1 cup	honey	250 mL
1 cup	walnuts, ground	250 mL
1/2 cup	almonds, ground	125 mL
2 tbsp.	cocoa	30 mL
1 tbsp.	flour	15 mL

Combine all ingredients in a saucepan. Cook for 15 to 20 minutes. Form into balls and roll in coconut or ground walnuts.

APRICOT PLETZLACH

2 lb.	dried apricots	1 kg
8 cups	sugar	2 L

Wash apricots well. Soak overnight in warm water to cover. Next day, simmer in the same water for 10 to 15 minutes, then mince well, and add sugar. Cook for a further 25 minutes. Spread onto a wet board. When dry, cut into squares and sprinkle with sugar.

KELSEY PLUM PLETZLACH

2 lb.	dried Kelsey plums	1 kg
6 cups	sugar	1.5 L

In a large saucepan, soak plums overnight in water to cover. Boil, taking care that fruit does not burn. When plums are dissolved, add sugar and boil another 30 to 40 minutes, stirring constantly. Jam should start lifting from pot. Cool 5 minutes, then pour onto a wet board. When set, cut into squares. Store in an open jar.

POMERANTZEN

5	grapefruit	5
5 cups	sugar	1.25 L
1/2 cup	water	125 mL
1/2 cup	orange juice	125 mL
3 tbsp.	icing sugar	45 mL

Carefully peel skin off fruit in quarters. Cover skins with water and cook until soft. Cool, and cut off thin, coloured rind. Combine sugar, water, and orange juice in a saucepan. Cook for approximately 30 minutes until sugar thickens. Mix in icing sugar and beat well. Pour onto rind arranged on a wet board. Cool overnight. Cut into squares. (Note: Oranges may be substituted for grapefruit.)

MUNDLACH (POPPY SEED TREATS)

2 cups	poppy seed	500 mL
3 1/2 cups	honey	875 mL
1 cup	filberts	250 mL
2 tbsp.	sugar	30 mL

Soak poppy seeds in water for 6 hours. Hang overnight in a cheesecloth bag to drain. Place in a shallow pan and dry in a 250°F (130°C) oven. Grind or chop very fine. Melt the honey. Add ground poppy seed and boil slowly for 30 minutes or until mixture forms a soft ball in cold water. Add nuts and sugar. Boil for 5 minutes. Pat onto a moistened board and cut into diamond shapes. When cold, remove to a platter. Will keep indefinitely if stored in a cold place.

overleaf:
Brisket and Carrot Tzimmes (page 107);
Chicken Soup (page 24) and Knaidlach (page 258)

Ritual Occasions

Passover

Passover is a time of remembering when the Jewish people were slaves, and the bitter herbs we eat with the sweet Charoses is to remind us that life is a mixture of the bitter and the sweet. It is a time to think not only of the past, but of the present, of justice and injustice, and to give thanks that we are free to celebrate Passover, each in our own way.

Passover—the festival of freedom and the celebration of Spring. The time when families and friends get together, and those living away from home return. The table is set with a fine tablecloth, special china, and candles. Grandparents and children are honoured in song and ceremony, the Four Questions are asked, and every night for the week of Passover, dinner is a party.

The most influential factor in keeping everyone happy is the dinner. The First Seder dinner is a grand ritual occasion, each dish lovingly prepared in keeping with the Jewish tradition. First the fish, made by the grandmother the way her mother used to make it; then soup with Knaidlach and Almond Balls; two kinds of meat, chicken and brisket of beef; Stuffed Helzel; Potato Kugel and a vegetable side dish. Then the dishes are cleared away and tea is served. And there is a little something to go with the tea: Sponge Cake, Ingberlach, Chremzlach, Taiglach, Honey Prunes, and maybe an Orange Almond Torte.

The next night is the same.

And the next night is the same.

By the fourth day, a fifth question is asked in every household: "Why can't this night be different from other nights?"

The answer is, it can. Because matzo, as old and wise as the Bible, can make a chameleon-like transition into modern cuisine and become sophisticated and urbane. Egg Rolls are served as an hors d'oeuvre, Matzo and Liver Pie is the first course, followed by Eggplant Casserole with Farfel Pilaf. Dessert is a suspiciously *hometz*-looking Chocolate Mousse or Chocolate Almond Cake.

By the last night of Passover, everyone at the table is delighted to partake once again of the traditional dishes and the matzo, and to re-kindle the bond that ties us to our forefathers.

CHAROSES

1	apple, pared	1
1/2 cup	nuts, chopped	125 mL
1/2 tsp.	cinnamon	2 mL
1 tsp.	sugar or honey	5 mL
1 1/2 tbsp.	red wine	20 mL
	dash of ginger	
1/2 tsp.	lemon rind, grated	2 mL

Grate the apple coarsely and mash thoroughly with remaining ingredients. Beat until mixture is smooth and free of lumps. Correct seasoning to taste.

MANDLEN

1/3 cup	schmaltz or oil	75 mL
2/3 cup	water	150 mL
1 1/2 tsp.	salt	7 mL
1/4 tsp.	pepper	1 mL
2 cups	matzo meal	500 mL
6	eggs	6

Mix schmaltz, water, and seasonings in a saucepan, and bring to a boil. Pour liquid gradually onto matzo meal, mixing well with a fork. Beat eggs into mixture, and knead thoroughly. Grease hands. Roll pieces of dough into marbles about 1/2" (1 cm) thick. Place on a greased cookie sheet and bake at 400°F (200°C) until brown. Serve with soup.

ALMOND BALLS FOR SOUP

1	egg, separated	1
1/4 cup	almonds, chopped	50 mL
1/4 tsp.	lemon rind, grated	1 mL
	pinch of salt	

Beat egg yolk until light; add almonds, lemon rind, and salt. Whip egg white until stiff. Fold into mixture. Drop from a teaspoon into boiling fat and deep fry to golden brown. Drain on brown paper. Add to soup just before serving.

KNAIDLACH

2	eggs	2
2 tbsp.	schmaltz or margarine	30 mL
2 tbsp.	chicken bouillon	30 mL
1 tsp.	salt	5 mL
1/2 cup	matzo meal	125 mL

Mix all ingredients together very well. Refrigerate 1 hour. With wet hands, form into 1" (2 cm) balls and drop into boiling salted water or chicken soup. Cover and boil for 1 hour. Remove with a slotted spoon and serve with soup. Serves 4 – 6.

KNAIDLACH

3	eggs, separated	3
1/2 cup	cold water	125 mL
1/2 tsp.	salt	2 mL
1/4 tsp.	pepper	1 mL
1/2 tsp.	cinnamon	2 mL
2 tbsp.	schmaltz or oil	30 mL
1 1/2 tsp.	onion, grated	7 mL
1 1/2 cups	matzo meal	375 mL

Beat egg whites until stiff. Beat the yolks and combine with the next 6 ingredients. Fold in egg whites. Add enough matzo meal to make a light dropping consistency. Adjust seasoning. Put in freezer for 25 to 35 minutes. Form into balls. Drop into boiling soup or water and cook, covered, about 20 minutes. Do not lift lid. Makes about 10 large balls.

LIVER KNAIDLACH

8 oz.	liver	250 g
1	onion, sliced	1
1 1/2 cups	boiling water	375 mL
1 3/4 cups	matzo meal	425 mL
3	eggs	3
1/4 cup	schmaltz or oil	50 mL
1 tsp.	salt	5 mL
1/4 tsp.	pepper	1 mL

Broil liver and grind with onion. Pour boiling

water over matzo meal; let cool. Combine all ingredients and mix thoroughly. Roll into walnut-sized balls. Drop into boiling salted water and boil, covered, for 20 minutes.

POTATO KNAIDLACH

6 medium	potatoes, peeled	6 medium
1½ tsp.	salt	7 mL
2	eggs	2
¾ cup	matzo meal	175 mL

Boil potatoes, then mash with salt. When cool, add slightly beaten eggs and just enough meal to hold mixture together. Mould into egg shape and drop into boiling salted water. Boil, covered, for 20 minutes. Remove with a slotted spoon, spread with schmaltz, and brown in a 400°F (200°C) oven. Serve with browned onions. Serves 6 – 8.

FILLED POTATO KNAIDLACH

10 large	potatoes, peeled	10 large
1 tbsp.	schmaltz or oil	15 mL
1 tbsp.	matzo meal	15 mL
	salt	
	pepper	
1	egg	1

Grate potatoes; place in a muslin or cheesecloth bag, and squeeze out all liquid. Combine with remaining ingredients. Form into small balls and press a deep dent into each. Fill each hollow with 1 tsp. (5 mL) of the filling, close up and roll knaidlach into smooth round balls. Drop them carefully into a large pot of boiling salted water. Boil for 2½ to 3 hours. Serve with clear soup. Serves 6 – 8.

Filling

4 tbsp.	matzo meal	60 mL
1 tbsp.	schmaltz or oil	15 mL
	salt	

Crumble ingredients together.

BEEF CASSEROLE

2½	matzos	2½
¼ cup	hot water	50 mL
2 tbsp.	parsley, chopped	30 mL
2 tbsp.	onion, minced	30 mL
2 tbsp.	schmaltz or oil	30 mL
¾ tsp.	salt	3 mL
½ cup	cold water	125 mL
1 lb.	chuck, ground	500 g
1	egg, beaten	1
11 oz.	tomato-mushroom sauce	312 g
2	tomatoes, sliced	2
1	green pepper, sliced	1

Soak 1½ sheets matzo in the hot water to soften, then drain. Combine with parsley, onion, schmaltz, and ¼ tsp. (1 mL) of the salt. Grease an 11½'' x 7½'' (2 L) utility pan and spread mixture on bottom. Soak remaining matzo in cold water and drain. Combine with ½ tsp. (2 mL) salt, meat, and egg. Spread over mixture in utility pan. Top with tomato sauce and tomato slices. Bake at 350°F (180°C) for 45 minutes. Add green pepper slices and bake 5 minutes more. Serves 4.

PINEAPPLE SHORT RIBS

4 lb.	beef or veal ribs	2 kg
1 tbsp.	potato starch	15 mL
1 tbsp.	matzo meal	15 mL
½ cup	brown sugar	125 mL
4 tsp.	dry mustard	20 mL
1 tsp.	salt	5 mL
½ tsp.	pepper	2 mL
½ tsp.	garlic powder	2 mL
1 cup	tomato sauce	250 mL
½ cup	water	125 mL
14 oz.	pineapple chunks	398 mL

Have ribs cut in 2'' (5 cm) pieces. Broil to remove all fat. Combine dry ingredients in a plastic bag, add meat a few pieces at a time, and shake to coat well. Place in a roasting pan or large casserole and let stand for 30 minutes. Combine tomato sauce and water and pour over meat. Bake, covered, at 375°F (190°C) for 1½ hours. Remove cover, and add pineapple with juice. Continue to bake until the meat is tender, stirring often. Serves 6 – 8.

POTATO MEAT CASSEROLE

4 large	potatoes	4 large
2 tbsp.	schmaltz or oil	30 mL
1 tbsp.	onion, chopped	15 mL
6 tbsp.	matzo meal	90 mL
3	eggs	3
	salt	
	pepper	
	dash of cinnamon	

Boil 1 potato, and mash. Finely grate 3 potatoes; drain. Combine with mashed potato and remaining ingredients. Arrange half the mixture on the bottom of a greased casserole. Spread meat filling over, and top with remaining potato mixture. Bake at 350°F (180°C) for 1½ hours. Serves 4.

Meat Filling

8 oz.	ground beef	250 g
1	onion, chopped	1
	salt	
	pepper	
	cinnamon	

BEEF AND LATKES

3 tbsp.	oil	45 mL
½ cup	green pepper, diced	125 mL
½ cup	onion, chopped	125 mL
1 cup	mushrooms, sliced	250 mL
3 cups	roast beef, diced	750 mL
2 tbsp.	potato flour	30 mL
1½ cups	cold water	375 mL
2 tsp.	instant beef bouillon	10 mL
	salt	
	pepper	

Sauté green pepper, onion, and mushrooms in oil until tender, but not brown. Add meat and heat through. Mix potato flour and a little of the water to a paste, then stir in remaining water with soup mix. Add to meat mixture. Stir and cook slowly until sauce thickens. Season to taste. Keep hot while preparing latkes.

Potato Latkes

6	potatoes, grated	6
½	onion, grated	½
2	eggs, beaten	2
¼ cup	matzo meal	50 mL
	salt	
	pepper	
	oil for frying	

Combine potatoes and onion. Stir in eggs, then matzo meal. Season with salt and pepper. Drop by spoonfuls into hot oil and fry on both sides until golden brown. Drain, place on a warm serving platter, and pour a spoonful of meat mixture onto each. Serves 4 – 6.

MATZO STUFFING

4	matzos	4
¼ cup	water	50 mL
2	eggs, beaten	2
1 tsp.	salt	5 mL
¼ tsp.	ginger	1 mL
¼ tsp.	pepper	1 mL
1 tbsp.	parsley, chopped	15 mL
2 tbsp.	onion, chopped	30 mL
1 stalk	celery, chopped	1 stalk

Crumble matzos and sprinkle with additional warm water. Add remaining ingredients. This stuffing may be used for any meat or fowl.

MATZO AND LIVER PIE

1 lb.	liver, sliced	500 g
2 large	onions, chopped	2 large
2 tbsp.	schmaltz or oil	30 mL
2	eggs, hard-boiled	2
2½ tsp.	salt	12 mL
¼ tsp.	pepper	1 mL
5	eggs	5
4 – 5	matzos	4 – 5
¼ cup	matzo meal	50 mL
½ cup	water	125 mL

Broil liver for 15 minutes. Remove outer skin and

veins, and chop. Brown onions in schmaltz, and add to liver. Add chopped hard-boiled eggs, 2 tsp. (10 mL) of the salt, and ⅛ tsp. (0.5 mL) pepper. Mix in 2 beaten eggs. Dip matzos briefly in cold water but do not soften. Cut them to fit an 8'' square (2 L) baking pan, cutting enough for 3 layers. Mix matzo meal with water and remaining 3 eggs and seasonings. Dip the pieces of matzo in this mixture. Put a layer of matzos in the greased baking pan, then a layer of liver mixture. Repeat. Top with a layer of matzos. Bake at 350°F (180°C) until brown, about 45 minutes. Serves 4.

BLINTZES

Batter

¾ cup	potato flour	175 mL
1 cup	cake meal	250 mL
	pinch of salt	
3	eggs, beaten	3
2 cups	water	500 mL

Sift dry ingredients together and add to eggs. Mix with enough water to make a smooth batter. Grease a heated pan lightly with schmaltz. Pour batter to cover base of pan thinly, and turn out onto a cloth when dry. Place a spoonful of filling on cooked side of each pancake. Fold into envelope shape and fry until golden. Yields 10–12.

Alternative Batter

3	eggs, beaten	3
1½ cups	water	375 mL
½ tsp.	salt	2 mL
¾ cup	cake meal	175 mL

Combine eggs and water with salt. Stir in cake meal until smooth. This makes a very thin batter. Fry thin sheets on a hot, slightly greased pan. Turn out on a clean towel. Fill, roll up, and fry or bake. Yields 6 blintzes.

Cheese Filling

1 lb.	dry cottage cheese	500 g
2	eggs	2
½ tsp.	salt	2 mL
2 tbsp.	sour cream	30 mL
1 tbsp.	sugar	15 mL

Mix all ingredients together well. Serve blintzes with sour cream.

Any cooked ground meat or poultry, seasoned with salt and pepper and moistened with a beaten egg.

PASSOVER CHEESE KREPLACH

3	eggs	3
3 tbsp.	butter, melted	45 mL
3 tbsp.	milk	45 mL
1 tsp.	salt	5 mL
1 cup	matzo meal	250 mL
1 cup	dry cottage cheese	250 mL
½ tsp.	sugar	2 mL

Beat eggs, adding melted butter, milk, and half the salt. Add matzo meal gradually, mixing well, and let stand 10 minutes. In a separate bowl, mix cheese with sugar and remaining salt. Roll dough into balls, dip fingers into water and press a hollow into each ball. Fill each dent with 1 tbsp. (15 mL) of cheese mixture. Press edges of hollow together to seal in cheese. Drop balls into boiling salted water and boil, covered, for 15 minutes. Serve warm with sour cream.

BAKED MATZOS AND CHEESE

1 lb.	dry cottage cheese	500 g
5	eggs	5
½ tsp.	salt	2 mL
6	matzos	6
2 tbsp.	butter	30 mL
½ tsp.	cinnamon	2 mL
1 tsp.	sugar	5 mL

Mix cheese with 3 of the eggs and the salt. Lightly beat remaining 2 eggs, and dip in whole matzos. Alternately layer matzos and cheese in a greased baking dish, sprinkling cheese layers with cinnamon and sugar, and ending with a cheese layer. Bake at 350°F (180°C) for 25 to 30 minutes. Serves 6.

GESMIRTE MATZOS

matzos
milk
cinnamon
sugar

Dip matzos carefully in milk just to moisten. Spread thickly with cheese mixture, and sprinkle with cinnamon and sugar. Bake at 350°F (180°C) until golden brown. Cut into serving-sized pieces while warm.

Cheese Mixture

1/2 lb.	cream cheese	227 g
1	egg	1
1 tsp.	potato flour	5 mL
1/4 cup	butter, melted	50 mL
1/2 cup	sour cream	125 mL
	salt	
	sugar	

Blend all ingredients together until smooth, adding salt and sugar to taste.

ROYAL APPLE KUGEL

Mixture A

2/3 cup	brown sugar	150 mL
4 tsp.	oil	20 mL

Combine these ingredients in a bowl. Set aside.

Mixture B

5	matzos	5
2	apples, grated	2
1 1/2 tsp.	cinnamon	7 mL

3 tsp.	sugar	15 mL
1 tsp.	lemon rind, grated	5 mL
2	eggs, beaten	2

In a large bowl, break up the matzos, cover with water, and let soak for 2 minutes. Drain. Add grated apples, then remaining ingredients. Mix together and set aside.

Mixture C

4	apples	4
2 tbsp.	lemon juice	30 mL
1 cup	raisins	250 mL
4 tbsp.	jam	60 mL
1/4 cup	sugar	50 mL

Peel and slice the apples, and mix with remaining ingredients in a third bowl.

To Assemble Kugel

Sprinkle the bottom of a 12" x 8" (2 L) greased utility pan with brown sugar. Spread on Mixture A. Top with half of Mixture B, then spread on Mixture C. End with balance of Mixture B.

Set utility pan in a large roasting pan and add just enough water to roaster to come up sides of utility pan. Bake uncovered at 325°F (160°C) for 1 1/4 hours. Serve hot, as a side dish or dessert. Serves 6.

APPLE KUGEL

1/2 cup	sugar	125 mL
8	eggs, separated	8
6 large	apples, grated	6 large
1/2 cup	matzo meal	125 mL
1 tsp.	lemon rind, grated	5 mL
	blanched almonds	

Blend sugar and yolks well. Mix in grated apples, then add matzo meal and lemon rind. Lastly fold in stiffly beaten egg whites. Sprinkle a handful of blanched almonds on top. Bake in an ungreased springform pan at 325°F (160°C) for approximately 1 hour. Serves 6.

GRATED APPLE PUDDING

4	eggs, separated	4
2/3 cup	sugar	150 mL
2 cups	apple, grated	500 mL
1 tbsp.	lemon juice	15 mL
1/2 tsp.	lemon rind, grated	2 mL
1 cup	matzo meal	250 mL
1/2 tsp.	cinnamon	2 mL
	pinch of salt	
	cinnamon and sugar	

Beat yolks and sugar. Add apple, lemon juice, rind, matzo meal, and cinnamon. Fold in stiffly beaten egg whites and salt. Pour half the batter into a greased 8'' square (2 L) ovenproof dish. Sprinkle with mixed cinnamon and sugar. Add remaining batter. Bake at 350°F (180°C) for 1 hour. Serves 4.

FARFEL KUGEL

1 cup	matzo farfel	250 mL
1 cup	boiled water, cooled	250 mL
1/2 cup	sugar	125 mL
3	eggs, separated	3
2	apples, grated	2
	cinnamon	

Mix farfel and water. Add sugar, egg yolks, and apple. Fold in stiffly beaten egg whites. Pour into a greased baking dish and dust with cinnamon. Bake at 375°F (190°C) for 45 minutes. Serves 4.

SWEET KUGEL

3	eggs	3
1/2 cup	matzo meal	125 mL
1 cup	water	250 mL
1/2 cup	sugar	125 mL
1/2 tsp.	cinnamon	2 mL
	pinch of salt	
1 tsp.	vanilla	5 mL
3 tbsp.	schmaltz or oil	45 mL
1 cup	dried fruit	250 mL
1	apple, cut up	1
1	orange or lemon	1

Beat eggs, add matzo meal and water, and let stand 15 minutes. Add remaining ingredients, including juice and grated rind of orange or lemon if desired. Bake in a greased 8'' square (2 L) pan at 350°F (180°C) about 45 to 60 minutes until firm on top. Serves 4.

SOUR CREAM KUGEL

5	matzos	5
2 cups	sour cream	500 mL
2 cups	dry cottage cheese	500 mL
3	eggs	3
1/4 cup	sugar	50 mL
	pinch of salt	

Moisten matzos with cold water. Mix remaining ingredients together. Place matzo and sour cream mixture in alternating layers in a buttered 8'' square (2 L) pan, beginning with matzo and ending with sour cream. Dot with butter. Bake at 300°F (150°C) for 40 minutes. Serves 8 – 10.

POTATO KUGEL

2 1/2 cups	potato, grated	625 mL
1/4	onion, grated	1/4
	oil	
4	eggs, separated	4
1/2 cup	matzo meal	125 mL
4 tbsp.	schmaltz or oil	60 mL
1 tsp.	salt	5 mL
1/4 tsp.	pepper	1 mL

Rinse grated potatoes thoroughly in a strainer under cold water to remove excess starch. Fry onion in oil until translucent but not brown. Combine potatoes, onion, and egg yolks with remaining ingredients. Beat egg whites until stiff and fold into potato mixture. Grease a utility pan well, leaving excess oil on bottom, and preheat in a 350°F (180°C) oven. Pour mixture into hot pan. Bake for 1 hour. Serves 4 – 6.

Variation
Make in muffin tins for individual kugels, reducing baking time a little.

MOCK POTATO KNISHES

6 medium	potatoes	6 medium
1	egg	1
3/4 cup	matzo meal	175 mL
1/2 lb.	liver, broiled	250 g
1/2 cup	gribene (cracklings)	125 mL
1/3 cup	schmaltz or oil	75 mL
	salt	
	pepper	

Peel and cook potatoes and mash well. Stir in egg, and add enough matzo meal to make mixture easy to handle and shape. Chop liver and gribenes and combine, using schmaltz to bind and seasoning to taste. Shape potato mixture in greased palm of hand. Place a little liver mixture in centre, roll quickly into a ball, and dip lightly in matzo meal. Flatten into patty shape and place in a hot greased pan. Bake at 375°F (190°C) for 45 minutes until golden brown. Yields 12.

CARROT PUDDING

8	eggs, separated	8
1 1/2 cups	berry sugar	375 mL
2 tbsp.	matzo meal	30 mL
1/4 cup	potato flour	50 mL
1 1/2 cups	carrots, grated	375 mL
1 tbsp.	wine	15 mL
1/2 tsp.	lemon rind, grated	2 mL
1 cup	almonds, crushed	250 mL

Beat egg yolks and sugar together. Add matzo meal and flour, carrots, wine, lemon rind, and almonds. Fold in beaten whites. Bake in a greased, floured pan at 300°F (150°C) for 1 hour. Serves 6.

EGGPLANT CASSEROLE

3 tbsp.	butter, melted	45 mL
1 large	onion, sliced	1 large
1 1/2 lb.	eggplant	750 g
1/2 cup	green pepper, diced	125 mL
1/4 tsp.	pepper	1 mL
1 tsp.	salt	5 mL
11 oz.	tomato-mushroom sauce	312 g
2	tomatoes, diced	2
1 lb.	dry cottage cheese	500 g
1 1/2 cups	matzo farfel	375 mL

Sauté onion in butter. Pare the eggplant and cut into 1/2'' (1 cm) cubes. Combine onion, eggplant, green pepper, seasonings, and sauce in a saucepan. Cover, and simmer for 15 minutes or until eggplant is tender. Stir in tomatoes. Arrange alternate layers of vegetables, cheese, and farfel in a greased 2 quart (2 L) casserole, beginning and ending with vegetables. Bake uncovered at 350°F (180°C) for 25 minutes. Serves 6 – 8.

EGG ROLLS

Blintzes

3	eggs	3
1 cup	water	250 mL
1/2 tsp.	salt	2 mL
4 tbsp.	potato starch	60 mL

Mix ingredients well. Fry thin crepes on a greased, hot skillet, tipping to spread batter and browning on one side only. Turn out on a cloth. Stir batter each time before making a blintz.

Vegetable Filling

1 cup	celery, sliced	250 mL
1/2 cup	onion, sliced	125 mL
1/4 cup	green onion, chopped	50 mL
1 cup	bean sprouts	250 mL
2 tsp.	oil	10 mL
1 tsp.	salt	5 mL
1/4 tsp.	pepper	1 mL
2 tsp.	soy sauce	10 mL

Cook vegetables in oil for 5 minutes until tender. Season and add soy sauce. Place 2 tbsp. (30 mL) filling in the centre of each blintz. Brush 3 edges with slightly beaten egg. Fold unbrushed edge towards centre of filling; fold over opposite edge to overlap, and fold over remaining 2 sides to seal in filling. Deep fry. Makes 6.

Chicken Variation

Add ¾ cup (175 mL) chopped cooked chicken with the soy sauce.

FARFEL PILAF

2 cups	matzo farfel	500 mL
2 tbsp.	schmaltz or oil	30 mL
1	onion, chopped	1
1 cup	mushrooms, sliced	250 mL
1½ cups	chicken soup	375 mL

Brown farfel in schmaltz. Set aside. Sauté onion and mushrooms and combine with 1¾ cups (425 mL) of the farfel. Place mixture in a greased casserole. Pour soup over top. Cover and bake at 350°F (180°C) for 30 minutes, until liquid is absorbed. Top with remaining dry farfel. Serve hot, plain or with gravy. Serves 4 – 6.

KNAIDLACH AND VEGETABLES SIDE DISH

1	Spanish onion, sliced	1
1 tbsp.	schmaltz or oil	15 mL
8 oz.	fresh mushrooms	250 g
1 large	green pepper, sliced	1
1 cup	celery, diagonally cut	250 mL
1	zucchini, sliced	1
	salt	
	pepper	
12	knaidlach	12

Brown onions in schmaltz. Add whole mushrooms and cook 10 minutes. Add green pepper, celery, and zucchini; season to taste. Carefully add knaidlach (see page 258), and warm over medium heat. Serves 4.

LATKES

5	eggs, well beaten	5
	salt	
	pepper	
1 tsp.	sugar	5 mL
½ cup	warm water	125 mL
½ cup	matzo meal	125 mL

Beat eggs with salt, pepper, sugar, and water. Add enough matzo meal to make a loose batter. Let stand 10 minutes to thicken. Drop by spoonfuls onto a thin layer of hot oil in frying pan. Brown on both sides. Transfer to a cookie sheet and keep in 300°F (150°C) oven until ready to serve. Serve plain or topped with sour cream, yogurt, or apple sauce. Serves 6 – 8.

MATZO MEAL PANCAKES

3	eggs, separated	3
1 tbsp.	sugar	15 mL
½ cup	matzo meal	125 mL
½ cup	water	125 mL
½ tsp.	salt	2 mL
	pinch of cinnamon	

Beat sugar with yolks until very light. Blend matzo meal with water, salt, and cinnamon, and add to egg yolks. Beat egg whites until stiff and fold into mixture. Drop by spoonfuls into hot oil in a frying pan, and fry until brown. Serves 4 – 6.

PANCAKES

½ cup	matzo meal	125 mL
1 tsp.	sugar	5 mL
½ tsp.	salt	2 mL
¾ cup	milk	175 mL
2	eggs, well beaten	2

Add milk to dry ingredients and stir well. Gradually add eggs, blending gently. Drop by spoonfuls onto a well-greased pan and fry on both sides until brown. Serve with sour cream, apple sauce, or jam. Serves 4 – 6.

FRIED MATZOS

Break matzos into quarters or smaller. Dip in boiling water, then in raw beaten egg. Fry in butter or hot oil until fairly dry and browned. Sprinkle with cinnamon and sugar, or serve with jam or buckwheat honey. Serve hot.

BEET ROSSEL

12 lb.	beets	6 kg
	water	

About 3 weeks before Passover, scrape beets, cut in pieces, and pour into a 12 quart (12 L) crock; fill with water. Place cover on crock, leaving a small opening, and cover with a clean cloth. Let stand in a warm place. After about 1 week, a white foam will form on top. Remove this completely and stir the whole mixture well. Cover again and let stand in a warm place until Passover, when rossel will be sour enough to use without having to add lemons.

CHREMZLACH

3 cups	beet rossel	750 mL
¾ cup	schmaltz or oil	175 mL
1 cup	sugar	250 mL
	matzo meal	
5	eggs	5
	jam	
2 cups	honey	500 mL
1 tbsp.	lemon juice	15 mL

Boil rossel with schmaltz and sugar. Mix in enough matzo meal to absorb all liquid. Cool. Add eggs. Shape into balls, and fill each one with jam. Fry until brown. Dissolve honey in a frying pan and add lemon juice. Roll cooled fried chremzlach in honey, basting well. Place in 400°F (200°C) oven until honey is well absorbed. Serves 6.

PIE CRUST

¼ cup	matzo meal	50 mL
½ cup	cake meal	125 mL
½ tsp.	salt	2 mL
2 tsp.	sugar	10 mL
¼ cup	pecan nuts, ground	50 mL
⅓ cup	oil	75 mL
	cold water	

Combine dry ingredients in a bowl and, with a fork or pastry blender, mix in oil and just enough water to make a moist dough. Pat into a 9'' (1 L) pie plate and bake at 400°F (200°C) for 10 minutes, or until brown. Makes 1 pie shell.

APPLE LEMON PIE

Crust

4	eggs, separated	4
¾ cup	sugar	175 mL
3 tbsp.	water	45 mL
¼ cup	potato starch	50 mL
¼ cup	cake meal	50 mL
	pinch of salt	

Beat egg whites with half the sugar until stiff. Beat yolks with remaining sugar, then add water and sifted dry ingredients. Fold in egg whites. Pour into a lightly greased 9'' (1 L) pie plate. Bake at 350°F (180°C) until golden.

Filling

¾ cup	sugar	175 mL
3 tbsp.	potato starch	45 mL
2 tsp.	lemon rind, grated	10 mL
3 tbsp.	lemon juice	45 mL
1 tbsp.	cold water	15 mL
1	egg, beaten	1
8	apples, grated	8
	pinch of salt	

In a saucepan, mix sugar and potato starch. Add remaining ingredients, and heat to boiling. Boil 2 minutes, stirring constantly. Cool. Pour into crust. Top with meringue and bake at 300°F (160°C) until golden.

Meringue

2	egg whites	2
1 tbsp.	sugar	15 mL

Beat egg whites until frothy. Gradually add sugar, beating constantly until stiff.

ALMOND TORTE

10	eggs, separated	10
3 cups	sugar	750 mL
3 cups	blanched almonds	750 mL
1 tsp.	lemon rind, grated	5 mL
2 tbsp.	lemon juice	30 mL
1 tsp.	almond extract	5 mL
1 1/4 cups	cake meal, sifted	300 mL

Beat egg yolks until light. Gradually add sugar, beating constantly. Grind almonds, and mix into egg yolks together with lemon rind, juice, and almond extract. Add cake meal gradually. Fold in stiffly beaten egg whites. Bake at 350°F (180°C) for 1 hour in a greased springform pan. Cool in oven with door open.

ORANGE ALMOND TORTE

8	eggs, separated	8
7/8 cup	sugar	220 mL
2	oranges	2
1/2 cup	lemon juice	125 mL
8 oz.	blanched almonds	250 g
2 tbsp.	matzo meal	30 mL

Beat egg whites with half the sugar until stiff. Scald oranges with hot water, then grate rinds. Mix orange rind and juice, lemon juice, and remaining sugar, and combine with well-beaten yolks. Add to egg whites. Fold in toasted ground almonds and matzo meal. Bake in an ungreased 10'' (2 L) tube pan at 325°F (160°C) for 50 minutes. Invert pan to cool before removing cake.

APPLE CAKE

8	eggs, separated	8
1/4 tsp.	salt	1 mL
1/4 cup	sugar	50 mL
8	apples, grated	8
1 cup	matzo meal	250 mL
1/4 cup	almonds, ground	50 mL
1 tsp.	cinnamon	5 mL
1 tbsp.	orange juice	15 mL

Beat egg whites with salt until stiff. Add sugar gradually, beating continuously. Beat in egg yolks. Add apples, matzo meal, almonds, and cinnamon. Mix, then add orange juice. Pour into a pan lined with wax paper and bake at 325°F (160°C) for 1 1/4 hours.

FILLED APPLE CAKE

Dough

5	eggs, separated	5
5 tbsp.	sugar	75 mL
2 tbsp.	lemon juice	30 mL
1 tsp.	lemon rind, grated	5 mL
3 tbsp.	potato flour	45 mL
2 tbsp.	cake meal	30 mL

Whip egg whites stiff. Add yolks one at a time and beat well. Stir in sugar slowly, then lemon juice and rind. Fold in flour and cake meal, and mix gently but thoroughly with a wooden spoon. Grease 2 round, 9'' (2 L) cake pans and divide dough between them. Bake at 400°F (200°C) for 20 minutes. When cool, sandwich together with apple filling.

Apple Filling

3 large	apples	3 large
1/2 cup	wine	125 mL
1/2 cup	raisins	125 mL
	sugar	
	cinnamon	
1/2 cup	nuts, chopped	125 mL

Peel and slice the apples and poach in wine until tender. Add raisins and cook for 3 minutes. Remove from heat, season with sugar and cinnamon, and fold in chopped nuts.

BANANA CAKE

7	eggs, separated	7
1 cup	sugar	250 mL
1 cup	bananas, mashed	250 mL

¼ tsp.	salt	1 mL
¼ cup	potato starch	50 mL
¼ cup	cake meal	50 mL

Beat egg whites stiff. Combine sugar and 2 yolks; beat well. Add mashed bananas and salt. Fold into whites with potato starch and cake meal. Pour into an ungreased 10'' (2 L) tube pan and bake at 350°F (180°C) for 1 hour. Invert and cool before removing cake from pan.

BANANA NUT CAKE

8	eggs, separated	8
¾ cup	sugar	175 mL
2	bananas, mashed	2
2 tbsp.	wine	30 mL
¼ tsp.	salt	1 mL
6 tbsp.	potato flour	90 mL
6 tbsp.	cake meal	90 mL
¾ cup	nuts, chopped	175 mL

Beat egg yolks until light. Add sugar and beat until light and fluffy. Add mashed bananas and wine. Whip egg whites with salt until stiff, and fold in. Sift flour and cake meal; add a little at a time to egg mixture until well blended. Fold in chopped nuts. Bake in an ungreased 10'' (2 L) tube pan at 325°F (160°C) for 70 minutes. Invert pan, and allow cake to cool for 1 hour before removing.

BURNT SUGAR CAKE

7	eggs, separated	7
1¾ cups	sugar	425 mL
¾ cup	cake meal	175 mL
¼ cup	potato flour	50 mL
	pinch of salt	
½ cup	cold water	125 mL
2 tbsp.	lemon juice	30 mL

Beat egg whites, gradually adding ¾ cup (175 mL) sugar. Beat egg yolks with ½ cup (125 mL) of sugar until light, then fold into whites. Sift cake meal and potato flour twice with salt, and fold in.

Melt remaining sugar over high heat, add water, and bring to boil. Fold syrup into cake mixture, together with lemon juice. Pour into a 12'' x 6'' (1.5 L) loaf pan, greased and lined with heavy wax paper. Bake at 350°F (180°C) for 1¼ hours.

CHOCOLATE ALMOND CAKE

8	eggs, separated	8
1½ cups	sugar	350 mL
⅓ cup	cocoa	75 mL
½ tsp.	salt	2 mL
4	apples, grated	4
1 cup	matzo meal	250 mL
1½ cups	almonds, ground	375 mL
1 tsp.	lemon rind, grated	5 mL
2 tbsp.	lemon juice	30 mL
½ tsp.	cinnamon	2 mL

Beat egg whites stiff, gradually adding half the sugar. In a separate bowl, beat egg yolks until thick. Add remaining sugar and other ingredients. Fold in egg whites. Pour into a greased 9'' x 13'' (3 L) pan and bake at 350°F (180°C) for 45 minutes.

WINE CHOCOLATE CAKE

8	eggs, separated	8
1½ cups	sugar	375 mL
2 tbsp.	cocoa	30 mL
1 tsp.	orange rind, grated	5 mL
¼ cup	orange juice	50 mL
¼ cup	wine	50 mL
¾ cup	cake meal	175 mL

Beat egg yolks until thick and lemon coloured. Add sugar, cocoa, orange rind and juice, wine, and cake meal, mixing thoroughly. Lightly fold in the stiffly beaten egg whites. Bake in 2 lightly greased, 10'' (2 L) tube pans at 350°F (180°C) for 40 minutes.

DATE CAKE

8	eggs, separated	8
1¼ cups	sugar	300 mL
2 tbsp.	lemon juice	30 mL
1 tsp.	lemon rind, grated	5 mL
1 tsp.	cinnamon	5 mL
1 tsp.	cloves	5 mL
1 cup	cake meal	250 mL
2 cups	dates, chopped	500 mL
½ cup	nuts, chopped	125 mL

Beat yolks and sugar until light. Add lemon juice and rind, spices, cake meal, dates, and nuts. Fold in stiffly beaten egg whites. Pour into an ungreased 10'' (2 L) tube pan. Bake at 325°F (160°C) for 1 hour.

DATE AND NUT TORTE

1 cup	sugar	250 mL
6 tbsp.	cake meal	90 mL
	pinch of salt	
¾ cup	walnuts, chopped	175 mL
1 lb.	dates	500 g
2 tbsp.	lemon juice	30 mL
1 tsp.	lemon rind, grated	5 mL
3	eggs, beaten	3

Combine sugar, cake meal, and salt. Add remaining ingredients, beating thoroughly. Pour into a greased cake pan. Bake at 350°F (180°C) for 45 minutes.

HONEY CAKE

10	eggs, separated	10
1 cup	sugar	250 mL
¼ cup	oil	50 mL
1 cup	buckwheat honey	250 mL
1 cup	cake meal	250 mL
1 tbsp.	potato starch	15 mL
1 tsp.	cinnamon	5 mL
1 tsp.	allspice	5 mL
	salt	

Beat egg yolks, sugar, oil, and honey. Add sifted dry ingredients. Beat egg whites with a pinch of salt until stiff. Fold into batter. Pour into an ungreased tube pan and bake at 350°F (180°C) on second lowest rack in oven for 65 minutes. Invert cake pan until cold before removing cake.

HAZELNUT CAKE

5	eggs	5
6 tbsp.	sugar	90 mL
8 oz.	hazelnuts, ground	250 g
1 tbsp.	lemon juice	15 mL
¼ cup	apple, grated	50 mL

Beat eggs well with sugar. Add hazelnuts, lemon juice, and apple. Bake in a springform pan at 350°F (180°C) for approximately 40 minutes. Ice with water icing, and decorate with hazelnuts.

Water Icing

1 cup	sugar	250 mL
½ cup	water	125 mL
2	egg whites	2
1	apple, grated	1

Cook sugar and water until mixture drops from a spoon in long threads. Pour slowly into stiffly beaten egg whites. Beat until firm. Fold in grated apple. Use immediately.

NUT CAKE

9	eggs, separated	9
1¼ cups	sugar	300 mL
1½ cups	walnuts, ground	375 mL
	pinch of salt	
¼ cup	cake meal	50 mL
1 tbsp.	lemon juice	15 mL

Beat egg yolks well, gradually adding sugar. Blend in nuts, salt, cake meal, and lemon juice. Beat well. Lastly fold in stiffly beaten egg whites. Bake in an ungreased tube pan at 275°F (140°C) for 1 hour. Invert to cool before removing cake from pan.

ORANGE NUT CAKE

1/2 cup	cake meal	125 mL
2 tbsp.	potato flour	30 mL
6	eggs, separated	6
1 cup	sugar	250 mL
1/2 cup	nuts, ground	125 mL
1 tsp.	orange rind, grated	5 mL
1 tsp.	orange extract	5 mL
1/4 tsp.	salt	1 mL

Sift cake meal and potato flour together. Beat egg yolks until light. Beat in sugar until light and creamy, then stir in sifted meal. Add nuts, orange rind, and extract. Whip egg whites with salt until stiff but not dry, and fold in gently. Turn into a greased and paper-lined utility pan and bake at 325°F (160°C) for 45 to 60 minutes.

SPONGE CAKE

1/3 cup	water	75 mL
1 cup	sugar	250 mL
2 tbsp.	orange juice	30 mL
1 tbsp.	lemon juice	15 mL
9	eggs, separated	9
	salt	
3 tbsp.	cake meal	45 mL
3 tbsp.	potato starch	45 mL

Boil water, sugar, orange and lemon juice together for 5 minutes. Beat egg whites with a little salt until stiff. Add boiled mixture gradually, beating constantly. Beat egg yolks until thick, and add. Sift cake meal and potato starch together several times. Fold batter into egg mixture. Bake in an ungreased tube pan at 300°F (150°C) for 1 hour. Invert pan to cool before removing cake.

CHIFFON SPONGE CAKE

5	eggs, separated	5
1/2 cup	sugar	125 mL
3/4 cup	matzo meal, sifted	175 mL
1/4 cup	potato flour	50 mL
1/2 cup	sugar	125 mL
1/2 tsp.	salt	2 mL
1/4 cup	oil	50 mL
1/4 cup	orange juice	50 mL
1 tsp.	lemon juice	5 mL
1 tsp.	lemon rind, grated	5 mL

Beat egg whites until they hold soft peaks. Gradually add sugar, beating until very stiff peaks form. Set aside. Sift dry ingredients together into mixing bowl. Make a well in centre. Add egg yolks, oil, juices and rind, and beat until smooth. Gently fold batter into egg whites until well blended. Pour into an ungreased 9'' (1 L) tube pan. Bake at 325°F (160°C) for 1 hour. Invert cake to cool before removing.

ORANGE SPONGE CAKE

8	eggs, separated	8
1 1/2 cups	sugar	375 mL
1/3 cup	orange juice	75 mL
1 cup	cake meal, sifted	250 mL
3/4 cup	potato starch, sifted	175 mL
1/4 tsp.	salt	1 mL
1 tsp.	orange rind, grated	5 mL

Beat egg whites until stiff. Slowly add half the sugar, beating continuously. In a separate bowl, beat egg yolks well. Add rest of sugar slowly, then juice. Fold in dry ingredients; add orange rind. Finally fold yolk mixture into whites. Pour into a lightly greased 10'' (2 L) tube pan. Bake at 350°F (180°C) for 1 hour. Invert pan, and remove cake when cool.

WINE CAKE

12	eggs, separated	12
1 cup	sugar	250 mL
1 cup	wine	250 mL
1 cup	cake meal, sifted	250 mL
1/2 tsp.	salt	2 mL
1 tsp.	cinnamon	5 mL
1 cup	walnuts, ground	250 mL

Beat egg whites until stiff but not dry; add sugar

gradually and beat until stiff. Beat egg yolks until very light. Add wine, cake meal, salt, cinnamon, and nuts. Fold in beaten whites. Bake at 325°F (160°C) for 1 hour, preferably in an angel food pan. Invert pan until cake is cool before removing. (Note: This is a large recipe, and will make 2 cakes if baked in angel food pans.)

JELLY ROLL

4	eggs, separated	4
1/2 cup	sugar	125 mL
1/2 cup	cake meal	125 mL
	pinch of salt	
1 tsp.	vanilla	5 mL
1/2 tsp.	almond extract	2 mL

Beat yolks well. Add sugar, cake meal, salt, and flavourings. Fold in stiffly beaten egg whites. Spread batter on a 10'' x 14'' (2.5 L) baking pan lined with wax paper, and bake at 375°F (190°C) for 10 minutes. Turn out on a towel sprinkled with icing sugar. Remove the paper, spread cake quickly with jam or lemon filling, and roll up. Wrap in wax paper and then in a damp towel for 20 minutes.

CREAM PUFFS

1 cup	water	250 mL
1/3 cup	oil	75 mL
1 cup	matzo meal	250 mL
1/2 tsp.	salt	2 mL
4	eggs	4

Boil water and oil in a saucepan. Pour matzo meal and salt into boiling water and cook, stirring, until batter no longer sticks to sides of pan. Remove from heat. Add eggs one at a time, beating well after each addition. Drop by spoonfuls onto a greased cookie sheet. Bake at 450°F (220°C) for 25 minutes. Reduce oven to 325°F (160°C) and bake 45 minutes longer. When cool, cut in half, remove all filaments of moist dough, and fill with Passover whipped topping, custard, fruits, or other fillings; sprinkle with icing sugar. Makes 12 medium-sized puffs.

CUSTARD FILLING

2	eggs	2
3/4 cup	sugar	175 mL
1 tbsp.	potato flour	15 mL
2 tbsp.	lemon juice	30 mL
1 tsp.	butter	5 mL
1 cup	water	250 mL

Beat eggs well. Add sugar and flour, beating slowly and continuously. Slowly add lemon juice, butter, and water. Cook in the top of a double boiler until thick, stirring constantly. Cool, stirring occasionally to prevent lumps.

LEMON JELLY ROLL

6	eggs, separated	6
3/4 cup	sugar	175 mL
1 tbsp.	lemon juice	15 mL
1/4 tsp.	salt	1 mL
1/2 cup	cake meal	125 mL

Beat egg whites until stiff. Add sugar and beat again. Beat in lemon juice and salt. Fold beaten yolks into the whites, and then lastly fold in the cake meal. Spread evenly onto a 10'' x 14'' (2 L) cookie pan lined with greased wax paper. Bake at 350°F (180°C) for 30 minutes. Turn out onto a towel sprinkled with icing sugar, and remove paper. Spread with lemon filling; roll up. Wrap in wax paper and then in a damp towel for 20 minutes.

Fluffy Lemon Filling

3	eggs, separated	3
1 tsp.	lemon rind, grated	5 mL
1/2 cup	sugar	125 mL
3 tbsp.	lemon juice	45 mL
1/4 cup	almonds, blanched	50 mL

Mix and beat together yolks, rind, and sugar in the top of a double boiler. Add lemon juice and cook until thick. Beat egg whites stiff. Add to lemon mixture and cook 1 minute longer. Stir in blanched almonds. Keeps in the refrigerator several days. (Note: This mixture may also be served on its own as a dessert.)

NEVER-FAIL LEMON FILLING

3	eggs, separated	3
1 cup	sugar	250 mL
3 tbsp.	lemon juice	45 mL
2 tsp.	lemon rind, grated	10 mL
1/4 tsp.	salt	1 mL
2 tbsp.	potato starch	30 mL
1 1/2 cups	water	375 mL

Mix egg yolks with sugar, lemon juice, rind, and salt. Make starch into a paste with the water, and add. Cook over boiling water in the top of a double boiler, stirring constantly, until mixture thickens. Reserve egg whites for meringues or macaroons.

PRUNE PUDDING

4	eggs	4
	pinch of salt	
1 cup	sugar	250 mL
1 cup	lukewarm water	250 mL
1 lb.	prunes, chopped	500 g
2 tbsp.	oil	30 mL
1 tsp.	cinnamon	5 mL
4	apples, sliced	4
1 cup	matzo meal	250 mL

Beat eggs, salt, and sugar well. Soak prunes in warm water, drain, and combine with remaining ingredients. Bake in a greased 8" (2 L) utility pan at 350°F (180°C) for approximately 1 hour.

HOT COMPOTE

14 oz.	canned apricots	398 mL
14 oz.	canned peaches	398 mL
14 oz.	canned pineapple	398 mL
10 oz.	canned mandarin oranges	284 mL
14 oz.	canned plums	398 mL
14 oz.	canned pears	398 mL
12 oz.	pitted prunes	340 g
	water	
3 tbsp.	sherry or apricot brandy	45 mL
19 oz.	canned cherries	540 mL
1 tbsp.	potato starch	15 mL

Drain apricots, peaches, pineapple, oranges, plums, and pears. Boil prunes for approximately 5 minutes in a small amount of water, to soften; drain. Layer drained fruit in an 8" square (2 L) casserole. Sprinkle liberally with sherry. Drain cherries, reserving juice. Arrange cherries on top of casserole. Thicken reserved cherry juice with potato starch, and pour over cherries. Bake at 350°F (180°C) for 1 1/4 to 1 1/2 hours. (Note: This is best made a day ahead, and reheated or served cold.)

CHOCOLATE MOUSSE

12 oz.	bitter chocolate	360 g
1/3 cup	sugar	75 mL
1/4 cup	water	50 mL
1 tbsp.	instant coffee	15 mL
2 tsp.	vanilla	10 mL
5	eggs, separated	5

In the top of a double boiler, stir the first 4 ingredients over hot water until smooth. Remove from heat. Stir in vanilla. Add egg yolks one at a time, beating well after each addition. Finally fold in stiffly beaten egg whites. Set in refrigerator overnight. Serves 4. (Note: May also be used as a filling.)

RASPBERRY DESSERT

6	eggs, separated	6
1 cup	sugar	250 mL
1 tbsp.	lemon juice	15 mL
3/4 cup	potato starch	175 mL
1/2 cup	sugar	125 mL
30 oz.	frozen raspberries	850 g

Beat egg yolks until light. Add 1/2 cup (125 mL) of the sugar, lemon juice, and 1/2 cup (125 mL) potato starch. Beat egg whites stiffly with remaining sugar, and fold in. Bake at 350°F (180°C) in an ungreased jelly roll pan for 15 minutes.

Drain thawed raspberries, reserving juice. Add remaining potato starch to juice and bring to a boil, cooking until thick. Cool, fold in raspberries, and spread onto cooled cake. Cover with meringue and brown slightly in oven.

Meringue

4	egg whites	4
1/2 cup	sugar	125 mL

Beat egg whites until frothy. Gradually add sugar, and continue beating until stiff.

STRAWBERRY ICE

4	eggs, separated	4
3/4 cup	sugar	175 mL
1 tbsp.	lemon juice	15 mL
15 oz.	sliced strawberries	425 g
1	banana, mashed	1

Beat egg yolks with 1 tsp. (5 mL) sugar, and the lemon juice and fruit. Beat egg whites until stiff, gradually adding remaining sugar. Fold egg whites into fruit mixture. Pour into a 9'' x 3'' (3 L) utility pan and freeze 1 hour. Pour into a mixing bowl, and beat well. Return to pan and freeze. Cut into squares to serve.

BROWNIES

3 3/4 oz.	bittersweet chocolate	105 g
1/4 cup	butter	50 mL
2	eggs	2
1/8 tsp.	salt	0.5 mL
2/3 cup	sugar	150 mL
1/2 cup	cake meal	125 mL
1/2 cup	nuts, chopped	125 mL

Melt chocolate and butter in the top of a double boiler. Cool. Beat the eggs with salt until thick. Add sugar, cake meal, and nuts. Fold in chocolate mixture. Pour into a greased 8'' square (2 L) pan. Bake at 325°F (160°C) for 20 minutes. Cut while hot into squares.

DATE AND NUT SQUARES

1 lb.	dates, chopped	500 g
1 cup	brown sugar	250 mL
2	eggs	2
2 cups	nuts, chopped	500 mL
1/2 tsp.	vanilla	2 mL
4 tbsp.	cake meal	60 mL

Combine all ingredients. Press into a greased 8'' (1 L) cake pan. Bake at 350°F (180°C) until golden brown. Sprinkle with icing sugar and cut into squares.

FILBERT MERINGUE SQUARES

3	eggs, separated	3
1/3 cup	oil	75 mL
1 3/4 cups	sugar	425 mL
1/2 cup	cake meal	125 mL
1/4 cup	potato starch	50 mL
2 cups	filberts, ground	500 mL
2 tbsp.	lemon juice	30 mL
2 tbsp.	lemon rind, grated	30 mL

Beat egg yolks with oil and 1/2 cup (125 mL) of the sugar. Mix cake meal and potato starch, and add. Pat into a greased 8'' (1 L) baking dish. Beat egg whites until stiff, gradually beating in remaining sugar with lemon juice and rind. Fold in filberts. Spread over batter in pan. Bake at 350°F (180°C) until light brown. Cut into squares.

APPLE AND ALMOND STRUDEL

Filling

2 lb.	apples	1 kg
2	lemons	2
2 cups	sugar	500 mL

Peel apples and grate coarsely. Slice peeled lemons finely. Mix together with sugar, and bake at 350°F (180°C) for 1 1/2 to 2 hours until filling is the consistency of thick, dark golden marmalade. (Note: The filling may be prepared in advance and refrigerated, but then it will be necessary to soften it with a fork before using.)

Dough

6	eggs, separated	6
1 cup	sugar	250 mL
1 lb.	almonds, ground	500 g
	almond extract	
1 tbsp.	cake meal	15 mL
1 tbsp.	icing sugar	15 mL

Beat yolks with sugar until light and thick. Fold in stiffly beaten egg whites. Add ground almonds, reserving about 1 tbsp. (15 mL) for topping, then fold in extract and cake meal. Pour half this mixture into a greased 10'' x 14'' (1.5 L) utility pan. Bake at 325°F (160°C) until set but not brown. Remove from oven and carefully spread filling over base. Cover with the balance of the dough. Combine reserved ground almonds with the icing sugar, and sprinkle over top of strudel. Return to oven and bake until light golden brown. Cut into squares to serve.

BAGELS

⅓ cup	oil	75 mL
⅔ cup	water	150 mL
1 cup	matzo meal	250 mL
1 tbsp.	sugar	15 mL
¼ tsp.	salt	1 mL
3	eggs	3
	cinnamon	
	sugar	

Bring oil and water to a boil. Combine matzo meal, sugar, and salt, and add. Beat together until fairly dry. Add eggs one at a time, beating well. Form into walnut-sized balls and roll in cinnamon mixed with sugar. Place on a greased pan. Make a hole in the middle with a finger dipped in cold water. Bake at 400°F (200°C) for 10 minutes, then at 300°F (150°C) for 1 hour. Yields 15. (Note: This recipe cannot be doubled.)

KICHEL

½ cup	oil	125 mL
1½ cups	water	375 mL
1 tsp.	salt	5 mL
2 tbsp.	sugar	30 mL
7	eggs	7
1½ cups	cake meal	375 mL

Boil oil, water, salt, and sugar. Remove from heat and stir in cake meal. Cool slightly. Add eggs one at a time, beating well. Grease muffin pans and heat well before filling three-quarters full. Bake at 450°F (230°C) for 20 minutes, then at 350°F (180°C) for 30 minutes. Yields 12.

NOTHINGS

3	eggs	3
3 tsp.	sugar	15 mL
½ cup	oil	125 mL
¾ cup	matzo meal	175 mL
3 tsp.	potato starch	15 mL
	sugar	
	sesame seeds	

Beat eggs, sugar, and oil together very well. Sift matzo meal and potato starch and add, beating well. Using a teaspoon of dough at a time, roll in sugar mixed with sesame seeds, and shape into twists. Place on an ungreased cookie sheet and bake at 400°F (200°C) for 10 minutes, then at 300°F (150°C) for 40 minutes.

KOMISH BROIT

4	eggs	4
1 cup	oil	250 mL
1 cup	sugar	250 mL
½ cup	almonds, crushed	125 mL
1 cup	matzo meal	250 mL
¾ cup	potato starch	175 mL
¼ tsp.	salt	1 mL
1 tsp.	cinnamon	5 mL

Mix all ingredients together well. Pour into 2

well-greased 9" x 5" (2 L) loaf pans, making pans about three-quarters full. Bake at 350°F (180°C) until golden brown. Remove from pans and cut into ½" (1 cm) slices. Places slices flat on a baking sheet; return to oven to dry out at 300°F (150°C) until brown, approximately 10 minutes on each side.

Variation
Chop a 3 oz. (85 g) chocolate bar, and add.

Sprinkle slices with a mixture of cinnamon and sugar before returning to oven to dry.

APRICOT DAINTIES

1 lb.	dried apricots	500 g
1 cup	sugar	250 mL
1 cup	walnuts, ground	250 mL

Wash apricots, and chop. Place in a saucepan with sugar and a little water; cook, stirring constantly, until very thick. Cool. Dip hands in cold water, then form apricots into small balls. Roll in nuts.

CHOCOLATE BALLS

8 oz.	bittersweet chocolate	250 g
1	egg	1
½ cup	icing sugar	125 mL
½ cup	coconut, shredded	125 mL
	toasted almonds	
	maraschino cherries	

Melt chocolate in the top of a double boiler. Remove from heat and beat in egg, icing sugar, and coconut. Roll a small amount of the mixture around an almond or cherry. Then roll in coconut or ground almonds. Keep refrigerated.

DROP COOKIES

1	egg white	1
¾ cup	sugar	175 mL
1 cup	toasted almonds	250 mL
1 cup	dates	250 mL
1 tsp.	lemon rind, grated	5 mL
2 tbsp.	lemon juice	30 mL
2 tbsp.	matzo meal	30 mL

Beat egg white with sugar until stiff. Chop almonds and dates, and fold into egg white with remaining ingredients. Drop from a spoon onto a greased pan. Bake at 375°F (190°C) for 8 to 10 minutes.

JELLY-FILLED COOKIES

3	eggs	3
1 cup	sugar	250 mL
1 cup	oil	250 mL
1 tbsp.	lemon juice	15 mL
2 cups	cake meal	500 mL
½ cup	potato starch	125 mL
1 cup	nuts, chopped	250 mL
	jelly	

Beat eggs well, slowly adding sugar. Add oil and juice. Sift cake meal and potato starch together, and add. Fold in nuts. Shape into walnut-sized balls, indent each ball with thumb, and fill hollow with jelly. Bake at 350°F (180°C) for 20 to 25 minutes.

MOCK OATMEAL COOKIES

1 cup	matzo meal	250 mL
¾ cup	sugar	175 mL
½ tsp.	cinnamon	3 mL
1 cup	matzo farfel	250 mL
¼ tsp.	salt	1 mL
½ cup	nuts, chopped	125 mL
½ cup	raisins	125 mL
2	eggs	2
⅓ cup	oil	75 mL

Mix together dry ingredients, including nuts and raisins. Beat in eggs and oil. Drop from a spoon onto greased cookie sheets, leaving room for cookies to spread. Bake at 350°F (180°C) for 30 minutes. Yields 24.

TAIGLACH

Dough

6	eggs	6
1 tbsp.	oil	15 mL
2½ cups	cake meal	625 mL

Beat eggs well. Add oil and just enough meal to form a soft dough. On a board sprinkled with meal, roll dough with hands into long thin strips. Cut in ½'' (1 cm) lengths. Bake on a pan sprinkled with potato flour at 350°F (180°C) for 10 minutes.

Syrup

1 lb.	honey	500 g
1 cup	sugar	250 mL
½ tbsp.	ginger	7 mL
½ lb.	walnuts, chopped	250 g

Mix honey, sugar, and ginger in a saucepan; bring to a boil. Add pieces of baked dough and nuts. Boil slowly, stirring frequently, until honey forms a firm ball in cold water. Pour onto a moistened board, immediately flatten with hands, and when cold cut into squares of desired size.

CARROT CANDY

1 lb.	carrots	500 g
1 tsp.	lemon rind, grated	5 mL
1 tsp.	orange rind, grated	5 mL
2 tbsp.	lemon juice	30 mL
1 lb.	brown sugar	500 g
½ cup	matzo meal	125 mL
1 cup	nuts, chopped	250 mL
1 tsp.	ginger	5 mL

Wash carrots well, but do not peel. Grate carrots coarsely into a saucepan and mix with grated lemon and orange rind. Stir in lemon juice and brown sugar. Bring to a boil; cook about 30 minutes. Add remaining ingredients. Cook 5 minutes longer, stirring continuously. Turn out onto a damp board, flatten, and sprinkle with nuts. Cut into squares when cool.

HONEY PRUNES

1 lb.	prunes	500 g
	nuts	
½ cup	beet rossel	125 mL
½ cup	honey	125 mL
1 tsp.	lemon juice	5 mL

Soak prunes in hot water until tender. Stone, and replace pit with a nut. Make a syrup of the rossel (see page 266), honey, and lemon juice. Simmer prunes, in syrup until sticky, and then roll in chopped nuts.

KRIMSEL

1 cup	matzo meal	250 mL
3 tbsp.	sugar	45 mL
	pinch of salt	
½ tsp.	cinnamon	2 mL
1 cup	boiling water	250 mL
2	eggs	2
	oil for frying	
	cinnamon	
	sugar	

Mix together first 4 ingredients. Add water and mix well, then beat in eggs. Let stand for 15 to 20 minutes. Drop by teaspoons into hot oil and fry until golden brown. Drain on brown paper before rolling in cinnamon mixed with sugar. Serve hot or cold. Yields 14.

INGBERLACH

1 lb.	brown honey	500 g
½ cup	sugar	125 mL
½ tsp.	ginger	2 mL
8 oz.	matzo farfel	250 g

Combine brown honey, sugar, and ginger in a saucepan and bring to a boil, stirring constantly. Add farfel and cook until syrup reaches soft ball stage (drops off spoon in chunks). Pour onto a wet board and pat flat. Cut while warm into triangles.

Menus for Holidays & Ritual Occasions*

Sabbath Eve

Sabbath eve is always a special family night; every week, in Jewish homes around the world, the atmosphere of a special occasion is recreated. Always there is a clean white tablecloth, and the candles, and the kiddush cup of wine, and the challah.

A sweet egg bread, the challah is rich in symbolism. Its familiar humped shape, achieved by braiding the dough, represents the twelve loaves of bread that were on the Temple altar on the Sabbath. The challah is usually topped with sesame or poppy seeds, symbolic of the manna that was dropped in the desert.

Fish, the symbol of fertility and prosperity, usually appears on the Sabbath table as Gefilte Fish, a tradition that arose more from poverty than from religious observance. Reflecting the thrift and ingenuity of a poor people, it is a dish that, like golden chicken soup and sweet carrot tzimmes, represents something more: the promise of a good rich life ahead.

Wine for Kiddush
Challah
Gefilte Fish with Horseradish
Chicken Soup with Noodles
Roast Brisket of Beef
Kasha
Carrot Tzimmes
Fruit Compote
Poppyseed Cookies/Komish Broit
Tea/Coffee

Sabbath Day

No fire may be lighted or food cooked on the Sabbath, the day of rest. Accordingly, lunch on the Sabbath day must be prepared ahead. For summer, meat roasted the day before and served cold with salad is ideal. For winter, a slow-cooking stew or pudding—like Cholent—that may be put in the oven before Sabbath eve, is the answer.

Cholent is believed to derive from the Old French word *chald* (modern French, *chaud*), meaning warm. A combination of bony meat, beans, and other vegetables, it is cooked over very low heat for ten hours or more, yielding a hearty stew with a thick, rich gravy.

Wine for Kiddush
Fresh Fruit Cup
Cholent/Cold Sliced Brisket
Carrot Salad
Sponge Cake
Tea/Coffee

After a Funeral or Unveiling

Following a momentous ritual occasion that marks the boundaries of life in this world, it is only fitting that the meal served should be solemn with symbolism. It is also, perhaps, typical of the Jewish faith that the symbols should be those of life, and not death.

*Recipes that appear in the book are high-lighted in blue.

The meal is known as the Meal of Consolation, and it is usually prepared by friends so that the mourners themselves do not have to be concerned with everyday chores. No meat is eaten following a funeral or unveiling. The table bears foods like eggs, lentils, bagels—round foods that symbolize the natural cycle and the continuity of life.

Challah
Rye Bread
Bagels
Smoked Salmon
Marinated Herring with Sour Cream
Tuna Salad
Whole Hard-boiled Eggs
Farmer's Salad
Fruit Plate
Honey Cake
Kuffles/Komish Broit
Tea/Coffee

Rosh Hashanah

Rosh Hashanah—the joyous and hopeful start of the new year—features lots of sweet foods, representative of the optimistic wish for a sweet and happy year to come. The meal traditionally starts with slices of apple dipped in honey, and the dishes that follow abound with honey, raisins, carrots, apples, and other sweet foods in season. Instead of the regular long braid, the challah is usually formed into a round, to symbolize a full year, and filled with raisins, to symbolize a sweet and rich one.

Wine
Apples and Honey
Challah
Tomato Consommé
Cabbage Rolls
Prime Rib Roast
Potato Knishes
Pickled Beets
Steamed Brussels Sprouts
Honey Chiffon Cake
Tea/Coffee

Wine
Apples and Honey
Challah
Seafood Cocktail
Barley Soup
Roast Turkey with Special Dressing
Roast Potatoes
Pea-filled Carrot Ring
Apple Cake
Tea/Coffee

Yom Kippur Eve

Yom Kippur, the Day of Atonement, is a solemn fast day. The fast is from sunset to sunset and, therefore, the meal on Yom Kippur eve is the last food or drink adult Jews will have for twenty-four hours. It is customary—and practical good sense—not to serve salty or highly spiced foods, nor to serve anything very rich and heavy.

The meat-filled kreplach have come to be closely associated with the Yom Kippur meal, as the symbol for God's mercy: the meat represents inflexible justice and the soft noodle dough, compassion; the hope is that God's strict justice will be mellowed by compassion, and his decision about whether to grant atonement for sins, and to inscribe the person in the Book of Life, will come down on the side of mercy.

Wine
Chicken Soup with Kreplach
Stuffed Veal Breast
Potato Kugel
Bibb Lettuce Salad with Grapes
Marble Chiffon Cake
Tea/Coffee

Meal After Yom Kippur Fast

Tomato Soup
Baked Sole with Mushrooms
Rissotto
Zucchini Creole
Chocolate Mousse
Tea/Coffee

Sukkot

The Feast of Tabernacles is a festival of thanksgiving. As a reminder of the forty years spent wandering in the desert, a temporary *sukkah* (booth) is built, roofed with leaves and branches through which the stars may be seen, and festooned with fruits and vegetables. For the seven days of Sukkot, meals are eaten in the *sukkah*.

Sukkot also has aspects of a harvest festival, and its principal symbols are agrarian ones—the "four species" of *lulav* (palm branch) and *etrog* (citron), myrtle and willow. The eighth day is a separate holiday, characterized by the special prayer for rain. And the whole season of rejoicing culminates in Simchat Torah, marking the completion of the annual cycle of Torah readings and the return to Genesis to begin the round again.

Wine
Sweet and Sour Meatballs
Sesame Chicken
Corn on the Cob
Party Cole Slaw
Lemon Meringue Pie
Tea/Coffee

Chanukah

Chanukah is the Feast of Dedication, also called the Festival of Lights. It commemorates the victory of the Maccabees over the Syrian-Greeks, the defilers of the Temple. It also celebrates the miracle whereby the one remaining cruse of holy oil, enough to burn the sacred eternal lamp for only one day, kept the flame alight for eight days while the Temple was rededicated.

In remembrance of the miracle of the oil and the cleansing of the Temple, Chanukah foods are cooked in lots of oil—deep-fried pancakes or latkes, doughnuts, and so on. The pancakes have a further significance: a mixture of flour and water quickly made, they are a reminder of the food hurriedly prepared for the Maccabees as they went off to battle.

Wine
Chopped Liver
Roast Brisket of Beef
Potato Latkes
Apple Sauce
Givetch
Soofganiyot
Tea/Coffee

Purim

Purim is a holiday made for children. It is a gay carnival of masquerades, plays, games, and parties, celebrating the dramatic and romantic story of Esther's successful rescue of the Jews of Persia from the evil plans of Haman.

As the last festival before Passover, Purim provides an excellent opportunity to use up the remainder of the year's flour, and one of the most attractive customs of the holiday is the sending of gifts of baked goods and sweets to friends and family. Hamantashen are the pastries most closely associated with Purim. Triangular in shape (like kreplach, which are also usually served on Purim), usually filled with poppy seeds (*mohn*) or prunes, they have given rise to any number of explanations of their name: a *mohn tash*, a pocket filled with poppy seed; expressing the wish that Haman's strength would weaken (*tash kocho*); or, the favourite with children, representing Haman's three-cornered hat.

Children's Fare
Hamantashen
Banana Muffins
Cream Puffs
Chocolate Marshmallow Roll
Brownies
Apples and Oranges
Fruit Punches

Passover

A grand ritual, the Passover Seder is the most impressive family meal of the year. The Passover table provides constant reminders of the significance of the holiday—the commemoration of the redemption of the Children of Israel from slavery, the Feast of Unleavened Bread, the Season of our Freedom, and the Festival of Spring.

The shank bone on the Seder plate represents the sacrifice offered by the Israelites in Egypt, and eaten on the eve of their exodus. The roasted egg recalls the festival offering from the Temple. The bitter herbs, usually horseradish, are a reminder of the bitter days of bondage. Parsley or celery is a symbol of the fresh growth of spring; it is dipped in salt water, representing the tears shed during the time of suffering. The muddy-looking Charoses mixture suggests the bricks made and used by the Israelites during their enslavement in Egypt.

Matzo is a symbolic sharing in the deliverance from slavery, a pervasive reminder of the unleavened bread baked in haste by the Israelites on their departure from Egypt. For the full eight days of Passover, no *hometz* (leaven) may appear in the home.

Seder Plate
a shank bone
a roasted egg
bitter herbs
parsley
Charoses

Also on the table for the Seder:

3 matzos (the Afikoman)
wine
salt water
a cup of wine for Elijah

First Seder
Gefilte Fish with Horseradish
Chicken Soup with Knaidlach

Roast Turkey with Cranberry Sauce
Farfel Pilaf
Carrot Tzimmes
Sliced Cucumbers and Tomatoes
Fruit Compote
Almond Torte
Tea/Coffee

Second Seder
Chopped Liver
Chicken Soup with Passover Mandlen
Roast Brisket of Beef
Potato Muffins
Steamed Fresh Broccoli
Royal Apple Kugel
Pickles and Olives
Fresh Fruit
Passover Strawberry Ice
Assorted Passover Cookies and Squares
Tea/Coffee

Shavuot

The dishes associated with Shavuot are all dairy foods, and the explanations for this are many and various. For one thing, Shavuot is a harvest festival, the Feast of the First Fruits, and the foods to celebrate it are all fresh fruits and vegetables and light dairy creations. Shavuot is also the religious festival commemorating the giving of the Torah on Mount Sinai, the Torah compared in the Bible to "milk and honey."

Whatever the reasons and interpretations, the custom is firmly established. For Shavuot, serve salads, fruits, vegetable dishes, and cheese blintzes, cheese kreplach, cheesecake, and other dairy foods.

Fresh Fruit Cocktail
Gefilte Fish with Horseradish
Chopped Herring
Cheese Blintzes with Sour Cream
Raw Vegetable Platter
Chocolate Pie
Tea/Coffee

Index